Fast Track Visual Basic .NET

Billy S. Hollis
Rockford Lhotka

Wrox Press Ltd. ®

Fast Track Visual Basic .NET

First Printed May 2002

Published by Wrox Press Ltd,
Arden House, 1102 Warwick Road, Acocks Green,
Birmingham, B27 6BH
United Kingdom
Printed in the United States
ISBN 1-861007-12-4

Trademark Acknowledgments

Wrox has endeavored to provide trademark information about all the companies and products mentioned in this book by the appropriate use of capitals. However, Wrox cannot guarantee the accuracy of this information.

Credits

Authors
Billy S. Hollis
Rockford Lhotka

Technical Reviewers
Martin Beaulieu
Maxime Bombardier
Rory Flaherty
Damien Foggon
Jacob Hammer
Hope Hatfield
Mark Horner

Commissioning Editor
Ian Blackham

Technical Editors
Mankee Cheng
Christian Peak
Dev Lunsford

Managing Editor
Viv Emery

Project Manager
Beth Sacks

Author Agent
Nicola Phillips

Production Coordinator
Abbie Forletta

Cover
Chris Morris

Indexers
Andrew Criddle
Martin Brooks

Proofreader
Chris Smith

About the Authors

Billy S. Hollis

Billy Hollis first learned BASIC over 25 years ago, and is co-author of the first book ever published on Visual Basic .NET, *VB.NET Programming with the Public Beta*, published Wrox Press, as well as several other .NET books. He is a frequent speaker at conferences, including Comdex, TechEd, Microsoft's Professional Developer Conference (PDC), and the Visual Basic Insiders Technical Summit (VBITS), often on the topics of software design and specification, object-based development in Visual Basic, and Microsoft .NET. He was chosen by Microsoft to train all 200 instructors for their 2001 .NET Developer Tour.

Billy is the MSDN Regional Director of Developer Relations in Nashville, Tennessee for Microsoft, and was named Regional Director of the Year for 2001 by Microsoft. He has hosted Developer Days in Nashville for the last four years. He has his own consulting company in Nashville, which focuses on training, consultation, and software development for the Microsoft.NET platform.

> *I need to thank several folks at Microsoft who have provided me with the opportunity to learn more about VB.NET, including Jennifer Ritzinger, Mike Iem, Ari Bixhorn, Susan Warren, Mark Boulter, and many others. Thanks also to Ken Spencer and Keith Pleas for getting me involved in early training projects on .NET.*

> *My family has been supportive as always as I've squeezed in the time to write for this book, often at their expense. Those of us in the software industry love this time of intense innovation, but I'm sure Cindy, Ansel, and Dyson will be happier when things get back to the normal pace of change.*

> *I'd like to dedicate this book to the entire .NET team at Microsoft. They have worked long and hard, and produced a revolutionary product that is changing this industry. They deserve more recognition than they get for their brilliant and tremendous effort.*

Rockford Lhotka

Rockford Lhotka is the Principal Technology Evangelist for Magenic Technologies, one of the nation's premiere Microsoft Gold Certified Partners dedicated to solving today's most challenging business problems using 100 percent Microsoft tools and technology. Rockford is an author for several Wrox Press titles, including *Professional Visual Basic Interoperability: COM and VB6 to .NET* and *Visual Basic 6 Distributed Objects* and is a columnist for *MSDN Online* and contributing author for *Visual Studio Magazine*. He regularly presents at major conferences around the world – including Microsoft PDC, TechEd, VS Live!, and VS Connections. He has over 15 years experience in software development and has worked on many projects in various roles, including software architecture, design and development, network administration, and project management.

> *This book is dedicated with love to my wife Teresa and my sons Tim and Marcus.*

Table of Contents

Introduction   1

Who is This Book For?   1

What is Covered in This Book?   2
The 80:20 Principle for Coverage of Topics   4

What You Need to Use This Book   4

Style Conventions   5

Customer Support and Feedback   6
Source Code and Updates   6
Errata   6
Technical Support   7
p2p.wrox.com   7

Chapter 1: Getting Started   11

The .NET Environment   12
.NET System Requirements   13
End User Requirements   14
Web Server Requirements   14
Application Server Requirements   14
Developer Requirements   15
Other Common Concerns   16
Mapped Network Drives   16
Optional Services   19
Installing and Configuring the Samples   19
Configuring the Samples   20
Running the Samples from other Machines   20
Configuring a Remote IIS Server   21

Getting Started with Hello World   21

Summary   26

Chapter 2: Introduction to the .NET Framework   29

What is .NET?   30
A Broad and Deep Platform for the Future   30
The Role of the .NET Enterprise Servers   31

Table of Contents

What's Wrong with DNA and COM?   32
    Difficulty in Integrating Internet Technologies   32
    Deployment Issues   33
    Poor Cross-language Integration   33
    Many Skills Required for Development   33
    Weaknesses in Visual Basic in COM/DNA applications   33
The Origins of .NET   34
An Overview of the .NET Framework   35
    A Common Substrate for all Development   35

The Common Language Runtime   **36**
Key Design Goals   37
    Simpler, Faster Development   37
    Automatic Handling of System-Level Tasks   37
    Excellent Tool Support   38
    Simpler, Safer Deployment   38
    Scalability   39
Metadata   39
Multiple Language Integration and Support   41
A Common Type System   41
    Reference Types vs. Value Types   41
    Everything is an Object   43
    Primitive Types in the .NET Framework   43
Namespaces   44
The Structure of a .NET Application   45
    Start with an Assembly, Build Up to an Application   45
    Assembly Structure   46
Deployment and Execution   47
    Execution   47
    Details on .NET Memory Management   47
    Managed vs. Unmanaged Code   48

The Next Layer – the .NET Class Framework   **49**
What is in the .NET Class Framework?   49

User and Program Interfaces   **51**
Windows Forms   51
    Client Applications Versus Browser-Based Applications   51
Web Forms   52
    Server Controls   52
Console Applications   53
Web Services   53

XML as the .NET 'Meta-language'   **54**

The Role of COM   **54**
No Internal Use of COM   55

The Role of DNA   **55**

Additional Benefits   **55**
Some Potential Downsides   56

The First Step – Visual Studio .NET   **56**

.NET Drives Changes in Visual Basic   **57**

How does .NET Affect Me?   **57**
    A Spectrum of Programming Models   58
    Reducing Barriers to Internet Development   58
    Libraries of Pre-Written Functionality   59
    Easier Deployment   59

Summary   **59**

Chapter 3: New IDE Features   **61**

A Tour of the Hello World Program   **62**
    Form Declaration, Initialization, and Termination   62
        Forms as Classes   62
        Forms Created by Inheritance   64
    Windows Form Designer-Generated Code   65
        The #Region Directive   66
        The Constructor Method   67
        The Dispose() Method   67
        Variable Declarations   68
        The InitializeComponent() Method   68
    Event Handler Code   69
        Event Parameters   70
        The Handles Clause   71
        Method Sytax   71

New IDE Features   **72**
    The Start Page   72
    Docking Windows   73
    Main Windows   75
        Graphical Designers   75
        Solution Explorer   77
        Properties Window   80
        Class View   80
        Dynamic Help   83
        Toolbox   84
        Server Explorer   86
        The Task List   87
        The Output Window   88
        The Command Window   89
    Macro Support   90
    Integrated Debugging   90
        The Call Stack Window   91
        The Breakpoints Window   91
        Watch and Value Display Windows   91

Summary   **91**

Table of Contents

Chapter 4: Language and Syntax   95

Namespaces   96
Using Namespaces   97
    Direct Addressing   97
    The Imports Keyword   98
    Aliasing Namespaces   99
Creating Namespaces   99
    Setting the Root Namespace   99
    The Namespace Keyword   100
The Microsoft.VisualBasic Namespace   100

Language and Syntax Changes   101
Option Statements   101
Data Type Changes   102
    Integer Type Changes (Byte, Short, Integer, Long)   103
    Floating-Point Division   103
    Replacing Currency with Decimal   104
    The Char Type   104
    The String Type   104
    Replacing Variant with Object   106
    The CType Statement   107
Changes in Declaration of Variables   107
    Declaring Multiple Variables   107
    Declaring Initial Values   108
    Declaring Constants   108
    Dim As New   108
    Scoping Changes   109
Changes to Arrays   109
    Zero-Based Arrays   109
    LBound and UBound   110
    Declaring Arrays   110
    ReDim   110
    ReDim Preserve   111
    Fixed Arrays   111
Changes to User-Defined Types   112
Changes to Collections   112
    VB6-Style Collections   113
    The System.Collections Namespace   113
    Creating Custom Collections   114
New Arithmetic Operators   116
Short-Circuited If...Then Statements   116
Using Reserved Words as Procedure Names   117
No Set Statement   117
Changes to Property Routines   118
    Consistent Scoping   119
    ReadOnly Properties   119
    WriteOnly Properties   120
    Default Properties   120

Structured Error Handling 120
The Try…Catch…Finally Structure 121
Catch Statement Variations 122
Exit Try 122
Exception Objects 123
Converting from On Error Goto 123
Converting from On Error Resume Next 125
Changes to Procedure Syntax 126
Parentheses Required on Procedure Calls 126
ByVal Default for all Parameters 126
Optional Parameters Require a Default Value 127
The Return Statement 128
Changes to Event Handling 129
Raising Events 129
Handling Events 129
Handling Multiple Events 130
Using AddHandler 131
Depreciated, Obsolete, and Unsupported VB Syntax 131
Gosub 131
DefType Statements 132

Delegates **132**

Attributes **134**

Summary **135**

Chapter 5: Windows User Interface Capabilities **137**

The Importance of Windows Forms **138**

Windows Forms Basics **139**

Architecture of Windows Forms **140**
Consistency with Web Forms 142

Comparing Windows Forms to VB6 Forms **142**
Using the Visual Designer for Windows Forms 143
Invisible Controls go in the Component Tray 143
Not All Controls Have to be Locked 144
Form Properties for Cancel and Default Buttons 144
Positioning and Layout 145
Location Property 145
Size Property 145
BringToFront() and SendToBack() Methods 145
New Layout Properties for Forms 145
Resizing Multiple Controls 146
Differences in Dialog Boxes 146
ShowDialog Instead of Show vbModal 148
DialogResult 148

Table of Contents

New Capabilities of Windows Forms — 150

Changing the Shape of the Form — 150
New Properties to Change a Form's Appearance — 151
 The Opacity Property — 151
 The TransparencyKey Property — 152
Owned Forms — 152
 AddOwnedForm() Method — 152
 Owner Property — 152
 OwnedForms Collection — 153
 TopMost Property of Forms — 153

Controls in Windows Forms — 153

New Properties of Controls — 154
 Anchor and Dock — 154
 Accessibility Properties of Controls — 156
 The Modifiers Property — 156
Adding New Controls at Run-Time — 156

Summary of Important Controls — 157

New Controls — 158
 Menu Controls — 158
 LinkLabel — 162
 UpDown Controls – DomainUpDown and NumericUpDown — 162
 CheckedListBox — 163
 DateTimePicker — 163
 MonthCalendar — 164
 Panel and GroupBox Container Controls — 164
 NotifyIcon — 165
 Extender Provider Controls — 166
 Working with Provider Controls in Code — 167
 PrintDocument — 168
 DataGrid — 168
Changes to Existing Controls — 168
 Renamed Properties of Controls — 169
 Different Default Names — 169
 Image Control no Longer Exists — 169
 New Capabilities for Existing Controls — 169
 No Control Arrays — 169

Multiple Document Interface (MDI) Forms — 170

Creating an MDI Parent Form — 170
Differences in MDI Parent Forms — 170
Differences in MDI Child Forms — 171
Arranging Child Windows in the MDI Parent — 171
An MDI Example in Visual Basic .NET — 171

Inheritance in Windows Forms — 173

The Inheritance Picker — 174

GDI+ — 176

System.Drawing Namespace — 177
 System.Drawing.Graphics Class — 177

Using GDI+ Capabilities in a Windows Form   178
System.Drawing.Drawing2D   181
System.Drawing.Imaging   181
System.Drawing.Text Namespace   181
Changes from VB6 and Earlier   182

Creating Custom Windows Forms Controls   **182**
Inheriting from an Existing Control   183
Step-by-Step Process to Create the Control   183
Composite Controls   184
Basing a New Control on the Control Class   185

Summary   **185**

Chapter 6: New Object-Oriented Capabilities   187

What is Object Orientation?   **188**

The Relationship of Objects to Components   **188**

Visual Basic .NET OO Implementation   **189**
Creating Classes   190
The Class Keyword   191
Classes and Namespaces   191
Nested Classes   192
Creating Methods   193
Creating Properties   195
Creating Events   197
Object Lifecycle   197
Object Construction   198
Object Destruction   202
Interacting with Objects   204
Object Declaration and Instantiation   204
Dereferencing Objects   206
Early vs. Late Binding   207
Shared Class Members   209
Shared Methods   209
Shared Variables   210
Shared Events   212
Inheritance   212
Creating Subclasses   214
Preventing Inheritance   216
Inheritance and Scoping   217
Overloading Base Class Methods in Subclasses   218
Overriding Base Class Methods   219
Overriding the Constructor Method   226
Shadowing Methods   226
Abstract Base Classes and Methods   229
The Effect of Inheritance on Events   231

Interfaces   233
    Interface Declaration   233
    Implementing an Interface   234
    Implementing Multiple Interfaces   235

Cross-Language Inheritance   **236**
    Creating the Visual Basic .NET Base Class   236
    Creating the C# Subclass   237
    Creating a Client Application   238

Visual Inheritance   **239**

Summary   **239**

Chapter 7: Web Capabilities   **241**

Why Replace Active Server Pages?   **242**

Overview of Web Forms   **243**
    A Web Form in Action   244
    Behind the Scenes   248
    ASP.NET as the Runtime Engine   248
      System.Web.UI Namespace   248
    Anatomy of a Web Form   249
      The Template for Presentation   249
      The Code-Behind Module   250
      A Subclassed Instance of the Page Class   250
    Web Forms Event Model   251
      Postback vs. Non-Postback Events   252
      Order of Events   252
      Built-in Events are Limited 252
      Application and Session Events   253
      State Management and the Life Cycle of a Web Forms Page   253
      Disabling State Management 254

Layout of Web Forms   **255**

Server Controls   **256**
    Why Are Server Controls Needed?   256
    ASP.NET Server Controls   257
    Validation Controls   258
      How to Use Validation Controls   259
      Summary of Available Validation Controls   259
      Regular Expressions   259
      Laying Out Error Messages on the Page   260
      Disabling Validation   260
    Custom Web Form Server Controls   260
      Differences for Extending an Existing Web Control   263

Data Binding in Web Forms   **263**

A Final Example – A Small Application Using Web Forms   **264**

Configuring Your Application with Web.config   **268**
    Securing an ASP.NET Web Site   269
    State Management Options   270

Overview of Web Services   **271**
    What are Web Services Used For?   271
    Understanding the SOAP Protocol   272
    Creating a Web Service in Visual Basic .NET   273
    Consuming a Web Service in Visual Basic .NET   275
    Creating and Consuming a Web Service   276
    Security in Web Services   277

Summary   **278**

Chapter 8: Data Access   **281**

ADO.NET vs. ADO   **282**
    ADO.NET Demands New Architectures   283

ADO.NET – Important Concepts   **283**
    Location of the ADO.NET classes   284
    Replacing Recordsets   284
    What is a DataSet?   284
    Data Flow Overview for a DataSet   285

Data Providers for Connected Operations   **287**
    Providers Included with .NET   287
        The OLE DB Data Provider   288
        The SQL Server Data Provider   288
    Classes Implemented by Data Providers   288
        Working With Data Provider Classes Using Wizards   289
        Combining Classes From Different Data Providers   289
        Working With Data Providers in Code   290
        Connection Classes   290
        Command Classes   291
        The DataReader Class   293
        The DataAdapter Class   295

How the ADO.NET Classes Work Together   **297**

Structure of a DataSet   **298**
    DataTable   299
    DataColumn   300
    DataRow   301
        Changing Data in a Row   301
        Examining Different Versions of Data in a Row   302
    Constraints   303
    DataRelation   304
        Using DataRelations for Master-Detail Data   305

Table of Contents

Working with a DataSet   **306**

Adding Rows to a DataTable   306
Finding a Particular Row in a DataTable   307
Deleting Rows from a DataTable   307
Creating a DataSet Manually   308
Creating a DataSet Using the DataAdapter Wizard   309
  Windows Form Example   310
  Web Forms Example   315

Using DataViews   **317**

Getting a Subset of Data into a DataView   317
Sorting a DataView   318

Typed DataSets   **319**

Using Stored Procedures in ADO.NET   **321**

Stored Procedures with Command Classes   321
Using Stored Procedures With DataAdapters   322

Exception Classes for ADO.NET   **323**

Data Binding   **324**

Data Binding with Listboxes and Combo Boxes   324
Data Binding to a Collection of Objects   325
Data Binding to any Property   326

Accessing XML through ADO.NET   **326**

Saving Changes to the Data   327
Persisting a DataSet in XML   328

Accessing XML through the DOM   **328**

The System.XML Namespace   328

Some General Guidelines for Using ADO.NET   **329**

When to Use DataReaders   329
When to use DataSets   329
Changes to the Business Tier with ADO.NET   330

When is Classic ADO Still Needed?   **330**

Pessimistic Concurrency   330
Applications that Need Server-Side Cursors   331

Summary   **331**

Chapter 9: Advanced Topics   **333**

Middle Tier Components   **334**

.NET Remoting   334
  Rules for Remote Access to Objects   336
  Implementing Remoting   339
Enterprise Services   349
  Transactional Processing   349

Using Microsoft Message Queue (MSMQ)   353
The System.Messaging Namespace   353

.NET Threading   **357**
Working with Threads   357
Thread Lifetimes   362
Interacting with the Current Thread   362
Passing Data to a Thread   363
Asynchronous Processing   365

Console Applications   **372**
Use of the System.Console Namespace   373

New Printing Model   **375**
PrintDocument and Related Objects   375
Implementing Printing   376
Basic Code Structure   376
Creating an Example   377
Rendering the Output   377
Invoking the Print Dialog   380
Invoking the Page Dialog   381

Creating a Windows NT/2K Service with VB   **382**
Creating a Windows Service   382
The Windows Service Project   382
Writing to the Application Log   383
Creating Worker Threads   384
Installing the Service   385

Monitoring the File System   **388**

Command Line Options   **390**
vbc Command Line Parameters   390
Description of Tools in the bin Directory   391
Configuration and Deployment Tools and Utilities   392
Windows Forms Design Tools and Utilities   393
Security Tools and Utilities   393
General Tools and Utilities   394

Summary   **395**

Chapter 10: Installation and Deployment   **397**

Build Configurations   **398**

The .NET Framework Redistributable   **399**

XCOPY Deployment   **400**
Windows Applications   400
Web Applications   401

Formal Installers   **403**

Windows Applications   405
    Creating a Test Application   405
    Running the Setup Wizard   406
    Running the Setup Program   410
Web Applications   411
    Creating a Test Application   411
    Running the Setup Wizard   412
    Running the Setup Program   413

Automatic Deployment   **414**

Launching a .NET Program from a URL   415
    Creating the NetRun Application   416
    Deploying an Application   417
    Adding NetRun to the Path   418
    Creating a Windows Shortcut   418
Using a Shell Program   419
    Creating the Shell Application   419
    Creating a Child Form   422
Security Considerations   423

Summary   **426**

Chapter 11: Interoperability and Migration   **429**

COM/DCOM Interoperability   **430**

Invoking COM Components From .NET   430
    Designing COM Components for .NET   430
    Calling a COM Component   434
    Using ADO from Visual Basic .NET   439
    DCOM   440
    Using ActiveX Controls from Windows Forms   441
Invoking .NET Components from COM   443
    Creating a .NET Assembly for COM   444
    Creating a COM Client   445

Calling Windows APIs   **446**

Using the Platform Invocation Services   446
    Calling a Simple API Function   447
    Aliasing a Function   448
    Hiding an API Interface   449
    Using Automatic ANSI/Unicode Location   449
    Passing Structures as Parameters   450

Using the Migration Wizard   **452**

The Migration Process   452
    Running the Wizard   452
    General Wizard Activities   454

Summary   **454**

Index   **457**

Introduction

As one of the languages forming part of the recently released .NET Framework, Visual Basic .NET is most likely to be the most popular tool to develop on this platform for years to come. As a result, thousands of existing Visual Basic developers will need to get to grips with the language's new features as well as modified old facilities.

This book is targeted at experienced Visual Basic 6 developers who are looking toward the future – Microsoft's .NET platform and its associated Framework. In porting Visual Basic to this new platform, Microsoft has had to make some important modifications to the language, adding features such as:

❑ Full object-orientation, including class inheritance, method overloading, parameterized constructors, and shared class members

❑ Structured error handling

❑ New threading models

The aim of this book is bring VB6 developers quickly up to speed in these (and other) new important features of Visual Basic .NET.

Who is This Book For?

This book covers not only a new version of Visual Basic, but also the new programming platform on which it runs. It is aimed at developers with a good working knowledge of VB, or ASP and VBScript. No attempt is made at providing a tutorial about the VB language, other than comparisons between VB6 and Visual Basic .NET code techniques, so a good familiarity with VB6 (or at least VBA or VBScript) is necessary to get the full benefit from this book.

Visual Basic .NET is also positioned to be a premier web development tool, not only for traditional web applications, but also for the creation of Web Services and web-based mobile applications.

As a result, this book will also appeal to web developers who are using ASP.NET and intend to use the VB language when developing their ASP.NET sites. The level of integration between ASP.NET and Visual Basic .NET far exceeds that between ASP and VB6, and a comprehensive understanding of Visual Basic .NET will be a huge asset to any web developer using ASP.NET.

In fact, the Visual InterDev development tool provided by Microsoft for ASP development has, in effect, been replaced. The functional equivalent to Visual InterDev in the .NET environment is the **Visual Studio .NET IDE**.

The .NET Framework provides a powerful new way to program for both Windows and the Internet, and this may well attract experienced developers from other platforms and languages to .NET and the Visual Basic .NET language. This book will appeal to these people as it provides discussion and examples of commonly performed programming tasks and techniques, allowing rapid transition from other platforms or languages to Visual Basic .NET.

What is Covered in This Book?

Chapter 1 of this book is about getting started with Visual Basic .NET – installing the required software, and coding and running our first 'Hello World' example.

All of the new features that we mentioned at the start of this *Introduction* are based on Microsoft's .NET Framework. We will start **Chapter 2** with an overview of the .NET Framework, emphasizing the details of importance to a VB developer.

While the .NET Framework offers the long-awaited new capabilities listed above, it also raises barriers to making the transition from older versions of VB to Visual Basic .NET. For a start, there is the new IDE, Visual Studio .NET. There are also a significant number of syntactical differences; fitting into the .NET Framework also required serious changes to the structure of the VB language – including rationalization of data types and syntax to bring VB in line with other languages. These changes pose difficulties that must be understood to allow developers to make a fast, efficient, and frustration-free leap to Visual Basic .NET. This is the focus of **Chapters 3 and 4**, which provide an overview of the new Visual Studio .NET IDE, and explore the syntactic and coding changes to the language.

For years, VB developers have worked with the forms engine built into the Visual Basic IDE. This forms environment is what allows VB developers to quickly and easily build applications with Windows user interfaces. The .NET Framework provides a common forms environment known as **Windows Forms** – Visual Basic .NET uses this and not Ruby, the VB6 forms engine. While Windows Forms offer the same powerful Windows GUI capabilities as the old VB forms engine, this is an entirely new environment, offering new capabilities and new ways to do the things we have been doing for years. **Chapter 5** tackles this new environment, demonstrating how to build the usual types of GUI interface and some of its exciting new capabilities.

With the introduction of version 4.0, VB developers gained the ability to use class modules to write OO programs, and to create reusable COM components. Since then, it has become apparent that the lack of a complete OO environment – in particular the lack of both visual and full class inheritance – was a limiting factor when building complex systems in VB. Visual inheritance is the ability to create a new Windows Form that inherits the attributes, controls, and behaviors from an existing form. Class (or 'implementation') inheritance is the ability to create a new class that 'inherits' the properties, methods, *and code* from an existing class.

Visual Basic .NET addresses this issue head-on by providing **full OO capabilities**, including both visual and code-based inheritance, method overloading, method overriding, and more. These capabilities are integral to the .NET environment in general, as well as being of great benefit to the VB developer. We will explore these new capabilities in **Chapter 6**, illustrating how all the benefits of OO programming are now available to VB developers.

Besides changing traditional VB development, Visual Basic .NET will also open up the possibility for web programming to hundreds of thousands of developers who did not embrace Active Server Pages (ASP) and its related technologies. **Chapter 7** provides a quick look at the **ASP.NET environment** – giving us a glimpse of how, with Visual Basic .NET, development of web-based screens and software will be quite similar to development of Windows screens and software with earlier versions of VB. ASP.NET makes it easy for VB developers to develop web systems.

The key technologies in Visual Basic .NET that simplify the transition are **Web Forms** and **XML Web Services**. While many of the features of these technologies will look familiar to VB developers, there are some significant differences and pitfalls to be avoided, such as the problem of using events extensively when communicating with a server. ASP.NET is a very large topic in itself, but **Chapter 7** should provide a good start on the concepts from a VB developer's perspective.

Over the years, Microsoft has developed a continual string of data access technologies that have been available to VB developers. We have worked with DAO, then RDO, and most recently the various versions of ADO. It should be no surprise then, that .NET comes with a whole new data access technology named **ADO.NET**. While it is possible for Visual Basic .NET programs to continue to use older data access technologies through interoperability mechanisms, most Visual Basic .NET developers will be likely to use ADO.NET, since it provides the easiest and most direct approach. **Chapter 8** discusses ADO.NET, demonstrating how to read, create, update, and delete data using the new technology.

The entire .NET platform, Visual Basic .NET included, is very reliant on data handled in an XML format. Therefore, **Chapter 8** also discusses how developers can use **XML** from Visual Basic .NET, both via ADO.NET and directly from VB itself.

We will discuss some more **advanced topics** in **Chapter 9**, such as the creation of middle tier and transactional components, the creation of console applications (Visual Basic .NET interacts easily with the standard console input/output mechanisms, `stdin` and `stdout`), and the set of very powerful external tools and utilities that come with the .NET Framework, including the VB compiler itself, which can be run directly from the command line if needed. We will also take a brief look at cross-language development with C#, how to write a program to monitor the file system for changes, and how to create a Windows NT service with VB.

One key goal of the .NET Framework is to simplify deployment and to eliminate **DLL Hell**, a topic we will enthusiastically cover in **Chapter 10** since it has been one of the biggest headaches for VB developers. Not only does Visual Basic .NET fix most DLL Hell issues, but we are also provided with the most **powerful and complete deployment technology** ever included with Visual Basic – a huge step forward as compared to previous Setup Wizard or Package and Deployment Wizard technologies. Add to this the ability to 'auto-deploy' components by running an application or parts of an application from a URL and things get very exciting indeed!

Obviously, most existing developers have substantial applications based on COM and other existing technologies such as ADO. **Chapter 11** will cover **interoperability and migration**, showing how Visual Basic .NET programs can make use of existing COM components, or can be used from COM components if necessary. We will also take a quick look at Microsoft's migration wizard here. This wizard helps upgrade existing VB6 applications to Visual Basic .NET.

The 80:20 Principle for Coverage of Topics

.NET obviously represents a very substantial platform change for Microsoft developers. While most of the component-oriented concepts from COM carry forward to .NET, there are some very major changes and enhancements in the new environment.

Whereas today a developer may interact with the Win32 API, in .NET, most interaction will be with the **.NET system class library**. In fact, any .NET program will make heavy use of this system class library to operate, requiring any developer who wishes to work in the .NET environment to learn the class library to a large degree.

On top of all these platform changes, there are the changes to VB itself. From a feature perspective, we now have inheritance and free-threading, to name just a couple of features. In addition to the feature changes, there are many syntax and coding changes that will impact upon day-to-day use of the language.

The VB IDE has now been merged into the Visual Studio .NET IDE, along with all the other .NET development tools. This integrated IDE is similar in some ways to the VB6 IDE, but there are some radical differences.

In fact, there are so many changes that a single book can't cover everything. Rather than trying to provide superficial coverage of every change, we have opted to apply the 80:20 rule – the idea being that if we cover 80 percent of the features, we will be providing a resource useful in most cases. In this book, we will provide thorough coverage of the most common changes developers will face. We will focus quite a lot on the IDE changes, the syntax changes, and the most important new features. To some degree we will also cover the .NET system class library, but only as it pertains to the types of scenarios most commonly faced by VB developers today.

What You Need to Use This Book

To run the samples in this book, you will need to have the following:

❑   Windows 2000 or Windows XP.

❑   Visual Basic .NET, which can be either the redistributable (included in the .NET SDK) or any version of the Visual Studio .NET development environment.

At least a few months of hands-on experience with Visual Basic is also assumed, as is some familiarity with data access via ADO.

The complete source code for the samples is available for download from our web site, http://www.wrox.com/. To download the code, click on the VB.NET link near the top of the page, find the **Fast Track Visual Basic .NET** link, and then click on the associated **Code Download** link. Alternatively, there is a link to the code download from the book overview page, http://www.wrox.com/Books/Book_Details.asp?isbn=1861007124.

Style Conventions

We have used a number of different styles of text and layout in this book to help differentiate between the different kinds of information. Here are examples of the styles we used and an explanation of what they mean.

Code has several font styles. If it is a word that we are talking about in the text – for example, when discussing a For...Next loop – it is in this font. If it is a block of code that can be typed as a program and run, then it is in a gray box:

```
Private Sub Button1_Click(ByVal sender As System.Object, _
   ByVal e As System.EventArgs) Handles Button1.Click
End Sub
```

Sometimes, you will see code in a mixture of styles, like this:

```
Private Sub Button1_Click(ByVal sender As System.Object, _
   ByVal e As System.EventArgs) Handles Button1.Click

   MsgBox(TextBox1.Text)

End Sub
```

In cases like this, the code with a white background is code that we are already familiar with. The line highlighted in gray is a new addition to the code since we last looked at it.

Advice, hints, and background information comes in this type of font.

> **Important pieces of information come in boxes like this.**

Important Words are in a bold type font.

Words that appear on the screen, or in menus like the File or Window, are in a similar font to the one you would see on a Windows desktop.

Keys that you press on the keyboard like *Ctrl* and *Enter* are in italics.

Commands that you need to type in on the command line are shown with a > for the prompt, and the input in **bold**, like this:

```
>something to type on the command line
```

Customer Support and Feedback

We always value hearing from our readers, and we want to know what you think about this book; what you liked, what you didn't like, and what you think we can do better next time. You can send us your comments, either by returning the reply card in the back of the book, or by e-mail to feedback@wrox.com. Please be sure to mention the book ISBN and the title in your message.

Source Code and Updates

As you work through the examples in this book, you may decide that you prefer to type in all the code by hand. Many readers prefer this because it is a good way to get familiar with the coding techniques that are being used. However, whether you want to type the code in or not, we have made all the source code for this book available at the Wrox.com web site.

When you log on to the Wrox.com site at http://www.wrox.com/, simply locate the title through our Search facility or by using one of the title lists. Then click on the Download Code link on the book's detail page and you can obtain all the source code.

The files that are available for download from our site have been archived using WinZip. When you have saved the attachments to a folder on your hard drive, you need to extract the files using a de-compression program such as WinZip or PKUnzip. When you extract the files, the code is usually extracted into chapter folders. When you start the extraction process, ensure your software (WinZip, PKUnzip, and so on) has Use folder names under Extract to: (or the equivalent) checked.

Even if you like to type in the code, you can use our source files to check the results you should be getting – they should be your first stop if you think you might have typed in an error. If you don't like typing, then downloading the source code from our web site is a must! Either way, it will help you with updates and debugging.

Errata

We have made every effort to make sure that there are no errors in the text or in the code. However, no one is perfect and mistakes do occur. If you find an error in this book, like a spelling mistake or a faulty piece of code, we would be very grateful for feedback. By sending in errata, you may save another reader hours of frustration, and of course, you will be helping us provide even higher quality information. Simply e-mail the information to support@wrox.com; your information will be checked and if correct, posted to the errata page for that title, and used in subsequent editions of the book.

To find errata on the web site, log on to http://www.wrox.com/, and simply locate the title through our Search facility or title list. Then, on the book details page, click on the Book Errata link. On this page you will be able to view all the errata that have been submitted and checked through by editorial. You will also be able to click the Submit Errata link to notify us of any errata that you may have found.

Technical Support

If you wish to directly query a problem in the book then e-mail support@wrox.com. A typical e-mail should include the following things:

❑ The **book name**, **last four digits of the ISBN** (7124 for this book), and **page number** of the problem in the Subject field

❑ Your **name**, **contact information**, and the **problem** in the body of the message

We *won't* send you junk mail. We need the details to save your time and ours. When you send an e-mail message, it will go through the following chain of support:

1. **Customer Support** – Your message is delivered to one of our customer support staff, who are the first people to read it. They have files on most frequently asked questions and will answer anything general about the book or the web site immediately.

2. **Editorial** – Deeper queries are forwarded to the technical editor responsible for that book. They have experience with the programming language or particular product, and are able to answer detailed technical questions on the subject. Once an issue has been resolved, the editor can post the errata to the web site.

3. **The Authors** – Finally, in the unlikely event that the editor cannot answer your problem, they will forward the request to the author. We do try to protect the author from any distractions to their writing, however, we are quite happy to forward specific requests to them. All Wrox authors help with the support on their books. They will mail the customer and the editor with their response, and again all readers should benefit.

> Note that the Wrox support process can only offer support to issues that are directly pertinent to the content of our published title. Support for questions that fall outside the scope of normal book support is provided via the community lists of our http://p2p.wrox.com/ forum.

p2p.wrox.com

For author and peer discussion join, the **P2P mailing lists**. Our unique system provides **programmer to programmer**™ contact on mailing lists, forums, and newsgroups, all *in addition* to our one-to-one e-mail support system. Be confident that your query is being examined by the many Wrox authors, and other industry experts, who are present on our mailing lists. At p2p.wrox.com you will find a number of different lists that will help you, not only while you read this book, but also as you develop your own applications.

To subscribe to a mailing list just follow this these steps:

1. Go to http://p2p.wrox.com/ and choose the appropriate category from the left menu bar.

2. Click on the mailing list you wish to join.

3. Follow the instructions to subscribe and fill in your e-mail address and password.

4. Reply to the confirmation e-mail you receive.

5. Use the subscription manager to join more lists and set your mail preferences.

1

Getting Started

In February 2002 at the VS Live! conference in San Francisco, Microsoft officially launched the **.NET Framework** and **Visual Studio .NET**. Microsoft's .NET Framework represents a major shift in the technical direction of Microsoft, and a major shift for those engaged in developing software using Microsoft tools. Microsoft has staked its future on the .NET Framework, shifting away from the COM-based world of today and towards a more distributed, open, and dynamic environment.

For the past several years **Visual Basic** (or abbreviated to simply **VB**) has been the most widely used programming language in the world. Unsurprisingly, Microsoft has brought VB forward into the .NET Framework in the form of **Visual Basic .NET**, sometimes referred to as just **VB.NET**. Visual Basic .NET is the natural progression for existing VB developers as they move to the .NET environment, and so, it is likely to be the most popular tool to develop in this framework for the next few years.

Microsoft has also introduced the new **C#** (pronounced *C sharp*) language. There is no doubt that C# will be used by many developers. However, for the typical VB developer it is likely that Visual Basic .NET will be the logical choice, since it preserves the same basic language structure and syntax as VB has, while providing access to all the new .NET platform features along with full **object-oriented** (OO) capabilities.

The .NET Framework is a large change from the existing Windows DNA COM development environment, and Visual Basic .NET has some substantial changes from previous versions of VB. At the same time, most existing VB developers will probably have enough to learn, without having to become familiar with a new language syntax and structure such as C#.

Perhaps even more important is the fact that the Visual Basic .NET and C# languages have the same basic capabilities, so neither offers a clear advantage over the other from an objective standpoint. C# offers a couple features that Visual Basic .NET doesn't (such as operator overloading), while Visual Basic .NET in turn offers a couple features that C# doesn't (such as late binding syntax). Your choice of language between C# and Visual Basic .NET really does come down to which one decreases the learning curve and makes you more comfortable and productive as a developer.

.NET has been in development for more than three years. Parts of it have gone under the names COOL, Next Generation Windows Services (NGWS), Windows DNA 2000, COM+ 2.0, and Visual Studio 7.0. All these have now been consolidated within the .NET umbrella, providing a level of consistency.

The released .NET software we have today, though still new by software standards, is not entirely new, having been in development for some time. Also, for the first time, Microsoft bolstered its development process with several open beta releases, so many people have already been working and building systems with Microsoft .NET for a year or more prior to its official launch.

Additionally, the .NET environment builds on a great deal of existing software, including the Windows 32-bit operating systems, COM, COM+, MSMQ, and previous versions of Visual Studio. The .NET Framework also builds on a number of new or existing standards such as HTML, CSS, XML, and SOAP.

.NET is arguably the biggest thing to hit the VB community since VB4, when the ability to create 32-bit applications, classes, and COM components was introduced. In fact, .NET is a much bigger and broader-reaching change since it provides a whole new inter-object communication mechanism that doesn't rely directly on COM.

That means hundreds of thousands, if not millions, of existing VB developers will need to make the transition from VB6 to Visual Basic .NET; and it is a major leap. This book is intended to help smooth the transition by:

- Discussing the new capabilities of Visual Basic .NET

- Illustrating the important changes and differences from previous versions

- And most importantly, by providing experienced developers' understanding of the changes and, where possible, the reasoning behind them

We feel that Visual Basic .NET and the .NET Framework are the most exciting and revolutionary technologies to come from Microsoft in many years. We hope that, through this book, we can share our enthusiasm and help developers get rapidly up to speed in this new environment.

The .NET Environment

The .NET Framework, Visual Basic .NET, and Visual Studio .NET are separate, but related, things. The .NET Framework includes the **Common Language Runtime** (or **CLR**), the system class libraries, and other tools. Visual Basic .NET is one of the languages provided with the .NET Framework. Visual Basic .NET is typically used within the Visual Studio .NET (sometimes shortened to VS.NET) package. Visual Studio .NET is a development tool and IDE for use by developers, and it requires the .NET Framework in order to operate.

There is also the **.NET runtime**, which must be installed on a machine before it can run .NET applications. The runtime is included within the .NET Framework, so it is automatically available on your development workstations, but must be installed on client machines or servers before they can run .NET code.

Microsoft .NET also includes the **.NET Enterprise Servers**. These include SQL Server 2000, Biztalk Server, Exchange Server 2000, and others. These servers are not written using the .NET Framework, but rather, are written using Windows and COM technologies. Thus, they are not only able to support .NET development, but they can also support Windows and COM development. We won't focus on these servers in this book other than the occasional use of SQL Server for data.

The following diagram helps illustrate how the various parts of Microsoft .NET fit together:

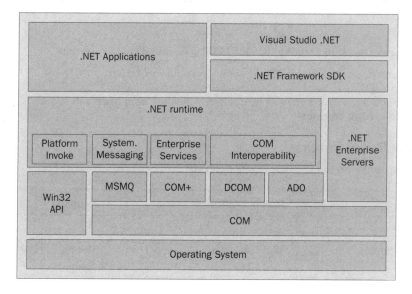

.NET System Requirements

It is important to understand the basic requirements needed to run each of these technologies. This includes minimum operating system versions and any other dependencies. To make this simpler, we have broken the problem into three parts:

- ❑ **End user** requirements
- ❑ **Server** requirements, encompassing both web server and application server
- ❑ **Developer** requirements

End User Requirements

The following table lists the end user operating system requirements:

Minimum	Recommended	Supported
Windows 98	Windows XP	Windows 98 Windows Me Windows NT 4 (SP6a) Windows 2000 (SP2) Windows XP Home Windows XP Pro

Other notes:

❑   System.Messenging requires that MSMQ be installed on the system

❑   EnterpriseServices require COM+ (Windows 2000 or higher)

The .NET runtime redistributable can be freely downloaded from Microsoft at http://msdn.microsoft.com/net.

Web Server Requirements

The following table lists the web server requirements:

Minimum	Recommended	Supported
IIS 5.0 Windows 2000	Windows 2000	Windows 2000 (SP2) Windows XP Pro

Other notes:

❑   As with any web server, the more memory the better

Application Server Requirements

The following table lists the application server requirements:

Minimum	Recommended	Supported
IIS 5.0 (for XML Web Services) Windows NT 4(SP6a)	Windows 2000	Windows NT 4 (SP6a) Windows 2000 (SP2) Windows XP Pro

Other notes:

- ❏ XML Web Services require Windows 2000 or higher
- ❏ .NET Remoting requires Windows 98, Windows NT 4, or higher
- ❏ System.Messenging requires that MSMQ be installed on the system
- ❏ EnterpriseServices require COM+ (Windows 2000 or higher)

Developer Requirements

Visual Basic .NET development can be done with nothing more than the .NET Framework SDK and a text editor. Of course, we'll typically use Visual Studio .NET, as it is a much more productive environment in most cases.

Either way, many developers tend to not only do development on their machine, but also run a web server, database server, and other tools. The key to making this work effectively is to have a lot of RAM on the system. When programming with the Framework SDK, 256 MB of RAM is typically sufficient, and with Visual Studio .NET, it is ideal to have at least 384 MB. Obviously, it is possible to work with less than these amounts, but if it is possible to get more memory, that is better.

The following table lists the developer requirements when working with the .NET Framework SDK:

Minimum	Recommended	Supported
Windows 98	Windows XP Pro	Windows 98 Windows Me Windows NT 4 (SP6a) Windows 2000 (SP2) Windows XP Home Windows XP Pro

Other notes:

- ❏ Web development requires access to a web server running .NET (see earlier)
- ❏ XML Web Services development requires access to a web server running .NET (see earlier)
- ❏ System.Messenging requires that MSMQ be installed on the system
- ❏ EnterpriseServices require COM+ (Windows 2000 or higher)
- ❏ Developing with just the SDK requires you to bring your own text editor

The .NET Framework SDK can be freely downloaded from Microsoft at http://msdn.microsoft.com/net.

Most developers will tend to use Visual Studio .NET for development, as it provides a much richer and more productive environment than the command line and a text editor. Visual Studio .NET is available in several versions, including Professional and the more comprehensive Enterprise Architect. For information about the specific versions available please refer to http://msdn.microsoft.com/vstudio/default.asp.

The following table lists the developer requirements when working with the Visual Studio .NET:

Minimum	Recommended	Supported
Windows NT 4 (SP6a)	Windows XP Pro	Windows NT 4 (SP6a) Windows 2000 (SP2) Windows XP Pro

Other notes:

❏ Visual Studio .NET requires a lot of memory; 256 MBs is the minimum recommended

❏ Web development requires access to a web server running .NET (see earlier)

❏ XML Web Services development requires access to a web server running .NET (see earlier)

❏ `System.Messenging` requires that MSMQ be installed on the system

❏ EnterpriseServices require COM+ (Windows 2000 or higher)

Visual Studio .NET comes in several editions that can be purchased commercially. Visual Studio .NET is also available to all MSDN Universal subscribers as part of their subscription and via the MSDN subscriber download web site.

In this book, we'll do our Visual Basic .NET development using Visual Studio .NET, and so, it is recommended that you, as a developer, should use Windows 2000 or Windows XP Professional as your development platform as you go through the book.

Other Common Concerns

At this point, we have a good grasp on the basic environment and requirements for our end users, servers, and developers. There are some other issues or concerns that are common when configuring an environment for .NET, and we will cover them here.

Mapped Network Drives

Visual Studio .NET cannot be installed to a mapped drive – it must be installed to a physical local drive to operate.

Additionally, extra steps are required if we want to store our code on a mapped drive during development. By default, .NET security treats a mapped drive as an Intranet site and this prevents that code from having full trust or full security. Most development assumes full security, and so, we need to either have our development code on a local drive, or change the .NET security settings for the mapped drive where we are storing our code.

To change the security to allow development code to reside on a network server, we can use the .NET Framework Configuration tool, which can be found under Start | Settings | Control Panel | Administrative Tools. This tool allows us to configure various aspects of .NET on our system, including security:

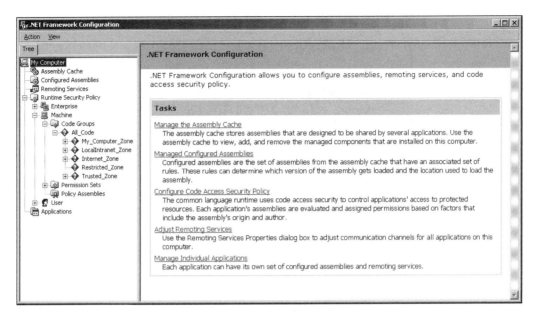

In this screenshot, the security policy for the development machine is expanded, listing all the **code groups** defined for the system. A code group defines the security for a specific .NET assembly, or location containing assemblies.

Code groups are maintained in a tree structure. Since a network server is considered part of the intranet, we will need to add a new code group for our server under the LocalIntranet_Zone node. Our new code group will add extra capabilities to a specific server within this zone.

Right-click on the LocalIntranet_Zone node and choose New.... This will bring up a dialog allowing us to add a child code group for this zone. Name the code group and give it a description:

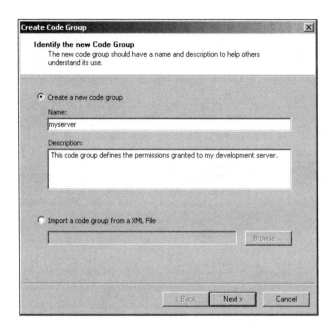

After clicking on **Next**, the following window of the wizard allows us to specify the assembly or location to which this code group applies. In our case, we want to add a server. This is done by adding a URL entry:

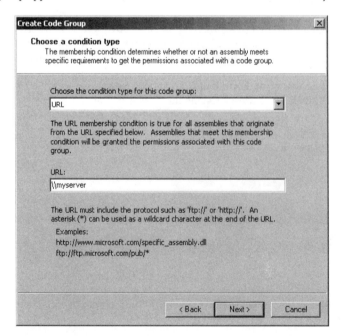

The URL itself is the network name of our server. This code group will now apply to any location on this particular server, adding any security settings we specify to those already granted by the LocalIntranet_Zone code group.

In the next panel of the wizard, we specify the permissions to be granted. For development purposes, we want to have full security, and that is defined by the FullTrust permission set.

The final panel of the wizard simply confirms the code group we are about to add. When we are finished, our new code group will be listed in the configuration tool, and any code residing on that server will have full security permissions. This means we can use network mapped drives on that server for development.

Optional Services

To fully explore the capabilities of Visual Basic .NET, we will need an environment that supplies a set of services. Not all of these services are required for basic applications, but they are required to gain the full benefit of the technology:

- ❑ **Database** – Many of the sample projects in .NET require a SQL Server database to operate. This will probably be true of most applications we create, since many business applications interact with a database. At a minimum, we will run the Microsoft SQL Server 2000 Desktop Engine (MSDE 2000), which is a sub-set of Microsoft SQL Server 2000. It is often nicer to have a full installation of Microsoft SQL Server 2000 available for use, however. This server can run on our development workstation, or on a separate server as long as it is available for use by our applications.

- ❑ **Message Queuing Services (MSMQ)** – The .NET system class libraries include the System.Messaging namespace. These classes provide support for queued messaging and they rely on an installation of MSMQ. We might install MSMQ directly on our development workstation, or it can be running on a server in our network, with only the MSMQ client software installed on our workstation. Either way, MSMQ is required to work with the System.Messaging classes.

- ❑ **Distributed Transaction Coordinator (DTC)** – The .NET environment supports transactional components. These components rely on COM+ and the DTC to provide transactional support. If we are going to build transactional components, we will need the DTC service enabled and running on our Windows 2000 or Windows XP system.

Installing and Configuring the Samples

As part of the Visual Studio .NET installation, the .NET Framework SDK is also installed. This occurs during the Windows Component Update process. When the SDK is installed, it includes a large number of sample applications that can be very helpful in figuring out how to do many things in .NET. Before these samples can be run, however, the system must be configured.

The configuration includes installing the MSDE, a free developer edition of SQL Server. If your system already has a version of SQL Server 2000 installed, a new server instance will be added for the sample databases.

Configuring the Samples

Under the Start menu is an option to access the samples. Choosing
Start | Programs | Microsoft .NET Framework SDK | Samples and Quickstart Tutorials will bring up a
web page in your browser that includes instructions on how to configure the machine. Basically, this
involves clicking the two links on the page – the first to install the MSDE (or add the database instance)
and the second to configure IIS and the MSDE databases. Step one may require a reboot of the machine
when it completes. The second link in the process goes through a series of steps, and displays a helpful
dialog during the process to keep us informed.

When it completes, the samples are ready to run. If we refresh this web page, the configuration steps
will no longer be displayed, and instead it will act as an entry point to the sample code. The Quickstart
Tutorials are very valuable and are now accessible either via the current web page or directly at
http://localhost/quickstart.

Running the Samples from other Machines

Once installed and configured, the samples are ready to run from our machine. However, we may want
to access some of the web samples from other machines on our network or even on the Internet.

By default, the security setting on the virtual roots created for the web samples preclude running the
samples on machines other than the server itself. For those samples that should be available to a wider
audience, we will need to update the security.

To do this, open up the **Internet Information Services MMC** console by choosing
Start | Settings | Control Panel | Administrative Tools and then choosing Internet Services Manager.

Log in as an **Administrator** and open the Internet Services Manager window, expand the
Default Web Site entry in the tree on the left. Locate the QuickStart virtual root. Right-click on this and
choose the Properties option:

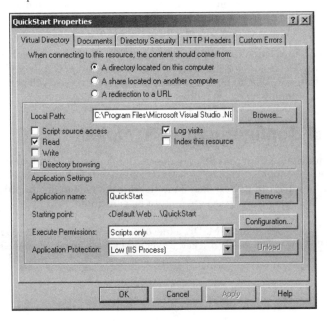

Switch to the Directory Security tab and click the Edit button in the
IP address and domain name restrictions panel. This will bring up another dialog indicating that this
virtual root is restricted for use only by the local machine. To make the root available to all other
machines, simply click the Granted Access option, then click OK. This change removes the machine
restriction from the virtual root, making it available to all machines on the network. If your machine is
available via the Internet, the virtual root will now be available to anyone on the Internet.

This method is only available for a Windows 2000 Server installation.

> **Configuring the virtual roots in this manner can cause a security issue. Be aware of
> the potential risks before opening these sites up for general Internet access.**

Configuring a Remote IIS Server

To develop applications using Web Forms or Web Services, we must have access to a machine with an
IIS installation. That machine might be your development workstation, in which case we're all set.
However, it might be a separate machine – especially if your development workstation is running
Windows NT 4.

If the web server is a separate machine, we need to configure that machine before it can be used for
.NET applications. The remote web server must be running IIS 5.0 or higher, along with FrontPage
2000 Server Extensions, so it must be either a Windows 2000 or Windows XP Professional machine.

The easiest way to configure a web server for use with .NET is to use the Visual Studio .NET installer to
perform the Windows Component Update process – thereby upgrading all required components on the
server and also installing the .NET Framework SDK. With that done, the server machine can run .NET
applications, but it is not fully configured to provide debugging support for Visual Studio .NET.

To provide full debugging support, continue with the Visual Studio .NET installation, choosing Step 2
in the process. When prompted for the various installation options by the installer, uncheck all the
options except for the Server Components. Then expand the Server Components element and make
sure all items within it are checked – in particular the Remote Debugger option.

By allowing the installer to run through the Windows Component Update process, and then configuring
the server machine with the server components, we'll be assured that the server has everything we need
both to host web applications and to integrate with the development environment on our workstations.

Getting Started with Hello World

In this section we will walk quickly through the process of building the traditional Hello World
program. We will return to this program in Chapter 3 to explain everything that is going on. So, for
now, let's just roll with it, even though there may be a number of things that look a bit odd to any VB6
developer. The primary goal of this section is just to get our feet wet with a very brief introduction to
the development environment and process.

This book was written using the Enterprise Architect version of Visual Studio .NET, but the following code and process should work with any version of the product.

To get started, open up the Visual Studio .NET IDE by choosing
Start | Programs | Microsoft Visual Studio.NET | Microsoft Visual Studio .NET. This will bring up the IDE for the first time.

The Visual Studio .NET IDE is common across Visual Basic .NET, Visual C# .NET, and Visual C++, and Microsoft licenses the IDE such that other vendors can add languages to it as well. This could make it a very complicated place – just think about pressing *F1* for help on a keyword in Visual Basic .NET and getting a description of that word for something like COBOL.

On top of this, various IDEs have historically had different key mappings. VB has typically used *F5* to launch an application in debug mode for instance, but that is not true for all language environments.

To avoid these sorts of issues, the IDE allows us to specify the profile we want to use within it. The My Profile link defines the keyboard shortcuts that apply, the default layouts of the windows, and the default filter to be used when searching for help, along with some other configuration items.

For most existing VB developers, the appropriate choice will be to select Visual Basic Developer from the list in the Profile dropdown. Choosing this will change the other options, causing the screen to appear as shown in the following screenshot:

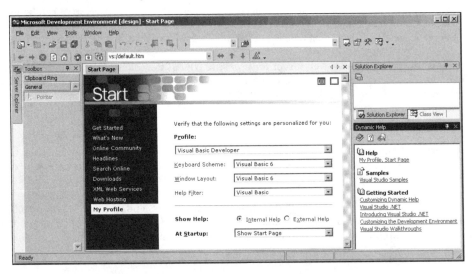

From here, we can simply click Get Started to proceed to the regular Visual Studio .NET start page. If you ever feel the need to change the profile you have selected, you can return here by clicking on the My Profile link again.

Notice the tack or pin icon in the top right of the Toolbox pane. This icon indicates that the Toolbox is pinned open. While this is typical for the VB environment, it also consumes a large amount of screen space, so you may want to click the pin icon to allow the Toolbox to fold into the left side of the screen.

We now find ourselves at the default start page for Visual Studio .NET, which is the screen you will typically see when starting Visual Studio .NET from this point forward. From here, we can open existing projects, start new projects, change our profile, search for help, and perform other useful operations.

In our case, you will want to choose the New Project button. This will bring up a new project dialog similar to the following:

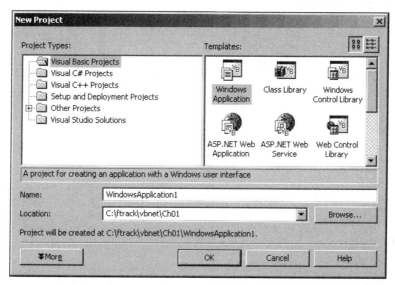

There are a lot of new and different options listed here – many of which we will explore throughout the remainder of this book. For now, however, let's stay focused on creating a simple program. Choose Windows Application in Visual Basic Projects – this is comparable to the regular Windows GUI applications you create with previous versions of Visual Basic.

Change the Name box to HelloWorld and click OK to set up the project. Visual Studio .NET will set up a new Windows application project called HelloWorld in a solution of the same name. In Visual Studio .NET, a solution can hold many projects of different languages and types – even multiple executable projects can be contained within a single solution. The screen will now appear as follows:

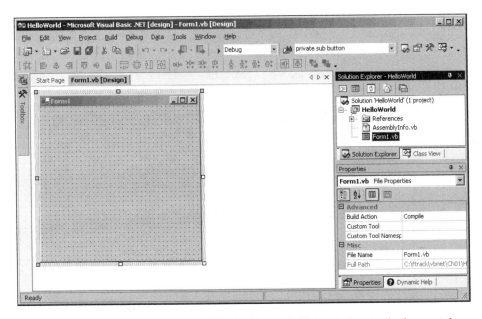

Again, we see a lot of enticing new features like the **Dynamic Help** window in the lower right corner. We will discuss many of these in Chapter 3, but for now, we will finish our application.

There are obviously a variety of ways to create a Hello World program, but we will make ours a little more complex than necessary to provide a decent introduction to Visual Basic .NET.

First off, move the mouse over **Toolbox** on the far left. This will cause the **Toolbox** window to extend out over our form designer so we can choose the controls to be added to the form. Double-click on both a **TextBox** and a **Button** to add them to the form. Alternatively, we can drag-and-drop them.

Arrange the controls so they don't overlap. Notice the **Properties** dialog in the lower right of the IDE, just where we would expect to find it in VB6. Find the **Text** property and change its value to **Show text** and press *Enter*.

Now double-click on the **Button** control in the form to bring up the code window and add a **Click** event.

So far, things aren't a whole lot different from anything you might have seen in VB in the past. The code we now see, however, does offer some interesting differences. Here is the default code we will see in the window:

```
Public Class Form1
    Inherits System.Windows.Forms.Form

Windows Form Designer generated code

    Private Sub Button1_Click(ByVal sender As System.Object, _
      ByVal e As System.EventArgs) Handles Button1.Click

    End Sub
End Class
```

Overall, it looks very much like regular VB code but there are some striking differences, like the fact that our form is a class, the use of the `Inherits` keyword, and the box indicating some **Windows Form Designer generated code**. Most of these changes will be covered in Chapters 3 and 4, with the `Inherits` keyword and associated OO features being discussed in Chapter 6.

To complete our application, let's make a message box pop up to display the text in the textbox when the button is clicked. This is done by adding the following code:

```
Private Sub Button1_Click(ByVal sender As System.Object, _
   ByVal e As System.EventArgs) Handles Button1.Click

   MsgBox(TextBox1.Text)

End Sub
```

In VB6, we could have achieved the same result like this:

```
Private Sub Button1_Click

   MsgBox TextBox1

End Sub
```

Other than the two new arguments to the `Button1_Click` event and the parenthesis around the `MsgBox` argument, there is not much different here from any VB code you might have written in the past. This will be generally true as we go through the rest of this book. Almost everywhere we look, there are changes to the IDE or the language – but a great deal of these changes are trivial or beneficial, and are easy to get used to.

Now press *F5* to run the program (sounds familiar?). After the solution is compiled, our application will run, displaying our form with its two controls. If we type **Hello World!!** into the textbox and click the **Show text** button, up pops our message box:

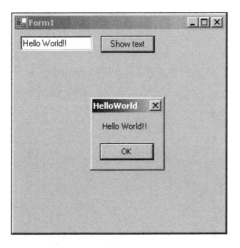

Obviously, this is a very simple example, but it illustrates how the basic process of developing a Windows application using VB has not radically changed from Visual Basic 6 to Visual Basic .NET. As we go through the book, we will see many things that are the same or similar, and many things that are quite different. By the end of the book, you should be well on your way to being a productive Visual Basic .NET developer.

Summary

Microsoft .NET is a very exciting and major technology change. While it builds on the concepts introduced by COM, it is quite different from anything we have today, promising to make us more productive as it merges the Windows GUI and browser-based Internet development environments closer together.

VB, the most popular development tool today, is fully supported in the .NET environment through Visual Basic .NET. Visual Basic .NET will likely be the most common development tool for the new .NET platform, since it offers the smoothest transition for existing VB developers, as well as being very accessible to developers who have used other languages and tools in the past.

At the same time, it is important to approach Visual Basic .NET for what it is – a substantially changed and enhanced language for the substantially changed and enhanced .NET platform. While a lot of Visual Basic .NET will seem familiar to existing developers, there are a great many changes to the IDE, the language, and features, providing a substantial challenge when moving to the new language and environment.

In this opening chapter, we have discussed the basic requirements for running .NET applications and servers. We have also discussed the requirements for setting up a development environment. Once we have Visual Studio .NET installed, we can configure the SDK samples, which provide valuable examples of many .NET techniques. Finally we wrapped up by creating a simple Hello World application, demonstrating that the general development process in Visual Basic .NET is not radically different from that in VB6.

In the next chapter, we will discuss the .NET Framework in more detail, comparing and contrasting it to the world of COM, and exploring all its new features and capabilities.

From there, we will dive into the features of Visual Basic .NET, including the IDE, the VB language changes, and how the .NET Framework and VB work together to create great applications.

2

Introduction to the .NET Framework

The impact of new technologies often forces industries to change their fundamental assumptions. In the computing industry, the latest such technology is the Internet. It has forced us to rethink how software should be created, deployed, and used.

Usually, when a powerful new technology comes along, it is first strapped onto existing platforms. This is not unique to computing. When the jet engine was first invented in the mid-1940s, the first ones were placed on aircraft that were very similar to propeller-driven designs. The result could fly, but was difficult to pilot, not very reliable, and failed to take full advantage of the new technology.

When the aircraft manufacturers went back to a blank piece of paper, they came up with a basic design for a jet aircraft in the late 1940s and early 1950s that has lasted for fifty years. The new design integrated the power of the new jet engine more transparently, and took advantage of its strengths.

We are now at the same point with respect to the Internet in the computing industry. For about seven years, we have been using older platforms with new Internet capabilities 'strapped on'. The resulting systems work, but they are expensive and difficult to produce, hard to use, and difficult to maintain. Realizing this, about four years ago, Microsoft decided it was time to design a new platform from the ground up specifically for the Internet world.

The result is called **.NET**. It represents a turning point in the world of Windows software for Microsoft platforms. Microsoft has staked its future on it, and publicly stated that close to 100 percent of its research and development will be done on this platform henceforth. It is expected that, eventually, almost all Microsoft products will be ported to the .NET platform.

What is .NET?

Microsoft's .NET initiative is broad-based and very ambitious. It includes the **.NET Framework**, which encompasses the languages and execution platform, plus extensive class libraries providing rich built-in functionality. Besides the core .NET Framework, the .NET initiative includes protocols (such as the **Simple Object Access Protocol**, commonly known as **SOAP**) to provide a new level of integration of software over the Internet, and a family of server-based products called the **.NET Enterprise Servers** that are the next generation of Microsoft's BackOffice. It also includes a family of services, called **.NET MyServices**, intended to allow packaged functionality to be used over the Internet.

In this chapter, we will look at the .NET Framework from the viewpoint of a Visual Basic developer. Since the .NET Framework is the foundation of most of the changes in Visual Basic .NET, an introduction to the .NET Framework is an essential first step in assimilating the changes that will be presented in the rest of this book.

The .NET Framework means changes for everyone who uses Microsoft technologies, and VB developers get more than their share. One goal Microsoft has for the .NET initiative is to bring together the best of all of its language platforms. In a broad sense, this means that other languages get many of VB's ease-of-use features, such as easy drag-and-drop generation of forms, while VB receives dramatic new capabilities, such as full object orientation, that take away many of the limitations VB developers have put up with in the past.

The first released product based on the .NET Framework is **Visual Studio .NET**, which was publicly launched in February of 2002. However, even before its public launch, hundreds of companies used pre-release versions to begin changing the way they do software development.

A Broad and Deep Platform for the Future

Calling the .NET Framework a *platform* doesn't begin to describe how broad and deep it is. It encompasses a virtual machine that abstracts away much of the Windows API from development. It includes a class library with more functionality than any yet created. It makes available a development environment that spans multiple languages, and it exposes an architecture that makes multiple language integration simple and straightforward.

At first glance, some aspects of .NET appear similar to previous architectures such as UCSD Pascal and Java. No doubt, some of the ideas for .NET were inspired by these past efforts, but there are also many brand-new architectural ideas in .NET. Overall, the result is a radically new approach to software development.

As mentioned earlier, this is the first development platform designed from the ground up with the Internet in mind. Previously, Internet functionality has been simply bolted on to pre-Internet operating systems like UNIX and Windows. This has required Internet software developers to understand a host of technologies and integration issues. The .NET Framework is designed, and intended, for highly-distributed software, making Internet functionality and interoperability easier and more transparent to include in systems than ever before, and significantly reducing the barriers to the usage of Internet technologies in all kinds of software systems.

The vision of Microsoft.NET is globally distributed systems, using XML as the universal glue to allow functions running on different computers across an organization or across the world to come together in a single application. In this vision, systems from servers to wireless palmtops, with everything in between, will share the same general platform, with versions of .NET available for all of them, and with each of them able to integrate transparently with the others.

This does not leave out classic applications as we have always known them, though. Microsoft .NET also aims to make traditional business applications much easier to develop and deploy. Some of the technologies of the .NET Framework, such as Windows Forms, demonstrate that Microsoft has not forgotten the traditional business developer.

The Role of the .NET Enterprise Servers

In addition to Visual Studio .NET, Microsoft had previously released several products, which it describes as being part of the **.NET Enterprise Servers** family. More of these are coming, and most will be released by the time this book is published. Products in the .NET Enterprise Servers family include:

- ❑ **BizTalk Server** (discussed in *Professional BizTalk* from Wrox Press, ISBN *1-861003-29-3*)
- ❑ **Commerce Server 2000**
- ❑ **Exchange Server**
- ❑ **Host Integration Server 2000** (the successor to SNA Server)
- ❑ **SQL Server 2000** (discussed in *Professional SQL Server 2000 Programming* from Wrox Press, ISBN *1-861004-48-6*)
- ❑ **SharePoint Portal Server**
- ❑ **Internet Security and Acceleration (ISA) Server** (the successor to Proxy Server)

Some of the marketing literature for these products emphasizes that they are part of Microsoft's .NET strategy. However, it is important that you understand the difference between these products and the .NET Framework upon which Visual Basic .NET is based. The .NET Enterprise Servers are *not* based on the .NET Framework. Most of them are successors to previous server-based products, and they use the same COM/COM+ technologies as their predecessors.

These .NET Enterprise Servers still have a major role to play in future software development projects. When actual .NET Framework projects are developed, most will depend on the technologies in the .NET Enterprise Servers for functions like data storage and messaging. However, the first actual product based on the .NET Framework is Visual Studio .NET, which includes Visual Basic .NET as the new generation of Visual Basic, as well as a new version of C++ and a new language from Microsoft called C# (pronounced C-sharp).

What's Wrong with DNA and COM?

The pre-.NET technologies used for development on Microsoft platforms encompassed the **COM (Component Object Model) standard** for creation of components, and the **DNA model** for multi-tier software architectures. As these technologies were extended into larger, more enterprise-level settings, and as integration with the Internet began to be important, several major drawbacks to them began to be apparent. These included:

- ❑ Difficulty in integrating Internet technologies:
    - ❑ Hard to produce Internet-based user interfaces
    - ❑ No standard way for systems and processes to communicate over the Internet
    - ❑ Expensive, difficult, and undependable deployment
    - ❑ Poor cross-language integration
    - ❑ Too many skills required to do effective development
- ❑ Weaknesses in the most popular Microsoft tool – VB:
    - ❑ Lack of full object orientation, which made it impossible to produce frameworks in VB
    - ❑ One threading model that did not work in some contexts
    - ❑ Poor integration with the Internet
    - ❑ Other weaknesses such as poor error handling capabilities

It is important to note that all pre-.NET platforms, such as Java, also have some of these drawbacks, as well as unique ones of their own. The drawbacks related to the Internet are particularly ubiquitous.

Let's take a brief look at these drawbacks to pre-.NET Microsoft technologies before taking up how .NET addresses them.

Difficulty in Integrating Internet Technologies

Starting in late 1995, Microsoft made a dramatic shift towards the Internet. It had to make some serious compromises to quickly produce Internet-based tools and technologies. The main result, **Active Server Pages**, was a tool that was not oriented around structured and object-oriented development. Designing, debugging, and maintaining such unstructured ASP code is also a headache. While many viable systems were produced with ASP pages, these obvious flaws needed to be addressed.

Later in the evolution of the Internet, it became apparent that communicating to the user via HTTP and HTML was limiting. To get, for example, a stock quote from an Internet server, it was often necessary for a program to pretend to be a user, get an HTML page, and then take it apart to get the information needed. This was fussy development, and the result was quite brittle because of the possibility that the format of the page might change, and thus, need new parsing logic.

Developers needed a standard way for **processes** to communicate over the Internet, rather than the communication being directed only at **users**. DNA and COM lacked any such standard.

Deployment Issues

Microsoft's COM standard was developed for use on small systems with limited memory running Microsoft Windows. The design tradeoffs for COM were oriented around sharing memory, and quick performance on hardware we would now consider slow.

This meant that **Dynamic Link Libraries (DLLs)** were shared between applications to save memory, and a binary interface standard was used to give good performance. To quickly find the components needed to run an application, DLLs had to register their class IDs in the local Windows Registry.

Besides the registration logistics needed to make DLLs work at all, COM components could be rendered inoperable by versioning issues. The resulting morass of problems related to versioning was colloquially known as 'DLL Hell'.

The need to register components locally also resulted in other limitations. It was not possible for a COM application to be placed on a CD-ROM or a network drive, and then run from that location without an installation procedure.

Poor Cross-language Integration

COM/DNA typically required the use of three separate development models. Business components were most often written in Visual Basic, and VB could also be used for local Win32 user interfaces. Browser-based user interfaces required Active Server Pages. System components sometimes required use of C++.

Each of these languages had difficulties integrating with the others. Getting Visual Basic strings properly transferred to and from C++ routines is a challenge for example. ASP pages required a COM interface with only `Variants` for data, which negated the strong typing available in VB and C++. Getting all three languages to work together required several arcane skills.

Many Skills Required for Development

Perhaps worst of all, this multitude of programming models significantly raised the barrier to developing sophisticated COM/DNA applications. Developers had to learn a host of technologies to be effective. Knowledge gained in writing code for ASP pages was not necessarily very useful in writing VB programs or C++ components.

Weaknesses in Visual Basic in COM/DNA applications

VB was easily the most popular language for developing applications with the DNA model. As noted above, it can be used in two major roles – forms-based VB clients and COM components (either on the client or the server).

There are other options, of course, including C++, J++, and various third-party languages such as Delphi and Perl, but the number of VB developers outnumbers developers using them all put together.

Despite its popularity, VB suffered from a number of limitations in the COM/DNA environment. Some of the most serious limitations include:

❑ No capability for multi-threading

❑ Lack of implementation inheritance and other object-oriented features

❑ Poor error handling ability

❑ Poor integration with other languages such as C++ (as discussed above)

❑ No effective user interface for Internet-based applications

Lack of multi-threading implies, for example, that VB can't be used 'out of the box' to write an NT-type service. There are also situations in which the apartment threading used by components created in VB limits performance.

VB's limited object-oriented features, in particular, the lack of inheritance, made it unsuitable for development of object-based frameworks, and denied design options to VB developers that were available to C++ or Java developers.

VB's archaic error handling becomes especially annoying in a multi-tier environment. It is difficult in VB to track and pass errors through a stack of component interfaces.

Perhaps the biggest drawback to using VB became apparent when many developers moved to the Internet. While VB forms for a Win32 client were state-of-the-art, for applications with a browser interface, VB was relegated mostly to use in components because of the difficulties (discussed above) with alternatives such as WebClasses and browser-based ActiveX components.

Microsoft tried to address this problem in Visual Basic 6 with WebClasses and DHTML pages. Neither caught on. WebClasses offered an obscure programming model, and limited control over visual layout. DHTML pages in Visual Basic 6 must send a (usually large) DLL to the client, and so, needed a high bandwidth connection to be practical, limiting their use mostly to intranet applications.

All of these limitations needed to be addressed, but Microsoft decided to look beyond just VB and solve these problems on a more global level. All of these limitations are solved in Visual Basic .NET through the use of technology in the .NET Framework.

The Origins of .NET

At the beginning of 1998, a team of developers at Microsoft had just finished work on a new version of Internet Information Services (version 4.0), including several new features in ASP pages. While developers were pleased to see new capabilities for doing Internet development on Microsoft NT applications, the development team at Microsoft had many ideas for improvement. That team began to work on a new architecture implementing those ideas. This project eventually came to be known as **Next Generation Windows Services (NGWS)**.

After Visual Studio 6 was released in late 1998, work on the next version of Visual Studio (then called Visual Studio 7) was folded into NGWS. The COM+/MTS team brought in their work on a universal runtime for all the languages in Visual Studio, which they intended to make available for third-party languages as well.

The concepts in .NET are inspired from many sources. Previous architectures, from p-code in UCSD Pascal up through the Java Virtual Machine, have similar elements. Microsoft has taken many of the best ideas in the industry, combined them with some great ideas of its own, and brought them all into one coherent package.

An Overview of the .NET Framework

First and foremost, .NET is a framework that covers all the layers of software development above the operating system. It provides the richest level of integration among presentation technologies, component technologies, and data technologies ever seen on a Microsoft, or perhaps any, platform. Secondly, the entire architecture has been created to make it as easy to develop Internet applications, as it is to develop for the desktop.

The .NET Framework actually 'wraps' the operating system, insulating software developed with .NET from most operating system specifics such as file handling and memory allocation. This prepares for a possible future in which the software developed for .NET is portable to a wide variety of hardware and operating system foundations.

The first release version of Visual Studio .NET supports all versions of Windows 2000 plus Windows NT4 and Windows XP. Programs created for .NET can also run under Windows 98 and Windows Me, though Visual Studio .NET does not run on these systems.

A Common Substrate for all Development

The major components of the Microsoft.NET Framework are shown in the following diagram:

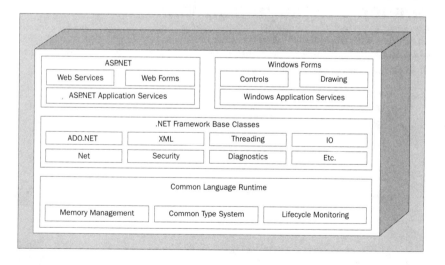

The framework starts all the way down at the memory management and component loading level, and goes all the way up to multiple ways of rendering user and program interfaces. In between, there are layers that provide just about any system-level capability that a developer would need.

At the base is the **Common Language Runtime**, often abbreviated to **CLR**. This is the heart of the .NET Framework – it is the engine that drives key functionality. It includes, for example, a common system of data types. These common types, plus a standard interface convention, make cross-language inheritance possible. In addition to allocation and management of memory, the CLR also does reference tracking for objects, and handles garbage collection.

The middle layer includes the next generation of standard system services such as classes that manage data and XML. These services are brought under control of the framework, making them universally available and making their usage consistent across languages.

The top layer includes user and program interfaces. **Windows Forms** is a new and more advanced way to do standard Win32 screens (often referred to as 'smart clients'). **Web Forms** provides a new web-based UI. Perhaps the most revolutionary is **Web Services**, which provides a mechanism for programs to communicate over the Internet, using SOAP. Web Services provides an analog of COM and DCOM for object brokering and interfacing, but based on Internet technologies so that allowance is made even for integration to non-Microsoft platforms. Web Forms and Web Services, which compose the Internet interface portion of .NET are implemented by a part of the .NET Framework referred to as **ASP.NET**.

For completeness, there is a console interface that allows creation of character-based applications. Such applications were very difficult to build with previous versions of VB. Chapter 9 discusses how these applications are written in Visual Basic .NET.

All of these capabilities are available to any language that is based on the .NET platform, including, of course, Visual Basic .NET.

The Common Language Runtime

We are all familiar with runtimes; they go back further than DOS languages. However, the **Common Language Runtime** is as advanced over traditional runtimes as a machine gun is over a musket. Here is a quick diagrammatic summary of the major pieces of the CLR:

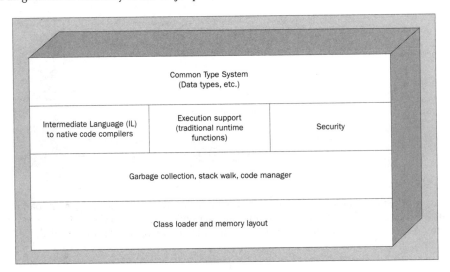

That small part in the middle called Execution support contains most of the capabilities normally associated with a language runtime (such as the VBRUNxxx.DLL runtime used with Visual Basic). The rest is new, at least for Microsoft platforms.

The CLR is required on every machine where you want to run .NET applications and code.

Key Design Goals

The design of the CLR is based on the following goals:

- ❑ Simpler, faster development
- ❑ Automatic handling of system-level tasks such as memory management and process communication
- ❑ Excellent tool support
- ❑ Simpler, safer deployment
- ❑ Scalability

Notice that many of these design goals directly address the limitations of COM/DNA. Let's look at each of these in detail.

Simpler, Faster Development

A broad, consistent framework allows developers to write less code, and reuse code more. Less code is possible because the system provides a rich set of underlying functionality. Programs in .NET access this functionality in a standard, consistent way, requiring less 'hardwiring' and customization logic to interface to the functionality than is typically needed today.

Programming is also simpler in .NET because of the standardization of data types and interface conventions. As will be discussed below, .NET makes knowledge of the intricacies of COM much less important.

Automatic Handling of System-Level Tasks

A lot of programming infrastructure is either automatically handled by the CLR or rendered completely unnecessary. That is, some of it is hidden, and some of it is just not there any more.

Memory management is an example of hidden infrastructure. VB developers stopped worrying much about memory long ago. Developers in other .NET languages now have the same luxury.

Hiding this infrastructure simplifies many programming tasks. As we will see in the section below on memory management in .NET, *Details on .NET Memory Management*, this simplification does not come without a price.

Excellent Tool Support

Though much of what the CLR does is similar to operating system functionality, it is designed first and foremost to support development languages. It furnishes a rich set of object models that are useful to tools like designers, wizards, debuggers, and profilers, and since the object models are at the runtime-level, such tools can be designed to work across all languages that use the CLR. It is expected that third parties will produce a host of such tools.

It's also important to note that Microsoft is not restricting use of the CLR to Microsoft languages. Third party language vendors are encouraged to re-architect their languages to use the CLR, which offers a host of benefits. Besides taking advantage of all the CLR functionality (and thereby not having to write it or support it), using the CLR enables never-before-seen levels of cross-language integration. More on this later on, under *Multiple Language Integration and Support.*

This capability of the CLR to work transparently with multiple languages has huge benefits for developers. Debuggers offer the best example. The CLR makes it possible to write a source-level debugger that treats all languages equally, jumping from one language to another as necessary. VB developers will benefit by having access to these more powerful tools.

Simpler, Safer Deployment

It is hard for an experienced Windows component developer to see how anything can work without registration, GUIDs, and the like, but the CLR does. Applications produced in the .NET Framework can be designed to install with a simple XCOPY. That's right – just copy the files onto the disk and run the application. We haven't seen this since the days of DOS (and some of us really miss it).

This works because compilers in the .NET Framework embed identifiers (in the form of **metadata**, discussed very soon) into compiled modules, and the CLR manages those identifiers automatically. The identifiers provide all the information needed to load and run modules, and to locate related modules.

As a great by-product, the CLR can manage multiple versions of the same component (even a shared component), and have them run side by side. The identifiers tell the CLR which version is needed for a particular compiled module because such information is captured at compile-time. The run-time policy can be set in a module to use the exact version of a component that was available at compile-time, to use the latest compatible version, or to specify an exact version. The bottom line is that .NET is intended to eradicate DLL Hell once and for all.

This has implications that might not be apparent at first. For example, if a program needs to run directly from a CD or a shared network drive (without first running an installation program), that was not feasible in Visual Basic after version 3. That capability reappears with Visual Basic .NET. This dramatically reduces the cost of deployment in many common scenarios.

Another significant deployment benefit in .NET is that applications only need to install their own core logic. An application produced in .NET does not need to install a runtime, for example, or modules for ADO or XML. Such base functionality is part of the .NET Framework, which is installed separately and only once for each system. The .NET Framework will eventually be included with the operating system and probably with various applications. Those four-diskette installs for a VB 'Hello world' program will be a thing of the past.

Making all of this work automatically requires a sophisticated security infrastructure. The .NET Framework captures the origin of a piece of code, and the publisher of a module can be identified with a public encryption key. The bottom line is that a system can be set up to not run untrusted software, which provides mechanisms to block viruses and other malicious code. In fact, as of Service Pack 1 of the .NET Framework, the default security settings disable downloaded code until permission to run it has been specified in the local machine's security policy.

Scalability

Since most of the system-level execution functions are concentrated in the CLR, they can be optimized and architected to allow a wide range of scalability for applications produced in the .NET Framework. As with most of the other advantages of the CLR, this one comes to all applications with little or no effort.

Memory and process management is one area where scalability can be built in. The memory management in the CLR is self-configuring and tunes itself automatically. Garbage collection (reclaiming memory that is no longer being actively used) is highly optimized, and the CLR supports many of the component management capabilities of MTS/COM+ (such as object pooling). The result is that components can run faster, and thus support more users.

This has some interesting side effects. For example, the performance and scalability differences among languages become smaller. All languages compile to a standard bytecode called **Microsoft Intermediate Language** (**MSIL**), often referred to simply as **IL**, and there is discussion later on how the CLR executes IL. Code compiled to IL is also known as **managed code**. With all languages compiling down to similar bytecode, it becomes unnecessary in most cases to look to other languages when performance is an issue. The difference in performance among .NET languages is minor – Visual Basic, for example, gives about the same performance as any of the other .NET languages.

Versions of the CLR are expected to be available on a wide range of devices. Eventually, the vision is for .NET to be running at all levels, from smart palmtop devices all the way up to web farms. That means the same development tools should work across the entire range – news that will be appreciated by those who have tried to use Windows CE development kits.

Metadata

The .NET Framework needs lots of information about an application to carry out so many automatic functions. The design of .NET requires applications to carry that information around inside them. That is, applications are **self-describing**. The collected information that describes an application is called **metadata**.

The concept of metadata is not new. COM components use a form of it called a type library, which contains metadata describing the classes exposed by the component and is used to facilitate OLE Automation. Using the facilities of COM+ also requires supplying more metadata to specify, for example, whether a component supports transactions.

One of the drawbacks to metadata in COM and COM+ is that metadata is stored in different places, and outside the component. A component's type library may be stored in a separate file. The component's registration GUID (which would be considered metadata related to identification of the component) is stored in the Windows Registry.

In contrast, the metadata in .NET is stored in one place – *inside* the component it describes. Metadata in .NET also contains more information about the component, and is better organized.

In .NET, the metadata is generated by a compiler and stored automatically in an EXE or DLL. Here are some of the items in the metadata defined for the .NET Framework:

- ❑ Description of a deployment unit (called an assembly):
  - ❑ Name, version, culture (which could determine, for example, the default user language)
  - ❑ A public key for verification
  - ❑ Types exported by the assembly
  - ❑ Dependencies – other assemblies that this assembly depends upon
  - ❑ Security permissions needed to run

- ❑ Base classes, and interfaces
- ❑ Custom attributes:
  - ❑ User defined (inserted by the developer)
  - ❑ Compiler defined (inserted by the compiler to indicate something special about the language)

Some of these, such as the custom attributes, are optional – the tools manage all the required ones automatically.

The metadata is one of the ways the CLR can support a wide variety of tools. Here are some of the possible consumers of .NET metadata:

- ❑ Designers
- ❑ Debuggers
- ❑ Profilers
- ❑ Proxy Generators
- ❑ Other .NET IL compilers (to find out how to use a component in their language)
- ❑ Type/Object browsers
- ❑ Schema generators

Compilers are some of the most extensive users of metadata. A compiler can examine a module produced by a different compiler and use the metadata for cross-language type import. This allows, for example, the VB compiler to look at components produced in C#, or a .NET version of COBOL, and expose those C# or COBOL components to a VB developer. The components would look the same way components developed in VB would look. Also, of course, a compiler can produce metadata about its own compiled modules, including such elements as flags that a module was compiled for debugging, or a language-specific marker.

This extendable store of data about a compiled module greatly facilitates the simpler deployment available under the .NET Framework. An API, called the **Reflection API**, is available for scanning and manipulation of metadata elements.

Metadata is key to the easy deployment in .NET. When a component is upgraded or moved, the necessary information about the component cannot be left behind. Metadata can never get out of sync with a .NET component because it is not in a separate file. Everything the CLR needs to know to run a component is supplied with the component.

Multiple Language Integration and Support

The most ambitious aspect of the CLR is that it is designed to support multiple languages and allow unprecedented levels of integration among those languages. By enforcing a common type system, and by having complete control over interface calls, the CLR allows languages to work together more transparently than ever before. The cross-language integration issues of COM discussed earlier simply don't exist in .NET.

It is straightforward in the .NET Framework to use one language to subclass a class implemented in another. A class written in VB can inherit from a base class written in C++, or in COBOL for that matter. The VB program doesn't even need to know the language used for the base class, and we are talking full implementation inheritance with no problems requiring recompilation when the base class changes.

How can this work? The information furnished in metadata makes it possible. A class interface looks the same, regardless of the language that generated it. The CLR uses metadata to manage all the interfaces and calling conventions between languages.

While there will always be benefits to having programming teams use a common language, Microsoft .NET raises the practicability of mixed-language projects. Complex systems that derive their functionality from different organizations using different language are far easier to create and manage in .NET. Besides the support for multiple languages in the CLR, Visual Studio .NET also makes it much easier to incorporate multiple languages into a single application by supporting multiple projects in different languages simultaneously.

A Common Type System

A key piece of functionality that enables multiple language support is a **common type system**, in which all commonly used data types, even base types such as `Long` and `Boolean`, are actually implemented as objects. Coercion among types can now be done at a lower level for more consistency between languages. Also, since all languages are using the same library of types, calling one language from another doesn't require type conversion or weird calling conventions.

This results in the need for some readjustment, particularly for VB developers. For example, what we called an `Integer` in VB6 and earlier, is now known as a `Short` in Visual Basic .NET. The adjustment is worth it to bring VB in line with everything else, though, and, as a byproduct, other languages get the same support for strings that VB has always had.

Reference Types vs. Value Types

There are two families of types in .NET. **Value types** are what VB developers would call data variables and user-defined types (UDTs). **Reference types** are basically classes.

One reason to understand this classification is that value types are tested for equality differently from reference types. Another major reason it is helpful to differentiate these types is that their memory management is handled differently. This will be described in the section below on how the CLR manages memory.

Notice that reference types and value types are also treated differently in assignment statements. Consider this code:

```
Dim nRooms As Integer
Dim nAvailableRooms As Integer
nAvailableRooms = 10
nRooms = nAvailableRooms
```

After this code is executed, there are two variables, nRooms and nAvailableRooms, which have the same value in them. From this point forward, changing the value in nRooms will not affect the value in nAvailableRooms – there is no implicit connection between the two variables. That's because Integer is a value type.

By contrast, consider the following code in VB6:

```
Dim objRoom As clsRoom
Dim objAvailableRoom As clsRoom
Set objAvailableRoom = New clsRoom
Set objRoom = objAvailableRoom
```

In this case, there is a connection between objRoom and objAvailableRoom. Both point to the same underlying object. Changing the object with one of the references means the other reference will reflect the changes. That's because objRoom and objAvailableRoom are a reference type, namely the class clsRoom.

The VB6 code in the above example would not be the same in Visual Basic .NET. Instantiation is done somewhat differently and the Set statement is not used. Here is the equivalent Visual Basic .NET code:

```
Dim objRoom As clsRoom
Dim objAvailableRoom As New clsRoom()
objRoom = objAvailableRoom
```

Chapter 4 will discuss these changes in detail.

A final difference between value types and reference types concerns how instances of a type are initialized. A variable declared as a reference type is initialized to Null and does not contain a reference to a valid object until assigned such a reference (by setting to a new instantiation of the class, or by assigning a reference from an existing valid object).

A variable containing a value type, on the other hand, always refers to a valid object. Note that all types, even native data types, are actually objects in .NET – see more on that in the next section. A primitive type (a type supported natively by the compiler such as an `Integer`, a `Boolean`, a `String`, and so on) will be initialized to an appropriate value (0 for `Integer`, `False` for `Boolean`, and so on). We discuss primitive types in the *Primitive Types in the .NET Framework* section.

Everything is an Object

As previously mentioned, every type supported by the common type system is an object. That means every type is derived from the `System.Object` class. This gives every type in .NET the ability to support the following methods:

Method	Description
`Boolean Equals(Object)`	Used to see if two objects are equal. For a reference type, the method returns `True` if the base object and the `Object` parameter both reference the same object. Value types should return `True` if the `Object` parameter has the same value as the base object.
`Int32 GetHashCode()`	Generates a number that is mathematically derived from the value of an object. If two objects of the same type are equal, then they must return the same hash code. The handling of collections by the .NET Framework depends on values from this method.
`Type GetType()`	Gets a `Type` object that contains useful information about the type. It is used, for example, in place of the `VarType` function in earlier versions of VB.
`String ToString()`	For primitive types such as `Integer`, `Boolean`, and `String`, this returns a string representation of the type's value. For other types, the string returned varies. The default implementation of this method returns the fully-qualified name of the class of the object. However, the method is usually overridden to output data that is more appropriate for the type, such as the value for primitive types mentioned above.

Primitive Types in the .NET Framework

As mentioned earlier, data types that are natively supported by a compiler are called primitive types. The .NET primitive types are:

Type	Referred to in Visual Basic .NET as	Description	Size
Boolean	Boolean	Boolean value of either true or false.	8 bits
Byte	Byte	An unsigned positive integer between 0 and 255.	8 bits
Char	Char	A Unicode character value.	16 bits

Table continued on following page

Type	Referred to in Visual Basic .NET as	Description	Size
DateTime	Date	A date and time value.	64 bits
Decimal	Decimal	Positive and negative values with 28 significant digits, ranging from negative 79,228,162,514,264,337,593,543,950,335 to positive79,228,162,514,264,337,593,543,950,335.	96 bits
Double	Double	Double precision, floating-point number ranging from negative 1.79769313486231570E308 to positive 1.79769313486231570E308.	64 bits
GUID	GUID	Represents a globally unique identifier (GUID).	128 bits
Int16	Short	Signed integer value that can range from negative 32768 to positive 32767.	16 bits
Int32	Integer	Signed integer value that can range from negative 2,147,483,648 to positive 2,147,483,647.	32 bits
Int64	Long	Signed integer value that can range from negative 9,223,372,036,854,775,808 to positive 9,223,372,036,854,775,807.	64 bits
Sbyte	Sbyte	Signed integer value that can range from negative 128 to positive 127.	8 bits
Single	Single	Single precision, floating-point number that can range from negative 3.402823E38 to positive 3.402823E38.	32 bits

The set of primitive types supported by .NET has a lot of overlap with the primitive types supported by previous versions of VB, but the overlap is not complete. There are some new types, and some changes to old types in VB. Chapter 4, which summarizes changes in Visual Basic .NET, discusses these data type changes.

Namespaces

One of the most important concepts in Microsoft.NET is **namespaces**. They help organize object libraries and hierarchies, simplify object references, prevent ambiguity when referring to objects, and control the scope of object identifiers.

Namespaces are discussed in more detail in Chapter 4., but for now, you can think of a namespace as a group of related classes. For example, all the classes having to do with access to XML are in a namespace called System.XML.

The DLL that contains a set of classes must be referenced in a project before it can be used, just as DLL in VB6 had to be referenced. However, in VB6, classes were not grouped into namespaces, and were just referenced directly. In .NET, namespaces form a hierarchical tree, and the full identifier of a class can be quite long. For example, the class for a Windows Form (the .NET analog to a VB form) is referred to as `System.Windows.Forms.Form`.

It can get tedious to type in such references to classes, so .NET languages have a mechanism for abbreviating namespace references. The abbreviation allows the types to be used in the code without using the full reference. In VB, this is done with an `Imports` statement. For example, a typical Windows Form code module in .NET might have the following line at the beginning:

```
Imports System.Windows.Forms
```

This line simply makes all of the standard classes for forms and controls available to the code in the form module. With this line in place for example, a textbox can be referred to in code as the type `TextBox` instead of having to type out `System.Windows.Forms.TextBox`.

The Structure of a .NET Application

.NET functionality requires a new structure for applications. The way these applications are executed and the way memory is managed are also new.

Start with an Assembly, Build Up to an Application

The unit of deployment, as previously mentioned, is an **assembly**. It can consist of one or more files and is self-describing. It contains a **manifest** which holds the metadata describing everything exported from the assembly, and what is needed to deploy and run the assembly.

There really isn't a VB6 equivalent of an assembly. A compiled EXE or DLL file comes closest in concept, but the fact that a .NET assembly can contain more than one file makes the comparison inexact.

An assembly has its own version. Assemblies are combined to become applications.

An application has one or more assemblies, and also may contain application-specific files or data. Applications may have their own private versions of assemblies, and may be configured to prefer their private version to any shared versions.

Assembly Structure

An assembly has the following general structure:

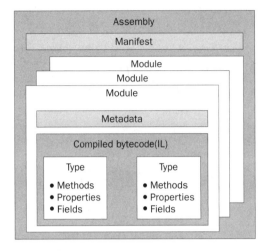

Here are details of the individual elements in an assembly:

Manifest – Every assembly must have a manifest. It may be a separate file in the assembly, or it may be contained in one of the modules. It contains the following information:

❑   Name and version number for the assembly

❑   Other assemblies that this assembly depends upon (including exact version numbers of those assemblies)

❑   Types (classes and members) exposed by the assembly

❑   Security permissions required by the assembly

Module – A module is either a DLL or an EXE in the Windows PE (Portable Executable) format. The compiled code in the module is in Microsoft Intermediate Language (IL), which is discussed next. A module also contains its own necessary associated metadata, and one module in an assembly may contain a manifest for that assembly.

Type – A type is a contained unit of data and logic affecting that data. It exposes information through properties, fields, and methods. Properties and fields look similar to a consumer of the type, and represent a piece of data. The difference is that properties have logic associated with them to verify or construct data, and fields are more like public variables. Methods, of course, are actions or behaviors of the type.

Deployment and Execution

With all the intelligence in the .NET framework and the CLR, there is a lot more going on at execution-time than we are accustomed to. Programs or components can't just load and go– there are several things that must happen for the whole structure to work. However, the steps required are all handled automatically by the CLR, so you as a developer, do not have to worry about them.

Execution

Source code modules for an assembly are compiled (at development-time) into the CLR's Intermediate Language (IL). Then, IL is compiled into native code before execution. That compilation can take place in several ways, and at various times. Normally, however, compilation into native code is done only once and the results are cached for future use.

The compilation into native code is done by a just-in-time (JIT) compiler. Code can be pre-compiled into native code if appropriate. That is, an installation of a package can be set to pre-compile the IL code into native code during the installation.

Scripting also fits into this model, actually being compiled before it is used. In current systems-interpreted script (in ASP pages or the Windows Scripting Host, for example) it is never compiled, but in .NET, such script (which is not explicitly compiled by the developer) is automatically sent through a language compiler the first time it is accessed, and transformed into IL. Then, the IL is immediately transformed into native code, and cached for future use. Scripts are created in .NET the way they are now, with any editor you like, and require no explicit compilation step. The compilation is handled in the background, and is managed automatically so that a change to the script results in appropriate recompilation.

The bytecode in IL is very high level. There is a bytecode for the action of inheritance, for example. Compilers for .NET languages don't have to understand how to make an inheritance work – that's the runtime's job. The compiler just places a bytecode in a module indicating that the module inherits from another compiled class, and the runtime takes care of loading that class at execution and integrating it with the subclass.

With software compiled into a processor-independent intermediate language, .NET makes it possible to achieve future platform independence. A CLR can be produced for non-Windows platforms, and applications produced on Windows 2000 should be able to run on them. Or, applications produced today with .NET could run without source code recompilation on a future 64-bit version of Windows. The capabilities of the CLR in some respects parallel those of the Java Virtual Machine, which is designed for platform independence.

Details on .NET Memory Management

One of the strong points of the CLR is automatic memory management and garbage collection. The CLR takes care of loading components and laying out the memory for them, and then reclaims and cleans up the memory when the component is finished. That happens when the component has no more references pointing to it (such as when it falls out of scope).

Older versions of VB take care of these functions too. However, there is one critical difference in the way objects are de-allocated with the CLR versus the old way objects are handled in VB6 and earlier. Older versions of VB performed reference counting of object instances, and when the reference count reached zero, the object's `Class_Terminate` event was immediately called. In Visual Basic .NET, the CLR performs garbage collection only when memory needs dictate that it is required. This implies that the equivalent of the `Class_Terminate` event, named the `Dispose()` method of the object, does not necessarily get called immediately. It is called when the CLR decides that garbage collection is needed, which depends on when the area of memory reserved for object instances (called the **managed heap**) gets full and needs compacting.

The old way, used by VB6 and earlier, is called **deterministic finalization**. This just means that it is possible for the developer to know with confidence when the finalization logic (in the `Class_Terminate` event) is run.

The .NET Framework does not have deterministic finalization. Since the CLR only does garbage collection as necessary, it is not possible to predict exactly when the finalization logic in a component (in the `Dispose()` method) will be run. Once all references to an object are gone, the object may sit around in memory for quite a while before the CLR decides to do anything about it. It could even be several minutes or longer before a garbage collection is done if the system has plenty of memory to work with.

This can lead to several development issues. Behavior of a program can vary with the memory needs of other programs on the system, leading to those dreaded intermittent program errors. Code converted from VB6 that depends heavily on `Terminate` events may need manual adjustment to work correctly in all cases in Visual Basic .NET.

The preferred programming practice in the .NET Framework is for developers to take an increased level of responsibility for making sure that an object instance gets cleaned up when the program is through, usually with explicit calls either to a built-in `Dispose()` method or to a custom method that takes care of finalization. This higher level of responsibility goes a bit against the grain of VB philosophy, and many VB developers are upset about it. However, it is a small trade-off for the huge advances available in Visual Basic .NET.

The new memory management scheme does have some advantages. It is expected to yield better performance. It also solves the 'circular reference' problem in Visual Basic, where object A had a reference to object B, and object B also had a reference to object A. In such a case, the reference count for neither object ever drops to zero, so the garbage collection algorithm in VB was unable to cope. The memory management algorithm in .NET detects such cases and manages them appropriately so that the objects can be deallocated when there is no reference to the objects from outside the circular loop.

Managed vs. Unmanaged Code

Code for which the memory is completely managed by the CLR (as described above and mentioned earlier in the chapter) is called **managed code**. This simply means the CLR takes all responsibility for allocating memory for objects in the code, for managing the memory while the objects are in use, and for reclaiming the memory when the objects are no longer needed. All code produced in Visual Basic .NET is managed code.

It is also possible, using the C++ compiler in Visual Studio .NET to produced **unmanaged code**. In such code, the code must explicitly allocate memory (using the `malloc` function, for example) as was done pre-.NET. The CLR takes no responsibility for the layout of such memory, or for reclaiming memory when objects are no longer needed. All such operations must be undertaken by the C++ code. (C++ can also produce managed code in .NET, but unmanaged code is the default.)

The Next Layer – the .NET Class Framework

The next layer up in the framework provides the services and object models for data, input/output, security, and so forth. It is called the **.NET Class Framework**, sometimes referred to as the **.NET base classes**. For example, the next generation of ADO, called ADO.NET, resides here (though a version of regular COM-based ADO is installed with .NET to provide compatibility for older code). Also included is the core functionality to do things with XML, including the parsers and XSL transformer. Some of the additional functionality in the .NET Class Framework is listed in the following section.

You might be wondering why .NET includes functionality that is, in many cases, duplication of existing class libraries. There are several good reasons:

❑ The .NET Class Framework libraries are implemented in the .NET Framework, making them easier to integrate with .NET-developed programs.

❑ The .NET Class Framework brings together most of the system class libraries needed into one location, which increases consistency and convenience.

❑ The class libraries in the .NET Class Framework are much easier to extend than older class libraries, using the inheritance capabilities in .NET.

❑ Having the libraries as part of the .NET Framework simplifies deployment of .NET applications. Once the .NET Framework is on a system, individual applications don't need to install base class libraries for functions like data access.

What is in the .NET Class Framework?

The .NET Class Framework contains literally thousands of classes and interfaces. Here are just some of the functions of various libraries in the .NET Class Framework:

❑ Data access and manipulation

❑ Creation and management of threads of execution

❑ Interfaces from .NET to the outside world – Windows Forms, Web Forms, Web Services, and console applications

❑ Definition, management, and enforcement of application security

❑ Encryption, disk file I/O, network I/O, serialization of objects, and other system-level functions

❑ Application configuration

❑ Working with directory services, event logs, performance counters, message queues, and timers

❑ Sending and receiving data with a variety of network protocols

❑ Accessing metadata information stored in assemblies

Much functionality that a programmer might think of as being part of a language has been moved to the base classes. For example, the VB keyword `Sqr` for extracting a square root is no longer available in .NET. It has been replaced by the `System.Math.Sqrt()` method in the framework classes.

It's important to emphasize that all languages based on the .NET Framework have these framework classes available. That means that COBOL, for example, can use the same function mentioned above for getting a square root. This makes such base functionality widely available and highly consistent across languages. All calls to Sqrt look essentially the same (allowing for syntactical differences among languages) and access the same underlying code. Here are examples in Visual Basic .NET and C#:

```
' Example using Sqrt in Visual Basic .NET
Dim dblNumber As Double = 200
Dim dblSquareRoot As Double
dblSquareRoot = System.Math.Sqrt(dblNumber)
Label1.Text = dblSquareRoot.ToString

' Same example in C#
Double dblNumber = 200;
Double dblSquareRoot = System.Math.Sqrt(dblNumber);
dblSquareRoot = System.Math.Sqrt(dblNumber);
label1.Text = dblSquareRoot.ToString;
```

Notice that the line using the Sqrt() function is exactly the same in both languages.

As a side note, a programming shop can create its own classes for core functionality, such as globally available, already-compiled functions. This custom functionality can then be referenced in code the same way as built-in .NET functionality.

Much of the functionality in the base framework classes resides in a vast namespace called System. The System.Math.Sqrt() method was mentioned just now. Here are just a few other examples of the subsections of the System namespace, which actually contains dozens of such subcategories:

Namespace	What it contains	Example Classes
System.Collections	Creation and management of various types of collections	Arraylist, Hashtable, SortedList
System.Data	Classes and types related to basic database management	DataSet, DataTable, DataColumn, SqlClient.SQLConnection, OleDb.OleDbConnection
System.Diagnostics	Classes to debug an application and to trace the execution of code	Debug, Trace
System.IO	Types that allow reading and writing to files and other data streams	File, FileStream, Path, StreamReader, StreamWriter
System.Math	Members to calculate common mathematical quantities, such as trigonometric and logarithmic functions	Sqrt (square root), Cos (cosine), Log (logarithm), Min (minimum)
System.Reflection	Capability to inspect metadata	Assembly, Module
System.Security	Types that enable security capabilities	CryptoStream, Permissions, Policy

The list above merely begins to hint at the capabilities in the `System` namespace. Some of these namespaces are used in later examples in other chapters. For example, the `System.Data` namespace is covered extensively in Chapter 8.

User and Program Interfaces

At the top layer, .NET provides three ways to render and manage user interfaces:

- ❏ **Windows Forms**
- ❏ **Web Forms**
- ❏ **Console applications**

and one way to handle interfaces with remote components:

- ❏ **Web Services**

We will cover these interfaces in this section.

Windows Forms

Windows Forms is a more advanced and integrated way to do standard Win32 screens. All languages that work on the .NET Framework, including new versions of Visual Studio languages, use the Windows Forms engine instead of whatever they were using before (MFC or direct Win32 API calls in the case of C++, the VB forms engine in the case of Visual Basic). This provides a rich, unified set of controls and drawing functions for all languages, as well as a standard API for underlying Windows services for graphics and drawing. It effectively replaces the Windows graphical API, wrapping it in such a way that the developer normally has no need to go directly to the Windows API for any graphical or screen functions.

Windows Forms is part of the framework base classes – it is in the `System.Windows.Forms` namespace. Since Windows Forms duplicates the functionality of the VB forms engine, it gives every single .NET language the capability of doing forms just as Visual Basic does. The drag-and-drop designer for Windows Forms (which is in Visual Studio .NET) can be used to create forms visually for use with any .NET language that has been integrated into Visual Studio .NET.

In Chapter 5 we will look at Windows Forms in more detail and note significant changes in Windows Forms versus older VB forms.

Client Applications Versus Browser-Based Applications

In the Windows DNA world, many internal corporate applications are made browser-based simply because of the cost of installing and maintaining a client application on hundreds or thousands of workstations. Windows Forms and the .NET Framework have the potential to change the economics of these decisions. A Windows Forms application will be much easier to install and update than an equivalent VB client application today. With a simple XCOPY deployment and no registration issues, installation and updating become much easier.

That means 'smart client' applications that need a rich user interface for a large number of users are more practicable under .NET than under Windows DNA. It may not be necessary to resort to browser-based applications just to save installation and deployment costs. There is even capability in .NET to deploy these 'smart client' applications over the Internet from a web server, with automatic updating of changed modules on the client. We will discuss that in more detail in Chapter 5.

Web Forms

A part of ASP.NET, Web Forms is a forms engine. It provides a web browser-based user interface. Web Forms applications can be produced by constructing 'pages' that conceptually resemble ASP pages, though Web Forms are much more advanced. However, VB developers will often prefer the impressive visual layout capabilities built into Visual Studio .NET, which allow drag-and-drop development of sophisticated web interfaces.

Divorcing layout from logic, Web Forms consist of two parts:

❑   A **template**, which contains HTML-based layout information for all user interface elements

❑   A **component**, which contains all logic to be hooked to the user interface

It is as if a standard Visual Basic form were split into two parts: one containing information on controls and their properties and layout, and the other containing the code. Just as in VB, the code operates 'behind' the controls, with events in the controls activating event routines in the code.

To make this new UI concept work, Web Forms have lots of built-in intelligence. Controls on Web Forms run on the server but make their presence known on the client. This takes lots of coordination and behind-the-scenes activity. However, the end result is web interfaces that can look and behave very much like Win32 interfaces today, and the ability to produce such interfaces with a drag-and-drop design tool. These web interfaces can also have the intelligence to deal with different browsers, optimizing their output for different browser classes. Supported browsers cover a broad range. At the top end are advanced modern versions like Internet Explorer 6.0, which support DHTML. At the other end are simpler, less capable browsers on hardware such as wireless palmtop devices. Web Forms will render themselves appropriately on all of these.

As with Windows Forms, Web Forms will be available to all languages. The component handling logic for a form can be in any language that supports .NET. This brings complete, flexible web interface capability to a wide variety of languages.

Server Controls

VB developers are familiar with the idea of controls. They are the reusable user interface elements used to construct a form. The analogs in Web Forms are called **server controls**.

Server controls essentially create a proxy on the server for a user interface element that is on a Web Form or ASP page. The server-side control communicates with local logic as necessary, and then intelligently renders its own UI as HTML as necessary, in any pages that are sent out containing the control. It also handles its own HTML responses, and incorporates the returned data.

Server controls need significant intelligence to render HTML for different levels of browsers, and to coordinate events with the client on which the page is running. A wide variety of controls are included with Visual Studio .NET, bringing web-based interfaces much closer to Win32 interfaces. Third party tools vendors add even more options for server-side controls.

One of the most important and amazing features of server-side controls is that they manage their own state. In ASP.NET, it is no longer necessary to write a lot of tedious code to reload state information into HTML controls every time a page is refreshed. Web Forms handle state by sending a tokenized (compressed) version of the state information to the client browser each time a page is sent. The page then posts that state information back to the server when changing the page. The server controls grab the state information, use or process it as necessary, and then send it out again with the next rendering of the page.

Chapter 7 introduces Web Forms in Visual Basic .NET. Server controls are discussed in detail, and an example application demonstrates how Web Forms are constructed. Other aspects of ASP.NET are extensively discussed in the Wrox book *Professional ASP.NET 1.0 Special Edition*, ISBN *1-861007-03-5*.

Console Applications

Though Microsoft doesn't emphasize the ability to write character-based applications, the .NET Framework does include an interface for such console apps. Batch processes, for example, can now have components integrated into them that are written to a console interface.

As with Windows Forms and Web Forms, this console interface is available for applications written in any .NET language. Writing character-based applications in previous versions of VB, for example, has always been a struggle because it was completely oriented around a GUI interface. Visual Basic .NET can be used for true console applications.

An introduction to console applications is included in Chapter 9.

Web Services

Application development is moving into the next stage of decentralization. The oldest idea of an application is a piece of software that accesses basic operating system services, such as the file system and graphics system. Then we moved to applications that used lots of base functionality from other, system-level applications, such as a database – this type of application added value by applying generic functionality to specific problems. The developer's job was to focus on adding business value, not on building the foundation.

Web Services represent the next step in this direction. In Web Services, software functionality becomes exposed as a service that doesn't care what the consumer of the service is (unless there are security considerations). Web Services allow developers to build applications by combining local and remote resources for an overall integrated and distributed solution.

In .NET, Web Services are implemented as part of ASP.NET, (diagrammed at the top level of the .NET Framework in the first figure in this chapter), which handles all web interfaces. It allows programs to talk to each other directly over the web, using the SOAP standard. This capability requires very little additional work on the part of the developer compared to developing typical subroutines and functions. All that is needed is to indicate that a member should be included in the Web Services interface by marking it with a `<WebMethod>` attribute, and the .NET Framework takes care of the rest. This has the capacity to dramatically change the architecture of web applications, allowing services running all over the Web to be integrated into a local application.

It is hard to over-emphasize the potential importance of Web Services. Consider, for example, the potential for Web Services to replace packaged software. A commercial software company could produce a Web Service that, for instance, calculates sales tax for every jurisdiction in the nation. A subscription to that Web Service could be sold to any company needing to calculate sales tax. The customer company then has no need to deploy the sales tax calculator because is it just called on the Web. The company producing the sales tax calculator can dynamically update it to include new rates and rules for various jurisdictions, and its customers using the Web Service don't have to do anything to get these updates.

There are endless other possibilities. Stock tickers, weather information, current financial rates, shipping status information, and a host of other types of information could be exposed as a Web Service, ready for integration into any application that needs it.

Chapter 7 contains a detailed discussion of Web Services.

XML as the .NET 'Meta-language'

Much of the underlying integration of .NET is accomplished with XML. For example, Web Services depends completely on XML for interfacing with remote objects. Looking at metadata usually means looking at an XML version of it.

ADO.NET, the successor to ADO, is heavily dependent on XML for remote representation of data. Essentially, when ADO.NET creates what it calls a **dataset** (a more complex successor to a recordset), the data is converted to XML for manipulation by ADO.NET. Then, the changes to that XML are posted back to the datastore by ADO.NET when remote manipulation is finished.

Chapter 8 discusses ADO.NET and its use with XML in more detail.

With XML as an 'entry point' into so many areas of .NET, future integration opportunities are multiplied. Using XML to expose interfaces to .NET functions allows developers to tie components and functions together in new, unexpected ways. XML can be the glue that ties pieces together in ways that were never anticipated, both to Microsoft and non-Microsoft platforms.

The Role of COM

When the .NET Framework was first introduced, some uninformed journalists interpreted it as the death of COM. That is completely incorrect. COM is not going anywhere for a while. In fact, Windows will not boot without COM.

.NET integrates very well with COM-based software. Any COM component can be treated as a .NET component by native .NET components. The .NET Framework wraps COM components and exposes an interface that .NET components can work with. This is absolutely essential to the quick acceptance of .NET, because it makes .NET interoperable with a tremendous amount of older COM-based software.

Going in the other direction, the .NET Framework can expose .NET components with a COM interface. This allows older COM components to use .NET-based components as if they were developed using COM.

Chapter 11 discusses COM interoperability in more detail. The co-authors of this book have also produced a complete book on interoperability between VB6 and VB.NET published by Wrox Press, *Professional Visual Basic Interoperability – COM and VB6 to .NET*, ISBN *1-861005-65-2*.

No Internal Use of COM

It is important, however, to understand that native .NET components *do not* interface using COM. The CLR implements a new way for components to interface, one that is not COM-based. Use of COM is only necessary when interfacing to COM components produced by non-.NET tools.

Over a long span of time, the fact that .NET does not use COM internally may lead to the decline of COM, but that is for the very long term. For any immediate purposes, COM is definitely important.

The Role of DNA

Earlier in the chapter, we discussed the limitations of the current DNA programming model. These limitations are mostly inherent in the technologies used to implement DNA today, not in the overall structure or philosophy. There is nothing fundamentally wrong with the tiered approach to development specified by the DNA model. It was specifically developed to deal with the challenges in design and development of complex applications. Many of these design issues, such as the need to encapsulate business rules, or to provide for multiple user interface access points to a system, do not go away with .NET.

Applications developed in the .NET Framework will still, in many cases, use a DNA model to design the appropriate tiers. However, the tiers will be a lot easier to produce in .NET. The presentation tier will benefit from the new interface technologies, especially Web Forms for Internet development. The middle tier will require far less COM-related headaches to develop and implement, and richer, more distributed middle tier designs will be possible by using Web Services.

The architectural skills that experienced developers have learned in the DNA world are definitely still important and valuable in the .NET world.

Additional Benefits

The major benefits of Microsoft .NET discussed thus far can be summarized as:

- ❑ Faster development (less to do, the system handles more)
- ❑ Lots of built-in functionality through a rich object model
- ❑ More stable code through built-in, comprehensive memory management and use of prepackaged, widely-used functionality

❑   A variety of ways to interface and integrate with the outside world

❑   More reuse

❑   Easy integration of different languages into one system

❑   Easier deployment

❑   Higher Scalability

❑   Easier building of sophisticated development tools

There are a couple of additional benefits that are worth mentioning:

❑   **Fewer bugs in applications** – The architecture and capabilities of the CLR should wipe out whole classes of bugs. Memory leaks, failure to clean up at the end of execution, and other memory management related problems should become rare or non-existent. Instancing of classes is handled automatically, and they are managed throughout their lifecycle.

❑   **Potentially better performance** – The built-in capabilities of the CLR are to be used almost universally. Microsoft knows that, for .NET to succeed, these capabilities must be reliable and efficient, and it can invest the efforts of its very best architects and developers to make that happen.

This heavy investment in system-level code should have the result of speeding up performance for all but the most optimized applications. Critical and frequently used functions, no matter how ordinary, will usually be optimized to the hilt in the CLR.

Some Potential Downsides

Nothing comes completely for free. Here are a couple of ways in which there is a price to be paid to get the advantages of .NET:

❑   **Incompatibilities with existing code** – Making languages work in this new framework usually means adjustment to the language syntax. This introduces compatibility problems in moving existing code into the .NET Framework. Visual Basic is a particular problem, as we shall see throughout this book.

❑   **Transparency of 'source code'** – The bytecodes in the IL are much higher level than the processor instructions that programs are compiled into today. While we can disassemble a program in current environments, the assembler-based result is of limited use. .NET programs disassembled from IL, on the other hand, more closely resemble actual source code. They also contain the information needed to understand data structures. Such disassembled programs make algorithms and code processes more transparent than with older environments, making it more difficult to protect intellectual property.

Third party vendors are expected to introduce tools that 'obfuscate' the code to make such disassembly more difficult, but the details on that are not known as of the time this is written.

The First Step – Visual Studio .NET

As mentioned earlier, the first technology released on the .NET Framework is the next generation of Visual Studio, which has been tagged Visual Studio .NET. It will include Visual Basic .NET, Visual C++, and a new language called C# (pronounced *C sharp*).

The Visual Studio .NET Integrated Development Environment (IDE) is much enhanced over previous versions. However, it will feel relatively comfortable for developers experienced with previous versions of Visual Basic. Chapter 3 goes through the details on the IDE and discusses many of the new features.

.NET Drives Changes in Visual Basic

We previously covered the limitations of Visual Basic in today's DNA programming model. To recap, they were:

- ❑ No capability for multi-threading
- ❑ Lack of implementation inheritance and other object features
- ❑ Poor error handling ability
- ❑ Poor integration with other languages such as C++
- ❑ No effective user interface for Internet-based applications

Since Visual Basic .NET is built on top of the .NET Framework, all of these shortcomings have been eliminated. Visual Basic basically piggybacks on the stuff that was going to be implemented anyway for C++, C#, and third party .NET languages.

In fact, VB gets the most extensive changes of any existing language in the Visual Studio .NET suite. These changes pull VB in line with other languages in terms of data types, calling conventions, error handling, and, most importantly, object-orientation. Chapter 4 covers the changes to Visual Basic, especially the syntax changes, in detail. It will discuss several incompatibilities along with new features and capabilities.

Microsoft has supplied a conversion tool, which will assist in porting VB6 projects to .NET, but it will not do everything required. There will be some areas where the conversion tool merely places a note that indicates something needs to be done. Migration of existing code to Visual Basic .NET will certainly not be nearly as transparent as migrating code among older versions of Visual Basic.

How does .NET Affect Me?

One of the reasons you are probably reading this book is because you want to know how Visual Basic .NET will affect you as an existing Visual Basic developer. Here are some of the most important implications.

A Spectrum of Programming Models

In previous Microsoft-based development tools, there were a couple of quantum leaps required to move from simple to complex. And sometimes the complex programming models were required to get more power. A developer could start simply with ASP pages and VB Script, but when those became cumbersome, it was a big leap to learn component-based, three-tier development in Visual Basic. And it was another quantum leap to become proficient in C++, ATL, and related technologies for system-level work.

A key benefit of Visual Basic .NET and the .NET Framework is that there is a more gradual transition in programming models from simple to full power. ASP.NET pages are far more structured than ASP pages, and code used in them is often identical to equivalent code used in a Windows Forms application. Internet development can now be done using real Visual Basic code instead of VBScript.

Visual Basic itself becomes a tool with wider applicability, as it becomes easy to do a web interface with Web Forms, and it also becomes possible to do advanced object-oriented designs. Even system-level capabilities, such as Windows Services can be done with Visual Basic .NET. Old reasons for using another language, such as lack of performance or flexibility, are mostly gone. Visual Basic will do almost anything that other .NET languages can do.

This increases the range of applicability of Visual Basic. It can be used all the way from 'scripts' (which are actually compiled on the fly) written with a text editor, up through sophisticated component and web programming in one of the most advanced development environments available.

Reducing Barriers to Internet Development

With current tools, programming for the Internet requires a completely different programming model from programming systems that will be run locally. The differences are most apparent in user interface construction, but that's not the only area of difference. Objects constructed for access by ASP pages, for example, must support `Variant` parameters, but objects constructed for access by Visual Basic forms can have parameters of any data type. Accessing databases over the Internet requires using technologies like RDS instead of the ADO connections that local programming typically uses.

The .NET Framework erases many of these differences. Programming for the Internet and programming for local systems are much more alike in .NET than with today's systems. Differences remain – Web Forms still have significant differences from Windows Forms, for example, but many other aspects, such as the way data is handled, are much more unified under .NET.

A big result of this similarity of programming models is to make Internet programming more practicable and accessible. With functionality for the Internet designed in from the start, developers don't have to know as much or do as much to produce Internet systems with the .NET Framework.

Libraries of Pre-Written Functionality

The evolution of Windows development languages, including Visual Basic, has been in the direction of providing more and more built-in functionality so that developers can ignore the foundations and concentrate on solving business problems. The .NET Framework continues this trend.

One particularly important implication is that the .NET Framework extends the trend of developers spending less time writing code and more time discovering how to do something with pre-written functionality. Mainframe COBOL programmers could learn everything they ever needed to know about COBOL in a year or two, and very seldom need to consult reference materials after that. In contrast, today's Visual Basic developers already spend a significant portion of their time digging through reference material to figure out how to do something that they may never do again. The sheer expanse of functionality available, plus the rapidly changing pace, makes it a requirement that an effective developer is also a researcher. .NET accelerates this trend, and will probably increase the ratio of research time to coding time for a typical developer.

Easier Deployment

A major design goal in Microsoft .NET is to simplify installation and configuration of software. With DLL Hell mostly gone, and with installation of compiled modules a matter of a simple file copy, developers should be able to spend less time worrying about deployment of their applications, and more time concentrating on the functionality of their systems. The budget for the deployment technology needed by a typical application will be significantly smaller.

Summary

This chapter has provided some background to the whole development strategy regarding Microsoft's .NET Framework, and in particular how this will affect VB developers. It is clear that .NET provides a raft of new challenges for developers, but simultaneously provides them with greatly enhanced functionality. In particular, Visual Basic developers now have the ability to develop web-based applications far more easily and cheaply.

In the next chapter, we move on to take a closer look at the Visual Studio .NET IDE, beginning with the Hello World example we created in Chapter 1. Then, coverage is devoted to the new features available in the Visual Studio .NET IDE.

3

New IDE Features

Visual Basic .NET preserves VB6's general approach to programming with a 'what you see is what you get' development environment, click-through forms to get at the underlying code, and so forth. The new Visual Studio .NET IDE incorporates these capabilities, providing Visual Basic .NET developers with a relatively familiar development environment that is tailored for developing on the .NET platform.

Some of the key features of the Visual Studio .NET IDE include:

- ❑ Graphical designers for Windows Forms and Web Forms
- ❑ Solution Explorer
- ❑ Class View
- ❑ Dynamic Help
- ❑ An integrated task list
- ❑ Integrated debugging

In this chapter, we will discuss the various new features of the Visual Studio .NET IDE. This new IDE not only supports Visual Basic .NET, but also provides support for all the .NET languages, including Visual C# .NET and Visual C++, and offers a wide range of powerful capabilities for us as developers.

To explore the Visual Studio .NET IDE, we will revisit the Hello World program from Chapter 1 and walk through it in more detail. This will give us both a good tour of the IDE and a bit more understanding of how Visual Basic .NET applications are constructed.

A Tour of the Hello World Program

To get started, open up Visual Studio .NET. At the start page you should be presented with the options to open an existing project, or start a new one:

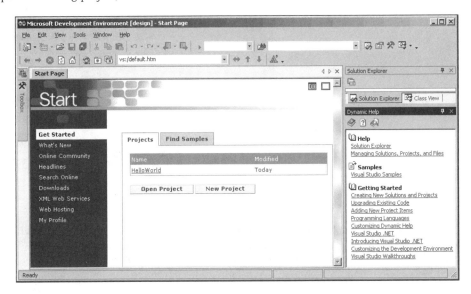

Click on the HelloWorld project to open it up in the environment and we are ready to go.

If you don't have the HelloWorld project, either return to Chapter 1 to recreate it, download the code from http://www.wrox.com/, or just follow along with the code in the book. We will cover everything pretty thoroughly, so it probably isn't critical to have the project right in front of you.

Let's walk through the code behind Form1. Bring up the code window by selecting Form1 in the Solution Explorer on the right side of the window and then clicking the View Code button at the top of the explorer window.

Form Declaration, Initialization, and Termination

Visual Studio .NET now shows us the code for our form. When compared to VB6, there is some extra code here. Though at first this may seem odd, it is exactly the same code for every form we add to a project, so it will soon fade into the background and become commonplace. Let's walk through the code to see what it means.

Forms as Classes

The first line of code declares a class named Form1:

```
Public Class Form1
```

Since VB4 we have been able to treat a form module like a class, but form modules have never really *been* classes.

Now, in Visual Basic .NET, forms really *are* classes. They are just classes that happen to create a window and work with controls placed on that window. Since we have been able to treat forms as classes for some time now, this isn't a huge change.

On the other hand, up to now we have been able to refer to a form in two different ways. The first way is to use the form 'directly', which would be done using the following VB6 code:

```
Form1.Show
```

This is referred to as interacting with the **default instance** of a form. We didn't explicitly create a Form1 object – the VB6 runtime created the instance on our behalf behind the scenes. This was nice because it was simple, but this syntax is really a holdover from far earlier, since it originated with VB1 or thereabouts.

We could also *explicitly* create an instance of the form using the following VB6 code:

```
Dim, MyForm As Form1

Set MyForm = New Form1
MyForm.Show
```

In this case, we have manually created an object of type Form1. Our code then interacts with this specific instance of the form. This type of syntax was required to fully support MDI forms, since an MDI parent could contain several child windows all of the same type and we needed some way to create more than one instance of a given form.

The unfortunate side effect of having these two ways of creating a form was the dreaded bug created by the following VB6 code:

```
Dim MyForm As Form1

Set MyForm = New Form1
Form1.Show
```

Notice how we create an explicit instance of Form1, then turn around and use the default instance to display the form. Of course the form that is displayed is the default instance, *not* the instance we explicitly created, and now we have got this extra form floating around in memory. This is one of the most common bugs in novice programmers' VB applications – all caused by the inconsistent treatment of a form module as both object and class.

Visual Basic .NET resolves this issue by always treating forms as classes. Now the only valid approach is to treat a form as a class and to create an instance of the form to interact with. This is illustrated by the following Visual Basic .NET code:

```
Dim MyForm As Form1

MyForm = New Form1()
MyForm.Show()
```

If we have typically created applications using the default instances of forms, this new approach will take a little getting used to. For those who regularly work with explicit instances of forms, there is no real change involved in the idea of a form being a class.

Forms Created by Inheritance

The next line of code uses the new keyword, Inherits:

```
Inherits System.Windows.Forms.Form
```

This statement indicates that Form1 is actually a subclass of the System.Windows.Forms.Form class. This class is the root of all .NET GUI forms; any form we create in Visual Basic .NET will be inherited from this base class.

Many of the behaviors we expect from forms are actually implemented in this base class, meaning that we don't need to implement them in our own forms. These behaviors include:

- Activation/deactivation
- Closing
- Detecting mouse clicks and mouse movements
- Drag-and-drop functionality
- Getting and losing focus
- Key press events
- Menu handling
- Form movement and resizing
- Managing the controls on a form

Also, this base form class implements the events that we typically associate with a Windows form, including:

- Click and DoubleClick
- Resize
- LostFocus

and many more.

Since our Form1 class is a subclass of System.Windows.Forms.Form, we automatically gain all the methods, properties, behaviors, and events common to all forms. We can use them as they are, or we can override them to alter their behavior as necessary.

Inheritance and overriding are discussed more thoroughly in Chapter 6.

Windows Form Designer-Generated Code

When the Visual Studio .NET IDE created our form, it automatically generated the code we have seen so far. It also generated another section of code that we normally never need to see or interact with. This section of code is collapsed by default:

```
⊞  Windows Form Designer generated code
```

Clicking on the plus (+) symbol expands this collapsed block of code, which is called a **region**.

> *In fact, to the left of most of our class and method declarations, we see a minus symbol. Clicking on this will collapse our own code into a box similar to this one.*

The code in this region is generated and maintained by the Visual Studio .NET IDE on our behalf.

> **Since this code is automatically created and maintained, we should never directly edit this code as this can cause unpredictable and undesirable side effects within the IDE.**

Typically we don't need to see this code or worry about what is going on within it. However, since we are in the process of learning how Visual Basic .NET works, it is worth walking through this hidden code once, just to get a feel for what goes on inside.

> *As we look at this code, it will become apparent that we could create a Visual Basic .NET form **without** the Visual Studio .NET IDE. Everything required to make the form work is entirely in code – nothing is hidden in a separate FRX file or anything like that. Of course the IDE makes development so easy, it would be hard to give it up, but it is interesting to consider that we could have created this entire application by just using Notepad.*

Click on the aforementioned plus symbol to expand this section of code. We can see how the code creates instances of the various controls on the form and sets their positions, initial values, and so forth:

```
#Region " Windows Form Designer generated code "

  Public Sub New()
    MyBase.New()

    'This call is required by the Windows Form Designer.
    InitializeComponent()

    'Add any initialization after the InitializeComponent() call

  End Sub

  'Form overrides dispose to clean up the component list.
  Protected Overloads Overrides Sub Dispose(ByVal disposing As Boolean)
    If disposing Then
      If Not (components Is Nothing) Then
        components.Dispose()
      End If
```

```
      End If
      MyBase.Dispose(disposing)
    End Sub

    'Required by the Windows Form Designer
    Private components As System.ComponentModel.IContainer

    'NOTE: The following procedure is required by the Windows Form Designer
    'It can be modified using the Windows Form Designer.
    'Do not modify it using the code editor.
    Friend WithEvents TextBox1 As System.Windows.Forms.TextBox
    Friend WithEvents Button1 As System.Windows.Forms.Button
  <System.Diagnostics.DebuggerStepThrough()> Private Sub InitializeComponent()
      Me.TextBox1 = New System.Windows.Forms.TextBox()
      Me.Button1 = New System.Windows.Forms.Button()
      Me.SuspendLayout()
      '
      'TextBox1
      '
      Me.TextBox1.Location = New System.Drawing.Point(8, 8)
      Me.TextBox1.Name = "TextBox1"
      Me.TextBox1.TabIndex = 0
      Me.TextBox1.Text = "TextBox1"
      '
      'Button1
      '
      Me.Button1.Location = New System.Drawing.Point(120, 8)
      Me.Button1.Name = "Button1"
      Me.Button1.TabIndex = 1
      Me.Button1.Text = "Show text"
      '
      'Form1
      '
      Me.AutoScaleBaseSize = New System.Drawing.Size(5, 13)
      Me.ClientSize = New System.Drawing.Size(292, 273)
      Me.Controls.AddRange( _
        New System.Windows.Forms.Control() {Me.Button1, Me.TextBox1})
      Me.Name = "Form1"
      Me.Text = "Form1"
      Me.ResumeLayout(False)

    End Sub

#End Region
```

The #Region Directive

The region of code is bounded at the top by a #Region directive and at the bottom by an #End Region directive. These directives allow the code editor to understand what code is to be included when this section is collapsed or expanded. The #Region directive also takes an argument – the text that is to be displayed in the box when the region is collapsed:

```
#Region " Windows Form Designer generated code "
```

The #Region directive is a powerful tool that we can use to help make our code more manageable, or even to create an initial outline for our application.

The Constructor Method

Since Form1 is actually a class, it has a **constructor** method. Constructor methods are also new to Visual Basic .NET. The constructor method is called as an instance of the class is created, somewhat like the Class_Initialize event in previous versions of VB. We will discuss constructor methods in depth in Chapter 6 when we discuss the object-oriented features of Visual Basic .NET.

In Visual Basic .NET, constructor methods are always named New(). Here is the New() method for Form1:

```
Public Sub New()
  MyBase.New()

  'This call is required by the Windows Form Designer.
  InitializeComponent()

  'Add any initialization after the InitializeComponent() call

End Sub
```

The first thing that all constructor methods *must* do is call the constructor in their base class. If we try to move this line of code later in the routine we will get a syntax error.

> *Actually, Visual Basic .NET will automatically call the base class constructor for us in many cases, so we don't need to write this line. This is discussed in more detail in Chapter 6.*

A class's base class is known by the keyword MyBase – just as the current instance of any class is known by the keyword Me. So, to call the base class's constructor, we have the line:

```
MyBase.New()
```

The constructor code then calls the InitializeComponent() method – a call that is required for the form to work properly. Again the code for InitializeComponent() is hidden inside a section of collapsed code, as we will see shortly.

Following this method call is a comment to mark the location where we might add our own code to do whatever we want as the form comes into being. Normally, we won't write any code here, as this type of code goes in the Form_Load event just as it does in VB6. However, if we need to write code that really runs before virtually anything else happens, the constructor is the place to do it.

The Dispose() Method

If New() is somewhat comparable to Class_Initialize, then it should come as no surprise that we also have a method that is similar to Class_Terminate. This method is named Dispose() and it is called when the form is being destroyed, just like the Class_Terminate method was in previous versions of VB:

```
'Form overrides dispose to clean up the component list.
Protected Overloads Overrides Sub Dispose(ByVal disposing As Boolean)
   If disposing Then
     If Not (components Is Nothing) Then
       components.Dispose()
     End If
   End If
   MyBase.Dispose(disposing)
End Sub
```

Again, we see that this method interacts with the base class by calling its `Dispose()` method. This is important, as it allows the code in the base class to perform any required cleanup before the form is destroyed. We also call the `Dispose()` method on a variable named `components`. This is another variable that is declared in the collapsed code section, which we will discuss next.

Variable Declarations

Within the bounds of this region, we find the declarations of all the variables available form-wide. This includes the `components` variable we saw in the `Dispose()` method. Also declared as variables, are the button and textbox controls we placed on the form:

```
'Required by the Windows Form Designer
Private components As System.ComponentModel.IContainer

'NOTE: The following procedure is required by the Windows Form Designer
'It can be modified using the Windows Form Designer.
'Do not modify it using the code editor.
Friend WithEvents TextBox1 As System.Windows.Forms.TextBox
Friend WithEvents Button1 As System.Windows.Forms.Button
```

Notice also that the control variables are declared using the `WithEvents` keyword. This ensures that any events that are raised by the controls are available for our use within the form. The end result is that we can receive events such as `Click` from the controls just as we did in VB6.

The InitializeComponent() Method

In this section of code we also find the `InitializeComponent()` method that we saw called earlier from the `New()` method.

True to its name, this method initializes our form – first by creating instances of the constituent objects such as the button and textbox controls:

```
Me.TextBox1 = New System.Windows.Forms.TextBox()
Me.Button1 = New System.Windows.Forms.Button()
```

The `SuspendLayout()` method is called to prevent the form from updating its display while all the control properties are initialized:

```
Me.SuspendLayout()
```

Next comes the code to initialize the properties of our controls. These properties are set and modified using the IDE and should not be directly changed here:

```
'
'TextBox1
'
Me.TextBox1.Location = New System.Drawing.Point(8, 8)
Me.TextBox1.Name = "TextBox1"
Me.TextBox1.TabIndex = 0
Me.TextBox1.Text = "TextBox1"
'
'Button1
'
Me.Button1.Location = New System.Drawing.Point(120, 8)
Me.Button1.Name = "Button1"
Me.Button1.TabIndex = 1
Me.Button1.Text = "Show text"
```

Finally, the properties of the form itself are set. Again, these properties are set and modified using the IDE and should not be directly changed here:

```
'
'Form1
'
Me.AutoScaleBaseSize = New System.Drawing.Size(5, 13)
Me.ClientSize = New System.Drawing.Size(292, 273)
Me.Controls.AddRange( _
  New System.Windows.Forms.Control() {Me.Button1, Me.TextBox1})
Me.Name = "Form1"
Me.Text = "Form1"
```

Now that all the properties are initialized, the ResumeLayout() method allows the form to update its display as needed:

```
Me.ResumeLayout(False)
```

While all this code is generated and maintained on our behalf by the IDE, it is still good to have some basic understanding of what is going on behind the scenes. This sort of thing was also done in previous versions of VB, but it was entirely hidden within the VB runtime. Now we can, if we choose, see what is going on throughout the entire process of creating and initializing a form. This can make debugging much easier.

Event Handler Code

We are almost done with the code in our simple application. The only thing left is the code that we wrote to handle the Click event from Button1:

```
Private Sub Button1_Click(ByVal sender As System.Object, _
  ByVal e As System.EventArgs) Handles Button1.Click
```

```
    MsgBox(TextBox1.Text)

  End Sub
```

While very similar to the type of event handler code we'd expect in VB6, there are some differences. In VB6, the code would have been as follows:

```
  Private Sub Command1_Click()

    MsgBox Text1.Text

  End Sub
```

Of course, there is the obvious and trivial difference that, in VB6, our command button was named Command1, while in Visual Basic .NET, the command button is Button1. Several control names have been changed from VB6 to Visual Basic .NET – this is something to be aware of, but also something that is pretty inconsequential.

More important, however, is the fact that the Button1_Click event handler accepts a couple of parameters and has a Handles clause on the end.

Event Parameters

Click event handlers didn't accept parameters in VB6 – in fact, *most* event handlers didn't accept parameters. In .NET GUI programming however, *all* event handlers accept two parameters:

Parameter	Description
sender As System.Object	This argument always contains a reference to the object that raised the event we are receiving. This means that our event handler may be called from more than one object – for instance, our Click event could be attached to more than one control – so we can use this parameter to tell which control raised the event.
e As System.EventArgs	This argument contains any arguments the sending object wanted to provide us. For a Click event, there are no arguments, but for events such as OnMouseMove we will be provided with the coordinates of the mouse pointer.

Things are actually a bit more complex than this. Sometimes, sender is declared as a specific type of object, and sometimes e is of a type that is a subclass of EventArgs. Still, the general formula of receiving two parameters is consistent throughout all of .NET.

By having all event handlers accept two parameters, we gain a great deal of consistency and flexibility in our code. Any event handler can count on knowing where the event came from – via the sender parameter, and if any further information is required we know it will be contained in the EventArgs object.

The Handles Clause

The `Click` event handler also has a new clause attached to the end – the `Handles` clause. We will discuss this clause in more detail in the next chapter when we cover the changes to the way Visual Basic .NET works with events. For now it is enough to know that it is this clause that links the control's `Click` event to this specific method. Unlike VB6, the *name* of the method itself is unimportant; it is the `Handles` clause that causes it to handle any given event.

Method Sytax

The final difference worth noting is that we called `MsgBox` like this in VB6:

```
MsgBox TextBox1
```

while in Visual Basic .NET, the parameter passed to the `Show` property of `MsgBox` is within parentheses:

```
MsgBox(TextBox1.Text)
```

The .NET system class libraries also include a new way to invoke a message box:

```
MessageBox.Show(TextBox1.Text, "Test", messagebox.IconInformation)
```

This is virtually identical to the `MsgBox` command from VB, but is not VB-specific.

The `MessageBox` class comes from the `System.Windows.Forms` namespace, so that namespace must be referenced within the project for this to work. The VB `MsgBox` class comes from the `Microsoft.VisualBasic` namespace, which is automatically referenced by Visual Basic .NET projects, and so, is always available. We will discuss referencing and importing libraries such as `System.Windows.Forms` later in this chapter.

> *Throughout this book, we will use a little of each syntax. Neither offers a clear advantage over the other and there is some benefit in becoming familiar with both approaches.*

> **Parentheses are now always required for procedure, method, and function calls that accept parameters. They are typically inserted by the IDE even when a method doesn't accept parameters.**

While this is not a huge change, it is pervasive and it can take some getting used to before new habits form.

This quick tour through the code behind our simple Hello World application has shown some similarities and some differences between Visual Basic .NET and prior versions of VB. Next, we will take a look at features of the new Visual Studio .NET IDE.

New IDE Features

The development environment for Visual Basic .NET is Visual Studio .NET – an environment shared with the other major .NET languages, Visual C# .NET, JScript, and Visual C++. Visual Studio .NET also includes development support for ASP.NET, Web Forms, XML Web Services, XML, HTML, and other web related technologies.

> *For many years now, we have been hearing that the IDEs for the major development languages would merge together. In Visual Studio 6.0 we got closer, since the VID and J++ IDE was common and had a very similar look and feel to the VB IDE. Now, with Visual Studio .NET, the promise of a unified development environment is finally a reality.*

As we might expect, merging all these languages into the same IDE makes the IDE itself pretty complex. There are a lot of features and capabilities built into the environment – some are of more use than others. Fortunately, for the most part we only need to see or interact with the parts of the IDE that we find useful.

The Start Page

Let's quickly go back to the home page by clicking on the Start Page tab:

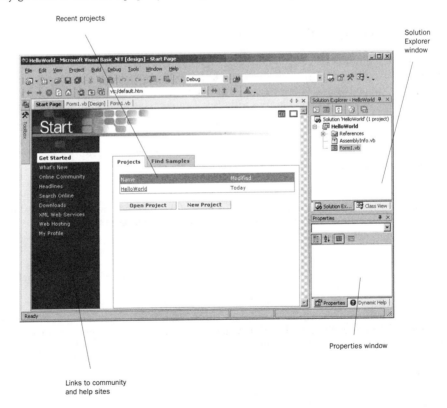

Recent projects

Solution Explorer window

Properties window

Links to community and help sites

In the center of the display is the main window, which includes a list of helpful links, including the link to edit your profile. In this area, we also find a list of recently opened projects, each one a link, which you can click on to quickly open that project and begin work. Below that list are buttons that allow us to open existing projects or create a new project. All these links make the IDE much more like a browser.

Docking Windows

On the right-hand side we see both the Solution Explorer and Properties windows. We will cover these in a bit, but first notice that both of these windows have tabs at the bottom. Along with the Solution Explorer we can also see a tab for a Class View, and along with the Properties window we have a tab for Dynamic Help.

This is a major feature of the Visual Studio .NET IDE – the ability to dock and arrange windows – including docking several windows in the same location such that they are displayed via tabs as we see here.

Using the mouse, we can click and drag the title bar for the Solution Explorer out into the main window, undocking it and making a free-floating window. Notice that the Class View tab comes along for the ride:

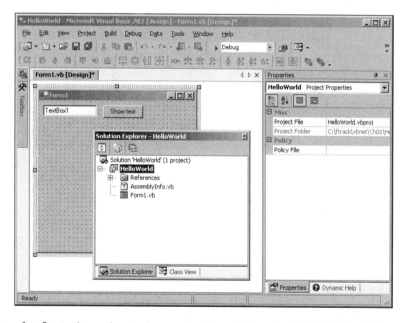

When we say *free-floating* here, the window really is free. It is not an MDI child window, so it can be dragged totally outside of the Visual Studio .NET main window.

To separate the Class View into its own window, click and drag the Class View tab away from the Solution Explorer window – now we have two free-floating windows:

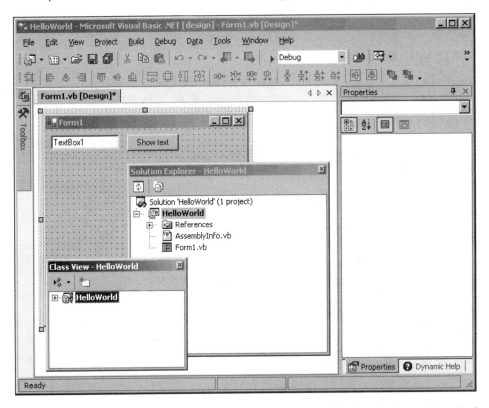

To recombine the two windows, drag one on top of the other such that they display with a tab-shaped outline at the bottom of the window.

To dock the window back where it was, drag the window near the edge of the Visual Studio .NET main window until an outline appears indicating where it will be docked. With a little playing around it will be apparent that these windows can be docked and combined in a wide variety of ways. Even the tabs can be rearranged by dragging them to left or right.

> It can take a bit of practice to get windows to dock and combine as desired. One tip is to keep in mind that the process keys off the location of the mouse pointer, not the original size or position of the window being dragged.

As we proceed through the rest of this section, we won't focus too much on *where* windows appear as much as what they do. This is because we can always dock, undock, combine, separate, and even auto-hide the windows to make the environment comfortable – whatever happens to be comfortable for each individual developer.

Main Windows

The Visual Studio .NET IDE provides us with access to a wide range of capabilities. Most of these capabilities have associated windows that can be docked and combined as we see fit.

To view any of the windows that are not visible, simply choose the View menu and then select the window to be displayed. All of them have default start locations, but can be moved as needed.

Graphical Designers

When we have a project open and are working with that project's files, we will typically be focused on the large main window in the center of the Visual Studio .NET display. This is the main interface where the **designer** will be displayed for our particular file.

Designers were introduced in VB5 and were heavily used in VB6, but they really come of age in Visual Studio .NET. Any time we edit a file – be it creating a WYSIWYG form, editing code, or even creating a non-visual item like a regular class – we are presented with a designer appropriate for that type of file.

One of the most commonly used designers is the graphical Windows Forms designer, which allows us to drag-and-drop controls onto a form. However, there are several other types of designer that we will encounter when working on projects in Visual Basic .NET. These include:

❑   Windows Forms designer – For creation of GUI interfaces

❑   Web Forms designer – For creation of web interfaces

❑   Component designer – For creation of non-visual components

❑   XML designer – For creation of XML documents and XSD schemas

> *The Web Forms designer is used for creating ASP.NET applications. Such applications can be created in many languages, including Visual Basic .NET; hence two different groups of people use it –ASP developers moving to ASP.NET and VB developers moving to Visual Basic .NET to do web development.*

And, of course, the regular code designer where we author our code. This understands a great many types of code, including:

❑   Visual Basic

❑   C#

❑   C++

❑   HTML and DHTML

❑   CSS files

❑   XML

❑   JScript

Each of these file types gets automatic color-coding, and most get auto-formatting, auto-completion, and IntelliSense functionality.

Tabbed Navigation

Along the top of the designer window we find a row of tabs:

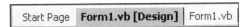

We have used these before – they let us easily navigate through all the open designer windows to find the one we need. Additionally, we can press *Ctrl-Tab* and *Shift-Ctrl-Tab* to cycle back and forth through the open designers.

Component Tray

In previous versions of VB, we had the concept of an 'invisible' control – an ActiveX control (or VBX if we go way back) that is visible on a form at design-time but is invisible at run-time.

Visual Basic .NET formalizes and generalizes this concept through the use of a new designer feature – the **component tray**. The component tray is a separate region in each graphical designer (Windows Forms, Web Forms, Component, and so on) where invisible controls are displayed.

We can see this in our `HelloWorld` application by adding a `Timer` control. Double-click on **Form1** in the **Solution Explorer** to bring up the form designer. Then hold the mouse over the **Toolbox** tab on the far left until it expands. Locate the **Timer** control under **Components** and double-click on it.

> *The **Toolbox** may be pinned out as well, in which case you don't need to expand it. Given the immense flexibility of the IDE in terms of positioning and configuration of windows, it is impossible to know for sure that any description of window access will apply to every developer's environment, as they may have changed windows around in many ways.*

The result is that a `Timer` control is added to our form – but not directly on the form, as it was in the past. Instead, it is displayed in a new region at the bottom of the designer:

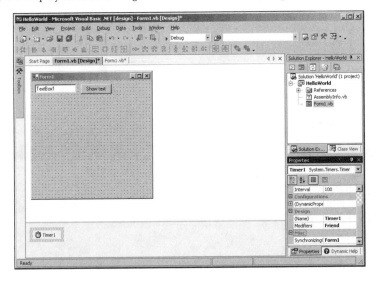

`Timer1`, the new control, is now part of our form just as much as the `Button` and `TextBox` controls. The only difference is where it is displayed in the designer; it is located in the component tray. Notice how the **Properties** window to the right is displaying the control properties – allowing us to view and manipulate them just like any other control.

The component tray is a particularly nice feature when working with invisible controls, since we don't need to worry about them being obscured behind other controls – they are always available for our use.

This is even more important when using the **component designer**. This designer is geared towards the creation of non-visual components (somewhat comparable to COM DLLs), and so, there is no WYSIWYG concept. It is used when creating non-graphical components such as an XML Web Service. However, the graphical designer does provide the component tray, so it is possible to drag-and-drop controls or other components onto the designer and thus, make them available for use by the code within the component.

Solution Explorer

By default, on the right-hand side of the main Visual Studio .NET display we have the Solution Explorer, which is similar to the Project Explorer in previous versions of VB. The Solution Explorer is a bit more advanced, however, since it allows us to construct solutions out of several different projects – including those written in different languages. This makes it very easy to debug and jump between components.

In VB6 we had the concept of a **project group**, which was a group of related projects that could all be opened in the IDE at once. A **solution** is similar in concept, but is more advanced since it allows many different types of project, in many different languages – and even allows us to include arbitrary miscellaneous files that aren't in a formal project at all.

> *When combined with the Server Explorer, which allows us to work with databases and the other features of the IDE, we can do pretty much any development activity directly from within Visual Studio .NET. This helps simplify our tasks, since we don't need to switch out to another IDE, or to the SQL Enterprise Manager to do common tasks – they are all right here in the integrated environment.*

Notice how the Solution Explorer displays our HelloWorld solution, with the HelloWorld project inside:

The HelloWorld project itself is composed of some **References**, an `AssemblyInfo.vb` file and our `Form1.vb` code module, which contains our `Form1` class.

Files and Extensions

The `Form1` file has a vb extension. In VB6, this would have had an `frm` extension instead, indicating it is a form. However, we now know that all forms in Visual Basic .NET are just classes, so there is no need to distinguish between various types of VB source files. In fact, all source files containing VB code will end in a vb extension, regardless of whether they contain forms, classes, or general code.

> **All Visual Basic .NET code modules, or files, end in a vb extension, and any of these vb files can contain more than one class.**

Another new feature of Visual Basic .NET is the ability to have more than one class in a file. In previous versions of VB, physical files could only contain one code module – one class, one form, and so on. In Visual Basic .NET, a physical file can contain several classes, forms, or a mix of different types of code – as long as it is all written in the same language.

Technically, it is possible to create an entire application in a single code file, including classes, forms, and modules all in that one file. This approach is probably not ideal since it makes navigating through code more difficult. On the other hand, there are cases where it may make sense to put some tightly related classes together in the same file to help keep them organized.

References

The Solution Explorer shows a References entry under our project. This is where we manage the assemblies or components referenced by our project – much like the Project | References menu option in VB6. In fact, there is still a Project | Add Reference... menu option in Visual Basic .NET.

To add a reference to our project, we can either right-click on the References item in the Solution Explorer, or we can choose the Project | Add Reference... menu option. Either way, we will be presented with a references dialog:

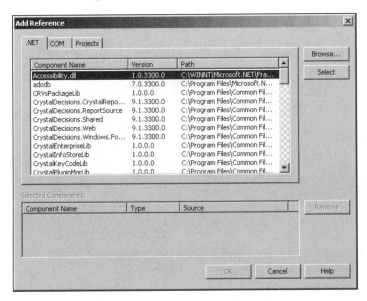

This dialog allows us to add references for .NET Framework components, COM objects, or other projects we are working on.

Once a reference has been added, it will be listed in the Solution Explorer under the References entry. To remove a reference, simply right-click on the reference to be removed, and then choose the Remove option.

Adding a reference makes the namespaces and classes within the assembly or component available for use by our code. Namespaces and how they are used are discussed in the next chapter.

The AssemblyInfo File

All projects have some project-wide configuration settings. These are contained within the AssemblyInfo.vb file, where we can edit them as needed. By default, this file contains the following code:

```
Imports System.Reflection
Imports System.Runtime.InteropServices

' General Information about an assembly is controlled through the following
' set of attributes. Change these attribute values to modify the information
' associated with an assembly.

' Review the values of the assembly attributes

<Assembly: AssemblyTitle("")>
<Assembly: AssemblyDescription("")>
<Assembly: AssemblyCompany("")>
<Assembly: AssemblyProduct("")>
<Assembly: AssemblyCopyright("")>
<Assembly: AssemblyTrademark("")>
<Assembly: CLSCompliant(True)>

'The following GUID is for the ID of the typelib if this project is
'exposed to COM
<Assembly: Guid("F9BF3851-BFEF-42D1-8196-42CDC24C4FF5")>

' Version information for an assembly consists of the following four values:
'
'        Major Version
'        Minor Version
'        Build Number
'        Revision
'
' You can specify all the values or you can default the Build and Revision
' Numbers by using the '*' as shown below:

<Assembly: AssemblyVersion("1.0.*")>
```

At the top of this file some namespaces are *imported* for use by the code. We will discuss the Imports keyword in more detail in the next chapter when we discuss namespaces. For now, it is enough to know that these Imports statements simplify the use of the classes and data types found in those namespaces.

The remainder of the code is either comments or **attributes**. Attributes are extra information that can be attached to a variable, method, class, or assembly. Since an assembly is a project, these attributes all apply to our project as a whole. Most are self-explanatory, allowing us to specify the author of the project, any copyright information, and so forth.

The Guid() attribute is created just in case we want to expose our assembly to the world of COM.

See Chapter 11 and Professional Visual Basic Interoperability: COM and VB6 to .NET published by Wrox Press, ISBN 1-861005-65-2 for more information about interacting with COM.

The AssemblyVersion() attribute is used to specify the version of our assembly. By default, the build and revision numbers are automatically generated and incremented each time we build our project. If we want, we can set them specifically here.

Properties Window

Beneath the Solution Explorer on the right-hand side of the Visual Studio .NET main window is the Properties window. This is very similar to the Properties window in previous versions of VB. It displays the properties for the currently selected object in the main window, allowing us to alter these properties at design-time in a graphical fashion. The properties may be sorted or organized in different ways by clicking on the icons in the mini-toolbar within the Properties window.

In the Solution Explorer, double-click on Form1 to bring up its designer, and then click on Button1, the Show text button. This will cause the Properties window to display the properties for that object:

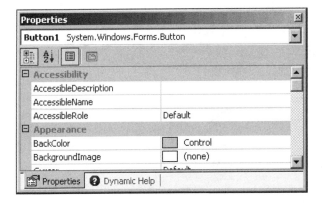

As this window is very, very similar to its VB6 counterpart, we will forgo further discussion of it, other than to point out that changes to properties in this window cause the IDE to alter the code in the collapsed region where the generated code is kept – as we discussed earlier.

Class View

The Class View window is somewhat similar to the Solution Explorer, in that it provides a view into our solution and project. However, the Class View gives us a view of classes, methods, and properties rather than a view of files. This is a very powerful tool in the object-oriented world of .NET.

If we open the Class View window and expand the HelloWorld and Form1 items, we will get a display similar to the following:

Double-clicking on an element in this display will bring up the code window for that element. This makes it a convenient way to move through the code in our project.

In this very graphical display, the icons to the left of each item give meaning:

Icon	Meaning	Scope
	class	public
	class	protected (key)
	class	private (padlock)
	class	friend (envelope)
	interface	public
	module	public
	module	private (padlock)

Icon	Meaning	Scope
	module	friend (envelope)
	method	public
	method	protected (key)
	method	private (padlock)
	method	friend (envelope)
	method returning a value	public or friend (which does not have an envelope in this particular instance)
	method returning a value	protected (key)
	method returning a value	private (padlock)
	field or attribute	public
	field or attribute	protected (key)
	field or attribute	private (padlock)
	field or attribute	friend (envelope)
	property	any scope
	event	public
	event	protected (key)

Table continued on following page

Icon	Meaning	Scope
	event	private (padlock)
	event	friend (envelope)
	structure	public
	structure	protected (key)
	structure	private (padlock)
	structure	friend (envelope)

So Form1 is marked as a public class, New() is marked as a public method, Button1 is marked as a friend attribute and Button1_Click is marked as a private method.

Since Form1 is a subclass of another class, we see an item named Bases and Interfaces. This element appears any time a class is a subclass or implements another interface, and it allows us to drill up into the base class or interface definition. Through this mechanism, we can see virtually everything there is to see about our class and its ancestors.

There are two buttons in the window's toolbar. The left-hand button allows us to change the sort order of the display, while the right-hand one allows us to create a new folder. This new folder is really a specialized view into which we can drag-and-drop elements from the main display. The elements remain in the primary list as well, but within our folder we can have a narrower view of just those elements of interest.

Dynamic Help

One of the nicest new features of the Visual Studio .NET IDE, at least for beginning programmers or those getting used to the new environment and language changes, is the Dynamic Help window. This is a context-sensitive help system, so the window is constantly being updated with links to help on whatever is appropriate.

For instance, with the `Timer1` control selected in our HelloWorld project, the Dynamic Help window appears as:

As we click on different controls or move our cursor into different keywords within our code, the list of topics will change to show help appropriate to that control, component, or keyword.

There is a performance implication to having this window open. The process of monitoring our context, searching for appropriate topics, and displaying the list takes memory and processor time. If your development workstation is nearer the minimum hardware requirement, the performance hit may be more than it is worth.

Toolbox

The Toolbox, found by default on the left-hand side of the display, is a powerful window. It is where we find the controls to create our forms, but it is also a place to find non-graphical components, such as database connections and code fragments that we can drag directly from the Toolbox into our code window.

Tabs

The Toolbox is organized into different tabs, each containing related components, controls, or code. We can add our own tabs to the Toolbox by right-clicking and choosing the Add Tab option.

The default tabs will vary depending on the type of project we are currently building, but some tabs are consistent across all project types:

Tab	Description
Data	Contains components that provide access to data and data sources
Components	Contains various components such as reporting, message queuing, and so on
General	Empty by default, this is a place for us to store general controls, components, and code fragments

When we are building a Windows Forms project such as our HelloWorld example, an additional Windows Forms tab will be available, containing Windows Form controls for use as we create our forms.

When we are building a Web Forms project, two additional tabs become available. The first is a Web Forms tab, containing server-side Web Form controls that we can use to create our web pages. The second is an HTML tab, containing controls that correspond to the standard HTML tags. The Web Form controls are substantially more sophisticated than their HTML counterparts and offer extra capabilities. We will discuss this more in Chapter 7.

Many other tabs are available and will appear as appropriate. To see all the tabs, right-click on the Toolbox and select the Show All Tabs option. The list is quite extensive and covers a wide range of capabilities for the different tools found within the Visual Studio .NET IDE. Many of the options may appear disabled, either due to the current project type or the type of designer that is currently active.

As we noted in Chapter 1, this is a very large and complex product – and there is far more here than can be covered in a single book. As such, we will stay focused on the concepts and tools that are most useful when developing a typical application with Visual Basic .NET. For more information on using the IDE comprehensively, see Effective Visual Studio .NET, published by Wrox Press, ISBN 1-861006-96-9.

Working with the Clipboard Ring

The Clipboard Ring tab is visible when we are editing code, and always lists the last few items copied to the system clipboard. This includes items copied to the clipboard from other applications, such as Word.

We can drag-and-drop items from the tab into our code or other designers where appropriate. This can be a very nice way to grab code or HTML fragments from various locations and quickly integrate them with our application.

Working with Code Fragments

Somewhat similar to the Clipboard Ring is the capability to grab fragments of code from a Visual Studio .NET code window and store a copy of that code in the Toolbox. Typically, these fragments are stored on the General tab, though we can create our own tab for the purpose if we so desire.

To store a code fragment on the General tab, simply open up a code window – say for the Form1 module of our HelloWorld application – highlight some text in the code window, then drag-and-drop that highlighted text onto the General tab.

This will add the code and expand the General tab. We will see an entry like the following:

Just as with the items in the Clipboard Ring, these items can be dragged back into a code window at any point and the appropriate text will be added.

This is a great way to keep common code templates and routines quick at hand – just drag them into the code window and away you go. It can be particularly useful to store standard comment blocks, which we can drag into our code and then fill in the details.

Server Explorer

By default, there is another tab to the far left of the Visual Studio .NET display – the Server Explorer. This is an exciting new feature of Visual Studio .NET, as it allows us to explore and access server components in a nice graphical environment.

In the following display we see the explorer listing the tables available in a SQL Server database:

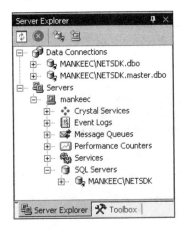

The elements displayed in the **Server Explorer** are more than just for show. Most can be dragged directly onto a designer (Windows Forms, Web Form, Component, and so on) making them available for use from our application.

For example, we can drag a stored procedure from the display onto a designer and Visual Basic .NET will automatically add the appropriate connection and command objects to make the stored procedure available via code. This is a very powerful capability.

This means that gaining access to a database, a message queue, or a Windows 2000 performance counter is as easy as drag-and-drop. When an element is dropped onto a designer, the IDE automatically adds code into the code region for automatically generated code. This code, in general, declares and instantiates an object of the appropriate type and sets its properties so the object ends up representing the item we selected from the explorer window. At that point, the object is available for use by our code – all set up and ready for our use.

The Task List

One nice feature from Visual InterDev was the task list. This feature has been carried over and developed for Visual Studio .NET, providing a quick list of all the current build and syntax errors in our application. If it is not visible already, click on **View | Show Tasks | All**.

As we program, the automatic syntax checker is constantly checking our code for errors, just as in previous versions of VB. However, now the errors are not only indicated in the code window with a wavy underline – they are listed conveniently in the **Task List** window too.

Double-clicking on an error listed in the window will take us right to the troublesome point in our code. To see this in action, go into the code of a project and intentionally create a syntax error. The error will be displayed in the window and double-clicking the error will return us to the code window to fix the error:

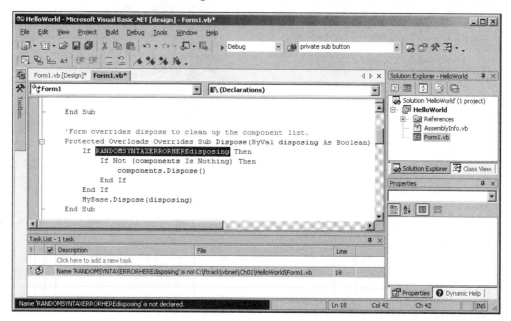

The tasks shown in this window can be filtered by various criteria. To set the filtering, right-click on the window and choose the Show Tasks menu option. Then choose the appropriate option to filter for the tasks of interest.

TODO Comments

In addition, we can add special TODO comments to our code and they too will be displayed in the task list. In code the comments appear as:

```
' TODO: here is my comment
```

This is a great feature since it is quite common to leave bits of programming for later, and using this technique allows us to easily mark and find places where further work is required.

Custom Comments

Better still, we can have the task list display comments based on other tokens of our choice. To configure this, choose the Tools | Options menu and go to the Task List option:

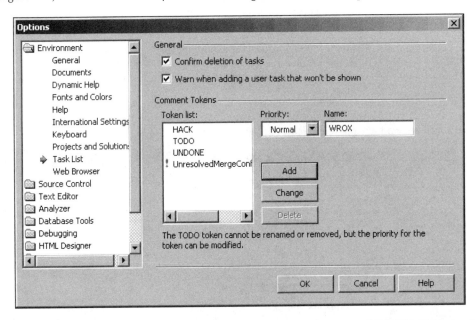

In the diagram, we are in the process of adding a Normal priority token named WROX. If this is added, then any comments starting with WROX will be listed in the task list, just as TODO comments are by default.

The Output Window

In previous versions of VB we had the Immediate window, which allowed us to view debug output from our application, and to interact with the environment by entering bits of code or even calling procedures within our code. Visual Studio .NET splits this functionality up a bit, with the output portions being handled within the Output window. The window is automatically invoked during a build process, or you can use *Ctrl-Alt-O* to see it.

The Output window is also the place where debug output is displayed, as shown in the following diagram:

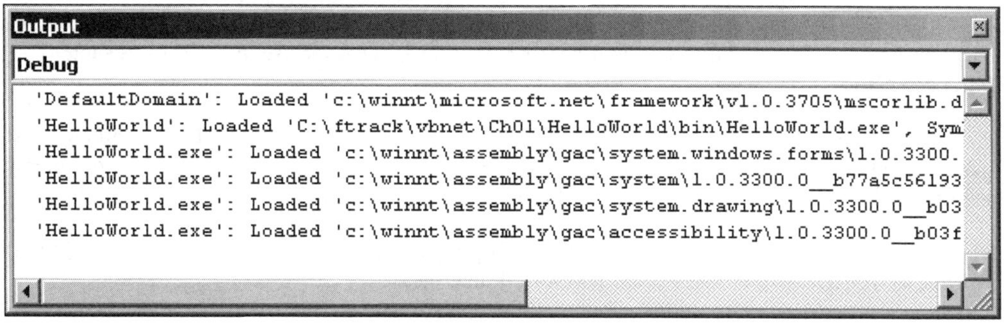

This diagram shows the output from the process of running an application in the debugger, including a list of the modules that were loaded into the debugger. The penultimate line is generated from code using the System.Diagnostics.Debug class:

```
Debug.WriteLine("Test")
```

This is the Visual Basic .NET equivalent of the Debug.Print command in VB6.

The Command Window

The Command window provides us with command line access to the Visual Studio .NET environment and IDE. Through this window, we can enter commands to manipulate the IDE, execute macros and macro commands, and so forth.

To view this window, go through View | Other Windows | Command Window. It may be convenient to drag the title bar of the new Command window onto the tab bar of the existing Task List and Output window.

If we enter a command such as:

```
File.AddNewProject
```

the IDE will respond by displaying the Add New Project dialog.

This window is not a direct replacement for the Immediate window familiar to experienced VB developers, since it does not allow us to directly enter and execute VB code during design-time. However, like VB6's Immediate window, it can be used to interact with our application itself at run-time and evaluate lines of code.

Macro Support

While we are discussing IDE commands and macros, we should take a quick look at the macro capabilities of the Visual Studio .NET environment. *Macro*, in this context, means a macro to control Visual Studio .NET – *not* a development environment for macros for use in other tools such as Microsoft Office.

Previous versions of VB have had some degree of macro programming support, since much of the IDE was exposed through COM. Until now, however, we have never had the ability to record and playback a simple set of actions, nor the total access to the environment that is provided by Visual Studio .NET.

Under the Tools | Macros menu are a number of options that allow us to record and play temporary macros, as well as create, explore, and run stored macros.

These quick macros can be an immense time saver when we are applying repetitive changes to a lot of code. We might record a macro to find some specific text, change it, and then do a couple other code fixes in the surrounding code before moving on to find the next instance of the text.

To quickly record a macro press *Ctrl-Shift-R*. Do any steps necessary for the macro, then click the appropriate button in the pop-up tool bar to stop recording. To play back the macro, simply press *Ctrl-Shift-P*.

There are many examples of repetitive code changes that can be quickly streamlined by recording a quick macro to play back.

Integrated Debugging

One of the strengths of VB ever since version 1 has been its integrated debugging capabilities. Few other tools have ever approached the ease with which VB applications can be debugged.

The Visual Studio .NET IDE provides a comparable integrated debugger, continuing to provide us with the same capabilities. The debugger is invoked by pressing *F5* to run an application from within the IDE – just as it has been for a decade.

The debug commands are available via the Debug menu. This includes an option to run our application from the IDE without invoking the debugger – a convenient feature.

As we edit our code, we can set breakpoints by pressing *F9* or left-clicking in the left margin area at the line where we want to set the breakpoint. Alternatively, we can right-click in the code to get a full list of options.

When running a program in the debugger, right-clicking in the code provides an expanded list of options, including one that lets us add a watch for variables, much the same as in VB6.

F8 is used to step through code line-by-line.

> *Keep in mind that the specific keys used for these purposes can vary depending on the profile chosen for Visual Studio .NET. The keys described here are for the Visual Basic .NET profile, but they may be different for other language profiles.*

We have already discussed the Output window and its role in providing output from the debugger and from our application via the `System.Diagnostics.Debug` class. However, there are a number of other windows directly related to the debugging capabilities of Visual Studio .NET.

The Call Stack Window

As our application executes, methods call other methods, which in turn call other methods. If we have a breakpoint in a method, it can often be useful to know how we got to where we are in the code. The list of methods that were invoked to get us to where we are in the code is called the **call stack**. As we debug our code, we can use the call stack to trace back through the steps in our application.

The Call Stack window displays the current location of execution in our application, and the entire call stack that brought us to this point.

While more complex than the VB6 Call Stack window, the Visual Basic .NET display is more complete, showing not only our code, but also all the various methods that were called that eventually led us to the current method.

The Breakpoints Window

Another window available while debugging is the Breakpoints window. This window lists all the breakpoints currently set in our application. Double-clicking on a breakpoint in this window will take us to the location of the breakpoint in the code, making it very easy to move from point to point.

Also, each breakpoint has a checkbox to the left – allowing us to quickly enable or disable breakpoints. Unchecking a breakpoint doesn't remove it from the code, it just temporarily disables it – a very nice feature when debugging within loops.

Watch and Value Display Windows

Several other windows are at our disposal, including a Watch window that displays information about variables we have marked for watching.

There is also an Autos window and a Locals window, which display valuable information about the state of our application's variables.

Obviously, there is a lot more to the Visual Studio .NET IDE than we have discussed here. There are some other windows and designers available, and some other capabilities that may be very useful. However, we have covered the features and capabilities that are most likely to impact upon us on a day-to-day basis as we use the tool. Some other features are specific to the development of Windows Forms, which are covered in Chapter 5, or to developing Web Forms, which are covered in Chapter 7.

Summary

Though Visual Basic .NET has some obvious differences compared to VB6, our walkthrough of the Hello World program should have illustrated that there is also a great deal of commonality. Visual Basic .NET is a substantial evolutionary step for VB, which goes right along with .NET, which is a substantial evolutionary step forward from COM.

Though it is possible to program in Visual Basic .NET using nothing more than the .NET Framework SDK and a text editor, Visual Studio .NET provides us with a truly powerful and productive environment in which to work. In this chapter, we covered merely the most important and commonly used parts of Visual Studio .NET – there is a lot more to explore.

Visual Studio .NET gives us the ability to create Windows Forms applications in a manner comparable to how we created Windows applications in VB6. It also extends much of that graphical designer capability forward to web development through its support for Web Forms. By also integrating support for server-side resources such as databases and message queues, Visual Studio .NET provides an environment in which we can perform virtually all the programming tasks we will need to build applications.

We will continue to use and explore Visual Studio .NET throughout the rest of the book. In the next chapter however, we will focus more on the language and syntax of Visual Basic .NET.

Language and Syntax

By this point in the book, you should have a good understanding of a basic Visual Basic .NET application and the Visual Studio .NET development environment, so we are ready to explore the language and syntax changes to the Visual Basic language itself. There are quite a number of changes and enhancements, some very useful and others that are less so, but that are necessary for operation in the .NET environment. In some cases, we will show both VB6 and Visual Basic .NET examples to better illustrate the differences and similarities.

Visual Basic .NET is obviously still Visual Basic, sharing the same basic syntax, keywords, and programming approach. However, Visual Basic .NET does have a large number of new features, new or different keywords, and some new syntax and data types and changes.

These include:

- ❏ The introduction of namespaces
- ❏ Data type changes
- ❏ Declaration of variables and arrays
- ❏ Enhanced collection types
- ❏ Structured error handling
- ❏ Various other syntactic changes to the language

In this chapter, we will discuss these changes and more. Also note that Visual Basic .NET is now a fully object-oriented language, and we will cover the new object-oriented features separately in Chapter 6.

It is also important to understand the close relationship between Visual Basic .NET and the .NET Framework that we discussed in Chapter 2. Visual Basic .NET applications always make heavy use of the .NET Framework, as it is this that compiles and runs our applications. Additionally, it is virtually impossible to create any application that does not make use of the .NET system class libraries – another key part of the .NET Framework.

Namespaces

Namespaces are a naming scheme that helps organize the various classes available to our application so that they are more easily found. All code in .NET, VB or otherwise, is contained within a namespace.

This is true of code in the .NET system class libraries. For instance, the Windows Forms classes are in the `System.Windows.Forms` namespace and the classes that support collections are in the `System.Collections` namespace.

All of the code in our applications is also contained in namespaces.

In VB6, much of our code was contained within a form of namespace as well. Any code in a COM component was addressed as *componentname.classname* – otherwise known as the `PROGID`. This technique was somewhat limited, however:

❑ The address of a class was tied directly to the component in which it was contained

❑ Classes not in COM components were not in a namespace

❑ `PROGID` naming is only one level deep

❑ Component naming is always global to the entire computer

Namespaces in .NET overcome these limitations.

Several assemblies (EXEs or DLLs) can be in the same namespace, meaning that classes from more than one component can be found in the same namespace. This also allows for multi-language namespaces, where a class written in VB can be in the same namespace as a class written in C#, for instance.

Likewise, a single assembly can contain multiple namespaces. Typically, each assembly has a namespace for all of the classes it contains. Often, however, we will subdivide those classes into sub-namespaces using namespace nesting – a concept we'll discuss shortly.

> *An **assembly** is roughly the .NET equivalent of a COM component. All code in .NET is contained in assemblies. Assemblies were explained more thoroughly in Chapter 2.*

In .NET, *all* code is in a namespace, whether that code is in an official component or a regular Windows Forms client application. If we don't provide an explicit namespace for our code, a namespace is generated for us based on the name of our assembly/application (the project name in Visual Basic .NET). This means that our code is always accessible via a consistent naming scheme.

Namespaces can also be nested, allowing for a great deal of clarity and readability when using them to organize classes. For example, if we were building a comprehensive manufacturing application, we might create a high-level namespace `MyMfgApp`. Within that namespace we might have namespaces for various parts of the application:

- ❑ `MyMfgApp.Accounting.GL`
- ❑ `MyMfgApp.Accounting.AP`
- ❑ `MyMfgApp.MRP`
- ❑ `MyMfgApp.Inventory`

and so forth. So, we have defined a base `MyMfgApp` namespace, with other namespaces contained within it – each one possibly containing classes, modules, enums, structures, and other namespaces.

Each of these namespaces would contain the classes appropriate to that part of the overall application, but due to the namespace addressing it is always clear where the class belongs.

Class names only need to be unique within a namespace. This means that, even though Windows Forms has a `Form` class, we can create our own namespace that has a `Form` class, perhaps for a data entry application where the data is entered on forms. This helps reduce the number of reserved words that we are prevented from using effectively in our applications.

Using Namespaces

It is impossible to create a .NET application without using namespaces. While this is true, namespaces are so well integrated into the environment that we may often use them without thinking – it becomes second nature.

We can use namespaces explicitly through direct addressing or implicitly through the `Imports` keyword.

> **Either way, our application must first reference the assembly that contains the namespace we wish to use. This is done with the Project | Add References menu option.**

Adding a reference to an assembly (DLL or EXE) makes all the namespaces, classes, and other types contained within that assembly available to our application. All the classes and data types in the assembly will be contained within a namespace, but the assembly itself may contain multiple namespaces.

Referencing an assembly makes the namespaces and types available for our use. The `Imports` statement merely simplifies how we write code to use the functionality in the assembly.

Direct Addressing

Any namespaces contained by assemblies referenced by our application are available for use in our code. For instance, if we want to read or write from `stdio` (the console input/output stream) the `System.Console` namespace is required. We can access any class in this namespace directly by providing its fully qualified name. For example:

```
System.Console.WriteLine("This is a test")
```

This line of code invokes the `WriteLine()` method in the `System.Console` namespace, using it to print a line of text to an output window.

This is true of any namespace available to our application, but it is somewhat lengthy to type. Fortunately, IntelliSense kicks in and helps to auto-complete the text on our behalf.

The Imports Keyword

Another way to avoid typing quite so much, and to make our code more concise, is to use the `Imports` keyword. This statement allows us to implicitly address namespaces by making them available to our code, somewhat like a shortcut.

If you want to make all the classes in a given namespace available to your code without the need to type the entire namespace each time, you can use the `Imports` statement. For example:

```
Imports System.Console

Some code...
```

```
WriteLine("This is a test")
```

By importing the namespace at the top of our code module, we avoid having to explicitly reference the namespace each time we use a class within that namespace. This can save typing since we don't always need to use the fully-qualified name.

The only exception to this is where a given class name is used within two namespaces. If we import both namespaces, we will still need to explicitly use enough of the fully qualified name when using that class, otherwise the name will be ambiguous.

For instance, say we have two namespaces, `MyMfgApp.Inventory` and `MyMfgApp.Sales`, both of which have a `Product` class. The following code would have trouble:

```
Imports MyMfgApp.Inventory
Imports MyMfgApp.Sales

Public Sub DoSomething()
  Dim obj As New Product()
End Sub
```

There is no way for the compiler to tell *which* `Product` class we are referring to from the context. To avoid this problem, we can change the code to:

```
Dim obj As New Sales.Product()
```

thus removing the ambiguity around the `Product` class.

Aliasing Namespaces

At first glance, it seems that having the same class name in more than one namespace should be fairly rare. Unfortunately, it is pretty common, meaning that we can find ourselves typing explicit namespace addresses quite often.

To help avoid typing quite so much, we can provide an **alias** for a namespace. Rather than simply importing a namespace as is, we can give it a new name:

```
Imports Inv = MyMfgApp.Inventory
Imports MyMfgApp.Sales

Public Sub DoSomething()
  Dim obj As New Inv.Product()
End Sub
```

Here, we are aliasing `MyMfgApp.Inventory` with the shorter name `Inv`. Then, we can use `Inv.Product()`, which really means `MyMfgApp.Inventory.Product()`.

Creating Namespaces

Any code we create using Visual Basic .NET will be contained within a namespace. We have control over how the namespace is named, though Visual Studio .NET does provide a default – the name of our project, as mentioned earlier.

Setting the Root Namespace

Every project in Visual Studio .NET has a **root namespace**, which is set in the project's Property page. For example, our `HelloWorld` project's namespace is `HelloWorld` by default. Highlight the HelloWorld node in the Solution Explorer and then select View | Property Pages. You should then see a form like this:

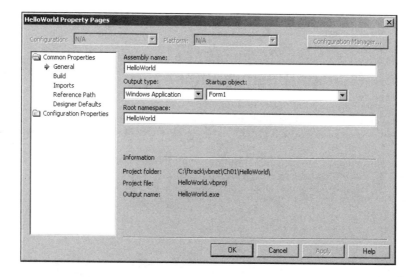

Notice the Root namespace field where the namespace is set. We can override this value if we desire, causing all the classes in our project to belong to a different namespace. If we wanted the classes from multiple projects to co-exist in the same namespace, we would need to override this field in all the projects to ensure that they have the same value.

In our `HelloWorld` project, we have a `Form1` class that is more properly named:

```
HelloWorld.Form1
```

Within our project, we don't need to use this full name, but if we were to make `Form1` or some other class from our project available to other applications, this is the address that would be used.

The Namespace Keyword

While Visual Studio .NET provides our code with a root namespace via the project properties, we know from earlier that namespaces can be nested so that we can further organize our classes.

This is where the `Namespace` keyword comes into play. In a Visual Basic .NET project, a class will always be contained within the root namespace. However, if we want it to be in a more specific namespace, we can put the class within a `Namespace` block:

```
Namespace MyNamespace

Class MyClass
End Class

End Namespace
```

This class will now have the address of:

```
MyRootNamespace.MyNamespace.MyClass
```

Using this technique, we can be very specific in the naming of our classes, allowing us to organize our code as we desire.

The Microsoft.VisualBasic Namespace

Most languages are composed of not only their keywords, but also a set of runtime functions, methods, and constants. This is certainly true of all modern Basic languages including Visual Basic. It is hard to envision programming Basic without using `Len()`, `Mid()`, and a variety of other common functions.

These runtime functions, methods, and constants are located in the `Microsoft.VisualBasic` namespace. This assembly and namespace are automatically referenced and imported for our use in any Visual Basic .NET project.

Language and Syntax Changes

Now that you have got a basic understanding of namespaces and how they are used to organize and address our code, we can move on to discuss the various language and syntax changes you will encounter in Visual Basic .NET.

Option Statements

VB has had `Option` statements for some time, allowing us to control the behavior of the compiler and thus affect how we code. Visual Basic .NET continues this tradition, using the `Option` keyword to allow us to override default behaviors as we desire.

Our options are:

Option Statement	Value	Description
Option Explicit	On	Requires declaration of all variables before they are used (default).
	Off	Variables may be used without being declared.
Option Compare	Binary	Strings are compared using a binary comparison algorithm (default).
	Text	Strings are compared using a text comparison algorithm.
Option Strict	On	Automatic type coercion will not take place. We must explicitly convert types when desired – for example, we must use `CLng()` to convert an `Integer` to a `Long` data value.
	Off	Automatic type coercion will take place much as it did in VB6, where data of one type will be automatically converted to other types without warning or error (default).

These options can be set within the project's properties so they are global to the entire project. Right-click on the project and choose **Properties** from the menu and select the **Build** tab. Here we can define the default options for this project. Any option default set in the properties window can be changed on a per-file basis through the use of explicit `Option` statements in the code – just as in previous versions of VB.

`Option Explicit` works largely as it did in the past. With this option turned On, we are forced to declare variables before using them. Any undeclared variables are of type `Object`.

Notice that `Option Base` is no longer available. This option was used to indicate whether arrays should begin with a 0 element or a 1 element. In Visual Basic .NET all arrays are zero-based, starting with a 0 element.

Also, `Option Strict` is new. One of the most controversial features in the recent versions of VB has been the liberal way in which VB would convert data from one type to another. In VB6 we could have code such as:

```
Dim MyLong As Long
Dim MyInt As Integer

MyLong = 5
MyInt = MyLong
```

While convenient, this code could be viewed as unsafe or unclear. Hidden in the assignment of `MyLong` to `MyInt` is a type conversion – changing the value 5 from an `Integer` to a `Long`. With `Option Strict On` in Visual Basic .NET, this code will not run and must be changed to:

```
Dim MyLong As Long
Dim MyInt As Integer

MyInt = 5
MyLong = CLng(MyInt)
```

Depending on your view, this is either a nice new feature or a serious step backwards. It should certainly reduce the potential for coding errors. Regardless, it is important to be aware of the new general type coercion statement, `CType()`, which we will discuss in this chapter.

Data Type Changes

Visual Basic .NET introduces a number of data type changes – something that can be disconcerting at first. Some of these changes have been introduced to provide new capabilities, others to support future systems such as the 64-bit processors that will be supported by 64-bit versions of Windows 2000 and the new Windows .NET Server operating systems.

A common underlying change to the data types is that they are all now technically derived from type `Object`. This means that a simple `Integer` is of type `Object` and can be treated like any other object. Normally, this has little impact on us as developers, but it is important to keep in mind, since any method parameter of type `Object` can not only accept 'real' objects, but can also accept native data types, since they too are objects.

The process of converting a value type, such as `Integer`, into and out of the `Object` type is called **boxing and unboxing**. There is a performance implication here, since some work is involved in converting a simple value type into the more general `Object` type, and so, we should generally avoid treating value types as `Object` when possible.

Integer Type Changes (Byte, Short, Integer, Long)

Perhaps the most striking changes in data types are those to the integer data types:

Data Type	Size	Range
Byte	8-bit	0 to 255 (unsigned)
Short	16-bit	-32,768 to 32,767
Integer	32-bit	-2,147,483,648 to 2,147,483,647
Long	64-bit	-9,223,372,036,854,775,808 to 9,223,372,036,854,775,807

Integer and Long are the most commonly used data types in VB, and both have changed sizes. Integer used to be 16-bit and is now 32-bit, while Long used to be 32-bit and is now 64-bit.

This means that those people who used Long to achieve optimal performance on 32-bit processors will want to switch to using Integer, while those who used Integer as a general rule need to be aware that their favorite data type will contain values higher than 32,767.

These changes also bring the VB data types more in line with their counterparts in SQL Server, which can help reduce bugs for those people interacting with databases on a regular basis.

Floating-Point Division

Visual Basic .NET still has the same basic Single and Double data types, though we will see some different behaviors when it comes to division. **Floating-point** numbers are often designed to conform to the specifications from the IEEE standards body. Conformance with this specification leads to some interesting results from the following code:

```
Dim d1 As Double
Dim d2 As Double

d1 = 1
d2 = 0
Debug.WriteLine(d1 / d2)
```

where we would expect to get a division by zero error, the output instead is the word Infinity.

Likewise, the following does not cause an error:

```
Dim d1 As Double
Dim d2 As Double

d1 = 0
d2 = 0
Debug.WriteLine(d1 / d2)
```

This prints the text result of NaN.

These results, while a bit surprising, conform to the IEEE standard governing floating-point numbers.

Replacing Currency with Decimal

Previous versions of VB had a Currency data type that was used to represent large floating-point values. The idea was to provide support for large currency values.

Visual Basic .NET has no Currency data type, but does have a 128-bit Decimal data type, which provides support for very large values that can be scaled by powers of 10. It is divided into two parts – a 96-bit integer and an associated 32-bit integer. These allow representation of very large values. This means that the Decimal data type can act as a decent replacement for the Currency data type.

Decimal values can have anywhere from 0 to 28 digits to the right of the decimal point. The more digits to the right of the decimal point, the higher our precision, but the lower the overall range of values can be.

The Char Type

Visual Basic .NET has both a Byte and a Char data type.

Byte contains a numeric value in the range 0-255 and consumes 1 byte of space and is a numeric value, not a character value. On the other hand, it is often used to store ASCI character values in numeric form.

Char contains values from 0-65535 and consumes 2 bytes of space. This is a Unicode value, meaning it directly supports international character sets.

The Char data type is intended for use in manipulating single character values or for creating arrays of character values. This can be confusing at first, since Byte is useful in working with characters as well.

However, Byte is only useful for simple ASCI characters, and we live in a Unicode world – which is where Char comes into play. Unicode characters are 2 bytes in length, and so the Char data type exists to support this 2-byte character scheme.

The String Type

The String data type in Visual Basic .NET is different from that found in previous versions of VB. The Visual Basic .NET String data type flows from the .NET system class library, where we find namespaces devoted to dealing with text and String data.

The String data type comes from the System.String class, and is designed as an **immutable** string of text. This means it cannot be changed, so any attempt to change a String results in a new String being created to store the changed value, while the original is destroyed.

This is not all that different from the behavior in previous versions of VB, since even then, any increase to a string's length would cause the same effect. However, in VB6 we could alter a string inplace:

```
MyString = "Hello"
Mid$(MyString, 5, 1) = "X"
```

In Visual Basic .NET, this code causes a new `String` to be created. While the code continues to work transparently, there are obviously performance implications to be considered.

Another change to the `String` data type is that the concept of a fixed-length string has changed somewhat. In VB6 we could declare a variable as:

```
Dim MyString As String * 50
```

This variable is a `String` of exactly 50 characters and is fixed at that length – no longer, no shorter. In Visual Basic .NET, this syntax is invalid. Instead we need to use an attribute:

```
<VBFixedString(50)> Private MyString As String
```

Other namespaces with important string handling classes and methods include:

- ❏ `System.String`
- ❏ `System.Text`
- ❏ `System.IO`

Typically, we will use the VB run-time functions for `String` data, such as `Mid`, `Right`, `Left`, and so forth. Optionally, we can also choose to use the classes and methods found in these other namespaces.

One key example of this is string concatenation. Concatenating a string with a large series of other strings is very expensive in terms of performance. This means that:

```
MyString = "Hello "
MyString = MyString & "world, "
MyString = MyString & "How "
MyString = MyString & "are "
MyString = MyString & "you "
MyString = MyString & "today? "
```

is very slow. It is much faster to use the `StringBuilder` class from the `System.Text` namespace:

```
Dim sb As New System.Text.StringBuilder()
sb.Append("Hello ")
sb.Append("world, ")
sb.Append("How ")
sb.Append("are ")
sb.Append("you ")
sb.Append("today? ")
```

Both of these code fragments do the same thing, but when concatenating many little strings together, the `StringBuilder` is a definite performance winner.

Replacing Variant with Object

One of the most powerful, flexible, and dangerous data types in previous versions of VB is the `Variant` data type. A variable of type `Variant` could hold virtually any value, automatically adjusting its internal data type to accommodate the value so it could be stored. The price of this flexibility was a serious loss of performance and the substantial potential for unintentional bugs due to automatic type coercion. The `Variant` data type also consumed a lot of memory, as its flexibility required a lot of memory to track all the possible types of data it could represent or store.

Visual Basic .NET does not have a `Variant` data type, thus avoiding some of the negatives that came along with it – but what about the positives?

Visual Basic .NET *does* have the `Object` data type. In fact, at least conceptually, all data types in .NET are technically objects, and so, the `Object` data type is somewhat comparable to `Variant` in that a variable of type `Object` can hold virtually any value.

This means that `Object` is somewhat of a replacement for `Variant`, in that it provides comparable functionality. However, it is worth noting that the implementation of `Object` behind the scenes is not the same as the implementation of `Variant` in previous versions of VB.

> *We will discuss the `Object` data type again in Chapter 6 when we cover the object-oriented features of Visual Basic .NET. The `Object` class is the base type for all types in the .NET Framework, and so, is very important for object-oriented programmers.*

Also, `Option Strict` comes into play here, changing the way code is typically written. For instance, in VB6 we might have code like:

```
Dim x1 As Variant
Dim x2 As Variant

x1 = 5
x2 = "10.5"
Debug.Print x1 + x2
```

In Visual Basic .NET, with the default of `Option Strict Off`, we would write pretty much the same code:

```
Dim x1 As Object
Dim x2 As Object

x1 = 5
x2 = "10.5"
Debug.WriteLine(x1 + x2)
```

but if we turn `Option Strict On`, our code would appear as:

```
Dim x1 As Object
Dim x2 As Object
```

```
x1 = 5
x2 = "10.5"
Debug.WriteLine(CInt(x1) + CSng(x2))
```

While we have the flexibility of the Variant, we have greater clarity in this code because the type conversions are explicit rather than automatic. In all three cases, the result is the number 15.5.

The CType Statement

One common use of both the Variant and Object data types in VB6 was to store object references. Methods and properties on those objects could then be called by using the variable. For example, in VB6 we might have:

```
Dim x As Object

Set x = New Customer
Debug.Print x.LastName
```

While Visual Basic .NET does continue to have the Object data type, and a variable of type Object can hold any object reference, just like in VB6, things are a bit more complex due to Option Strict. As a result of Option Strict, a variable of type Object can't be automatically coerced into any specific object type – we must do this explicitly by using the CType() statement. For example:

```
Dim x As Object

x = New Customer
Debug.WriteLine(CType(x, Customer).LastName)
```

The CType() statement converts a value of one type into a value of another type. The new type is supplied as the second parameter to the statement – providing a lot of flexibility. It can be argued whether this code is more or less readable than its VB6 counterpart. However, we could also declare another variable of type Customer and set our generic Object value into that variable to make the code more clear.

Changes in Declaration of Variables

Along with the data type changes, Visual Basic .NET also enhances the way that we declare and work with variables.

Declaring Multiple Variables

In VB6, we could declare several variables on one line:

```
Dim x, y, z As Integer
```

The deceptive result of this statement is that x and y are declared as type Variant, while z is declared as Integer. Visual Basic .NET alters this behavior so all three variables are declared as type Integer – a result that is more intuitive.

Declaring Initial Values

Frequently, when declaring a variable, we also want to set its initial value. In VB6, we would do:

```
Dim x As Integer
x = 5
```

In Visual Basic .NET, we can shorten this to:

```
Dim x As Integer = 5
```

This is shorter and more concise, though it does make the `Dim` statement into an actual executable line of code.

Declaring Constants

Constants in Visual Basic .NET must be declared with a specific type:

```
Public Const MY_CONSTANT As String = "The constant value"
Private Const MAX_VALUE As Integer = 42
```

While this is a small change, it is important to recognize it.

Dim As New

In VB6, we could use the `New` keyword while declaring an object variable:

```
Dim x As New Customer
```

This was not recommended, however, due to the way VB6 implemented this functionality. While it appears that a new `Customer` object was created by this code, no object is created until the variable x is actually used in code. This deceptive behavior was the cause of some bugs, which were very hard to find in many applications.

Additionally, the way this was implemented behind the scenes meant that the VB compiler inserted code before *any* use of the variable x – code to check and see if the object already existed or if it needed to be created. All this extra code reduced the performance of our application.

Visual Basic .NET addresses these concerns by making the syntax work as we might expect, by creating the object immediately. This means the following line:

```
Dim x As New Customer()
```

will cause a new `Customer` object to be created immediately – the variable x represents the object right away – avoiding many of the bugs and performance issues from VB6.

We will cover the instantiation of objects in far more detail in Chapter 6 when we discuss objects and the object-oriented features of Visual Basic .NET.

Scoping Changes

Variables declared in Visual Basic .NET may be subject to some different scope restrictions from those declared in previous versions of VB. In particular, Visual Basic .NET introduces the concept of **block-level scope**, where variables can be declared within specific blocks of code, such as an `If...End If` block.

In VB6, we could write code such as:

```
If True Then
  Dim x As Integer
  x = 5
End If
x = 15
```

In Visual Basic .NET, however, this code is invalid, since the variable x is not valid outside of the `If...End If` block. The same is true for any type of block structure, including `Do...Loop`, `While...Wend`, `For...Next`, and so forth.

For most people, who declare variables at the top of routines, this won't be an issue. For those who declare variables throughout their code as the variables are needed, this will require some changing of habits.

Changes to Arrays

In previous versions of VB, arrays were a native data type of the language itself. In Visual Basic .NET, arrays flow from the .NET system class libraries and are common across all .NET languages.

This means that arrays can be easily passed around within the .NET environment from component to component regardless of the language used to create each component, but this does represent a change from what we are used to as VB developers. Fortunately, the basic syntax for using arrays remains relatively consistent, so, for the most part, the changes are transparent in day-to-day coding.

Zero-Based Arrays

Perhaps the biggest change is that all arrays are now zero-based, meaning that the lowest array element of any array is 0 rather than 1. In VB6, we had the `Option Base` statement, which allowed us to specify whether arrays were zero-based or one-based. In Visual Basic .NET, this statement is gone and all arrays are zero-based.

In Visual Basic .NET, we can declare an array as:

```
Dim myarray(10) As Integer
```

The result is an array with subscripts that range from 0 to 10 rather than from 1 to 10.

Another side effect of this change is that the `To` syntax is no longer supported, so we can no longer declare an array as:

```
Dim myarray(1 To 10) As Integer
```

This will cause an error. Effectively, all arrays in Visual Basic .NET are declared as being (0 To x) where x is our upper bound.

LBound and UBound

In the past, the LBound statement would return the lowest valid index value for an array. This functionality remains intact, though obviously, since all arrays are zero-based, the LBound statement will always return the value 0.

The UBound statement also continues to work, returning the highest valid index value for an array:

```
Dim myarray(5) As String

MessageBox.Show(CType(UBound(myarray), String))
```

This code will display a message box with the value 5, the highest valid array index for this array.

Declaring Arrays

As with previous versions of VB, we can declare arrays with explicit sizes such as:

```
Dim myarray(5) As String
```

or we can declare them with no explicit size, relying on the use of a ReDim statement to size the array later:

```
Dim myarray() As Decimal
```

Visual Basic .NET allows us to preload an array with data as it is being declared. This is conceptually the same as initializing any other variable as it is being declared, but with arrays, the syntax is a bit different since we are supplying a list of values instead of a single value:

```
Dim myarray() As Integer = {1, 3, 6, 2}
```

This has the effect of sizing the array to hold the data elements we provide, as well as placing those values into the array. To use this feature, we can't explicitly define the size of the array.

ReDim

The ReDim statement remains valid in Visual Basic .NET. This statement can be used to change the number of elements in an array, though it cannot be used to change the number of dimensions. This means we can write code such as:

```
Dim myarray() As String

ReDim myarray(5)
```

This declares an array and then changes the number of elements in the array to 6 (0 through 5).

We can also redimension more complex arrays such as:

```
Dim myarray(0, 0) As String

ReDim myarray(10, 20)
```

Notice that the ReDim statement doesn't alter the number of dimensions, just the number of elements in each dimension.

It is important to note that each time we use the ReDim statement, we are telling Visual Basic .NET to create a brand new array for our use. This can be an expensive operation and must be used with care.

ReDim Preserve

When using the ReDim statement, all existing data in the array is lost. To avoid losing this data, we can use the Preserve keyword. Use of this keyword places an additional restriction on the ReDim statement. In particular, when using the Preserve keyword, only the last dimension can be resized, so the following code is valid:

```
Dim myarray(0, 0) As String

ReDim myarray(5, 5)

ReDim Preserve myarray(5, 10)
```

This is valid because only the last (right-most) dimension is resized using the ReDim Preserve statement.

> *We can write code to use ReDim Preserve, which changes any dimension in the array without causing a build error. This code appears valid in the IDE, but will cause an error at run-time.*

The ReDim Preserve statement causes Visual Basic .NET to create a new array with the new dimensions, and then copy the existing data into the new array. This is an expensive operation and must be used with care.

Fixed Arrays

We can also create fixed-size arrays by using an attribute:

```
<VBFixedArray(10)> Dim FixedArray() As String
```

This attribute is specific to Visual Basic .NET, and can create one-or two-dimensional fixed-size arrays. It should be avoided if we intend to allow this array to be used by other .NET languages.

Changes to User-Defined Types

The concept of a **user-defined type**, or **UDT**, is a powerful one. It allows us to group a set of values together to form a more complex type. In VB6, this was done using code such as:

```
Public Type mytype
  Name As String
  Age As Integer
End Type
```

Visual Basic .NET preserves this functionality, but changes the syntax somewhat. Instead of using the keyword Type, we now use the Structure keyword:

```
Public Structure mystruct
  Public Name As String
  Public Age As Integer
End Structure
```

We have the same basic functionality, with just a slight change to syntax.

Notice that the individual elements of the structure are declared with a scope. This means that we can create a structure with some Public elements (the default), which are visible to other code, and also with elements that are more restricted in their scope.

A Structure can also have a constructor method. This is a method that accepts parameters and allows us to initialize the values of the Structure as it is being declared:

```
Public Structure mystruct
  Public Name As String
  Public Age As Integer

  Public Sub New(ByVal n As String, ByVal a As Integer)
    Name = n
    Age = a
  End Sub
End Structure
```

Now we can create a variable for this Structure using the following syntax:

```
Dim st As New mystruct("Fred", 33)
```

This will cause the constructor method to be run, loading the values into the Structure as it is declared.

Changes to Collections

In previous versions of VB, the Collection type was native to the language. In Visual Basic .NET we still have a Collection type, but more extensive support for collections, and similar functionality, such as a Dictionary class, comes from the .NET system class libraries.

VB6-Style Collections

Functionality directly comparable to the VB6-style `Collection` object is available in Visual Basic .NET through its `Collection` class. This means we can write code such as:

```
Public Sub DoSomething()
  Dim col As New Collection()

  col.Add("some data")
End Sub
```

This `Collection` object works in the same way as the `Collection` objects we are used to working with in previous versions of VB. However, this is not the recommended approach for new code because more powerful alternatives exist in the `System.Collections` namespace.

The System.Collections Namespace

The new collection functionality provided in the .NET system class libraries flows from the `System.Collections` namespace. This namespace not only provides support for the concept of a simple collection (or hashtable) as we have had in the past, but it also provides support for a `Dictionary`-style collection such as that provided by the Windows Scripting Host Library. Other types of collections are available as well. The following is a list of commonly used items:

Collection	Description
ArrayList	Implements a single-dimension array that grows dynamically as elements are added. This is a close approximation of the VB6 `Collection` object.
BitArray	Implements a single-dimension array of `Boolean` values, which are stored internally as single bits, providing a very compact way to manage a list of `Boolean` values.
Hashtable	Implements a collection of key-value pairs that are organized based on the hash value of the key. This allows very fast and efficient storage and retrieval of data based on the key value.
Queue	Implements a FIFO (first in, first out) queue structure.
SortedList	Implements a sorted list of key-value pairs.
Stack	Implements a LIFO (last in, first out) stack structure.

Additionally, there are some other collection classes in `System.Collections.Specialized`:

Class	Description
BitVector32	Stores `Boolean` and small integer values.
HybridDictionary	Implements a `Dictionary` that optimizes its behavior for both small and large data sets.

Table continued on following page

Class	Description
ListDictionary	Implements a Dictionary that is optimized for small data sets.
NameValueCollection	Implements a collection with String values and keys and a numeric index value. This is also somewhat similar to the VB6 Collection object.
StringCollection	Implements a simple collection of String values.
StringDictionary	Implements a Dictionary that only accepts String keys.

The variety of classes available can seem overwhelming when compared to the simplicity of a single Collection data type. However, we are now presented with substantially more options than we have had in the past, along with classes such as Hashtable and ObjectList, which provide functionality quite comparable to the Collection object with which we are familiar.

For instance, for Collection-style functionality where we don't care about the order of the elements, we might use the Hashtable class:

```
Imports System.Collections

Public Sub DoSomething()
    Dim ht As New Hashtable()
    Dim entry As DictionaryEntry

    ht.Add(1, "item 1")
    ht.Add(2, "item 2")

    For Each entry In ht
      Debug.WriteLine(entry.Value)
    Next
End Sub
```

As with all the key-value collection implementations, the elements of the collection are represented by DictionaryEntry objects, which provide us with access to the key and value data for each element.

While slightly different from a VB6 Collection object, this code is quite similar, and is generally consistent with the type of code we would write to work with any of the other collection classes available in the System.Collections namespace.

Creating Custom Collections

There are many cases where we need to create custom collections – most frequently because we want a collection that only contains a certain data type or type of object. Creating a custom collection in VB6 was somewhat of a black art, since it required us to implement the mysterious NewEnum property, along with setting its Procedure ID to the not-entirely-self-explanatory value of –4.

Things are much more clear in Visual Basic .NET, where we can use the object-oriented concept of **inheritance** to create a new collection that is based on one of the existing collection types provided in the system class library. In fact, we can base a new collection object on one of the base classes from the System.Collections namespace – they are designed for this purpose:

Base Class	Description
`CollectionBase`	Base from which to create simple value collections
`DictionaryBase`	Base from which to create key-value dictionaries
`ReadOnlyCollectionBase`	Base from which to create simple read-only value collections
`NameObjectCollectionBase`	Base from which to create name-value collections

Though we will cover inheritance thoroughly in Chapter 6, it is worth showing how a custom collection can be created while we are discussing collection functionality.

Suppose we have a simple `Structure` as follows:

```
Public Structure MyStruct
  Public Name As String
  Public BirthDate As Date
End Structure
```

and suppose we want a collection that only contains data in this structure. We can simply implement a subclass of the `CollectionBase` class – a pre-built class designed to allow us to create collections that are strongly typed. The following code implements such a collection:

```
Public Class MyCollection
  Inherits CollectionBase

  Default Public Property Item(ByVal Index As Integer) As MyStruct
    Get
      Return CType(List(Index), MyStruct)
    End Get
    Set(ByVal Value As MyStruct)
      List(Index) = Value
    End Set
  End Property

  Public Function Add(ByVal Value As MyStruct) As Integer
    Return List.Add(Value)
  End Function

  Public Sub Remove(ByVal Value As MyStruct)
    List.Remove(Value)
  End Sub
End Class
```

Notice that we don't need to re-implement any of the base functionality – all of that is provided through the inheritance mechanism, which we will discuss in Chapter 6. All we need to do is provide our own implementation of the `Add()`, `Item()`, and `Remove()` methods so they accept and return only the `MyStruct` type.

New Arithmetic Operators

Visual Basic .NET introduces some new arithmetic operators – shortcuts for existing syntax. The following table illustrates the new syntax:

Arithmetic Operation	Existing Syntax	New Shortcut
Addition	X = X + 4	X += 4
Subtraction	X = X – 10	X -= 10
Multiplication	X = X * 2	X *= 2
Division	X = X / 13	X /= 13
Integer division	X = X \ 13	X \= 13
Exponent	X = X ^ 3	X ^= 3
String concatenation	X = X & " text"	X &= " text"

The existing syntax continues to work – we just have more options now than before.

Short-Circuited If...Then Statements

When checking conditions in our code, we often have compound expressions. For instance:

```
Dim myInt As Integer

myInt = 0
If myInt <> 0 And 17 \ myInt < 5 Then
```

The If...Then statement here has two components. When using And and Or *both* components are checked, even if the first one would ensure that the entire expression's outcome is known. In this example, if myInt <> 0 evaluates to false, then we know immediately that the whole expression is false.

Worse yet, in this example, we will actually get a run-time error of division by zero because the second part of the expression will be evaluated.

It would be much more efficient if we could **short-circuit** the comparison and avoid evaluating any more of the statement as soon as we know the result.

To this end, Visual Basic .NET introduces the AndAlso and OrElse statements. We can now rewrite the code as:

```
Dim myInt As Integer

myInt = 0
If myInt <> 0 AndAlso 17 \ myInt < 5 Then
```

With this new code, as soon as the first part of the expression evaluates to false, the process is complete. There will be no division by zero error because the evaluation is short-circuited.

The only way to accomplish this in prior versions of VB was to use two If statements such as:

```
Dim myInt As Integer

myInt = 0
If myInt <> 0 Then
  If 17 \ myInt < 5 Then
```

The addition of these new keywords allows us to write much more concise and readable code.

Using Reserved Words as Procedure Names

There are many times when it would be nice to name a method or procedure using a word that is reserved by the language. For instance, we might want a method named Loop to loop through some data:

```
Public Sub Loop(ByVal Data() As String)
   Dim Index As Integer

   For Index = 0 To UBound(Data)
      ' do work here
   Next
End Sub
```

Unfortunately Loop is a reserved word, and so, this won't work. However, we can place the reserved word within square brackets and still use it, so this is valid:

```
Public Sub [Loop](ByVal Data() As String)
```

This should be used with care, however, since any code that calls the method will also need brackets:

```
Dim ar() = {"a", "b", "c"}

[Loop](ar)
```

If widely used, this can lead to some very obscure and hard to read code.

No Set Statement

One of the most confusing syntax elements of previous versions of VB is the use of the keyword Set when assigning objects to variables. This is confusing since it tends to set objects apart from any other data type.

In VB6, we might have statements such as:

```
Set x = New Customer
Set y = x
```

In Visual Basic .NET, the Set statement is gone, simplifying our code, and so in Visual Basic .NET, we have statements such as:

```
x = New Customer()
y = x
```

The result of this change is that object variables are treated the same as any other variable, simplifying the language syntax overall, and reducing much confusion, especially for new programmers or those coming from other languages.

Notice that you can still type Set, but Visual Basic .NET will automatically take it out once you have finished typing in the line!

Changes to Property Routines

Since we no longer have a Set statement, it should come as no surprise that the meaning of Property Set and Property Let are affected as well.

The concept of a Property Set doesn't exist as it did in VB6. Beyond this, however, there are other substantial syntax changes that affect how Property routines are built. In VB6, we might have code in a class module such as:

```
Private mstrName As String

Public Property Let Name(Value As String)
  mstrName = Value
End Property

Public Property Get Name() As String
  Name = mstrName
End Property
```

In Visual Basic .NET things are quite different. The same code is written in a Visual Basic .NET class as follows:

```
Private mstrName As String

  Public Property Name() As String
    Get
      Return mstrName
    End Get
    Set(ByVal Value As String)
      mstrName = Value
    End Set
  End Property
```

There are a few things to note here. First off, all the code for the entire property is contained within one `Property` routine, and this routine is subdivided into two blocks – a `Get` block and a `Set` block. Though the `Set` statement for assignment of object references is gone, we still use `Set` within `Property` routines. There is no longer a `Property Let` – this is included in the functionality of the `Set` block we see in the above code.

Also notice that the `Set` block uses a `Value` parameter to accept the new value. We can change this parameter name if needed, though the data type of the parameter must match the data type of the property itself.

Consistent Scoping

One consequence of consolidating both the assignment (`Set`) and accessor (`Get`) functionality into the same `Property` routine is that they both have the same scope. In VB6, we could have scoped these differently, such as:

```
Friend Property Let Name(Value As String)
  mstrName = Value
End Property

Public Property Get Name() As String
  Name = mstrName
End Property
```

thus restricting which code could change the value of `Name`, while allowing any code to read the value. We can't implement this the same way in Visual Basic .NET, since the entire `Property` routine is scoped the same.

To achieve similar functionality in Visual Basic .NET, we need to implement two separate properties – each with the appropriate scope – or use methods rather than properties.

ReadOnly Properties

In VB6, implementing a read-only property was as simple as writing a `Property Get` routine without a corresponding `Property Set` or `Property Let`. In Visual Basic .NET, this remains true, but the syntax is more explicit, lending clarity to our code:

```
Public ReadOnly Property Age() As Integer
  Get
    Age = 3
  End Get
End Property
```

Notice the use of the `ReadOnly` keyword, which causes the compiler to ensure that we only supply a `Get` routine for this `Property`.

WriteOnly Properties

If we have a ReadOnly keyword, it only makes sense that there would be a WriteOnly keyword for declaring write-only properties:

```
Public WriteOnly Property Data() As Integer
  Set(ByVal Value As Integer)
    mintData = Value
  End Set
End Property
```

This has the same general effect as the ReadOnly keyword, but the WriteOnly keyword ensures that we have a Set routine with no Get routine for this Property.

Default Properties

Visual Basic .NET changes the way we create default properties. In VB6, creating a default property involved using the **Procedure Attributes** dialog to change the **Procedure ID** to (default). This had no visible impact on our code and generally seemed to be quite obscure.

Visual Basic .NET improves this process by making the creation of a default property something that is declared directly in our code through the use of the Default keyword:

```
Default Public Property Name(ByVal Index As Integer) As String
```

Visual Basic .NET also imposes an extra restriction on default properties – they *must* have at least one required parameter. It is no longer legal to have a default property that accepts no parameter.

Structured Error Handling

One area where VB has long been criticized is its lack of structured **error handling**.

Certainly, we were able to do a lot with On Error Goto and On Error Resume Next, but these global error handlers lacked control and didn't lend anything to our program's readability. They also involved a huge amount of work.

> The older error handling options still exist in Visual Basic .NET, though a given procedure can use *either* the old *or* the new error handling capabilities, but not both in the same procedure.

Visual Basic .NET incorporates new structured error handling capabilities, addressing these concerns head-on. The structured error handling in Visual Basic .NET is quite similar to that found in many other languages, including:

- ❑ C++ and C#
- ❑ Java
- ❑ VAX Basic (from the OpenVMS world)

It provides us with a block structure that can be nested, controlled, and easily understood. This means that we can implement very robust error handling that actually increases the readability of our code.

Additionally, Visual Basic .NET introduces **exception handling** – including an `Exception` class to augment the existing `Err` object we have had in previous versions of VB.

The Try...Catch...Finally Structure

The error handling is accomplished via a basic block structure. For example, we could create a bit of code that divides two values and traps any possible division error (such as division by 0):

```
Try
   intResult = intValue1 \ intValue2
Catch
   intResult = 0
Finally
   Debug.WriteLine(intResult)
End Try
```

When using a `Try` block, at a minimum we must provide a `Catch` or a `Finally` block, or we will get a syntax error.

Let's take this apart to see what is going on.

The first part of our block structure is the `Try` section:

```
Try
   intResult = intValue1 \ intValue2
```

All code in the `Try` block is contained within an **error trap**. While this example shows just one line of code, it is possible to have many lines of code within a `Try` block – including nested `Try...Catch` blocks. If an error occurs in a `Try` block, the `Catch` block is invoked to handle the error:

```
Catch
   intResult = 0
```

This code is *only* run in the case that an error occurs in the `Try` block. If no error occurs, this code is entirely skipped and does not run. If we get here, we know that an error has occurred, and so, this code exists to handle the error as appropriate. Again, this example shows just one line of code, but the `Catch` block may contain many lines of code if needed.

We may also want some code to run regardless of whether there was an error or not. In many cases we need to perform cleanup or take other actions in any case. This is where the `Finally` block comes into play:

```
Finally
   Debug.WriteLine(intResult)
End Try
```

The `Finally` block is optional – we don't need to have one if it doesn't make sense in a given scenario. However, any lines of code that are contained in a `Finally` block are run after the code in the `Try` block if there is no error, or after the code in the `Catch` block if there is an error.

Also note that a `Catch` block is required to actually *trap* an error. If we only have a `Finally` block, with no `Catch`, then the `Finally` block will run *and then* the error will be raised as though no error handler was in effect!

Catch Statement Variations

The `Catch` statement can be more sophisticated than shown in our simple example. In particular, we can have more than one `Catch` statement in a `Try...End Try` block, each one set up to handle a specific error. For example:

```
Try
    ' our code goes here
Catch When Err.Number = 5
    ' handle error 5
Catch
    ' handle all other errors
End Try
```

In this way, we can have separate error handling blocks to handle different errors that may occur.

Another variation is to assign a specific variable to hold the error exception information within the `Catch` block:

```
Catch e As Exception
   MessageBox.Show(e.ToString)
```

This example code would display a dialog showing a text description of the error that has occurred.

The two syntax variations can be combined as well:

```
Catch e As Exception When Err.Number = 12
```

These variations on the `Catch` statement provide us with a great deal of power to handle errors.

If an error is not caught by any specific `Catch` statement, it will be handled by the generic `Catch` statement (the one with no `When` clause). If there is no generic `Catch` statement, then the error will be raised up the call stack as though there was no error handler at all. Even in this case the `Finally` block will be executed before the error is raised.

Exit Try

As with any block structure, it is very nice to be able to jump out of the structure when needed. This is the purpose of the `Exit Try` statement. This statement can exist within the `Try` block of our overall structure, and causes the flow of execution to jump to the first line of code following the `End Try` statement:

```
Try
  ' protected code goes here
  If MyFlag = True Then Exit Try
  ' more protected code goes here
Catch
  ' error handling goes here
End Try
' execution resumes here
```

If we have a `Finally` block, that block of code must still be run before the `Try` block is exited:

```
Try
  ' protected code goes here
  If MyFlag = True Then Exit Try
  ' more protected code goes here
Catch
  ' error handling goes here
Finally
  ' execution resumes here
End Try
```

Based on the flow of your code, you can jump out of the protected region at any point with the `Exit Try` statement.

Exception Objects

From a general syntax or coding level, the only real change to VB error handling is the introduction of the `Try...End Try` structured error handling. However, behind the scenes, Visual Basic .NET uses a substantially more sophisticated, and capable, error handling mechanism than was available in previous versions of VB. This new error mechanism is based on the concept of **exceptions**, which can be **thrown** to raise an error and **caught** when that error is handled.

The `Err` object now has a `GetException()` method that will return the `Exception` object containing the details of the underlying exception that caused the error.

While largely hidden from day-to-day VB programming, this underlying exception mechanism will be a welcome addition to programmers from other languages, who are used to dealing with exceptions and having access to that information.

Converting from On Error Goto

While the older `On Error` statements still exist in Visual Basic .NET, we may want to convert to the newer, more structured alternatives. Let's take a look at two different examples that cover the most common ways `On Error` is used within VB6.

First, we may have an `On Error Goto` statement, with an error handler later in our routine:

```
Sub DoSomething()
  On Error Goto Handler

  ' protected code goes here
```

```
    Exit Sub

Handler:
  ' error handling code goes here
End Sub
```

In Visual Basic .NET, this code would appear as:

```
Sub DoSomething()
  Try
    ' protected code goes here
  Catch
    ' error handling code goes here
  End Try
End Sub
```

The result is pretty similar, but is somewhat easier to read and understand.

However, keep in mind that there is no Resume equivalent for Try blocks. If our current error handler resumes the protected code, then in some cases, things get more complex. For instance, in VB6 we might have:

```
Sub DoSomething()
  On Error Goto Handler

  ' protected code goes here
  Exit Sub

Handler:
  ' error handling code goes here
  Resume
End Sub
```

The Resume statement will cause us to re-run the line that originally cause the error, jumping back into the normal flow of execution. This functionality doesn't exist within the context of a Try block. We cannot call Resume from within a Catch block to re-enter the Try block.

This is a major limitation of the structured error handling scheme, and requires a bit more work on our part. Typically, the Resume statement is used when we are handling an 'expected' error within our code – meaning it is an error that we can fix in the handler and thus allow the original code to continue as planned.

This scenario is now covered through the use of nested Try blocks. For instance, perhaps we expect that we might have a division by 0 error in one line of our code, but the rest of our code would work if the result was just forced to be a zero rather than an error. Our Visual Basic .NET code might appear as:

```
Sub DoSomething()
  Try
    ' protected code goes here
    Try
      x = x / y
```

```
      Catch
        x = 0
      End Try
      ' more protected code goes here
    Catch
      ' error handling code goes here
    End Try
  End Sub
```

This addresses the typical use of Resume, and potentially adds a great deal of clarity to our code, since we can see exactly what lines of code are *expected* to cause an error.

Converting from On Error Resume Next

Another very common error handling approach in VB6 is to use On Error Resume Next, and then to simply check the Err.Number value to see if an error has occurred. While you can continue to use this technique in Visual Basic .NET, you may want to change your code to use a Try block.

In VB6, we might have code such as:

```
  Sub DoSomething()
    On Error Resume Next
    ' protected code goes here
    If Err Then
      ' error handling code goes here
    End If
    On Error Goto 0
    ' unprotected code goes here
  End Sub
```

This type of error handling code is typically directed at catching a specific error that we expect to occur within our code. For instance, many applications use On Error Resume Next immediately prior to attempting to open a file that may or may not exist, providing a relatively readable technique for catching that error and handling it inline.

Structured error handling is a much better way to handle these scenarios. We can convert this VB6 code to Visual Basic .NET as follows:

```
  Sub DoSomething()
    Try
      ' protected code goes here
    Catch
      ' error handling code goes here
    End Try
    ' unprotected code goes here
  End Sub
```

We achieve the same end result, trapping and handling the potential error in our protected code, but structured error handling is much easier to read, and thus, to maintain.

Changes to Procedure Syntax

Visual Basic .NET introduces a number of changes to the way procedures (Function, Sub, and other methods) are called, and the way in which they are created or declared.

Parentheses Required on Procedure Calls

One striking syntactical difference in Visual Basic .NET is that all method calls require parentheses unless the method accepts no parameters. In the past, parentheses were only required when calling a Function – a method that returns a value – with parameters, such as:

```
x = DoSomething(y, z)
```

Now, however, parentheses are required for any method that accepts parameters, whether the method returns a result or not. This means that many methods declared as Function and methods declared as Sub, with or without parameters, require parentheses. So, method calls now appear as:

```
x = DoSomething(x)
x = DoSomethingElse(y, z)
```

In fact, the IDE will often automatically insert parentheses even for those methods that don't accept parameters, even though the parentheses are technically optional:

```
DoMoreStuff()
```

While more consistent overall, this change in syntax does take some getting used to, and for consistency, it is probably best to get used to just putting parentheses after all method calls – parameters or not.

Though we will discuss this more in Chapter 6, it is also worth noting that object creation also requires parentheses in Visual Basic .NET:

```
x = New Customer()
```

This is because any creation of an object causes an implicit call to the constructor method for that class – and all method calls require parentheses.

ByVal Default for all Parameters

When creating procedures (either Function or Sub) it is important to note that Visual Basic .NET changes the way parameters are passed into the procedure.

In VB6, most parameters were passed ByRef, meaning that the procedure gained a reference to the variable, and any changes to the value of a parameter within a procedure would be carried back to the original calling code. Even though the ByRef keyword wasn't required, it was implicit in all parameter declarations. For us to pass a variable by value, we had to use the ByVal keyword.

In VB6, we could have code such as:

```
x = 5
DoSomething x
Debug.Print x

Private Sub DoSomething(value As Integer)
  value = 10
End Sub
```

The value printed as a result of this code is 10 rather than 5. This is because the variable x was passed by reference to the procedure – allowing the procedure to change the value at will.

Visual Basic .NET changes this default behavior, passing all parameters ByVal – by value. This change was done to increase performance. Passing most data types by value is faster than passing them by reference. Additionally, defaulting to by value means that the opportunities for accidental side-effects causing bugs is reduced.

Converting the above code to Visual Basic .NET we have:

```
x = 5
DoSomething(x)
Debug.WriteLine(x)

Private Sub DoSomething(value As Integer)
  value = 10
End Sub
```

The value printed as a result of this code is 5, since the variable x is passed by value, meaning the procedure can't cause the original value to change.

Obviously, the ByRef and ByVal keywords can still be used when declaring parameters for a procedure, meaning we can have whichever behavior we require. However, it is important to note that the *default* behavior has changed.

Fortunately, Visual Studio .NET automatically inserts the ByVal keyword as we type our code, so the normal coding we will do in Visual Basic .NET is always explicit in its intent.

Optional Parameters Require a Default Value

Another change to the way parameters are handled deals with optional parameters. One thing that hasn't changed is that optional parameters must be the last parameters in the parameter list – and that remains true.

However, it used to be that optional parameters had to be of type Variant, and we could use the IsMissing statement to find out if the optional parameter was supplied or not. In more recent versions of VB this behavior changed, as we were allowed to have optional parameters of other data types. IsMissing remained valid, but only for Variant parameters.

In Visual Basic .NET we no longer have the `Variant` data type, and so, the `IsMissing` keyword has also been eliminated. `Optional` parameters still exist, but must now be declared with default values – making it easy for us to determine if a specific value was provided by the calling code since it would vary from the default value we have set.

The new syntax for declaring an optional parameter is:

```
Public Sub DoSomething(Optional ByVal param1 As String = "")
```

When using the `Optional` keyword for a parameter, we must also supply a default value for the parameter by adding an assignment after the type declaration.

As in previous versions of VB, optional parameters must be the last parameters on the parameter list. Once a parameter is marked as optional, all subsequent parameters must also be declared as optional.

The Return Statement

Visual Basic .NET enhances how we return result values from `Function` procedures. Long ago, we had to create our functions along this line:

```
Public Function GetCustomer(ID As Long) As Customer
   Dim objCust As Customer

   Set objCust = New Customer
   objCust.Load ID
   Set GetCustomer = objCust
End Function
```

More recently, we were able to use this syntax:

```
Public Function GetCustomer(ID As Long) As Customer
   Set GetCustomer = New Customer
   GetCustomer.Load ID
End Function
```

This syntax is highly disturbing for programmers used to recursion, since it appears to be a recursive bit of code, even though it is not recursive.

Now in Visual Basic .NET, we can use the `Return` keyword to return our value:

```
Public Function GetCustomer(ID As Integer) As Customer
   Dim objCust As New Customer(ID)

   Return objCust
End Function
```

The `Return` keyword sets the result value of the `Function` to the value provided as a parameter.

For those curious about the object creation process shown here, we will cover this in more detail in Chapter 6.

Apart from making obvious what is being returned, `Return` also facilitates changing the function name without having to run through all the code within the function to change the lines that set the return value.

Changes to Event Handling

Visual Basic .NET preserves the basic functionality of events as provided in VB6. In fact, raising events is unchanged, although handling events has been enhanced.

Raising Events

This means we continue to have event declarations in a class:

```
Public Event MyEvent()
```

Our events can also have parameters – values that are provided to the code receiving the event:

```
Public Event MyEvent(ByVal Info As String)
```

Within the class, our code can raise the event with the `RaiseEvent` statement:

```
Public Sub DoSomething()
  RaiseEvent MyEvent("Some info")
End Sub
```

So far, this is all the same as VB6 code.

Handling Events

Where things get a bit different is in the code that handles the events. In VB6, an event handler was created using what can only be described as a weird syntax. If we had an object variable named `myObject` that raised an event, we might have a routine such as this:

```
Private WithEvents myObject As MyClass

Private Sub myObject_MyEvent(Info As String)
  Debug.Print Info
End Sub
```

While the `WithEvents` keyword is pretty clear, the rest of this syntax was far from intuitive to new developers, as it doesn't explicitly indicate what the routine is for. To clarify this, Visual Basic .NET uses the `Handles` keyword instead, allowing us to create the following code:

```
Private WithEvents myObject As MyClass
```

```
Private Sub OnMyEvent(ByVal Info As String) Handles myObject.MyEvent

    Debug.WriteLine(Info)
End Sub
```

Note how the procedure is declared with the `Handles` keyword, indicating the event that it will be handling. The procedure can be scoped as desired, and can be called directly if we want, but it will also be automatically called when the event is raised.

This is not only much more clear than the VB6 equivalent, but it is more flexible, since the procedure that handles an event can be named anything. The only requirement is that its parameter list matches that of the event being raised.

The Visual Basic .NET IDE will create event handler methods for us, just like the VB6 IDE did. Simply select the object in the class name drop-down list in the upper-left of the code window, and then select the event to be handled in the method name drop-down list in the upper-right. The resulting method will appear as:

```
Private Sub myObject_MyEvent(ByVal Info As System.String) _
    Handles myObject.MyEvent
```

This is a pretty similar naming convention to what we are used to in VB6. If you don't like this name, you can change it as desired, as long as the `Handles` statement remains to link the method up to the event.

Handling Multiple Events

The `Handles` keyword offers even more flexibility. Not only can the method name be anything we choose, but a single method can also handle multiple events if we desire. Again, the only requirement is that the method and all the events being raised must have the same parameter list.

> As an aside, this explains why all the standard events raised by the .NET system class library have exactly two parameters – the sender and an `EventArgs` object. By being so generic, it is possible to write very generic and powerful event handlers than can accept virtually any event raised by the class library.

One common scenario where this is useful is when we have multiple instances of an object that raises events:

```
Private WithEvents myObject1 As MyClass
Private WithEvents myObject2 As MyClass

Private Sub OnMyEvent(ByVal Info As String)
    Handles myObject1.MyEvent, myObject2.MyEvent

    Debug.WriteLine(Info)
End Sub
```

Notice that we have now declared two different object variables based on `MyClass`. They both raise the event `MyEvent`, and we have changed the `Handles` clause to indicate that the method will handle the events from *both* objects.

This technique can be used to consolidate a lot of code in some cases. Many VB6 programs have a large number of event handling routines that all simply call into a single, central routine to do the actual work. With Visual Basic .NET, all those events can be directly routed to a single handler where they can be processed.

Using AddHandler

We can also link events to methods dynamically at run-time. While the new `Handles` clause is much nicer than the VB6 syntax, it has the same limitation in that it is only useful when hooking up an event to a handler at design-time.

Visual Basic .NET includes the `AddHandler()` method, which allows us to link an event to a handler at run-time dynamically. In this case, we don't use the `WithEvents` keyword or the `Handles` clause:

```
Private myObject1 As MyClass

Private Sub Form1_Load(ByVal sender As System.Object, _
    ByVal e As System.EventArgs) Handles MyBase.Load

   AddHandler myObject1.MyEvent, AddressOf OnMyEvent

End Sub

Private Sub OnMyEvent(ByVal Info As String)

   Debug.WriteLine(Info)

End Sub
```

When the form is loaded, the `AddHandler()` method will link the event from our object to the specified method. This can provide a lot more flexibility in terms of event handling, since events can be handled from dynamically loaded objects.

Depreciated, Obsolete, and Unsupported VB Syntax

By now, it has probably become apparent that there are a number of functions, keywords, and statements from previous versions of VB that are either unsupported in Visual Basic .NET, or are at least considered depreciated and should not be used as they may be removed in future versions. A couple of the most obvious are listed here.

Gosub

The `Gosub` keyword and related functionality has been entirely removed from Visual Basic .NET. Code that currently uses `Gosub` will need to be rewritten. For example:

```
Public Sub DoSomething()
   Dim x As Integer
```

```
' do some work
Gosub Mysub
' do some more work
Exit Sub

Mysub:
  ' do work in the subroutine using x
  Return
End Sub
```

We might re-write this code in a variety of ways. The most direct is to do something along this line:

```
Public Sub DoSomething()
  ' do some work
  Mysub(x)
  ' do some more work
End Sub

Private Sub Mysub(ByRef x As Integer)
  ' do work in the subroutine
End Sub
```

By passing the variable x as a ByRef parameter, we preserve the behavior where code in a Gosub routine could alter the value of variables in the main procedure.

DefType Statements

The little-used DefType statement has been a long time holdover from the days when BASIC shared some commonality with FORTRAN. This statement allowed us to declare all variables starting with certain letters to be certain data types. This has long been discouraged as a declaration mechanism, as it leads to code that is hard to read and maintain. Visual Basic .NET removes support for this keyword and this concept.

Delegates

There are times when it would be nice to be able to pass a procedure as a parameter to a method, a concept known as **function pointers** or **callbacks**. The classic case is when building a generic sort routine, where we not only need to provide the data to be sorted, but we need to provide a comparison routine appropriate for the specific data.

VB6 had the AddressOf operator, which would return the address of a procedure in a BAS module. This approach had two limitations. First off, the code had to be in a BAS module. Second, and more important, there was no way to *call* the method based on its address from VB. This meant that the operator was only really useful for calling Windows API functions.

While Visual Basic .NET preserves the AddressOf operator, it extends its functionality to include methods of objects as well as procedures in code modules. More importantly, through the mechanism of **delegates**, we can call these methods from within our VB code.

The concept of a delegate formalizes the process of declaring a routine to be called and calling that routine. In our code, we can declare what a delegate procedure must look like from an interface standpoint. This is done in a class by using the Delegate keyword:

```
Delegate Function IsGreater (v1 As Integer, v2 As Integer) As Boolean
```

Once a delegate has been declared, we can make use of it within our code:

```
Public Sub DoSort(ByRef theData() As Integer, GreaterThan As IsGreater)
  Dim outer As Integer
  Dim inner As Integer
  Dim temp As Integer

  For outer = 0 To UBound(theData)
    For inner = outer + 1 To UBound(theData)
      If GreaterThan.Invoke(theData(outer), theData(inner)) Then
        temp = theData(outer)
        theData(outer) = theData(inner)
        theData(inner) =  temp
      End If
    Next
  Next
End Sub
```

Note the use of the Invoke() method, which is the way a delegate is called from our code. All that remains is to actually create the implementation of the delegate routine and call our sort method. Typically, this would be done in a separate code module or class.

The only requirement of the method providing the delegate implementation is that its parameter list must exactly match that in our Delegate statement above:

```
Public Function MyIsGreater(v1 As Integer, v2 As Integer) As Boolean
  If v1 > v2 Then
    Return True
  Else
    Return False
  End If
End Function
```

We can then use this implementation when calling the sort routine with code such as:

```
Dim myData() As Integer = {3, 5, 2, 1, 6}
```

```
DoSort(myData, AddressOf MyIsGreater)
```

This is where the AddressOf operator comes into play. We can use it to gain the address of a regular procedure in a code module, a method of an object, or a shared method of a class – a concept we'll discuss in Chapter 6. Any procedure or method is valid as long as the parameters match the Delegate declaration.

Attributes

One major new addition to the VB syntax in Visual Basic .NET is the introduction of **attributes**. Attributes can be applied to classes, methods, and other code. They provide an extensible mechanism by which we can add tags to instruct the .NET runtime or other code to alter its behavior as it interacts with our code.

The .NET runtime supports a number of attributes that are very useful to VB developers. Additionally, we can use attributes as a mechanism to build advanced frameworks of our own, if we desire. In this book, we will stick to a discussion of attributes as they pertain to the .NET Framework and typical VB development.

Most attributes are instructions for some portion of the .NET Framework or for the Visual Studio .NET IDE itself. We will use and explain quite a number of them throughout the remainder of the book, as a lot of the functionality we will explore will require their use.

Attributes can be applied to assemblies, classes, methods, and variable declarations.

We specify an attribute on a class using the following syntax:

```
<theAttribute()> Public Class MyClass
```

As a convention for readability, it is typically best to use line continuation to place the attribute on a separate line above the class declaration itself.

Some attributes can also accept parameters, for example:

```
<Description("My useful class")> _
   Public Class MyClass
```

Often, attributes accept named parameters, in which case we use the standard VB named parameter assignment of := in the call:

```
<AnAttribute(SomeParam := parameterValue> _
   Public Class MyClass
```

Another common place where attributes are used is on methods or procedures:

```
<Description("My useful procedure")> _
   Public Sub DoSomething()
```

Attributes are defined as a type of class. This means they are syntax-checked by the IDE and offer benefits such as IntelliSense. This also means that we can define our own attributes by creating an attribute class, and then we can use reflection to interrogate a class or object about its attributes – a powerful mechanism for building frameworks.

Attributes are an integral part of the .NET Framework, so we will see lots of common examples of their use throughout the rest of this book.

Summary

Visual Basic .NET is most definitely still Visual Basic, providing the same syntax and coding style to which we are accustomed. At the same time, Visual Basic .NET has some language and syntax changes that allow it to fit very well into the .NET Framework, ensuring that it is a first-class .NET language.

While the syntax and language changes in Visual Basic .NET can take a little getting used to, most of them are well thought out and tend to make the language more intuitive and explicit. This leads to better readability and maintainability for our code.

There are a number of other language and syntax changes in Visual Basic .NET pertaining to objects and object-oriented programming – these are covered in Chapter 6.

Many of the other exciting new capabilities offered by Visual Basic .NET, such as multi-threading, flow from the .NET system class libraries rather than from Visual Basic .NET itself. Some of these are explored in Chapter 9 where we take a look at some more advanced concepts.

Before we explore the object changes, however, Chapter 5 will cover the creation of Windows GUI user interfaces using the .NET Framework's Windows Forms technology.

5

Windows User Interface Capabilities

The .NET Framework provides three ways to render and manage user interfaces:

❑   **Windows forms**

❑   **Web Forms**

❑   **Console applications**

In this chapter, we will look in detail at Windows Forms, and compare and contrast them with the VB forms used in previous versions of Visual Basic. We will also discuss the implications of .NET and Windows Forms, particularly an expected resurgence of 'smart client' designs for applications.

Web Forms are covered in Chapter 7, and console applications are covered in Chapter 9.

Windows Forms are basically a more advanced way to create standard Win32 screens. The technology behind Windows Forms was originally created for the Windows Foundation Classes (WFC), which were developed for Visual J++ (Microsoft's implementation of Java). This history accounts for the fact that Windows Forms are a very mature and robust technology, even in the first version of .NET.

All languages in the .NET Framework use Windows Forms for local, Win32 interfaces. This means that Windows Forms are the replacement for several different older technologies. For Visual Basic .NET, Windows Forms replace the VB forms engine. For C++, Windows Forms can be used instead of Microsoft Foundation Classes (MFC) and Active Template Library (ATL) technologies (though a .NET version of ATL is also available).

The basic architecture of Windows Forms is very similar to the VB forms used in earlier versions of Visual Basic. Windows Forms provide a rich, unified set of controls and drawing functions for all languages, as well as a standard API for underlying Windows services for graphics and drawing. With Windows Forms, it is mostly unnecessary to use the native Windows graphical API for any graphical or screen Functions.

Windows Forms are actually part of the .NET Framework base classes. The namespace used by Windows forms is System.Windows.Forms and will be examined in detail below.

The Importance of Windows Forms

When looking at the hype around .NET, it 's easy to get the idea that Windows Forms are just an afterthought. Web Forms and Web Services tend to get more attention in the press. This seriously underestimates the importance of Windows Forms, and their applicability for developers going forward.

The need for client-based applications with a rich, flexible, and responsive user interface is not going away. In fact, as was mentioned in Chapter 2, such 'smart client' applications may become more important under .NET. Many applications produced with earlier tools are made browser-based, in spite of the higher cost of development and a weaker user interface, just to get away from the deployment costs of client apps. With the XCOPY deployment of a Windows Forms-based application, the deployment and support costs are reduced. This may tip the scale towards a Windows Forms interface in the .NET world in some situations that today, would lean toward using a browser-based user interface.

Even more likely to tip the scale is the new capability for automatic deployment of an application over the Internet. With complete versioning, and a 'trickle-feed' model that only downloads what is immediately needed, smart-client applications can have deployment costs that approach those of browser-based applications. We will discuss internet deployment in Chapter 10.

The multi-tier programming model that we call Windows DNA today still applies in the .NET world, and that model leaves open the possibility that an application may have both a local Win32 interface *and* a web interface. For projects in the .NET Framework, this means that it will be desirable in some cases for an application to have one interface done with Windows Forms and another with Web Forms in ASP.NET. Both interfaces would sit on top of the same middle-tier components. For example, an ordering system might have a Win32 interface for telephone operators to enter orders using an interface optimized for speed, while another web interface allowed customers to enter orders directly into the same system.

It is possible to produce applications utilizing both Win32 and web interfaces with earlier tools, but it becomes much easier using .NET. The .NET Framework makes it easier to integrate components among tiers by providing a consistent component interface model for all .NET languages, including scripting languages. This means, for example, that it is unnecessary in .NET to have special versions of components that use Variants in their interface the way ASP interfaces require (and in fact, Chapter 4 mentioned that the Variant type is not even available in .NET, though is has been replaced by the Object type).

It is also just as easy to integrate Windows Forms with Web Services, as it is to integrate Web Forms with Web Services. Rich, Win32 interfaces based on Windows Forms can access and manage data on remote Internet servers through Web Services, just as Web Forms can. This allows applications to be 'internet-enabled' without necessarily using a browser-based interface.

Windows Forms Basics

Chapters 1 and 3 covered a Hello World program that was created in Windows Forms. Here is a summary of the main points made in that example:

- ❑ A Windows Form program is actually a class. There is no separate 'form module' syntax in Visual Basic .NET.

- ❑ Since a form is actually a class, it cannot be implicitly loaded. That is, simply referring to a form to get it to load is not valid syntax. It is necessary to instantiate the form and then show it – the way classes are used in VB6.

- ❑ The class inherits the capability to be a Windows Form by inheriting from the System.Windows.Forms.Form class.

- ❑ As with all classes in the .NET Framework, Windows Forms have constructors and destructors. The constructor, named Sub New, is a rough equivalent of Form Load in previous VB versions. A Form Load event still exists for form classes, however, and can be used in the same way as Form Load was used in VB6. That event is actually fired by the constructor for the form, so it doesn't really matter which you use, except that you can't pass arguments to the Form Load event, but you can to the constructor.

  The destructor, named Sub Dispose, is roughly equivalent to Form Unload, though there are differences related to the way .NET does its garbage collection, covered in Chapters 2 and 6.

- ❑ The visual forms designer inserts a lot of code in the class to instantiate and manage the form and the controls it contains. This designer code takes the place of the beginning section of a VB6 .frm file (which contains definitions and settings for controls in VB6 and earlier). This code is, by default, hidden in a special region of the source file, and it is normally unnecessary to look at it. You should also be extremely cautious about modifying it.

- ❑ Events are handled somewhat differently, and are more flexible than in VB6 forms. Events contain more information in their arguments, for example, and using advanced techniques a single event routine can be applied to multiple controls.

A program with a Windows Form interface is initially created by selecting File | New | Project... in the Visual Studio .NET IDE. The Windows Application template should be selected for a Windows Forms project, and an appropriate name should be entered. Upon pressing the OK button, a project is created with a blank form named Form1, just as in VB6.

The construction of Windows Forms is very similar to the construction of forms in earlier versions of VB. Controls reside in a toolbox, and are placed on the form surface through drag-and-drop. Double-clicking on a control activates the code window and places the cursor in an event handler for the control. The underlying actions are quite different, with the designer creating VB code to define the controls instead of using the header of a .frm file, but the actions from the developer's point of view are quite similar.

Architecture of Windows Forms

There are several generic classes in the System.Windows.Forms namespace that form an object hierarchy. Here are the classes in the hierarchy:

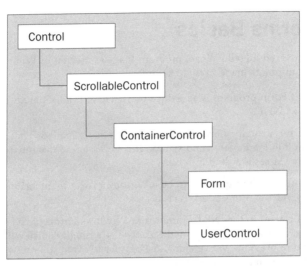

Of course, these classes ultimately inherit from the Object class (as all classes in .NET do); the hierarchy does not end here. The controls that reside on a Windows Form almost all descend from UserControl, and this base class can also be used by developers to create new controls via inheritance. This chapter contains a section later on inheritance in Windows Forms and controls.

Most of the properties and methods of forms and controls that Visual Basic developers will find familiar are actually not implemented in the Form or UserControl classes. Many commonly used properties and methods are implemented in classes above Form in the class hierarchy, and become available to the classes further down in the hierarchy through inheritance. For example, the Control class implements a BackColor property that works exactly like the BackColor property of a form or control in Visual Basic. All of the other classes in the hierarchy then inherit the BackColor property from the Control class.

Let's examine the hierarchy starting at the top.

Control Class

The Control class contains the basic functionality to define a rectangle on the screen, provide a handle for it, and process routine operating system messages. This gives the class the ability to perform such functions as handling user input through the keyboard and mouse. The Control class serves as the base class for any component that needs a visual representation on a Win32-type graphical interface. Application developers can inherit directly from this control for certain types of custom controls, and this is discussed in the section on inheriting forms and controls later in the chapter.

The complete list of members of the `Control` class is too long to include here, but it is available in the help files for Visual Studio .NET. Many of the properties, methods, and events of the `Control` class will be familiar to users of previous versions of VB. For example, the `Control` class implements `Enabled` and `Visible` properties that manage access to a control, properties related to size and position, and properties that set foreground and background colors (`ForeColor` and `BackColor`). Familiar methods such as `Show()`, `Hide()`, and `Refresh()` are implemented in the `Control` class, as are familiar events such as `Click`, `DoubleClick`, `GotFocus`, `KeyDown`, `KeyPress`, `KeyUp`, `MouseDown`, `MouseEnter`, `MouseMove`, `MouseUp`, and `Resize`.

New members in the `Control` class allow new functionality. For example, the developer now has more control over validation of data in controls, using the `CausesValidation` property. The `WndProc()` method gives access to Windows messages, and the `PropertyChanged` event lets the developer know when a property for a control has changed its value.

For positioning controls, the `Control` class features new properties called `Anchor` and `Dock`. These are some of the most useful new properties because they dramatically reduce the amount of code needed to position controls when a form resizes.

The `Anchor` property allows a control to maintain a constant distance to any combination of the container form's edges. The `Dock` property allows a control to be 'docked' to any edge of a form, much like the `Align` property of certain controls in VB6. However, `Dock` is available in all controls in Visual Basic .NET. We will see examples for both `Anchor` and `Dock` later, in the section on positioning and layout of forms and controls.

ScrollableControl Class

As the name suggests, the `ScrollableControl` class adds support for scrolling the client area of the control's window. While it can be inherited and used, it is typically not inherited directly by application developers. It is the base class for `ContainerControl`, so its capabilities are thereby passed down to forms and controls.

Almost all the members implemented by this class relate to scrolling. They include `AutoScroll`, which turns scrolling on or off, and controlling properties such as `AutoScrollPosition`, which gets or sets the position within the scrollable area.

ContainerControl Class

The `ContainerControl` class derives from `ScrollableControl`, and adds the ability to support and manage child controls. It manages the focus and the ability to tab from control to control. As with the `ScrollableControl` class, `ContainerControl` is not usually inherited from directly.

Form Class

Finally, we get to a class that VB developers will actually use a lot. However, keep in mind that the `Form` class inherits from all the classes discussed above, and so, it has all of the properties, methods, and events for those classes.

The `Form` class adds the ability to display caption bars and system menus, so that a form based on this class can look like a normal Windows Form. The `Form` class can also be used to create windows that are borderless or floating, or modal forms such as a dialog box. Capabilities that are specific to forms (but not controls), such as the capability to have default controls for pressing the *Enter* key and pressing *Esc* to cancel, are implemented in the `Form` class.

The new members of the Form class are discussed throughout this chapter in detail, so we will not list them here.

If you have experience with previous versions of VB, the properties, events, and methods of the Form class (including those members inherited from its parent classes) will look generally familiar to you. Many of the same properties, events, and methods are available. Some of the new members replace equivalent members in VB6. Some members, such as the Menu property that points to a MainMenu control, implement old functionality in a new way and replace the equivalents in VB6.

UserControl Class

An original innovation of VB was to have an extendable set of visual form elements, called controls. Controls in Visual Basic .NET are getting quite a facelift, but the concept is still similar. The UserControl class is the base class for most of the controls VB developers are most familiar with. It provides an empty container to implement visual controls.

The UserControl class can contain other child controls, but the interface of UserControl is designed to present a single, unified interface to outside clients such as forms or container controls. The external interface of the UserControl class consists almost completely of members inherited from other classes. It does implement the Load event and the associated OnLoad() method. The Load event is equivalent to the Load event of a form, and is fired before a control based on UserControl becomes visible.

Consistency with Web Forms

As we will see in Chapter 7 on web functionality in Visual Basic .NET, Windows Forms functionality and naming conventions are fairly consistent with Web Forms. There are no UI classes that are used in both, but the naming of the corresponding classes in each namespace is reasonably consistent. For example, both namespaces have a Button class with a Text property and an OnClick event. There is a UserControl class in both hierarchies, both of which serve as a container for visual form elements.

Comparing Windows Forms to VB6 Forms

Now that you understand the general architecture of Windows Forms, we can compare them to the forms you used in VB6 and earlier. In this section of the chapter, we will be looking at differences in:

❑   Designing Windows Forms

❑   Form properties for the cancel and default buttons

❑   Positioning and layout

❑   Dialog boxes

Before we do that, however, here are a few comments on the creation of menus and differences in MDI forms.

The form menu editor in VB6 is gone in Visual Basic .NET. Instead, menus are implemented with special controls, and those controls use a much nicer editor to create menu structures and set properties for menu options. The details on this are in the *Menu Controls* section later.

MDI form interfaces are handled differently in Visual Basic .NET from how they were in VB6. The differences can be summed up by saying that Visual Basic .NET has all the MDI functionality of VB6, with a few extra features, but that functionality is accessed differently. The section entitled *Multiple Document Interface (MDI) Forms* covers these differences.

Using the Visual Designer for Windows Forms

While creating Windows forms in Visual Basic .NET is basically similar to creating VB forms in VB6, there are some differences.

Invisible Controls go in the Component Tray

In VB6, even controls that had no visible manifestation at run time were still located on the form surface at design-time. The most common control used this way in VB6 was the Timer control.

In Visual Basic .NET, there is a separate pane of the design surface, called the **component tray**, for such invisible controls (which are actually components). This is a nice improvement, because there are a lot more of these controls in Visual Basic .NET. It also ensures that such controls are neither in the way, nor hidden on the form at design-time. The sections later in the chapter on provider controls and menu controls go into more detail on some of them.

To see how the component tray works, pull up a Windows Form in Visual Basic .NET, and drag a Timer control and a PrintDocument control (from the Windows Forms tab in the Toolbox) onto the form. You will see the extra pane appear below the normal form design surface. Here is a typical screen showing this extra pane, with a Timer control and a PrintDocument control added:

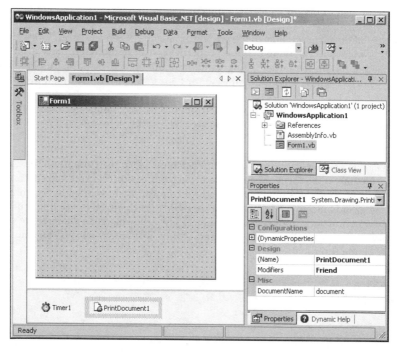

These controls can be highlighted in the extra pane, and then their properties show up in the properties box just as you would expect. The sample screen above shows the PrintDocument1 control's properties in the Properties window.

Not All Controls Have to be Locked

In VB6, there is a Lock Controls option on the Format menu. When this option is selected for a form, all controls are locked. Even new controls placed on the form are locked in place as soon as they are on the design surface.

In Visual Basic .NET, the Lock Controls menu option (still under the Format menu, and also available by right-clicking on the form) locks all controls currently on the form, but new controls remain unlocked until the option is selected again. This allows you to create some of the controls on the form, lay them out exactly as you would like, and then lock them in place while you lay out the rest of the controls.

Form Properties for Cancel and Default Buttons

In VB6, it is possible to set the button that is automatically activated (clicked) when the user presses the *Esc* key. It is also possible to set the button automatically activated by the *Enter* key. This is done by setting properties of the button. Setting the `Cancel` property of a button to `True` causes it to become activated when the user presses *Esc*. Setting the `Default` property of a button to `True` causes it to become activated when the user presses *Enter*, as long as the control with the focus is not already handling the *Enter* key.

The same functionality is available in Visual Basic .NET, but it is accessed differently. Now the *form* has the properties to determine the cancel and default buttons, rather than the button properties being used.

The properties of the form are named `CancelButton` and `AcceptButton`. They are normally set in the Properties window. When one of these properties is accessed, the property displays a drop-down list with all of the buttons on the form. Setting a button in the `CancelButton` property allows it to be activated by *Esc*, and setting a button in the `AcceptButton` property allows it to be activated by *Enter*.

The buttons assigned to these properties must be buttons that are on the current form or located within a container on the current form. The properties can only be set to a button, and not to any other type of control.

Though the cancel and accept buttons would typically be set in the Properties window and stay the same for the lifetime of the form, it is possible to set `CancelButton` and `AcceptButton` properties dynamically, at run-time. This might be done, for example, if you wanted to design a form that had both a 'normal' and an 'advanced' mode, and it was desirable for the form to use different buttons for the cancel and accept functions in the different modes. The following code changes the cancel and accept buttons to two buttons named `btnCancel2` and `btnAccept2`, respectively, assuming that these buttons already exist on the form:

```
Me.CancelButton = btnCancel2
Me.AcceptButton = btnAccept2
```

Positioning and Layout

Visual Basic .NET has similar functionality for positioning and layout to VB6, but various actions are performed differently. Here are the new ways that Visual Basic .NET allows control over the positioning and layout of forms and controls.

Location Property

In place of the traditional `Left` and `Top` properties in VB6, forms and controls in Visual Basic .NET have a `Location` property. The `Location` property returns or accepts a `Point` structure, which contains X and Y coordinates that correspond to the old `Left` and `Top` properties. (Point structures are also useful in many of the drawing methods discussed in the later section on *GDI+* in .NET.)

The `Top` and `Left` properties are actually still there for forms and controls, and can be manipulated in code (using syntax such as `Form1.Top`), but `Top` and `Left` do not show up in the property window for a form or control. Instead, the `Location` property has a plus sign next to it, and when you press it, you will see the X and Y properties show up in the Properties window.

Size Property

The `Size` property is similar in concept to the `Location` property, except that it corresponds to the `Height` and `Width` properties. It returns or accepts a `Size` structure, which allows the height and width to be set at the same time instead of setting the properties individually.

As with `Top` and `Left`, `Height` and `Width` can still be manipulated as properties of forms and controls in code. However, unlike `Top` and `Left`, they do show up in the Properties window once you click the plus sign next to the `Size` property.

BringToFront() and SendToBack() Methods

In VB6, the layered ordering of controls on a form was controlled by the `ZOrder()` method, which could set the `ZOrder` for a control or form. The concept of `ZOrder` is still available in Visual Basic .NET, but the way to manipulate `ZOrder` has changed. The `BringToFront()` method of a control causes it to appear on top of any other controls. Similarly the `SendToBack()` method causes a control to be behind any other controls that overlap it. These methods are the only mechanism available in Windows Forms to control `ZOrder`.

New Layout Properties for Forms

For a form, there are some additional properties affecting size and layout. These include `DesktopBounds`, `DesktopLocation`, `MaximumSize`, and `MinimumSize`.

`DesktopBounds` returns or sets a `Rectangle` that determines the size and location of the form on the current desktop – this ignores the Windows Task Bar size. A `Rectangle` in .NET is similar to a `RECT` structure from the Win32 API, but much more flexible. A `Rectangle` in .NET is a structure in the `System.Drawing` namespace, which is discussed in detail in the section on *GDI+*. Setting up a `Rectangle` and passing it to the `DesktopBounds` property sets both the size of the form and its location on the desktop all at once.

To set just the location, you can use the `DesktopLocation` property. It sets and gets a `Point` structure, just as the `Location` property above does. The difference in the `DesktopLocation` property is that it takes the Windows Task Bar into account, so that if the Task Bar is on top of the screen, for example, the form's position will be automatically adjusted downward by the height of the Task Bar.

`MaximumSize` and `MinimumSize` both get or set a `Size` structure, the same as the `Size` property discussed above. These properties have the effect of determining how large and small, respectively, a form can be. If you want to have a form that is always exactly 500 x 500 pixels, then you could create a variable of type `Size`, set the `height` and `width` properties of that variable both to 500, and then set the form's `MaximumSize` and `MinimumSize` properties to the same `Size` structure.

Resizing Multiple Controls

In the Windows Forms designer in the Visual Studio .NET IDE, there is a new capability to resize multiple controls simultaneously. Just select several controls at once, by clicking and dragging a rectangle around them, or by holding down the *Ctrl* key to select multiple controls by clicking on them individually. The last control selected will have white resize handles, while the rest have black resize handles. Resizing the control with the white handles will cause all the other controls to resize proportionately.

Differences in Dialog Boxes

In VB6 and earlier, forms were shown with the `Show()` method, and this technique is still used in Visual Basic .NET. In both VB6 and Visual Basic .NET, the `Show()` method by default displays *modeless* forms, which are forms that allow the user to click off of them onto another form in the application.

In VB6, dialog boxes were displayed with the `vbModal` parameter (or a hardcoded 1) after the form's `Show()` method. This caused the form to be a *modal* form, which meant that is was the only active form in the application until it was exited. This operation is done differently in Visual Basic .NET. Before we can describe the differences, it is helpful to go over the code for a typical dialog box scenario in VB6.

A dialog box form needs a way to communicate with the form that called it. In VB6, this was often done by placing a read-only property on the form to communicate the user action. I normally called such a property `Action`, so my dialog boxes in VB6 would have code like this in them:

```
' This is VB6 code!!
Public Enum enuAction
   actionOK = 1
   actionCancel = 2
End Enum

Dim mAction As enuAction

Public Property Get Action() As enuAction
   Action = mAction
End Property

Private Sub cmdOK_Click()
   mAction = actionOK
```

```
      Me.Hide
   End Sub

   Private Sub cmdCancel_Click()
      mAction = actionCancel
      Me.Hide
   End Sub
```

Notice the enumerated type `enuAction`, which has two values, `actionOK` and `actionCancel`. The `Action` property is set to be of this enumerated type. The command buttons set the `Action` property to an appropriate value and then hide the form. The form must be hidden and not unloaded, since the calling form will need to access the `Action` property to see what the user did in the dialog box.

Suppose such a dialog box form was named `DialogForm`. To call this form from another form requires code (in VB6) like this:

```
' This is VB6 code!!
Dim frmDialogForm As DialogForm
Set frmDialogForm = New DialogForm
frmDialogForm.Show vbModal
```

It is not enough just to call the form though. To know what action the user took, it is necessary to examine the `Action` property of the dialog box, which can be done by adding the following lines to the above code:

```
' This is VB6 code!!
Dim frmDialogForm As DialogForm
Set frmDialogForm = New DialogForm
frmDialogForm.Show vbModal

'When control returns, we assume the frmDialogForm
'is hidden but still loaded.

' Code to get information from frmDialogForm goes here
' ...
Select Case frmDialogForm.Action
   Case actionOK
     ' code goes here for normal processing
   Case actionCancel
     ' code goes here for user canceling
End Select
Unload frmDialogForm
```

There are two significant changes in Visual Basic .NET that affect the way this kind of logic is written. Let's examine the differences and compare the above code in VB6 to the equivalent code in Visual Basic .NET.

ShowDialog Instead of Show vbModal

The `vbModal` argument for the `Show()` method of a form is not supported in Visual Basic .NET. In its place, a Windows Form has a `ShowDialog()` method instead. Here is the comparison of equivalent code:

```
' VB6 code
Dim frmDialogForm As DialogForm
Set frmDialogForm = New DialogForm
frmDialogForm.Show vbModal

' Visual Basic .NET code
Dim frmDialogForm As New DialogForm
frmDialogForm.ShowDialog()
```

In the VB6 code, there is one line to `Dim` the form variable, and another line to instantiate the form. This is done to force an explicit instantiation instead of allowing an implicit instantiation when the form is first referenced. Since there is no implicit instantiation in Visual Basic .NET, it is not necessary to have both the `Dim` and `Set`, so those lines are replaced by one line which both declares and instantiates the form.

The last line in this example shows the switch from using the `Show()` method with a `vbModal` parameter to using the `ShowDialog()` method.

DialogResult

We saw above how it was common to create a custom form property to find out the user's action in a dialog box. Such homegrown properties, and their states, are usually not necessary in Windows Forms because a replacement is available. When a form is shown with the `ShowDialog()` method, the form has a property already present, called `DialogResult`, to indicate its state.

The `DialogResult` property can take the following enumerated results:

- ❑   `DialogResult.Abort`
- ❑   `DialogResult.Cancel`
- ❑   `DialogResult.Ignore`
- ❑   `DialogResult.No`
- ❑   `DialogResult.None`
- ❑   `DialogResult.OK`
- ❑   `DialogResult.Retry`
- ❑   `DialogResult.Yes`

When the `DialogResult` property is set, as a by-product, the dialog is hidden.

The `DialogResult` property of a dialog box can be set in two ways. The most common way is to associate a `DialogResult` value with a button. Then, when the button is pressed, the associated value is automatically placed in the `DialogResult` property of the form.

To set the `DialogResult` value associated with a button, the `DialogResult` property of the button is used. If this property is set for the button, it is unnecessary to set the `DialogResult` in code when the button is pressed. Here is an example that uses this technique.

In Visual Studio .NET, start a new Visual Basic .NET Windows Application. On the automatic blank form that comes up (named Form1), place a single button and set its Text property to Dialog.

Now, add a new Windows Form using the Project | Add Windows Form... menu, and name it DialogForm.vb. Place two buttons on DialogForm and set the following properties for the buttons:

Property	Value for First Button	Value for Second Button
Name	btnOK	btnCancel
Text	OK	Cancel
DialogResult	OK	Cancel

Do not put any code in DialogForm at all.

On the first form, Form1, place the following code in the `Click` event for `Button1`:

```
Private Sub Button1_Click(ByVal sender As System.Object, _
   ByVal e As System.EventArgs) Handles Button1.Click

   Dim frmDialogForm As New DialogForm()
   frmDialogForm.ShowDialog()

   ' We're back from the dialog - check user action.
   Select Case frmDialogForm.DialogResult
     Case DialogResult.OK
       MsgBox("The user pressed OK")
     Case DialogResult.Cancel
       MsgBox("The user pressed cancel")
   End Select

   frmDialogForm = Nothing

End Sub
```

Now, run and test the code. When a button is pressed on the dialog form, a message box should be displayed (by the calling form) indicating the button that was pressed.

This code is the equivalent of the VB6 code shown earlier to instantiate a dialog box and check the result. Notice that the code that was needed inside the dialog box in VB6 (to define and set the `Action` property) has been rendered completely unnecessary. Since the form class inherits and implements the functionality to expose and manage the `DialogResult` property, the VB developer does not have to create any code for this functionality.

The second way to set the `DialogResult` property of the form is in code. In a `Button_Click` event, or anywhere else in the dialog form, a line like this can be used to set the `DialogResult` property for the form, and simultaneously hide the dialog form, giving control back to the calling form:

```
Me.DialogResult = DialogResult.Ignore
```

This particular line sets the dialog result to `DialogResult.Ignore`, but setting the dialog result to any of the permitted values will also hide the dialog form.

New Capabilities of Windows Forms

We have seen that Windows Forms conceptually resemble VB6 forms, and the differences outlined above are relatively minor adjustments. However, Windows Forms also offer some dramatic new capabilities over VB6 forms. In this section, we shall examine some of these capabilities.

Changing the Shape of the Form

VB6 only supported forms that were rectangular. That is the default in Visual Basic .NET, but the `Form` class has a property called `Region` that allows you to specify a different shape for the form. This is useful for placing various 'skins' on an application such as a music player, or creating forms with an iconic shape that helps the user understand their function in a business application.

The shape is expressed in terms of a **graphics path**, which is defined by specifying the curves and lines that make up the path. Curves and lines can come from a variety of graphics sources. The curves that outline letters, for example, can be used, and of course, traditional lines and curves that are specified with coordinates, angles, and curvatures can make up part, or all, of the path.

The commands that define graphics paths are part of GDI+, which is covered in more detail later in the chapter. However, we can see a short example that demonstrates using the `Region` property to change the shape of a Windows Form.

Start a new **Windows Application** in Visual Studio .NET. For the default `Form1` that comes up, drag its borders to make it approximately twice its original size. Then, place a **Button** on the form, and place the following code behind it:

```
Private Sub Button1_Click(ByVal sender As System.Object, _
  ByVal e As System.EventArgs) Handles Button1.Click

    Dim myGraphicsPath As System.Drawing.Drawing2D.GraphicsPath = _
      New System.Drawing.Drawing2D.GraphicsPath()
    Dim stringText As String = "Wrox!"
    Dim family As FontFamily = New FontFamily("Arial")
    Dim fontStyle As FontStyle = fontStyle.Bold
    Dim emSize As Integer = 150
    Dim origin As PointF = New PointF(50, 50)
    Dim format As StringFormat = StringFormat.GenericDefault
    myGraphicsPath.AddString( _
        stringText, family, fontStyle, emSize, origin, format)
    myGraphicsPath.AddEllipse(New Rectangle(0, 0, 300, 400))
    Me.Region = New Region(myGraphicsPath)

End Sub
```

This code begins by instantiating a `GraphicsPath` object. This object has various methods to add pieces to the graphics path. Towards the bottom of the code, two of those methods are used, one to add a text string to the path, and another to add an ellipse. Adding the text string also requires several other declarations to specify the font, the size, the location, and so on.

Finally, the graphics path is applied to the `Region` property of the form. This makes the form change to the shape specified by the graphics path. You can see this in action by running the program and pressing the button:

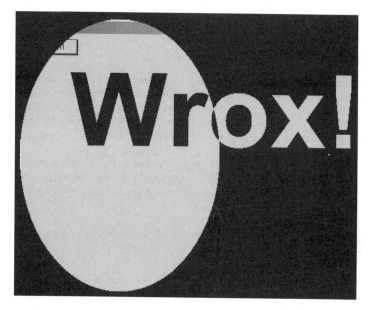

The new shape is not just cosmetic. You also must click inside the shape to click on the form. Clicking on a 'hole' in the form is actually clicking on the object behind the form. You can try that to see for yourself.

New Properties to Change a Form's Appearance

There are two new properties of the `Form` class that offer some additional advanced capabilities for altering the form's appearance. They are the `Opacity` and `TransparencyKey` properties.

The Opacity Property

The `Opacity` property is a percentage. The default is 100 percent, which gives a normal form appearance. Setting the `Opacity` property to a value less than 100 causes the form to become translucent. That is, the form's appearance begins to be mixed with the appearance of the objects behind the form. The lower the percentage, the more you can see what is behind the form showing through the form. At an `Opacity` setting of 0, the form, including its border and any controls on it, is present, but invisible, and it cannot be clicked on. At any `Opacity` greater than zero, the form and its controls can be clicked on, even though at very low levels, the form is effectively invisible because it does not show up enough to be seen.

This obviously gives you some opportunity to play jokes on your programmer friends, but the `Opacity` property is more often used to fade forms in and out. You can place a `Timer` on the form, and increase or decrease the `Opacity` setting each time the `Timer` fires.

The TransparencyKey Property

The `TransparencyKey` property allows you to specify a color that will become transparent on the form. For example, if `TransparencyKey` is set to a red color, and areas of the form that are that exact shade of red, they will be transparent. Whatever is behind the form will show through in those areas, and if you click in one of those areas, you will actually be clicking on the object behind the form.

Owned Forms

One of the common themes of .NET is to wrap up system-level functionality so that it can be accessed through object interfaces. One example is working with a form that floats above the application, but does not interfere with using the application. Examples would be a search-and-replace box, or a tutorial help box. It is possible to get a window to do this in VB6 with Windows API calls, but it is much easier in Windows forms using the concept of **owned forms**.

When a form is *owned* by another form, it is minimized and closed with the owner form. Owned forms are never displayed behind their owner form, but they do not prevent their owner form from gaining the focus and being used. However, if you want to click on the area covered by an owned form, the owned form has to moved out of the way first

A form can only have one owner at a time. If a form that is already owned by `FormA` is added to the owned forms collection for `FormB`, then the form is no longer owned by `FormA`.

There are two ways to make a form owned by another form. It can be done in the owner form, or in the owned form.

AddOwnedForm() Method

In the owner form, another form can be made owned with the `AddOwnedForm()` method. Here is code to make `Form2` become owned by `Form1`. This code would reside somewhere in `Form1`, and would typically be placed just before the line that shows `Form2` to the screen.

```
Me.AddOwnedForm Form2
```

Owner Property

The relationship can also be set up in the owned form. This is done with the `Owner` property of the form. Here is code that would work inside `Form2` to make it owned by `Form1`:

```
Me.Owner = Form1
```

However, in Visual Basic .NET, this statement requires an in-scope reference to `Form1`, because there is no 'global' reference to `Form1` available, as there is in VB6. Since it is not easy for a form to get such a reference without it being passed in, this technique is not used as often as using the `AddOwnedForm()` method in the `Owner` form.

OwnedForms Collection

The owner form can access its collection of owned forms with the `OwnedForms` property. Here is code to loop through the forms owned by a form:

```
Dim frmOwnedForm As Form
For Each frmOwnedForm In Me.OwnedForms
  Console.WriteLine(frmOwnedForm.Text)
Next
```

The owner form can remove an owned form with the `RemoveOwnedForm` method. This could be done in a loop like the one above, with code like this:

```
Dim frmOwnedForm As Form
For Each frmOwnedForm In Me.OwnedForms
  Console.WriteLine(frmOwnedForm.Text)
  Me.RemoveOwnedForm(frmOwnedForm)
Next
```

This loop would cause an owner form to stop owning all of its slaved forms. Note that those freed forms would not be unloaded – they would simply no longer be owned.

TopMost Property of Forms

Another way to get 'always-on-top' functionality is to use the `TopMost` property of a form. Setting the `TopMost` property to `True` will create a form that is always displayed in your application. A top-most form is a form that overlaps all the other forms, even if it is not the active or foreground form. Top-most forms are always displayed at the highest point in the application. A typical example would be a toolbar that must stay on the screen on top of many applications, such as the toolbar used in Microsoft Office.

The difference in using the `TopMost` property instead of making a form an owned form is that `TopMost` makes a form topmost for all forms of the application. An owned form is always on top of its owner form, but is not necessarily on top of other forms in the application. Also, a topmost form does not automatically get minimized or closed when other forms in the application are minimized or closed.

A form can be both a topmost form, and an owned form. In that case, when it is not minimized, it is on top of all other applications. However, when the owner is minimized, the form will be minimized automatically with the owner.

Controls in Windows Forms

As with forms, controls in Windows Forms conceptually resemble their VB6 counterparts. However, there are differences in implementation, and some nice new functionality. Let's first look at some new properties that are common to all controls in Windows forms.

New Properties of Controls

There are some new properties that are shared by all controls in Windows Forms. Here is a summary of some of the most significant.

Anchor and Dock

It is common in VB6 to have code in a form's `Resize` event to reposition and resize controls. For example, a grid control may need to be at the bottom of a form, and to always use the full width of the form. When the form is resized, the grid control's properties for size would need to be adjusted, and the code to do that would have to manually calculate distances on the form to work. The resulting code was tedious to write and hard to maintain.

Such code is unnecessary in Visual Basic .NET. Every control has two properties that can be used for that kind of manipulation.

The `Anchor` property forces one or more borders of a control to remain at a constant distance from the closest border of the form. It specifies which borders are to be controlled this way. For example, suppose we have a form with a ListBox that looks like this:

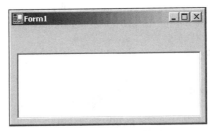

Now, suppose I would like to make the ListBox stay at the same distance from the form's edge on the left, right, and bottom whenever the form is resized. To do this, I set the Anchor property to Bottom, Left, Right in the Properties window. The Anchor property is set by clicking on a diagram containing the borders that can be used for anchors. Here is an example of a Properties window setting the Anchor property for the ListBox above:

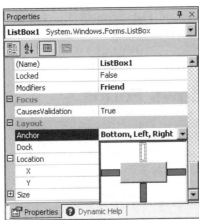

The dark gray rectangles indicate that the control is to be anchored to the left border, the right border, and the bottom border of the form. When this property diagram setting is accepted, the property value will show up as Bottom, Left, Right. Once the Anchor property is set, the ListBox will resize as needed when the form resizes.

The Dock property provides resizing functionality also, but it is more akin to the Align property of certain controls in VB6. Dock allows a control to 'stick' to one edge of the form. For example, if I replace the ListBox with a RichTextBox, and set its Dock property to Right like so:

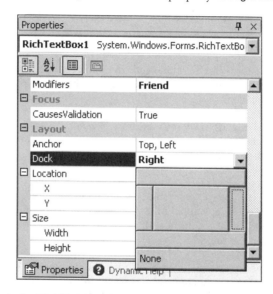

when the form is displayed, the RichTextBox will be against the form's right border, and it will extend from the top of the form to the bottom, like this:

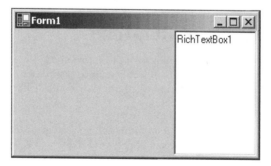

The Dock property can also be set to Fill, which makes a control fill the entire client area of the form.

Accessibility Properties of Controls

All controls inherit several members from the `Control` class relating to accessibility. All controls will show these properties (`AccessibleDescription`, `AccessibleName`, `AccessibleRole`) in the Properties window. These properties allow Windows Forms to work in Microsoft's Active Accessibility framework. In Active Accessibility, client programs can be created for users with special accessibility needs, such as poor vision. These properties provide information related to accessibility. For example, the `AccessibleDescription` property could be set for a button with a picture on it, so that those with visual handicaps could get a text-to-speech description of the button. For more information, check the overview of accessibility in the .NET documentation.

The Modifiers Property

In VB6, all controls on a form can be referenced from outside the form. That is, if `FormA` had a textbox named `TextBox1`, then any code outside the form (but in the same project) could access the textbox by referencing `FormA.TextBox1`.

Accessing a control from any arbitrary code location is generally not good practice. If it becomes necessary to change the control (say by replacing a set of option buttons with a drop-down list), then the calling code has to be changed as well.

Visual Basic .NET allows controls to have any of the standard settings for scope – `Public`, `Protected`, `Friend`, and `Private`. (Chapter 6 goes into more detail about the scope of objects in Visual Basic .NET.) The setting for scope is contained in the **Modifiers** property of a Windows Forms control. If you go to the **Properties** window for a control and access the **Modifiers** property, you will see a drop-down list with the possible scope settings.

The default setting is **Friend**, which allows the same level of access as VB6. However, if you think (as I do) that it is good programming practice to keep your controls private to the form, you can change the scope setting for each control to **Private**. Then, the control cannot be accessed by any code outside the form. You also have the option of making a control **Protected**, which will only allow access from your form and forms that inherit from your form.

Adding New Controls at Run-Time

Visual Basic has had the capability to add controls to forms at run-time, with the functionality increasing with various versions. Using the complete object-oriented capabilities of Visual Basic .NET, there is even more flexibility. However, the syntax for adding new controls has changed as a consequence of moving to object-orientation for this capability.

The new syntax is simple. For example, if a button's `Click` event needed to cause a new listbox control to be added, the `Click` event would contain code like this:

```
Private Sub Button1_Click(ByVal sender As System.Object, _
    ByVal e As System.EventArgs) Handles Button1.Click

    Dim lstNewListBox As New ListBox()
    lstNewListBox.Size = New Size(150, 200)
    lstNewListBox.Location = New Point(50, 50)
```

```
        lstNewListBox.Items.Add("First listbox item")
        lstNewListBox.Items.Add("Second listbox item")

        Me.Controls.Add(lstNewListBox)

    End Sub
```

As this code shows, a control is just a class that needs to be instantiated and have its properties set. In most cases, we need to set the control's size and location. Also, since it is a listbox in this example, some items are added to it.

However, instantiating the control is not enough. The form only manages controls that have been added to its `Controls` collection. The line just above the `End Sub` does that. The form's controls collection can be accessed in any form with `Me.Controls` (because `Me` refers to the current instantiation of any class, including a form). Then the `Add()` method takes a control as an argument and adds it to the controls collection. Once the control is in the controls collection, it is managed the same way a control added at design-time would be.

This capability is used in Visual Basic .NET for the same design situations as in VB6. For example, a form can have a variable number of checkboxes for a particular item, with new checkboxes added on the fly as new options to be checked are needed on the form. Or a generic data entry form can be created, with the actual fields needed for editing a specific record created and positioned on the form at run-time.

Summary of Important Controls

In this section, we will overview the controls available in Windows Forms, and highlight differences in controls and usage from VB6 to Visual Basic .NET.

Many of the controls in Windows Forms have almost exact equivalents in VB6 (either in the standard VB6 controls or the Windows common controls). While some properties are changed in name, and additional properties are present, the following controls are similar enough to their VB6 equivalents that detailed discussion is unnecessary:

Button (called Command Button in VB6)	ListBox	StatusBar
	ListView	TextBox
CheckBox	PictureBox	Toolbar
ComboBox	ProgressBar	Trackbar (called Slider in VB6)
HScrollBar	RadioButton (called Option Button in VB6)	TreeView
ImageList	RichTextBox	VScrollBar
Label		

There are also some controls that offer equivalent functionality, but require slightly different usage in code. These include:

❑ Common dialog boxes (File Open, File Save, Color, Font, Print)

❑ TabControl (combines VB6 SSTab and TabStrip)

New Controls

The remaining controls to be discussed have no exact VB6 equivalents. In some cases, such as the menu controls, these new controls are a new way to encapsulate functionality that was available in VB6. In these cases, while the functionality has not changed, the way in which it is used has been altered.

Other new controls, such as the DateTimePicker, have no equivalent functionality in the standard set of VB6 controls. However they may replace OCX equivalents that were available from Microsoft or various third parties, and some controls, such as the provider controls, are new in concept, with no major third-party controls that have provided that functionality in the past.

Menu Controls

VB6 has the ability to specify standard Windows menus that appear at the top of a form. It contains a menu editor specifically to design these menus. VB6 then associates menu options with events, so that when a menu option is chosen, an event is fired.

VB6 also provides the ability to make pop-up menus (typically activated with a right-click). Such menus are designed with the same menu editor as the one used for standard Windows menus. A portion of such a menu can be popped up with the PopUpMenu() method of a VB6 form.

In Visual Basic .NET, there are two controls that provide equivalent functionality. The MainMenu control allows a form to have a standard Windows menu at the top of the form. The ContextMenu allows creation of pop-up menus.

The MainMenu control contains a collection of MenuItem objects, which describe individual menu options. Properties can be set separately for each MenuItem object both at design-time (in the Properties window) and at run-time (in code), which allows menu items to be made visible or invisible, enabled or disabled, and so on.

Creating a menu with a MainMenu control is easy. There is a visual menu editor that appears at the top of a form containing a MainMenu control, and it is much easier to use than the old menu editor in VB6.

To create a standard menu on a form, first drag a MainMenu control (from the Windows Forms tab in the Toolbox) on to the form from the toolbox. The MainMenu control does not appear on the form surface, since it has no visible manifestation there. It appears in the component tray (which was discussed earlier in this chapter).

Dragging the MainMenu control onto the form automatically sets the form's Menu property to the MainMenu control. This Menu property determines whether a form has a menu, and if so, what MainMenu control is used for it. Typical forms will only *need* one MainMenu control, but it is possible for a form to have *more* than one, and for the form's menu to be changed by changing the Menu property of the form to point to a different MainMenu control.

When the MainMenu control is highlighted in the separate design pane, a visual menu designer appears close to the title bar of the form. Here is an example of a form with a MainMenu control dragged onto it, showing the visual menu designer:

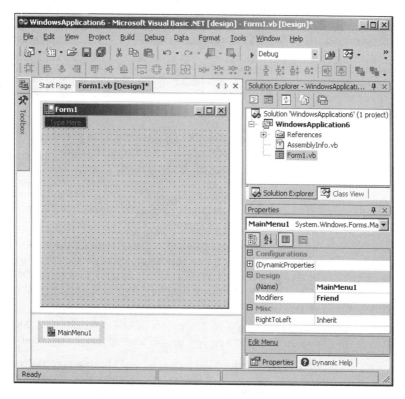

The visual menu designer is the shaded box close to the top of the form that says Type Here. Suppose we click on that box and type in the word File for the top-level File menu that usually begins a standard Windows menu. Then the area around the visual menu designer looks like this:

Now there are new areas to type in – one to the right of File that can accept the next top-level menu item and one under File that is for a submenu item inside the File menu when it is pulled down. Creating menu items is as easy as clicking on the appropriate box and typing them in. Double-clicking on a menu item brings up the event routine associated with the menu item, just as clicking on a control brings up the control's Click event routine. Also like VB6, entering an ampersand (&) character in the menu option text results in an *Alt-[key]* shortcut for the option.

Menu items are given default names just like other controls, and their names can be changed in the Properties window as described below. The default name for the first menu item added (typically the top-level File menu item) is MenuItem1. As with other controls, menu items should have an appropriate and consistent naming convention.

To change the properties for a menu item, just click on the menu item and change its properties in the Properties window. Here are the properties available for a MenuItem object:

Property	Usage
Checked	If True, the menu item has a checkmark beside it. If False, item is not checked.
DefaultItem	Indicates whether this item is the default item for the next higher menu in the hierarchy. If so, it becomes automatically selected if the user presses *Enter* for that next higher level. For example, if the menu item for Exit is the DefaultItem for the menu item File, then selecting File and pressing *Enter* will automatically select Exit.
Enabled	True if the menu item is currently available for selection, False if not. Items with the Enabled property set to False are grayed out on the menu.
MdiList	Only applicable for MDI parent forms. Allows a menu to contain as submenu items a list of the currently loaded MDI child forms. There is an example later in the chapter that uses this property.
MergeOrder	When this menu is merged with another menu in an MDI application, the MergeOrder determines the order in which the merged items are displayed. (When child menus receive the focus in an MDI application, some applications merge the menu of the active child form with the menu on the MDI parent form.)
MergeType	When this menu is merged with another menu, the MergeType property determines how this item is treated in the merged menu. This property is an enumerated value with possible settings of MenuMerge.Add, MenuMerge.MergeItems, MenuMerge.Remove, or MenuMerge.Replace. MenuMerge.Add is used to add the item to a merged menu. MenuMerge.MergeItems is the default and just causes the items to be merged. MenuMerge.Replace causes the item to replace an equivalent item from the merged menu. MenuMerge.Remove causes the item to be left off a merged menu.

Property	Usage
OwnerDraw	Normally set to **False** to allow the system to render (draw) the menu option for you. If you set this to **True**, you can actually render your own visual representation of the menu option. You do this using the drawing capabilities of GDI+. If you have always wanted the capability to make your menu options look really fancy, **OwnerDraw** gives it to you.
RadioCheck	If **True**, instead of using a checkmark to indicate that an item is checked, a radio button is used beside the item instead.
Shortcut	Allows any of the non-ASCII keys on the keyboard (such as function keys, *Insert*, *Delete*, and so on) to directly access this menu item. Such a shortcut key accesses the option immediately, without navigating the menu hierarchy. This is in contrast to the control key access (such as *Ctrl-F* for the **File** menu) that is indicated by placing an ampersand (&) in the **Text** property for the menu option, which is used to navigate the hierarchy.
ShowShortcut	If **True** and the **Shortcut** property is set to a key, then the shortcut key is shown in the menu.
Text	The text in the menu item.
Visible	Determines whether the menu item can be seen.

Any of these properties can be manipulated at run-time to dynamically affect the behavior of the menu.

Menu items can be added dynamically with code like this:

```
Dim mnuNewMenuItem As New MenuItem()
mnuNewMenuItem.Text = "New menu item"
MenuItem1.MenuItems.Add(mnuNewMenuItem)
```

This creates a new item and places it under the menu item identified as **MenuItem1**. For the example above, this would mean that the menu item would appear under **File**. Note that you don't have to add menu items to the form's `Controls` collection as we did in our earlier example because the **MainMenu** control that manages menu items is already in the `Controls` collection.

By default, new menu items added in code appear at the bottom of their menu. However, menu items have an **Index** property that can be used to manipulate the position of the item in the menu.

Pop-up menus are created with the **ContextMenu** control. It is also dragged onto the form and appears in the extra pane below the form's design surface. When the **ContextMenu** control is highlighted in the extra pane, the visual menu editor at the top of the form is used to design the pop-up menu.

To use one of these menus, it should be associated with a form or a control on the form. Highlight the form or control that will use the pop-up menu, and set the **ContextMenu** property on the form or control to the **ContextMenu** control that was previously defined. Then, when you right-click the form or control, the **ContextMenu** will pop up.

A form typically needs only one MainMenu control, but it can have any number of different ContextMenu controls, which may be associated with various other controls on the form or with the form itself. A context menu is associated with a form or control using the ContextMenu property of the form or control.

LinkLabel

A LinkLabel is a new control that looks like a hyperlink in a web page. It displays text in hyperlink format, and provides a way to link to another form in the application, or to a web site. It acts like a Label control, but has different screen cosmetics. The linking action is actually accomplished in code in the control's Click event. The LinkLabel control can also display an image instead of text.

Here is a Windows Form during execution with both types of LinkLabel controls, and examples of the UpDown controls discussed in the following section. The controls were just dragged onto the form and their Text properties changed:

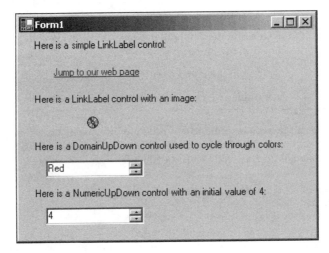

UpDown Controls – DomainUpDown and NumericUpDown

In VB6, an UpDown control (sometimes called a Spinner) is available. It has two common uses:

1. To allow the user to rotate through items in a combo box

2. To cause numeric items in a textbox to increment or decrement

The associated control in VB6 (combo box for function 1, textbox for function 2) is called the **buddy control**.

In Visual Basic .NET, there are separate controls for these two different functions. The first function is performed by the DomainUpDown control. The second is performed by the NumericUpDown control. Both are pictured in the sample screen above.

The biggest difference from VB6 is that the UpDown controls in Visual Basic .NET include both the control holding the values and the control providing the up-down navigation. The NumericUpDown control has a place for the number to be displayed and the up and down arrow keys to increment and decrement the number. No separate buddy control (such a textbox) is required. Similarly, the DomainUpDown control has a text area that holds the items being cycled through. Those items are loaded into the control the same way as they would be loaded into a combo box. No separate buddy combo box is needed.

CheckedListBox

The VB6 listbox can be set to place checkmarks beside items to indicate that they are selected. This is done by setting the Style property to Checkbox.

In Visual Basic .NET, such a listbox is a separate control, called a CheckedListBox. It works like an ordinary listbox (and is in fact derived from it), but adds the cosmetics to handle checkboxes beside each item.

DateTimePicker

Third party controls have long been used in VB6 for choosing dates and times in VB, and such a control was also included in a set of common controls distributed by Microsoft. However, Windows Forms includes its own sophisticated date/time control called the DateTimePicker, which can be found in the Windows Forms tab in the Toolbox. It is similar to the DTPicker included in the VB6 common controls, and is easy to use compared to many third party equivalents.

When placed on a form, the control looks like a combo box, and contains a date. When the drop-down arrow is pressed, a monthly calendar is displayed for choosing a date. Here are screens showing these two states:

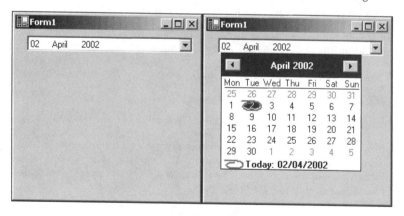

Properties control various options such as the date range that is available, the format of the date or time that is being selected, and the option to use a built-in UpDown control instead of the drop-down to change the date or time in the control. Here is a sample screen with the control's Format property set to Time (to make the control work with a time instead of a date), and with the ShowUpDown property set to True:

MonthCalendar

If you are only interested in allowing the user to select a date, and you would like the full month representation to be visible all the time (instead of just popped down when they ask for it), you can use a MonthCalendar control.

Panel and GroupBox Container Controls

In VB6, a frame control can be used as a container to group controls. A set of option buttons (the VB6 version of radio buttons) placed in a frame control automatically becomes related as one option group. Frames are also often used in VB6 to separate areas of a form into functional areas, or to group controls for showing and hiding. If a frame is hidden, all the controls in it are hidden. Sometimes, frames in VB6 are used with a border (with or without a title for the frame), and other times without a border.

The functionality in the frame control for VB6 is divided into two controls in Visual Basic .NET. They are called the GroupBox control and the Panel control.

Each is like the VB6 frame control in the following ways:

❑   They can serve as a container for other controls

❑   If they are hidden or moved, the action affects all the controls in the container

The GroupBox control is the one that most closely resembles a frame control visually. It acts just like a VB6 frame control, with one significant exception. There is no way to remove its border. It always has a border, and it can have a title if needed. The border is always set the same way. Here is a form with a GroupBox control containing two RadioButtons:

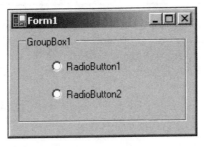

The Panel control has three major differences from GroupBox:

❏ It has options for displaying its border in the BorderStyle property, with a default of no border

❏ It has the capability to scroll by setting its AutoScroll property to True

❏ It has no ability to set a title or caption (it has no Text property)

Here is a form containing a Panel control with its border set to FixedSingle, with scrolling turned on, and with a ListBox that is too big to display all at once (which forces the Panel to show a scroll bar):

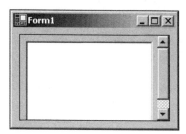

NotifyIcon

Here is a new control that is really nifty. The NotifyIcon control allows a form to display an icon in the Windows System Tray, which is the small tray of icons that is normally positioned on the right-hand side of the Windows Task Bar. Doing this in VB6 would require an inordinate amount of API code, but it is easy in Windows Forms. Dragging a NotifyIcon control onto the form places the control in the component tray in Visual Studio .NET. When the control is highlighted, its Icon property can be set to associate the icon that will appear in the System Tray.

The NotifyIcon's Click event is the event that is fired when the icon is double-clicked in the System Tray. By placing code in that event, you can make the icon in the tray take any action you wish. A pop-up menu can also be associated with the icon in the tray by setting up a ContextMenu control (discussed above) and setting the NotifyIcon control's ContextMenu property to point to the ContextMenu control. Below is a System Tray with an icon (the one that looks like a CD) and its associated pop-up menu, all set up by a Windows Form:

To replicate this example, create a new Windows Application, and drag over a ContextMenu control and a NotifyIcon control. Add three menu options to the ContextMenu control named Add contact, Find contact, and Delete contact. Then change the ContextMenu property of the NotifyIcon to point to the ContextMenu control (which will be named ContextMenu1 by default). Change the Icon property for the NotifyIcon control to an appropriate icon. (You can find icons in the Common7\Graphics\Icons subdirectory of your Microsoft Visual Studio .NET directory.)

Then run the program. When it starts, the icon will be in the System Tray. Right-click on it, and you will see the menu.

Extender Provider Controls

There is a new family of controls in Windows Forms that can only be used in association with other controls. Each of these controls, called **extender provider controls**, causes new properties to appear for every other control on the form.

Extender provider controls have no visible manifestation, so they appear in the component tray. The three extender provider controls currently available are the HelpProvider, the ToolTip, and the ErrorProvider. All three controls work in basically the same way. Each extender provider control implements the properties that are 'attached' to other controls. The best way to see how this works is to go through an example, so let's do that with a ToolTip control.

ToolTip

The ToolTip control is the simplest of the extender providers. It adds just one property to each control, named ToolTip on ToolTip1 (assuming the ToolTip control has the default name of ToolTip1). This property works exactly the same way the ToolTipText property works in VB6, and in fact, replaces it.

To see this in action, create a Windows Forms application. On the blank Form1 that is created for the project, place a couple of buttons. Take a look at the properties window for Button1. Notice that it does not have a ToolTip property of any kind.

Now drag over the ToolTip control, which will be placed in the component tray. Go back to the properties window for Button1. A property named ToolTip on ToolTip1 is now present. Set any string value you like for this property.

Now run the project, and hover the mouse pointer over Button1. You will see a tooltip containing the string value you entered for the ToolTip on ToolTip1 property.

HelpProvider

The HelpProvider control allows controls to have associated context-sensitive help available by pressing *F1*. When a HelpProvider control (named HelpProvider1 by default) is added to a form, all controls on the form get these new properties, which show up in the controls' Properties windows:

Property	Usage
HelpString on HelpProvider1	Provides a pop-up tooltip for the control when *F1* is pressed while the control has the focus. If the HelpKeyword and HelpNavigator properties (see below) are set to provide a valid reference to a help file, then the HelpString value is ignored in favor of the information in the help file.
HelpKeyword on HelpProvider1	Provides a keyword or other index to use in a help file for context-sensitive help for this control. The HelpProvider1 control has a property that indicates the help file to use. This replaces the `HelpContextID` property in VB6.

Property	Usage
HelpNavigator on HelpProvider1	Contains an enumerated value that determines how the value in HelpKeyword is used to refer to the help file. There are several possible values for displaying such elements as a topic, an index, or a table of contents in the help file.
ShowHelp on HelpProvider1	Determines whether the HelpProvider control is active for this control.

Filling in the HelpString property immediately causes the control to have tooltip help when pressing *F1* while the control has the focus. The HelpProvider control has a property to point to a help file (either an HTML help file or a Win32 help file), and the help topic in the HelpTopic property points to a topic in this file.

ErrorProvider

The ErrorProvider control presents a simple way to indicate to a user that a control on a form has an error associated with it. The added property for controls on the form when an ErrorProvider control is used is called Error on ErrorProvider1 (assuming the ErrorProvider has the default name of ErrorProvider1). Setting this property to a string value causes the error icon to appear next to a control, and the text to appear in a tooltip if the mouse hovers over the error icon.

Here is a screen with several textboxes, and an error icon next to one (with a tooltip). The error icon and tooltip are displayed and managed by the ErrorProvider control:

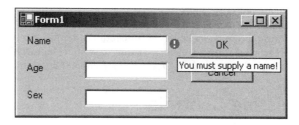

The ErrorProvider control's default icon is the red circle with an exclamation point. When the Error property for the textbox is set, the icon will blink for a few moments, and hovering over the icon will cause the tooltip to appear. The code for this behavior in the example screen above is explained in the next topic.

Working with Provider Controls in Code

Setting the Error property in the above example is not done with typical property syntax. By convention, extender provider controls have a method for each property they need to set, and the arguments for the method include the associated control and the property setting. To set the Error property in the above example, the following code was used in the OK button's Click event:

```
ErrorProvider1.SetError(txtName, "You must supply a name")
```

The name of the method to set a property is the word Set prefixed to the name of the property. The above line of code shows that the Error property is set with the SetError() method of the ErrorProvider.

There is a corresponding method to get the value of the property, and it is named with Get prefixed to the name of the property. To find out what the current Error property setting for txtName is, you would use the line:

```
sError = ErrorProvider1.GetError(txtName)
```

Similar syntax is used to manipulate any of the properties managed by an extender provider control. The discussion of the tooltip provider earlier talked about setting the ToolTip property in the Properties window. To set that same property in code, the syntax would be:

```
ToolTip1.SetToolTip(Button1, "New tooltip for Button1")
```

PrintDocument

The new PrintDocument control is another control that does not appear on the form, but just adds functionality. When one is added to a form, it appears in the component tray.

The PrintDocument control has properties to set a document to be printed, and to control the way the document is printed. The Print() method of the PrintDocument control causes the printing to take place. More details on this can be found in Chapter 9.

DataGrid

The new DataGrid control in Windows Forms is conceptually similar to previous grid controls such as the FlexGrid control. However, it is specifically written to support hierarchical datasets such as those used in ADO.NET. Chapter 8 discusses the DataGrid control and data binding.

Changes to Existing Controls

The changes that have occurred to existing controls fall into five groups:

- ❑ Some properties have been renamed
- ❑ Some controls receive different default names
- ❑ One entire control, the Image control, no longer exists
- ❑ Existing controls receive new capabilities, such as new data binding options
- ❑ Controls cannot be associated into control arrays

Let's take each of these changes in turn.

Renamed Properties of Controls

Some properties of controls have been renamed for consistency with .NET naming conventions.

> **The most significant change has been that all properties that get or set text in a control are now called `Text`.**

In VB6, some controls, such as command buttons, labels, and forms, had a `Caption` property that was used to set their text. These controls now have a `Text` property instead.

In the listbox and combo box, the old `ListIndex` property has been replaced with a `SelectedIndex` property. Also, the old `List` collection of items in the controls has been replaced in Visual Basic .NET with an `Items` collection.

Different Default Names

The default names that controls receive when dropped on to the form's design surface have changed for a few controls. Since the Command button in VB6 is now just called Button, the default name for a typical control of this type placed on the form has changed from Command1 to Button1. Other renamed controls, such as Option button (now RadioButton), and Slider (now Trackbar) similarly have their default names changed.

In addition, one control has a change in default naming even though the control's class name has not changed. The textbox control used default names such as TextBox1 in VB6, but the equivalent default name in Visual Basic .NET is Text1.

Image Control no Longer Exists

The Image control has traditionally been used in VB6 and earlier as a lightweight alternative to the PictureBox. Saving system resources is not the priority it once was, so the Image control is being retired. All of its functions can be fulfilled by the PictureBox control in Windows Forms.

New Capabilities for Existing Controls

We have already discussed that all controls now have the Anchor and Dock properties, which is functionality that did not exist in VB6. Some controls also receive additional new functionality.

We won't try to list all the new capabilities for existing controls, as that's a long list, however, a significant chunk of the new functionality is concerned with **data binding**. .NET implements data binding completely differently from VB6, and offers far more flexibility. Some of the most important new data binding features are discussed in Chapter 8.

No Control Arrays

In VB6, controls can be associated into control arrays, in which all the controls have the same name, but vary by index. Control arrays are not available in Visual Basic .NET. However, controls can be placed into arrays and various types of collections using code, providing a work-around.

A group of controls can also be set in code to share event routines, so that all radio buttons in a group can have the same click event, for example. This requires use of the new event capabilities of Visual Basic .NET, and these are discussed in Chapter 6.

Multiple Document Interface (MDI) Forms

There are several minor differences in working with an MDI interface in Visual Basic .NET. This section summarizes these differences, with an example at the end illustrating most of the changes.

Creating an MDI Parent Form

In VB6, an MDI parent form is created with an option on the Project menu called Add MDI Form. MDI forms are considered completely different from forms with a regular layout.

In Visual Basic .NET, a regular form is converted to an MDI parent form by setting the IsMDIContainer property of the form to True. This should normally be done in the Properties window. While a form can be made into an MDI parent at run-time by setting the IsMDIContainer property to True in code, the design of an MDI form is usually too different from that of a normal form for this to be useful.

Differences in MDI Parent Forms

In VB6, an MDI parent form automatically has a top-level menu, just like all forms do. It is only necessary to go into the menu editor and add options to the menu.

In Visual Basic .NET, a form never has a top-level menu automatically, as discussed in the section on menu controls (above). A MainMenu control must explicitly be dragged on to an MDI parent form (as with any form in Visual Basic .NET) to give it a top-level menu.

In VB6, an MDI parent form can only contain controls that have a property called Align. This property determines to which side of the MDI parent form the control is supposed to be docked. Typical controls like buttons and textboxes cannot be added directly to an MDI parent form. They must be added to a container control, such as a PictureBox, which has an Align property.

In Visual Basic .NET, an MDI parent can contain any control that a regular form can contain. Buttons, labels, and such can be placed directly on the MDI surface. The MDI surface can thus contain both controls (that are directly on the MDI surface, and can be freely positioned) and MDI child forms.

The controls will appear in front of the MDI child forms that are displayed in the MDI client area. That is, if the MDI parent form has a button in the middle of it, and a child form is displayed in that area, the button will be in front of the child form. This will look strange to a VB6 developer, because VB6 has no equivalent functionality.

It is still possible to use controls like PictureBoxes to hold other controls on a Visual Basic .NET MDI parent, and these controls can be docked to the side of the MDI form. In fact, every control in Visual Basic .NET has the equivalent of the Align property, called Dock.

The Dock property was discussed earlier in the chapter.

Differences in MDI Child Forms

In VB6, an MDI child form is created by setting a form's MDIChild property to True. Such a form can then only be used as an MDI child form, meaning it can only be loaded when an MDI parent is available for the form to use for display. Also, the MDIChild property can only be set at design-time. A form cannot be made into an MDI child at run-time.

In Visual Basic .NET a form becomes an MDI child at run-time by setting the form's MDIParent property to point to an MDI parent form. (The MDIParent property cannot be set at design-time – it must be set at run-time to make a form an MDI child.) This makes it possible to use a form as either a standalone form or an MDI child in different circumstances. For example, a form that was used to edit a document could be used in a standalone editing mode, or as a child window inside an MDI form. It would act the same in both settings.

As with VB6, it is possible to have any number of MDI child forms displayed in the MDI parent client area. And, as with VB6, the currently active child form can be determined with the ActiveForm property of the MDI parent form.

Arranging Child Windows in the MDI Parent

In VB6, child windows in an MDI parent are arranged into a specific layout with the `Arrange()` method. This method accepts values to tile the child windows horizontally or vertically, or to cascade them into a regular overlapping pattern.

In Visual Basic .NET, the same functionality is available with the `MDILayout()` method.

An MDI Example in Visual Basic .NET

In this exercise, we will go through the steps and show code relating to creation of an MDI parent, and allowing it to display an MDI child form.

1. Create a new Windows Application. It will have an empty form named Form1.

2. In the Properties window, set the IsMdiContainer property for Form1 to True. This designates the form as an MDI container for child windows. (Setting this property also causes the form to have a different default background color.)

3. From the Toolbox, drag a MainMenu control to the form. Create a top-level menu item with the Text property set to File and with submenu items called New MDI Child and Quit. Also create a top-level menu item called Window. The File | New MDI Child menu option will create and show new MDI child forms at run-time, and the Window menu will keep track of the open MDI child windows. (For more information on working with MainMenu controls, see the relevant section earlier in the chapter. Basically all you need to do it to type in the menu options on the bar that appears at the top of the form.)

4. In the menu option editor at the top of the form, right-click on the Window menu item and select Properties. In the Properties window, set the MdiList property to True. This will enable the Window menu to maintain a list of open MDI child windows with a checkmark next to the active child window.

5. Now we need to create an MDI child form to use as a template for multiple instances. To do this, select Project | Add Windows Form... and then Open in the Add New Item dialog box. This will result in a new blank form named Form2.

6. To make the child form more interesting, we will put a RichTextBox control in it to simulate a word-processing application. (Of course, the child form template could have any controls desired.) Drag a RichTextBox control onto Form2. In the Properties window for the RichTextBox, set the Dock property to Fill by clicking on the middle box in the user interface. This causes the RichTextBox control to completely fill the area of the MDI child forms, even when the form is resized.

7. Now go back to Form1 (the MDI parent form). In the menu editing bar, double-click on the New MDI Child option under File. The code editor will appear, with the cursor in the event routine for that menu option. Place the following code in the event:

```
Private Sub MenuItem2_Click(ByVal sender As System.Object, _
    ByVal e As System.EventArgs) Handles MenuItem2.Click

    Dim NewMDIChild As New Form2()
    'Fix the title string for the form so each will by different
    NewMDIChild.Text = "Form #" + Str$(Me.MdiChildren.GetUpperBound(0) + 1)
    'Set the parent form of the child window.
    NewMDIChild.MDIParent = Me
    'Display the new form.
    NewMDIChild.Show()

End Sub
```

8. Now go back to Form1 again (the MDI parent form). In the menu editing bar, double-click on the Quit option under File. The code editor will appear, with the cursor in the event routine for that menu option. Place the following code in the event:

```
Private Sub MenuItem3_Click(ByVal sender As System.Object, _
    ByVal e As System.EventArgs) Handles MenuItem3.Click

    End

End Sub
```

9. Now run and test the program. Use the File | New MDI Child option to create several child forms. Note how the Window menu option automatically lists them with the active one checked, and allows you to activate a different one:

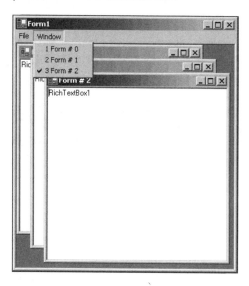

Inheritance in Windows Forms

Finally, VB gets inheritance in Visual Basic .NET. While Chapter 6 covers inheritance in depth, there are two aspects of it that relate to Windows Forms. The first is **visual inheritance** from one form to another, and the other is **authoring** new Windows Forms controls.

If you are unclear on the concept of inheritance, you may want to read Chapter 6 before reading this section, but it is simple enough to follow if you have a basic understanding of the concept of inheritance.

The basic syntax for inheritance is simple, and in fact, you have already seen it several times, starting with the Hello World program in Chapters 1 and 3. To quickly review, a class indicates it's base class using the Inherits keyword. The base class is referred to inside the subclass's code with a reference to MyBase.

We have already discussed the fact that a form in Windows Forms is really a class module, and that it inherits the capability to be a form from the .NET Framework classes. Here is an example of the code at the top of a Form class:

```
Public Class Form1
   Inherits System.Windows.Forms.Form
```

By inheriting from `System.Windows.Forms.Form`, the class representing the form automatically gets all the properties, methods, and events that a form is supposed to have. This is similar to the way that a form in VB6 or earlier automatically gets standard form properties and methods, but in Visual Basic .NET, the inheritance of those members comes specifically because the class has inherited from `System.Windows.Forms.Form`.

However, a class does not have to inherit directly from `System.Windows.Forms.Form` to become a Windows Form. A class can also become a form by inheriting from another form, which itself inherits from `System.Windows.Forms.Form`. Here is an example. Suppose we create a regular form named BaseForm, which looks like this in the visual designer (we will show how to do this in a moment):

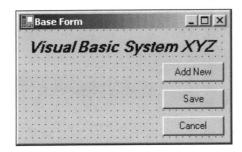

We want to create a form named DataForm that has these controls (the Label and three buttons) from BaseForm. This new form also needs to have controls of its own to do some data entry. This can be accomplished through inheritance. We can use BaseForm as a starting position to start our work on DataForm.

To get our terminology straight, the original form (the one in our example named BaseForm that inherits from `System.Windows.Forms.Form`) is referred to as the **base** form. The form that inherits from the base form (DataForm in our example) is called the **inherited** form.

The Inheritance Picker

Forms like our hypothetical DataForm, which inherit from another form instead of directly from `System.Windows.Forms.Form`, are created in Visual Studio .NET with the Project | Add Inherited Form... menu option. Once you have selected this option, and specified a name for the form, you will be asked what form it should inherit from. The dialog that shows the forms available for inheritance is called the **inheritance picker**.

However, a form must be compiled before it is available in the inheritance picker. The form to be inherited from can be in the current project, in which case it is compiled with the Build command, or it can be in an external DLL that was previously compiled, and then referenced in the current project.

To see this process in action, do the following:

1. Open a new Windows Application project in Visual Basic .NET.

2. On the empty Form1 that is created for the project, change the name of the form to BaseForm, and change the Text property for the form to Base Form. Then add controls so that the form looks like the example just above. This will require you to add a Label at the top that says Visual Basic System XYZ, and add three buttons that say Add New, Save, and Cancel. The buttons should be close to the right-hand portion of the screen, so that we will have room on the left to place some controls in our inherited form.

3. Build the project with the menu option Build | Build Solution.

4. Select the menu option Project | Add Inherited Form....

5. Name the form DataForm.vb. Then select the Open button, and a dialog will appear that shows the forms that can be used as a base form for inheritance. It looks like this:

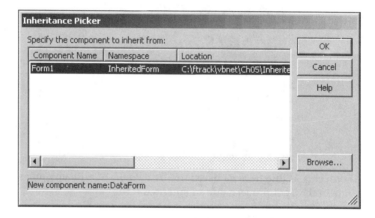

6. Choose Form1, and press OK. Then display the new DataForm in the visual designer. It will look something like this:

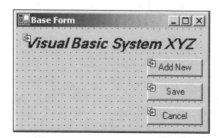

Notice the controls inherited from BaseForm have a small icon in their upper-left corner. These controls cannot be moved, nor can they be double-clicked to put code in their `Click` event routines – their event routines are actually in BaseForm.

At this point, you can place additional controls on DataForm, and they can be manipulated as usual. The running version of DataForm will have both types of controls on it, and the user won't be able to tell which controls come from the base form, and which are on the inherited form.

Now go back to BaseForm and select the top button (Add New). In the Properties window, change its Modified property to Protected, which gives access to the inherited subclasses of the form. Select Build | Build Solution again, and then go back to DataForm. Now you can move that button, and double-clicking on it does give a click event.

Any changes to BaseForm will not be displayed on DataForm until Build is selected and a successful build of BaseForm is performed. At this point, any changes to BaseForm will show up on DataForm. That's why you must access Build | Build Solution in the example above before returning to DataForm.

Suppose you now put some textboxes for entering someone's name and phone number on DataForm. Then make DataForm the startup form for the project (to do that, right-click on the project, select Properties, and set the startup object to DataForm.) Then start the project, and a running version of DataForm will look like this:

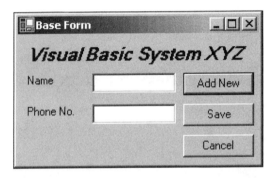

Note that DataForm gets its title from its base form by default. As with any other form, you should put an appropriate title in the Text property for an inherited form.

Suppose BaseForm is in another DLL separate from the project that contains DataForm, and you make some changes to BaseForm and recompile the DLL. It is not necessary to recompile the project with DataForm to see the changes in BaseForm take effect in DataForm. Of course, that means you need to be very careful about tampering with a base form once you have inherited from it.

GDI+

Another part of the System namespace that is important for Windows forms is **GDI+**. This is the new version of the old GDI (Graphics Device Interface) functions provided by the Windows API. GDI+ provides a new API for graphics functions, which then takes advantage of the Windows graphics library.

GDI+ functions are in the System.Drawing namespace. Some of the classes and members in this namespace will look familiar to developers who have used the Win32 GDI functions. Classes are available for such items as pens, brushes, and rectangles. Naturally, the System.Drawing namespace makes these capabilities much easier to use than the equivalent API functions.

Some of the features of the classes in the `System.Drawing` namespace are:

❑ Bitmap manipulation

❑ `Cursors` class, including the various cursors that you would need to set in your application such as an hourglass or an insertion 'I-beam' cursor

❑ `Font` class, including capabilities like font rotation

❑ `Graphics` class containing contains methods to do routine drawing constructs, including lines, curves, ellipses, and so on

❑ `Icon` class

❑ Various structures for dealing with graphics, including `Point`, `Size`, `Color`, and `Rectangle`

❑ `Pen` and `Brush` classes

This list is by no means exhaustive.

System.Drawing Namespace

The `System.Drawing` namespace includes many classes, and it also includes subsidiary namespaces called `System.Drawing.Drawing2D`, `System.Drawing.Imaging`, and `System.Drawing.Text`. An overview of these namespaces is included below. First, let's look at important classes in `System.Drawing`.

System.Drawing.Graphics Class

Many of the important drawing functions are members of the `System.Drawing.Graphics` class. Methods like `DrawArc()`, `DrawEllipse()`, and `DrawIcon()` have self-evident actions. There are over forty methods that provide drawing-related functions in the class.

Many drawing members require one or more points as arguments. A `Point` is a structure in the `System.Drawing` namespace. It has X and Y values for horizontal and vertical positions, respectively. When a variable number of points are needed, an array of points may be used as an argument. The next example below uses points.

The `System.Drawing.Graphics` class cannot be directly instantiated. That is, you can't just enter code like this to get an instance of the `Graphics` class:

```
Dim grfGraphics As New System.Drawing.Graphics()  ' will not work!!
```

There are several ways to get a reference to a `Graphics` class, but the most common one is to use an argument in an event for a form or control to get a reference to the `Graphics` class for that form or control. That technique is used in the next example.

Using GDI+ Capabilities in a Windows Form

Here is an example of a form that uses the `System.Drawing.Graphics` class to draw some graphic elements on the form surface. The example code gets a reference to a `Graphics` object for the form, and then uses it to draw an ellipse, an icon (which it gets from the form itself), and two triangles, one in outline and one filled.

Start a **Windows Application** project in Visual Basic .NET. A blank **Form1** will be created. Go to the code window for **Form1**. Insert a **Paint** event for **Form1** by selecting (**Base Class Events**) in the left hand drop-down at the top of the code window, and then selecting the **Paint** event in the right-hand drop-down. In that event, insert the following code:

```
Private Sub Form1_Paint(ByVal sender As Object, _
    ByVal e As System.Windows.Forms.PaintEventArgs) Handles MyBase.Paint

    ' Need a graphics object to use for the drawing
    ' The eventargs object has a property called Graphics to get it
    Dim grfGraphics As System.Drawing.Graphics
    grfGraphics = e.Graphics

    ' Need a pen for the drawing. We will make it violet
    Dim penDrawingPen As New _
        System.Drawing.Pen(System.Drawing.Color.BlueViolet)

    ' Draw an ellipse and an icon on the form
    grfGraphics.DrawEllipse(penDrawingPen, 30, 150, 30, 60)
    grfGraphics.DrawIcon(Me.Icon, 90, 20)

    ' Draw a triangle on the form
    ' First, we have to define an array of points
    Dim pntPoint(2) As System.Drawing.Point

    pntPoint(0).X = 150
    pntPoint(0).Y = 150

    pntPoint(1).X = 150
    pntPoint(1).Y = 200

    pntPoint(2).X = 50
    pntPoint(2).Y = 120

    grfGraphics.DrawPolygon(penDrawingPen, pntPoint)

    ' Do a filled triangle
    ' First, we need a brush to specify how it is filled
    Dim bshBrush As System.Drawing.Brush
    bshBrush = New SolidBrush(Color.Blue)

    ' Now relocate the points for the triangle
    ' We will just move it 100 pixels to the right
    pntPoint(0).X += 100

    pntPoint(1).X += 100

    pntPoint(2).X += 100

    grfGraphics.FillPolygon(bshBrush, pntPoint)

End Sub
```

Then start the program. The resulting screen should look similar to this one:

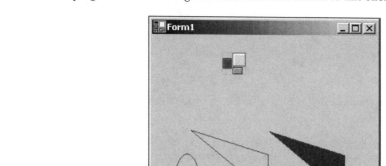

As you can see, the graphics functions are not difficult to use. The hardest part is figuring out how to initialize the objects needed, such as the `Graphics` object itself, and the necessary brushes and pens.

It is typical to use such drawing functions in the form's `Paint` event, but that's not the only option. Forms and controls have a `CreateGraphics()` method to allow you to get a graphics object for a form or control anywhere in code, but if you do graphics operations outside the `Paint` event, the results disappear the next time the form or control is painted to the screen.

The previous example used the namespace `System.Drawing.Graphics` with each class name in that namespace. This was done to emphasize where these classes reside. However, the `System.Drawing` namespace is available by default in Windows Forms, so that it is not necessary to use the full namespace identifier for the classes that are being used. For example, the `System.Drawing.Graphics` class that is used is declared just as type `Graphics`. The remaining examples will omit the namespace from classes in `System.Drawing`.

Some of the effects that you can achieve using the `System.Drawing` namespace can be very fancy. Here is the next example, using two of the fancier effects that are available; painting the inside of some text with a bitmap, and then washing out part of the form.

In a new **Windows Application** in Visual Studio .NET, emulate the previous example, inserting a `Paint` event in **Form1** and then insert this code:

```
Private Sub Form1_Paint(ByVal sender As Object, _
    ByVal e As System.Windows.Forms.PaintEventArgs) Handles MyBase.Paint

    ' Declare a brush, a font, and a graphics object to use
    Dim bshBrush As Brush
    Dim fntFont As Font

    ' We can get the graphic object directly from
```

```
    ' the PaintEventArgs parameter of the event
    Dim grfGraphics As Graphics = e.Graphics

    ' Fix up the brush and the font
    ' Substitute any bitmap you want in the next line
    bshBrush = New TextureBrush(New Bitmap("C:\WINNT\Rhododendron.bmp"))
    fntFont = New Font("Impact", 50, Drawing.FontStyle.Strikeout)

    ' Now draw some fancy text
    grfGraphics.DrawString(".NET", fntFont, bshBrush, 10, 60)

    ' Wash out part of the form, including some of the text
    ' We need a special kind of brush to do that
    Dim washBrush As Brush = New SolidBrush(Color.FromArgb(180, Color.White))

    grfGraphics.FillRectangle(washBrush, 100, 60, 100, 100)

    ' Dispose of all the graphics objects
    washBrush.Dispose()
    bshBrush.Dispose()
    fntFont.Dispose()
    grfGraphics.Dispose()
```

```
End Sub
```

Another change in this example is that we include code to dispose of all our graphics objects. This is good practice because these objects can take up significant system resources.

Run the program, and the following form should display:

Note the bitmap inside the text, the strikethrough effect on the text, and the 'washed out' appearance under the rectangular area that overlaps the text.

The remaining namespaces in System.Drawing add additional capabilities. We will not look at these in as much detail, but simply note what kind of functionality is in each namespace.

System.Drawing.Drawing2D

The `System.Drawing.Drawing2D` namespace adds capability for two-dimensional vector graphics. This is in contrast to the graphics functions we have previously looked at, which were bit-mapped. These vector-based functions include the capability to use such effects as gradient fills.

Another class in the `System.Drawing.Drawing2D` namespace is the `GraphicsPath` class we used earlier to change the shape of a form.

System.Drawing.Imaging

The `System.Drawing.Imaging` namespace includes functions to work with various image formats. The formats can be displayed from a file, and saved into a file. Some of the supported formats include:

Format	Description
BMP	Windows bitmap image format
EMF	Enhanced Windows metafile image format
EXIF	Exchangeable Image Format
FlashPIX	FlashPIX image format
GIF	Graphic Interchange Format
Icon	Windows icon image format
JPEG	JPEG image format
MemoryBMP	A memory bitmap image format
PhotoCD	Eastman Kodak PhotoCD image format
PNG	W3C PNG (Portable Network Graphics) image format
TIFF	Tag Image File Format (TIFF) image format
WMF	Windows metafile image format

The namespace includes support for reading and writing these formats, and for manipulating the image during rendering.

System.Drawing.Text Namespace

The `System.Drawing.Text` namespace adds additional capability for working with fonts. While the `System.Drawing` namespace includes basic font capability, `System.Drawing.Text` goes beyond this to supply capabilities such as control over line spacing.

Changes from VB6 and Earlier

Some of the functionality residing in `System.Drawing` replaces keywords or controls in VB6 and earlier. Here are the relevant keywords that are being retired, and their replacements in the `System.Drawing` namespace:

Retired VB element	Location in Visual Basic .NET (namespace)	Member of namespace
`Circle` keyword	`System.Drawing.Graphics` class	`DrawEllipse()` method.
`Line` keyword, `Line` control	`System.Drawing.Graphics` class	`DrawLine()` method.
`Shape` control	`System.Drawing.Graphics` class	`DrawRectangle()` method and `DrawPolygon()` method.
`Pset` keyword	`System.Drawing.Graphics` class, `System.Drawing.Image` class	No exact equivalent– most functions done by `Pset` in VB6 are done with a `Point` structure used in with various methods for Visual Basic .NET, or by the `SetPixel()` method of the `Image` class.
`Point()` method (of forms and picture boxes)	`System.Drawing.Image` class	No exact equivalent. The `GetPixel` and `SetPixel` methods of the Image class provide similar functionality.

Creating Custom Windows Forms Controls

VB6 has minimal capability to create new controls. The only type it allows are **composite controls** that merely combine the capabilities of other controls. Such controls were known as `UserControls` in VB6.

Visual Basic .NET goes far beyond this, and actually has several ways to create new controls. The three basic strategies for creating a new control are:

❑   Inherit from another control

❑   Build a composite control

❑   Write a control from scratch, using the `Control` class as a base class

We can't cover all the techniques for creating and working with custom controls in this chapter. You can refer to Chapter 13 in *Professional VB.NET 2nd Edition* from Wrox Press, ISBN *1-861007-16-7*, for an extended discussion.

To give you a flavor of what is possible, we will look in brief at a few quick examples of custom controls. These examples will not use all the techniques available. For example, we won't include the logic to make our controls take full advantage of integration with the properties window, but you should be able to get an idea of what you can do through these examples.

Inheriting from an Existing Control

Suppose an existing control does almost everything you need, but there is a little functionality you would like to add. For example, suppose you have many textboxes on your application that take two digit numbers. The normal textbox is fine, except that it allows any length, and allows any characters.

You could write event logic for every textbox throughout the application to check for too many digits and incorrect characters, but placing that logic inside a control has many advantages. As soon as the control is dragged from the toolbox, the editing capabilities are immediately available. Let's write such a textbox.

Step-by-Step Process to Create the Control

1. Start a new Windows Control Library project in Visual Studio .NET and give it the name SpecialTextbox, rename the resulting project module SpecialTextbox.vb (by default it will be named UserControl1.vb), and bring up the code window for this class.

2. The first two lines of the class will look like this:

```
Public Class UserControl1
    Inherits System.Windows.Forms.UserControl
```

As we need to inherit from a textbox, these lines should be changed so as to read:

```
Public Class SpecialTextBox
    Inherits System.Windows.Forms.TextBox
```

3. Next, we need to add the code for our new functionality. In our case, this is just one extra event routine that excludes the keys we don't want to handle. To do that, place an event routine for the KeyPress event in the code. This is done in a similar way to previous examples – selecting (Base Class Events) from the left-hand form design drop-down menu and then selecting KeyPress from the right-hand drop-down menu.

4. The following code should be added to the KeyPress event to monitor keystrokes from the user:

```
Private Sub SpecialTextBox_KeyPress(ByVal sender As Object, _
    ByVal e As System.Windows.Forms.KeyPressEventArgs) _
        Handles MyBase.KeyPress

    Dim KeyAscii As Integer
    KeyAscii = Asc(e.KeyChar)

    Select Case KeyAscii
```

```
      Case 48 To 57, 8, 13    ' These are the digits 0-9.
        ' See if we already have two digits. If we do, throw away the
        ' current keystroke
      If Me.TextLength >= 2 Then
        KeyAscii = 0
      End If

      Case 8, 14    ' backspace, carriage return
        ' These are fine - don't need to do anything

      Case Else
        ' provide no handling for the other keys
        KeyAscii = 0

    End Select

  ' If we want to throw the keystroke away, then set the event
  ' as already handled. Otherwise, let the keystroke be handled normally.
  If KeyAscii = 0 Then
    e.Handled = True
  Else
    e.Handled = False
  End If

End Sub
```

5. Build the project to create a DLL containing the SpecialTextbox control.

6. Create a new Windows Application project to test the control. Name the new project anything you like. Now right-click on the Windows Forms tab in the Toolbox, and select Customize Toolbox..., and then click the tab for .NET Framework Components. Hit the Browse button and navigate to the directory containing your SpecialTextbox project, in order to select the `SpecialTextbox.dll` file (found in the /bin subdirectory). Return to the Customize Toolbox dialog. The checkbox for the SpecialTextbox control will be checked. Click the OK button.

7. Scroll to the bottom of the controls on the Windows Forms tab. The SpecialTextbox control should be there.

8. Drag a SpecialTextbox control onto the form as you would a normal TextBox. Blank out the Text property of the control and start the project. Test the SpecialTextbox to check that it only accepts two digits of numeric input.

Composite Controls

The process of creating a composite control (one that combines other controls) is conceptually similar to the way it's done in VB6. The controls are dragged onto a design surface, and properties and methods of the composite control are created to get information into and out of the composite control.

The details of implementation are different and somewhat simpler in Visual Basic .NET. We will not show an example of this technique. You can refer Chapter 13 in *Professional VB.NET 2nd Edition* for a detailed example.

Basing a New Control on the Control Class

If you need the ultimate in flexibility, you can inherit from the `Control` class, and then handle all of the drawing and rendering of the control yourself. Typically that means using the GDI+ functions previously covered to 'paint' the control as necessary. You can precisely position any text and graphical elements you need to create the visual representation of your control. You also must create any properties, events, and methods needed by your control beyond what the `Control` class provides (which we discussed earlier in the chapter).

As with composite controls, we will not show an example. If you are doing advanced control creation, however, you will want to check out this option. Chapter 10 in *Professional VB.NET 2nd Edition* contains an example of such a control written from scratch.

Summary

With all the functionality available, Windows Forms will take a while to become familiar to Visual Basic developers. This chapter has only looked at some of the most important additions and changes. However, the net effect is an easier way to build more powerful Win32 applications – with less code and far easier deployment and implementation.

The new deployment options also mean that Windows forms 'smart client' applications become feasible for a wider range of scenarios. There are many situations in which a VB6 application has prohibitively expensive deployment for a large number of client machines. Windows Forms applications, with their much lower deployment costs, will be practicable to use in many of these situations.

New Object-Oriented Capabilities

When Visual Basic 4.0 was released, it introduced a whole new era of programming for VB. **Object-oriented programming (OOP)** was finally a possibility – at least to some degree. Unfortunately, not all OO features were included in the VB language at that point. Most notably lacking were inheritance capabilities, one of the key defining criteria for any OO language. VB was also missing a large number of secondary features such as method overloading and overriding, and constructors.

With Visual Basic .NET, the VB language finally completes the transition to a fully OO language, incorporating features such as:

- ❑ Abstraction
- ❑ Encapsulation
- ❑ Polymorphism
- ❑ Inheritance

In this chapter, we will discuss all these new features and what they mean to us as VB developers.

While it certainly remains possible to create applications that make no more use of objects than we did in VB3, these new capabilities are quite pervasive and so at least some basic understanding is required to become fully proficient in the use of Visual Basic .NET.

Let's start the chapter by discussing the object-oriented features we listed above in more detail.

What is Object Orientation?

Generally speaking, a language is considered to be OO if it supports four main features:

❏ **Abstraction** – VB has supported abstraction since VB4. Abstraction is merely the ability of a language to create 'black box' code – to take a concept and create an abstract representation of that concept within a program. A `Customer` object, for instance, is an abstract representation of a real-world customer. A `Recordset` object is an abstract representation of a set of data.

❏ **Encapsulation** – This has also been with us since version 4.0. It's the concept of a separation between interface and implementation. The idea is that we can create an interface to an object (`Public` methods in a class) and, as long as that *interface* remains consistent, the application can interact with the object. This remains true even if we entirely rewrite the code *within* a given method – thus the interface is independent of the implementation.

Encapsulation allows us to hide the internal implementation details of a class. For example, the algorithm we use to compute Pi might be proprietary. We can expose a simple API to the end user, but we hide all of the logic used for our algorithm by encapsulating it within our class.

❏ **Polymorphism** – Likewise, polymorphism was introduced with VB4. Polymorphism is reflected in the ability to write one routine that can operate on objects from more than one class – treating different objects from different classes in exactly the same way. For instance, if both `Customer` and `Vendor` objects have a `Name` property, and we can write a routine that calls the `Name` property regardless of whether we're using a `Customer` or `Vendor` object, then we have polymorphism.

VB, in fact, supports polymorphism in two ways – through late binding (much like Smalltalk, a classic example of a true OO language) and through the implementation of multiple interfaces. This flexibility is very powerful and is preserved within Visual Basic .NET, along with the addition of polymorphism through inheritance.

❏ **Inheritance** – Visual Basic .NET is the first version of VB that supports full (implementation) inheritance. Using full inheritance, a class can gain the pre-existing interface *and behaviors* of an existing class. This is done by *inheriting* these behaviors from the existing class through a process known as **subclassing**. With the introduction of full inheritance, VB is now a fully OO language by any reasonable definition.

Along with the addition of inheritance to VB, Visual Basic .NET also adds a large number of related syntax and capabilities, including constructors, shared methods, method overloading, overriding, and shadowing.

The Relationship of Objects to Components

Since version 4.0, VB has provided us with the ability to create not only objects, but also COM components. In fact, VB's ability to create objects, and the way VB objects worked, was very closely tied to COM and the way objects worked within and between COM components.

In COM, components are pre-compiled binary entities – typically a DLL, EXE, or OCX file. Each component contains one or more classes that can be used by client applications. In VB6 we could create ActiveX EXE, ActiveX DLL, or user control (OCX) projects – thus creating COM components. Even when we weren't creating these project types, the way VB6 allowed us to create and work with objects was defined by how objects were created within COM components.

Therefore it should come as no surprise then that Visual Basic .NET is very closely tied to the way .NET handles objects, and the way objects work within and between .NET assemblies or components. This represents a pretty significant change for VB, however, since .NET is substantially more advanced in terms of objects and components when compared to COM.

With COM, objects and components were interrelated, but the marriage of the two was far from seamless. In .NET on the other hand, OO and component-oriented concepts (as defined earlier) are very closely related in ways that we could only dream of in the COM environment.

In .NET we retain the component-oriented features we are used to:

❏   Component-level scoping (via the `Friend` keyword)

❏   Ability to implement interfaces (using the `Implements` keyword)

Component-level scoping allows us to create classes or methods that are available to all the other code in our component – but not to code outside our component. We will discuss this in more detail later, but basically it is a level of scoping that sits between `Private` and `Public` – and is accessed via the `Friend` keyword.

Implementing interfaces via the `Implements` keyword allows each of our classes to have several different 'identities' – each with its own interface. This is a powerful technique that is used widely within both COM and .NET, and is something we will discuss in more detail later.

In addition to these existing features, with .NET we also gain some strong capabilities, most importantly inheritance and the `Inherits` keyword. Visual Basic .NET benefits from this new, closer relationship between objects and components – making both types of concept central to the language and to the way we develop applications. Let's now walk through the OO features in Visual Basic .NET.

Visual Basic .NET OO Implementation

Visual Basic .NET not only provides us with new OO features, but it also changes the way we implement some of the features we are used to from VB6. As we go through these features we'll both cover the new capabilities and also explore the changes to existing features.

When building classes in previous versions of VB, each class got its own file. While simple, this solution could cause a larger OO project to have many files. Visual Basic .NET allows us to put more than one class in a single source file. While we don't have to take this approach, it can be useful since we can reduce the overall number of files in a project – possibly making it more maintainable.

Additionally, Visual Basic .NET provides support for the concept of .NET namespaces, as we discussed in Chapters 2 and 4. There are also changes to the syntax used to create `Property` methods, and we can overload methods in our classes. We will look at all these features shortly. First though, let's look at how we add a class to a project.

Creating Classes

Adding a class in Visual Basic .NET is similar to adding a class in VB6. In order to do this we need to create a new **Windows Application** project and choose the **Project | Add Class...** menu option to bring up the **Add New Item** dialog:

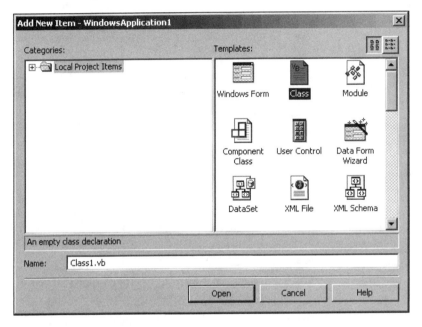

This is the common dialog used for adding any type of item to our project – in this case it defaults to adding a class module. Regardless of which type of VB source file we choose (form, class, module, and so on) we'll end up with a file ending in a .vb extension.

> It is the *content* of the file that determines its type, not the file extension. The IDE creates different starting code within the file based on the type we choose.

We can name the class file TheClass.vb in this dialog and, when we click **Open**, this new file will be added to our project, containing very simple code defining a class with the same name as the file:

```
Public Class TheClass

End Class
```

Though a .vb file can contain multiple classes, modules, and other code, the normal behavior from the IDE is the same as we've had in VB since its inception – one class, module, or form per file. We can manually add other code to the files created by the IDE with no problems, but when we ask the IDE to create a class for us it will always do so by adding a new file to the project.

At this point we're ready to start adding code.

The Class Keyword

As shown in this example, we now have a Class keyword along with the corresponding End Class. This new keyword is needed so that we can add more than one class to a particular single source file if we wish. Any time we want to create a class in Visual Basic .NET, we simply put all the code for the class within the Class...End Class block. For instance:

```
Public Class TheClass
  Public Sub DoSomething()
    MsgBox("Hello world")
  End Sub
End Class
```

Within a given source file (any .vb file) we can have many of these Class...End Class blocks, one after another.

Classes and Namespaces

We discussed the concept of a namespace in depth in Chapters 2 and 4. Namespaces are central to the .NET environment, as they provide a mechanism by which classes can be organized into logical groupings, making them easier to find and manage.

Namespaces in Visual Basic .NET are declared using a block structure. For example:

```
Namespace TheNamespace

    Public Class TheClass

    End Class

End Namespace
```

Any classes, structures, or other types declared within the Namespace...End Namespace block will be addressed using that namespace. In this example, our class is referenced using the namespace TheNamespace, so declaring a variable would be done as follows:

```
Private obj As TheNamespace.TheClass
```

Since namespaces are created using a block structure, it is possible for a single source file to contain not only many classes, but also many namespaces.

Also, classes within the same namespace can be created in separate files. In other words, within a Visual Basic .NET project we can use the same namespace in more than one source file – and all of the classes within those namespace blocks will be part of that same namespace.

For instance, say we have one source file with the code for TheClass in namespace TheNamespace as above, and we have a separate source file in the project with the following code:

```
Namespace TheNamespace

   Public Class TheOtherClass

   End Class

End Namespace
```

In this case, we will have a single namespace, TheNamespace, with two classes

❑   TheClass

❑   TheOtherClass

It is also important to remember that Visual Basic .NET projects, by default, have a **root** namespace that is part of the project's properties. By default this root namespace will have the same name as our project. When we use the Namespace block structure, we are actually adding to that root namespace.

So, in our example, if the project is named MyProject, then we could declare a variable as:

```
Private obj As MyProject.TheNamespace.TheClass
```

To change the root namespace, use the **Project | Properties** menu option. The root namespace can be cleared as well, meaning that all Namespace blocks become the root level for the code they contain.

Nested Classes

Classes can also contain other classes. This can be very beneficial in design, since often we'll have concepts that are logically contained by other concepts – such as an OrderLine object being contained by an Order. In such a case we may choose to physically place the contained class inside the parent or containing class.

The syntax for this is illustrated by the following:

```
Namespace TheNamespace

  Public Class TheClass

    Public Sub DoSomething()
      MsgBox("Hello world")
    End Sub

    Public Class InnerClass
      Public Sub DoInnerWork()
        MsgBox("Hello from inside")
      End Sub
    End Class

  End Class

End Namespace
```

By placing a class inside another class, the base class effectively becomes part of the namespace for the inner class. This means that the fully qualified name of `InnerClass` is:

```
MyProject.TheNamespace.TheClass.InnerClass
```

The relationship between the two classes is quite clear – `InnerClass` is subordinate to `TheClass`. This is perhaps illustrated most clearly by opening the **Class View** window:

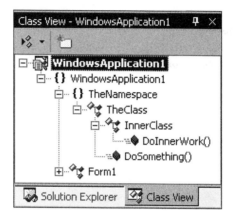

Here we can see graphically how `InnerClass` is nested within `TheClass`, which is contained within `TheNamespace` under the root `WindowsApplication1` namespace.

Creating Methods

Methods in Visual Basic .NET are created just like they are in VB6 – using the `Sub` or `Function` keywords. A method created with `Sub` does not return a value, while a `Function` must return a value as a result:

```
Sub DoSomething()

End Sub

Function GetValue() As Integer

End Function
```

Methods defined in a class are called **member methods**, since they are members of the class.

Method Scope

In Visual Basic .NET, we retain the three scoping keywords we are used to in VB6, but add a couple more:

- ❑ `Private` – callable only by code within our class
- ❑ `Friend` – callable only by code within our project/component

- ❑   `Public` – callable by code outside our class

- ❑   `Protected`

- ❑   `Protected Friend`

Both `Protected` and `Protected Friend` are used when we anticipate that our class may be inherited by another class. We will explain the use of both of these scoping keywords when we cover inheritance in depth at the end of the chapter.

Passing Parameters to Methods

Parameters to methods are now declared `ByVal` by default, rather than `ByRef`. We can still override the default behavior through explicit use of the `ByRef` keyword. We discussed these issues in depth in Chapter 4.

Overloading Methods

One of the more exciting new polymorphic features in Visual Basic .NET is the ability to **overload** a method. Overloading means that we can declare a method of the same name more than once in a class – as long as each declaration has a different parameter list, or **method signature**. This can be very powerful.

A different method means different data types in the parameter list. Consider the following method declaration:

```
Public Sub MyMethod(X As Integer, Y As Integer)
```

Here we need to pass two integer parameters to the method. To overload this method, we must come up with a different method signature – perhaps the parameter list contains an integer and a double instead of two integers. You should note that the order of the parameter types also matters, so the following method declarations represent overloaded methods too:

```
Public Sub MyMethod(X As Integer, Y As Double)
Public Sub MyMethod(X As Double, Y As Integer)
```

You will notice that the return type isn't even part of the method signature. Overloading cannot be done merely by changing the *return type* of a function (although the return type *can* be changed through overloading); it is the data types of the actual parameters that must differ for overloading to occur. However, both method declarations have the same method name – something that would be prohibited in VB6.

As an example, suppose we want to provide a search capability – returning an array of `String` data based on some criteria – so we create a routine such as:

```
Public Function FindData(ByVal Name As String) As String()
  ' find data and return result
End Function
```

In VB6, if we wanted to add a new searching option based on some other criteria, we would have to add a whole new function with a different name. In Visual Basic .NET however, we can simply overload this existing function, like this:

```
Public Function FindData(ByVal Age As Integer) As String()
  ' find data in a different way and return the result
End Function
```

When overloading a method we can have different scopes on each implementation – as long as the parameter lists are different as we discussed earlier. This means we could change our second `FindData()` method above to have a different scope:

```
Friend Function FindData(ByVal Age As Integer) As String()
  ' find data and return result
End Function
```

With this change, only other code in our Visual Basic .NET project can make use of the `FindData()` that accepts an `Integer` as its parameter. However, because the method signatures must be different for each overloaded method, we could not have overloads of the `FindData()` method that have the following signatures, even though they have different scopes:

```
Public Function FindData(ByVal Age As Integer) As String()
Friend Function FindData(ByVal Age As Integer) As String()
```

Creating Properties

In Chapter 4 we discussed the changes to the way `Property` routines are created. In the past we'd create separate routines for `Property Get` and `Property Let`. Now these are combined into a single structure:

```
Private mstrName As String

Public Property Name() As String
  Get
    Return mstrName
  End Get
  Set(ByVal Value As String)
    mstrName = Value
  End Set
End Property
```

You should refer to Chapter 4 for further discussion, including details on creating read-only and write-only properties.

The Default Property

When creating classes in VB6 we could declare a default method, or property, for our class. This was done using the **Tools | Procedure Attributes** menu option and by setting the **Procedure ID** to (default). Not an entirely intuitive process, since we couldn't look at the code to see what was going on.

Visual Basic .NET changes this behavior in a couple ways. First off, creating a default property is done through the use of a `Default` keyword – making the declaration much more clear and intuitive. However, Visual Basic .NET introduces a new limitation on default properties – to be default, a property must be a property array.

A **property array** is a property that is indexed – much like an array. The `Item` property on a collection or list object is an example:

```
strText = MyList.Item(5)
```

The `Item` property doesn't have a singular value, but rather is an array of properties accessed via an index. Since it is the default property, we can also use shorthand to reference it in our code:

```
strText = MyList(5)
```

By requiring default properties to be a property array, we allow the language to avoid ambiguities in the use of default properties. This is a key to the elimination of the `Set` keyword as we knew it in VB6. Consider the following code:

```
MyValue = MyObject
```

Does this refer to the object `MyObject`, or to its default property? In VB6 this was resolved by forcing us to use the `Set` command when dealing with the object, otherwise the default property was used. In Visual Basic .NET this statement *always* refers to the object since a default property would be indexed. To get at a default property we'd have code such as:

```
MyValue = MyObject(5)
```

This change means a property array procedure must accept a parameter. For example:

```
Private theData(100) As String

Default Public Property Data(ByVal Index As Integer) As String
  Get
    Data = theData(index)
  End Get
  Set(ByVal Value As String)
    theData(index) = Value
  End Set
End Property
```

In the end, this code is much clearer than its VB6 counterpart, but we lose some of the flexibility we enjoyed with default properties in the past. For instance, we'd often use default properties in VB6 when working with GUI controls, such as the default `Text` property:

```
TextBox1 = "My text"
```

This is no longer valid in Visual Basic .NET, since the Text property is not a property array. Instead we must now use the property name in these cases.

Creating Events

Objects can raise events by declaring them using the Event keyword and raising them with the RaiseEvent statement. This was discussed in Chapter 4. Later in this chapter we will consider the effect of inheritance on events.

Object Lifecycle

In VB6, objects had a clearly-defined and well-understood life cycle – a set of events that we always knew would occur over the life of an object. We encountered the following events:

Event	Description
Sub Main	Would run as the component was loaded, before an object was created (optional)
Class_Initialize	Called by the runtime as the object was being created, and run before any other code in the object
Class_Terminate	Called by the runtime as the object was being destroyed, would run after any other code in our object

With Visual Basic .NET, objects also have a lifecycle, but things are not quite the same as in the past. In particular, we no longer have the same concept of a component-level Sub Main that runs as a DLL is loaded, and the concept of the Class_Terminate event changes rather substantially. However, the concept behind the Class_Initialize event is morphed into a full-blown constructor method that accepts parameters.

Therefore, in Visual Basic .NET, we are only guaranteed the following:

Event	Description
New()	Will run before any other code in our object; called by the runtime as the object is being created.
Dispose()	Optionally called by the code using our object when it is done with the object. Nothing forces the code using our object to call Dispose(), so it may or may not ever be called – there are no guarantees.
Finalize()	If implemented, this method will be called by the .NET runtime right before our object is finally destroyed. Note that implementing this method will cause increased overhead and will therefore decrease the overall performance of our application.

This is quite a change so let's discuss the details further.

Object Construction

Object construction is triggered any time we create a new instance of a class. In Visual Basic .NET this is done using the `New` keyword – a level of consistency that didn't exist with VB6 where we had to choose between `New` and `CreateObject`.

The New() Method

In VB6 `Class_Initialize` is called before any other code in the object. In fact, it is called before the error handling mechanism is fully in place, making debugging very hard; errors show up at the client as a generic failure to instantiate the object. Additionally, `Class_Initialize` accepts no parameters – meaning there is no way in VB6 to initialize an object with data as it is created.

Visual Basic .NET eliminates `Class_Initialize` in favor of full-blown constructor methods, which have full error handling capabilities and do accept parameters. This means we can initialize our objects as we create them – a very important and powerful feature. The constructor method in Visual Basic .NET is `Sub New`. The simplest constructor method for a class is one that accepts no parameters – quite comparable to `Class_Initialize`:

```
Public Class TheClass
  Public Sub New()
    ' initialize object here
  End Sub
End Class
```

With this type of constructor, creating an instance of our class is done as follows:

```
Dim obj As New TheClass()
```

This example is directly analogous to creating a VB6 object with code in `Class_Initialize`.

However, more often than not we would prefer to actually initialize our object with data as it is created. Perhaps we want to have the object load some data from a database, or perhaps we want to provide it with the data directly. This is done by adding a parameter list to the `New()` method:

```
Public Class TheClass
  Public Sub New(ByVal ID As Integer)
    ' use the ID value to initialize the object
  End Sub
End Class
```

Now, when we go to create an instance of the class, we can provide data to the object:

```
Dim obj As New TheClass(42)
```

To increase flexibility we might want to optionally accept the parameter value. This can be done in two ways. The first is through the use of the `Optional` keyword to declare an optional parameter, as shown below:

```
Public Sub New(Optional ByVal ID As Integer = -1)
  If ID = -1 Then
```

```
      ' initialize object here
   Else
      ' use the ID value to initialize the object
   End If
End Sub
```

This approach is far from ideal, however, since we have to check to see if the parameter was or wasn't provided, and then decide how to initialize the object. It would be clearer to just have two separate implementations of the New() method – one for each type of behavior. This is accomplished through overloading:

```
Public Sub New()
   ' initialize object here
End Sub

Public Sub New(ByVal ID As Integer)
   ' use the ID value to initialize the object
End Sub
```

Not only does this approach avoid the conditional check and simplify our code, but it also makes the use of our object clearer to any client code. The overloaded New() method is shown by IntelliSense in the Visual Studio .NET IDE, making it clear that New() can be called both with and without a parameter.

In fact, through overloading we can create many different constructors if needed, allowing our object to be initialized in a number of different ways.

Constructor methods are not essential in Visual Basic .NET, except for when we are using inheritance and the only constructors the base class has require parameters. We will discuss inheritance later in the chapter.

Controlling Object Creation

In VB6, we could control the creation of an object by using the instancing property. By using this property we could control who could see, use, or create instances of our classes.

In Visual Basic .NET, we can still have this type of control, but instead of using the instancing property, our control comes through the scope of our class and its constructor methods. The following table shows the VB6 instancing property and the corresponding scopes needed for our Visual Basic .NET class and constructor methods. Keep in mind that we can have multiple constructors, with different scopes. The following table shows what will be allowed for each constructor scope:

Instancing property	Visual Basic .NET equivalent
| Private | ```
Friend Class TheClass
  Public Sub New()

  End Sub
End Class
```<br><br>Since the class is `Friend`, it cannot be created by any code outside our Visual Basic .NET project – meaning the class is private to our project. |
| PublicNotCreatable | ```
Public Class TheClass
  Friend Sub New()

  End Sub
End Class
```<br><br>Though the class is declared as `Public` – making it available to code outside our project – the constructor method is declared as `Friend`, meaning that only code *inside* our Visual Basic .NET project can actually create an instance of the class. |
| Multiuse | ```
Public Class TheClass
  Public Sub New()

  End Sub
End Class
```<br><br>Since both the class and constructor are `Public`, the class is available to code outside our project, and code outside our project can create objects based on the class. |
| GlobalMultiuse | ```
Public Class TheClass
  Private Sub New()

  End Sub
End Class
```<br><br>In .NET this is a class with a `Private` constructor so no object can be created based on the class. Therefore, if we wish to make use of the methods in the class, all of them should be declared using the `Shared` keyword, so that they are all callable directly from the class itself. |

We can also omit the constructor method entirely – in which case the Visual Basic .NET compiler will automatically create an empty constructor that is `Public` in scope and that requires no parameters. If we do manually implement a constructor then this empty constructor is *not* automatically created by the compiler.

Sub Main

Since VB6 was based on COM, creating an object could trigger a `Sub Main` procedure to be run. This would happen the first time an object was created from a given component – often a DLL. Before even attempting to create the object, the VB6 runtime would load the DLL and run the `Sub Main` procedure.

The .NET runtime doesn't treat components quite the same way, and so neither does Visual Basic .NET. This means that no `Sub Main` procedure is called as a component is loaded. In fact, `Sub Main` is only used once – when an application itself is first started. As further components are loaded by the application, only code within the classes we invoke is called.

It wasn't that wise to rely on `Sub Main` even in VB6, since that code would run prior to all the error handling infrastructure being in place. Bugs in `Sub Main` were notoriously difficult to debug in VB6. If we do have to use code that relies heavily on the `Sub Main` concept for initialization, we will need to implement a workaround in Visual Basic .NET.

This can be done easily by calling a central method from the constructor method in each class. For instance, we might create a centrally available method in a module such as:

```
Public Module CentralCode
  Private blnHasRun As Boolean

  Public Sub Initialize()
    If Not blnHasRun Then
      blnHasRun = True
      ' Do initialization here
    End If
  End Sub
End Module
```

This routine is designed to only run one time, no matter how often it is called. We can then use this method from within each constructor of our classes. For example:

```
Public Class TheClass
  Public Sub New()
    CentralCode.Initialize()
    ' regular class code goes here
  End Sub
End Class
```

While this is a bit of extra work on our part, it does accomplish the same effect we are used to with a VB6-style `Sub Main` routine.

Object Destruction

In VB6, an object was destroyed when its last reference was removed. In other words, when no other code had any reference to an object, the object would be automatically destroyed – triggering a call to its `Class_Terminate` event. This approach was implemented through reference counting – keeping a count of how many clients had a reference to each object – and was a direct product of VB's close relationship with COM.

While this behavior was nice – since we always knew an object would be destroyed immediately and we could count on `Class_Terminate` to know when – it had its problems. Most notably, it was quite easy to create circular references between two objects, which could leave them running in memory forever. This was one of the few (but quite common) ways to create a memory leak in VB6.

> *To be fair, the problem was worse prior to VB6. In VB6, circular references are only a problem across components. Objects created from classes within the same component would be automatically destroyed in VB6, even if they had a circular reference. Still, the circular reference problem exists any time objects come from different components. The issue is non-trivial and has created a lot of headaches for VB developers over the years.*

The clear termination scheme used in VB6 is an example of **deterministic finalization**. It was always very clear *when* an object would be terminated.

Garbage Collection

In .NET, reference counting is not part of the infrastructure. Instead, objects are destroyed through a garbage collection mechanism. At certain times (based on specific rules), a task will run through all of our objects looking for those that no longer have any references. Those objects are then terminated; the garbage is collected.

This means that we can't tell exactly when an object will really be finally destroyed. Just because we eliminate all references to an object doesn't mean it will be terminated immediately. It will just hang out in memory until the garbage collection process gets around to locating and destroying it. This is an example of **non-deterministic finalization**.

The major benefit of garbage collection is that it eliminates the circular reference issues found with reference counting. If two objects have references to each other, and no other code has any references to either object, the garbage collector will discover and terminate them, whereas in COM these objects would have sat in memory forever.

There is also a potential performance benefit from garbage collection. Rather than expending the effort to destroy objects as they are dereferenced, with garbage collection this destruction process typically occurs when the application is otherwise idle – often decreasing the impact on the user. However, garbage collection may also occur when the application is active in the case that the system starts running low on resources.

We can manually trigger the garbage collection process through code:

```
System.GC.Collect()
```

However, this process takes time, so it is not the sort of thing that should be done each time we want to terminate an object. It is far better to design our applications in such a way that it is acceptable for our objects to sit in memory for a time before they are finally terminated.

Finalize() Method

The garbage collection mechanism does provide some functionality comparable to the VB6 `Class_Terminate` event. As an object is being terminated, the garbage collection code will call its `Finalize()` method – allowing us to take care of any final cleanup that might be required:

```
Protected Overrides Sub Finalize()
  ' clean up code goes here
End Sub
```

This code uses both the `Protected` scope and `Overrides` keyword – concepts we'll discuss later as we cover inheritance. For now it is sufficient to know that this method will be called just prior to the object being terminated by the garbage collection mechanism – somewhat like `Class_Terminate`.

However, it is critical to remember that this method may be called long after the object is dereferenced by the last bit of client code (perhaps even minutes later).

It is also very important to recognize that any time we implement a `Finalize()` method, we force the GC to go through extra work to get rid of our object.

> Implementing a `Finalize()` method may have a negative impact on the performance of our application.

We should avoid implementing `Finalize()` methods on objects unless it is absolutely necessary.

Implementing a Dispose() Method

In some cases the `Finalize()` behavior is not acceptable. If we have an object that is using some expensive or limited resource – such as a database connection, a file handle, or a system lock – we might need to ensure that the resource is freed as soon as the object is no longer in use.

To accomplish this, we can implement a method to be called by the client code to force our object to clean up and release its resources. This is not a perfect solution, but it is workable.

This is accomplished by implementing the `IDisposable` interface, which in turn requires us to implement a `Dispose()` method. We'll discuss interfaces and how they work in Visual Basic .NET later in the chapter.

This can be done as follows:

```
Public Class TheClass
   Implements IDisposable

   Public Sub Dispose() Implements IDisposable.Dispose
     ' clean up code goes here
```

```
      End Sub

   End Class
```

It is up to our client code to call this method at the appropriate time to ensure cleanup occurs.

If we are also implementing a `Finalize()` method we should have it call the `Dispose()` method. This is important, because the client might *not* call the `Dispose()` method, meaning that our object may retain references to expensive resources even when `Finalize()` is invoked.

Not all objects take exactly this approach. For instance, database connection objects in ADO.NET do not implement a `Dispose()` method, choosing instead to implement a `Close()` method to release the expensive database connection resource. Typically however, `Dispose()` is the preferred method name for handling this scenario.

Interacting with Objects

With all the changes to the way we declare, construct, and implement classes in Visual Basic .NET, it makes sense that there are also some changes in the way we interact with objects. These changes impact on how we instantiate objects, how we reference and dereference objects, and how we use early and late binding techniques.

Object Declaration and Instantiation

The most obvious change in the way we work with objects comes as we try to create them and work with our object references. Visual Basic .NET doesn't use the `CreateObject` statement for object creation. `CreateObject` was an outgrowth of VB's relationship with COM, and since Visual Basic .NET doesn't use COM, it has no use for `CreateObject`.

*Technically Visual Basic .NET **can** use COM objects through an interoperability mechanism. This is discussed in Chapter 11. However, in typical .NET programming, COM doesn't enter the picture.*

The New Statement

Visual Basic .NET relies on the `New` statement for all object creation. We can use `New` in a number of different locations within our code – all of them perfectly valid.

The most obvious is to declare an object variable and then create an instance of the object:

```
Dim obj As TheClass

obj = New TheClass()
```

We can shorten this by combining the declaration of the variable with the creation of the instance:

```
Dim obj As New TheClass()
```

In VB6 this was a very poor thing to do, as it had negative effects on both performance and maintainability. However, in Visual Basic .NET there is no difference between our first example and this one, other than that our code is shorter.

Keep in mind that the scope of our variable comes into play here. If we declare a variable within a block structure, that variable will only be valid within that block structure. In many cases, we will want to declare the variable within the scope of our method, but possibly create instances of the object within a block structure such as a `Try...End Try` or loop structure. In such a case, combining the declaration with the instantiation may be inappropriate.

Also, realize that we have turned the `Dim` statement into an executable line of code in this case, and so it may raise an error as the object is created. This technique, while shorter, can complicate error handling in our code. We now need to wrap our `Dim` statements with error handling code – something that is not always intuitive. When doing this, remember that variables declared within a block structure are scoped *to that block structure* and so, cannot be used outside that block. Variables declared within a `Try...Catch` block are only valid within that same code block.

Another variation on the declaration and instantiation theme is:

```
Dim obj As TheClass = New TheClass()
```

Again, this both declares a variable and creates an instance of the class for our use. This syntax is perhaps more useful when working with inheritance or with multiple interfaces. We might declare the variable to be of one type – maybe an interface called `MyInterface`, but instantiate the object based on a class `TheClass` that implements that interface:

```
Dim obj As MyInterface = New TheClass()
```

We can employ more complex syntax at times too. Suppose that we have a method that requires an object reference. We can create an instance of the object right in the call to the method:

```
DoSomething(New TheClass())
```

This calls the `DoSomething()` method, passing a new instance of `TheClass` as a parameter. This new object will only exist for the duration of this one method call. When the method completes, the object will be automatically dereferenced by the .NET runtime.

> *Remember that dereferencing an object doesn't mean it is immediately destroyed. As we discussed earlier, objects are only destroyed when the .NET garbage collection process runs through and cleans up orphaned objects.*

This can be even more complex. Perhaps, instead of needing an object reference, our method needs a `String`. We can provide that `String` value from a method on our object – instantiating the object and calling the method all in one shot:

```
DoSomething(New TheClass().GetStringData())
```

Obviously we need to carefully weigh the readability of such code against its compactness – at some point having more compact code can detract from readability rather than enhancing it.

The Set Keyword

Notice that nowhere do we use the Set statement when working with objects. In VB6, any time we worked with an object reference we had to use the Set command – differentiating objects from any other data type in the language.

In Visual Basic .NET, objects are not treated differently from any other data type, and so we can use direct assignment for objects just like we do with Integer or String data types. The Set command is no longer valid in Visual Basic .NET. Refer to Chapter 4 for more details.

Dereferencing Objects

In VB6, we would dereference an object by setting our object reference to Nothing. The same is true in Visual Basic .NET:

```
Dim obj As TheClass

obj = New TheClass()
obj = Nothing
```

The *effect* of this statement is different in Visual Basic .NET, however. As we discussed earlier, Visual Basic .NET does not use reference counting to terminate objects, instead relying on a garbage collection mechanism. In VB6, when no more variables held a reference to an object, that object was immediately destroyed. In Visual Basic .NET this is not true – the object will be destroyed when the garbage collection process discovers that the object has no references. That is something that may happen seconds or even minutes after the last reference is removed.

This doesn't eliminate the value of dereferencing objects, however. If we have a long-running algorithm, it is a good practice to explicitly dereference objects within the process – thus allowing the garbage collector to remove them when possible. As long as our code retains a reference to an object, that object will remain in memory and will not be garbage collected.

That said, it is not a good practice to set an object to Nothing at the end of a method. At the end of a method all local variables will be dereferenced anyway. More importantly, however, the garbage collection mechanism is very intelligent and may collect local variables that are no longer used in our method. Therefore:

> Setting an object to Nothing at the end of a method may have a *negative* impact on the performance of our application.

Setting a variable to Nothing at the bottom means we're 'using' the variable at the bottom of the method and so prevents the garbage collection mechanism from being as efficient as possible.

Early vs. Late Binding

One of the strengths of VB has long been that we had access to both early and late binding when interacting with objects.

Early binding means that our code directly interacts with the object – knowing its data type ahead of time and thus being able to very efficiently interact with the object. Early binding allows the IDE to use IntelliSense to aid our development efforts and it allows the compiler to ensure that we are referencing methods that do exist and that we are providing the proper parameter values.

Late binding means that our code interacts with an object dynamically at run-time. This provides a great deal of flexibility since our code literally doesn't care what type of object it is interacting with as long as the object supports the methods we want to call. Since the type of the object isn't known by the IDE or compiler, neither IntelliSense nor compile-time syntax checking is possible – but in exchange we get unprecedented flexibility.

Visual Basic .NET continues this tradition, providing support for both early and late binding as we work with our objects.

By default, all objects are early bound. We can force the IDE and compiler to enforce this by setting `Option Strict` to `On`. The default is `Option Strict Off`, which provides us with the greatest compatibility with VB6, and also allows us to use late binding in our code as needed. `Option Strict` was discussed in Chapter 4.

Use of the Object Type

Late binding occurs when the compiler can't determine the type of object we will be calling. This level of ambiguity is achieved through the use of the `Object` data type. A variable of data type `Object` can hold virtually any value – including a reference to any type of object. Thus, code such as the following could be run against any object that implements a `MyMethod()` method that accepts no parameters:

```
Module LateBind
  Public Sub DoSomething(obj As Object)
    obj.MyMethod()
  End Sub
End Module
```

If the object passed into this routine *doesn't* have a `MyMethod()` method that accepts no parameters, then a run-time error will result. Thus, it is recommended that any code that uses late binding should always provide error trapping:

```
Module LateBind
  Public Sub DoSomething(obj As Object)
    Try
      obj.MyMethod()
    Catch
      ' do something appropriate given failure to call the method
    End Try
  End Sub
End Module
```

While late binding is flexible, it can be error prone and it is slower than early bound code. To make a late bound method call, the .NET runtime must dynamically determine if the target object actually has a method that matches the one we're calling, and then it must invoke that method on our behalf. This takes more time and effort than an early bound call where the compiler knows ahead of time that the method exists and can compile our code to make the call directly.

Late Binding and Reflection

The .NET Framework supports a concept known as **reflection**. This is the ability to write code that examines other .NET code to determine its composition. Reflection is supported by the `System.Reflection` namespace.

Reflection allows us to write code that discovers the classes within an assembly and the methods, properties, and events exposed by those classes. We can then use reflection to create instances of those classes and call those methods. This entire process can be very dynamic – much like late binding.

There are many reasons why we might use reflection in an application. One such reason would be to create an engine that uses metadata such as XML to load classes and call methods rather than hard-coding the entire process.

In fact, Visual Basic .NET uses reflection to implement late binding on our behalf. Rather than forcing us to write the code that uses reflection to find and invoke a method, Visual Basic .NET handles this for us when we use late binding coding techniques.

We could implement a limited form of reflection within VB6 by using the `typelib` DLL. The functions in this DLL allowed us to dynamically discover the classes and methods in a COM DLL, and then invoke them. Of course, COM components were described with IDL – a rather inaccurate description of the component. In .NET, assemblies are described by metadata that accurately describes each assembly, making reflection a much more robust solution.

Use of the CType Function

Whether we are using late binding or not, it can be useful to pass object references around using the `Object` data type – converting them to an appropriate type when we need to interact with them. This is done using the `CType` function, allowing us to use a variable of type `Object` to make an *early bound* method call:

```
Module LateBind
  Public Sub DoSomething(obj As Object)
    CType(obj, TheClass).MyMethod()
  End Sub
End Module
```

Even though the variable we're working with is of type `Object` – and thus any calls to it will be late bound – we are using the `CType` method to temporarily convert the variable into a specific type, in this case the type `TheClass`.

*This technique is often called **casting**. If we think of each interface or class type as a mold, we can cast an object of one type into the mold of another class or interface.*

The `CType` function can be very useful when working with objects that implement multiple interfaces (a concept we'll discuss later in the chapter), since we can reference a single object variable through the appropriate type as needed. For instance, if we have an object of type `TheClass` that also implements `MyInterface`, we can use that interface with the following code:

```
Dim obj As TheClass

obj = New TheClass
CType(obj, MyInterface).DoSomething()
```

In this way we can make early bound calls to other interfaces on an object without needing to declare a new variable of the interface type as we had to do in VB6.

Shared Class Members

While objects are very powerful and useful, there are times when we just want access to variables, functions, or routines that do useful work – without the need for an actual object instance. In the past, we would typically put this type of code into a simple code module, even if the routine was technically related to some class.

Shared Methods

In Visual Basic .NET we have a better alternative. Not only can a class have all the regular methods and properties we've seen so far – methods and properties only available after creating an instance of the class – but they can also have methods that are available *without* creating an instance of the class. These are known as **shared methods**.

These methods are also known as static methods or class methods.

A shared method is not accessed via an object instance like a regular method, but rather is accessed directly from the class. The following is a simple example of a shared method:

```
Public Class Math
  Public Shared Function Add(ByVal a As Integer, ByVal b As Integer) _
      As Integer
    Return a + b
  End Function
End Class
```

We can use this method – without instantiating a `Math` object – as follows:

```
Dim result As Integer

result = Math.Add(5, 10)
```

Notice how, rather than using an object variable, we use the actual class name to reference the method. With a normal method this would result in a syntax error, but with a shared method this is perfectly acceptable.

Shared methods can also be accessed via objects just like regular methods, but their most common use is to provide functionality without the requirement for creating an object. In fact, when a shared method is invoked, no object is created – the method is called directly, much like a procedure in a Module.

Shared methods can also be overloaded just like regular methods, so it is quite possible to create a set of variations on the same shared method, each having a different parameter list. In fact, it is possible to have both member and shared methods by the same name by using overloading, as long as their method signatures differ.

The default scope for a shared method is Public. It is possible to restrict the scope of a shared method to Friend, Protected, or Private by prefixing the declaration with the appropriate scope. In fact, when overloading a method we can have different scopes on each implementation – as long as the method signatures are different as we discussed when covering overloading.

A good example of how shared methods are used comes from the .NET system class libraries. When we want to open a text file for input we typically make use of a shared method on the File class:

```
Dim infile As StreamReader = File.OpenText("words.txt")
Dim strIn As String

strIn = infile.ReadLine()
```

No object of type File is created here. The OpenText() method is a shared method that opens a file and returns a StreamReader object for our use. Another example comes from the System.Guid data type. This class represents a globally unique identifier (GUID) value, but creating a new value is handled via a shared method:

```
Dim guidID As Guid

guidID = Guid.NewGuid()
```

The NewGuid() method is called directly from the Guid class. It creates a new Guid object and returns it as a result.

Shared Variables

There is another type of shared member we can create. There are times when it is nice to share a value across all instances of a class – when every object of a given type should share the same variable. This is accomplished through the use of **shared variables**.

A shared variable is declared using the Shared keyword, much like a shared method:

```
Public Class MyCounter
   Private Shared mintCount As Integer
End Class
```

As with shared methods, we can scope the shared variable as required. Where `Shared` methods are `Public` by default, `Shared` variables are `Private` by default.

> **In general, it is good practice to always explicitly define the scope of methods and variables to avoid confusion.**

The important thing about shared variables is that they are common across all instances of the class. We could enhance our class slightly as follows:

```
Public Class MyCounter
   Private Shared mintCount As Integer

   Public Sub New()
     mintCount += 1
   End Sub

   Public ReadOnly Property Count() As Integer
     Get
        Return mintCount
     End Get
   End Property
End Class
```

As we create each instance of the class the counter is incremented by one.

The += operator is new to Visual Basic .NET and is covered in Chapter 4.

At any point, we can retrieve the count value via the `Count` property. Thus, if we run the following client code we will get a resulting value of **3**:

```
Protected Sub Button1_Click(ByVal sender As Object, _
   ByVal e As System.EventArgs)
   Dim obj As MyCounter

   obj = New MyCounter()
   obj = New MyCounter()
   obj = New MyCounter()
   MsgBox(obj.Count)
End Sub
```

If we run it again we will get **6**, then **9**, and so forth. As long as our application is running the counter will remain valid. Once our application terminates the counter also goes away.

This technique can be very useful for server processes that run 'forever', since they can keep usage counters or other values over time very easily. The values are only reset when the process is restarted.

Global Values

Another common use for shared variables is to provide a form of global variable. Given a `Public` scoped shared variable:

```
Public Class TheClass
   Public Shared MyGlobal As Integer
End Class
```

We can then use this variable throughout our client code:

```
TheClass.MyGlobal += 5
```

This variable will be available to any code within our application, providing a very nice mechanism for sharing values between components, classes, modules, and so on.

Shared Events

Events may be declared as `Shared`. You should note that shared methods can only raise shared events, not non-shared events. For instance:

```
Public Class EventSource
   Shared Event SharedEvent()

   Public Shared Sub DoShared()
     RaiseEvent SharedEvent()
   End Sub
End Class
```

A shared event can be raised by both shared and non-shared methods:

```
Public Class EventSource
   Public Event TheEvent()
   Shared Event SharedEvent()

   Public Sub DoSomething()
     RaiseEvent TheEvent()
     RaiseEvent SharedEvent()
   End Sub

   Public Shared Sub DoShared()
     RaiseEvent SharedEvent()
   End Sub
End Class
```

Attempting to raise a non-shared event from a shared method will result in a syntax error.

Inheritance

While the OO features of VB have been very powerful and useful, we have been held back in many cases by the lack of implementation inheritance in the language.

Implementation inheritance is the ability of a class to gain the interface and behaviors of an existing class. The process by which this is accomplished is called **subclassing**. When we create a new class that inherits the interface and behaviors from an existing class, we have created a subclass of the original class. This is also known as an **'is-a' relationship**, where the new class 'is-a' type of original class.

Implementation inheritance, often just called inheritance, should not be confused with the concept of multiple interfaces, which is sometimes called **interface inheritance**. The term interface inheritance is somewhat misleading and mischaracterizes the nature of multiple interfaces as created using the `Interface` and `Implements` keywords. In this section we are talking about *real* inheritance. Later in the chapter we'll discuss multiple interfaces.

Much of this confusion stems from the way classes, objects, and interfaces worked in the world of COM. In COM (and thus prior versions of VB), the concept of a formal interface was central to the nature of the platform itself. A COM class always had a separate construct known as an interface. VB hid this fact from us in most cases, but we still tended to refer to the `Public` members of a class as belonging to that class's native or default interface.

In .NET the platform itself is fundamentally different and the interface is no longer so important. In .NET the class plays the central role, and classes often have `Public` methods that are directly part of the class. The concept of a native or default interface separate from the class doesn't really translate into .NET. You can think of all the `Public` members of a class as being a native or default interface if that helps the transition to the new platform – just remember that they are not part of some separate formal interface as they were in COM – they are directly part of the class itself.

*In .NET, a **class** has its own interface. This concept is key to understanding inheritance, since it is the interface and behaviors of each class that are inherited through the inheritance process.*

There is a lot of terminology surrounding inheritance. The original class, from which we inherit interface and behavior, is known by the following interchangeable terms:

❑ Parent class

❑ Superclass

❑ Base class

The new class that inherits the interface and behaviors is known by the following interchangeable terms:

❑ Child class

❑ Subclass

Inheritance is also sometimes called **generalization**. In fact this is the term used within the **Universal Modeling Language** (**UML**) – the most commonly used object diagramming notation.

Inheritance is often viewed through the lens of biology, where, for example, a dog is a canine and a canine is a mammal. Hence, by being a canine, a dog inherits all the attributes and behavior of a mammal. While useful for visualization, these analogies only go so far.

> For interested object-oriented aficionados, Visual Basic .NET does not allow multiple inheritance –
> where a subclass is created by inheriting from more than one base class. This feature is not
> supported by the .NET runtime and thus is not available from Visual Basic .NET. Visual Basic
> .NET does allow deep inheritance hierarchies where a class is subclassed from a class that is
> subclassed, but it doesn't allow a class to be subclassed from multiple base classes all at once.

We can contrast inheritance, an 'is-a' relationship, with another type of parent-child relationship – the **'has-a' relationship**. This is also known as aggregation or containment.

In a 'has-a' relationship, the parent object owns or contains one or more of the child objects, but the child objects are of different types from the parent. For instance, an Invoice has-a LineItem. The LineItem object isn't subclassed from Invoice – it is an entirely different class that just happens to be owned by the Invoice parent. This distinction is important, because the terms *parent* and *child* are used frequently when working with objects – sometimes when referring to inheritance and sometimes when referring to aggregation.

Within this section, we will use the terms base class, child, and subclass – all in the context of inheritance.

Creating Subclasses

To explore inheritance, consider a business example with a sales order that has line items. We might have product line items and service line items. Both are examples of line items, but both are somewhat different as well. While we could certainly implement ProductLine and ServiceLine classes separately, they would have a lot of common code between them. Redundant code is hard to maintain, so it would be nicer if they could somehow directly share the common code between them.

This is where inheritance comes into play. Using inheritance, we can create a LineItem class that contains all the code common to any sort of line item. Then we can create ProductLine and ServiceLine classes that inherit from LineItem – thus automatically gaining all the common code – including interface and implementation in an OO form.

A simple LineItem class might appear as:

```
Public Class LineItem
   Private mintID As Integer
   Private mstrItem As String
   Private msngPrice As Single
   Private mintQuantity As Integer

   Public Property ID() As Integer
     Get
       Return mintID
     End Get
     Set(ByVal Value As Integer)
       mintID = value
     End Set
   End Property
```

```
   Public Property Item() As String
     Get
       Return mstrItem
     End Get
     Set(ByVal Value As String)
       mstrItem = Value
     End Set
   End Property

   Public Property Price() As Single
     Get
       Return msngPrice
     End Get
     Set(ByVal Value As Single)
       msngPrice = Value
     End Set
   End Property

   Public Property Quantity() As Integer
     Get
       Return mintQuantity
     End Get
     Set(ByVal Value As Integer)
       mintQuantity = Value
     End Set
   End Property

   Public Function Amount() As Single
     Return mintQuantity * msngPrice
   End Function
End Class
```

This class has things common to any line item – some basic data fields and a method to calculate the cost of the item.

If a line item is for a product, however, we might have additional requirements. Perhaps we want to provide a product description as well:

```
Public Class ProductLine
  Inherits LineItem

  Private mstrDescription As String

  Public ReadOnly Property Description() As String
    Get
      Return mstrDescription
    End Get
  End Property

  Public Sub New(ByVal ProductID As String)
    Item = ProductID
    ' load product data from database
    mstrDescription = "Test product description"
  End Sub
End Class
```

Note the use of the `Inherits` statement:

```
Inherits LineItem
```

It is this statement that causes the `ProductLine` class to gain all the interface elements and behaviors from the `LineItem` class. This means that we can have client code like this:

```
Private Sub Button1_Click(ByVal sender As System.Object, _
    ByVal e As System.EventArgs) Handles Button1.Click

    Dim pl As ProductLine

    pl = New ProductLine("123abc")
    MsgBox(pl.Item)
    MsgBox(pl.Description)
End Sub
```

This code makes use of both the `Item` property (from the `LineItem` class) and the `Description` property from the `ProductLine` class. Both are equally part of the `ProductLine` class, since it is a subclass of `LineItem`.

Likewise, a line item for a service might have a date for when the service was provided, but otherwise be the same as any other line item:

```
Public Class ServiceLine
   Inherits LineItem

   Private mdtDateProvided As Date

   Public Sub New()
      Quantity = 1
   End Sub

   Public Property DateProvided() As Date
      Get
         Return mdtDateProvided
      End Get
      Set(ByVal Value As Date)
         mdtDateProvided = Value
      End Set
   End Property
End Class
```

Again, notice the use of the `Inherits` statement that indicates that this is a subclass of the `LineItem` class. The `DateProvided` property is simply added to the interface gained from the `LineItem` class.

Preventing Inheritance

By default any class we create can be used as a base class from which other classes can be created. There are times when we might want to create a class that cannot be subclassed. To do this we can use the `NotInheritable` keyword in our class declaration:

```
Public NotInheritable Class ProductLine

End Class
```

When this keyword is used, no other code may use the Inherits keyword to create a subclass of our class.

Inheritance and Scoping

When we create a subclass through inheritance, the new class gains all the Public and Friend methods, properties, and variables from the original class. Anything declared as Private in the original class will not be directly available to our code in the new subclass.

The exception to this is the New() method. Constructor methods must be re-implemented in each subclass. We will discuss this in more detail later in the chapter.

For instance, we might rewrite the Amount methods from the LineItem class slightly:

```
Public Function Amount() As Single
   Return CalcAmount
End Function

Private Function CalcAmount() As Single
   Return mintQuantity * msngPrice
End Function
```

With this change, we can see that the Public method Amount() makes use of a Private method to do its work.

When we subclass LineItem to create the ServiceLine class, any ServiceLine object will have an Amount() method because it is declared as Public in the base class. The CalcAmount() method, on the other hand, is declared as Private and so neither the ServiceLine class nor any client code will have any access to it.

Does this mean that the Amount() method will break when called through the ServiceLine object? Not at all. Since the Amount() method's code resides in the LineItem class, it has access to the CalcAmount() method even though the ServiceLine class can't see the method.

For instance, in our client code we might have something like this:

```
Protected Sub Button1_Click(ByVal sender As Object, _
   ByVal e As System.EventArgs)

   Dim sl As ServiceLine

   sl = New ServiceLine()
   sl.Item = "delivery"
   sl.Price = 20
   sl.DateProvided = Now

   MsgBox(sl.Amount)
End Sub
```

The result is displayed in a message box, thus illustrating that the CalcAmount() method was called on our behalf even though neither our client code, nor the ServiceLine code directly made the call.

Protected Scope

Sometimes Public and Private aren't enough. If we declare something as Private it is totally restricted to our class, while if we declare something as Public (or Friend) it is available to both subclasses and client code. There are times when it would be nice to create a method that is available to subclasses, but *not* to client code.

This is where the Protected scope comes into play. When something is declared as Protected, it is not available to any code outside of the class. However, it *is* available to classes that are derived from our class through inheritance. For example:

```
Public Class ParentClass
   Protected TheValue As Integer
End Class

Public Class SubClass
   Inherits ParentClass

   Public Function GetValue() As Integer
     Return TheValue
   End Function
End Class
```

Here we have a parent base class with a Protected member – TheValue. This variable is not available to any client code. However, the variable is fully available to any code within SubClass, because it inherits from the parent.

In this example, SubClass has a Public method that actually does return the protected value – but the variable TheValue is not directly available to any client code (that is, code outside the class).

Protected Friend Scope

A final scope we have at our disposal is Protected Friend. This is a combination of the Protected and Friend scopes, and acts like both at once.

Since it has the Friend attribute, a method declared with this scope will be accessible to any other code in our Visual Basic .NET project.

However, since it also has the Protected attribute the method will be accessible to any subclass that inherits from our class. This includes subclasses that are created *outside* of our Visual Basic .NET project.

Overloading Base Class Methods in Subclasses

Earlier in the chapter we discussed how methods can be overloaded within a class. All that is required is to create more than one method of the same name, but with different method signatures.

Overloading also works with inheritance. This allows our subclass to add new implementations of methods that already exist in the base class, as long as the new implementations have different method signatures. For instance:

```
Public Class ParentClass
  Public Sub DoSomething()
    MsgBox("Parent class")
  End Function
End Class

Public Class SubClass
  Inherits ParentClass

  Public Overloads Sub DoSomething(ByVal Text As String)
    MsgBox("SubClass: " & Text)
  End Function
End Class
```

Notice that both classes implement a DoSomething() method, but each has a different method signature. The SubClass implementation also includes the Overloads keyword:

```
Public Overloads Sub DoSomething(ByVal Text As String)
```

This is required to achieve overloading in subclasses. If we omit this keyword we will be doing **shadowing** – which will give us an entirely different effect. We will discuss shadowing later in the chapter.

Since the method is overloaded, we can now write client code such as:

```
Dim obj As New SubClass()

obj.DoSomething()
obj.DoSomething("hello world")
```

Both versions of the method are available. Our subclass has merely extended the original interface by adding a new version of the method.

Overriding Base Class Methods

One key attribute of inheritance is that a subclass not only gains the behaviors of the original class, but it can also override those behaviors. We have already seen how a subclass can *extend* the original class by adding new Public, Protected, and Friend methods. However, by using the concept of overriding, a subclass can *alter* the behaviors of methods that were declared on the base class.

By default, methods cannot be overridden by a subclass. To allow them to be overridden, the base class must declare the method using the Overridable keyword:

```
Public Class Parent
  Public Overridable Sub DoSomething()
    MsgBox("Hello from Parent")
  End Sub
End Class
```

We can also explicitly disallow overriding through the use of the `NotOverridable` keyword. Of course since this is the default, this keyword is rarely used.

> *However, it may be a good practice to explicitly define whether a method can or cannot be overridden to increase the clarity of code and to protect against the possibility that the default behavior might change.*

If we then create a subclass, we can optionally override the behavior of `DoSomething()` by using the `Overrides` keyword:

```
Public Class SubClass
  Inherits Parent

  Public Overrides Sub DoSomething()
    MsgBox("Hello from SubClass")
  End Sub
End Class
```

Now we can write client code such as:

```
Dim obj As New SubClass()

obj.DoSomething()
```

Since we created an object of class `SubClass`, and then called the `DoSomething()` method on it, the result will be a message dialog containing the text Hello from SubClass.

Virtual Methods

Consider the following client code:

```
Dim obj As Parent

obj = New SubClass()
obj.DoSomething()
```

First off, it seems odd to declare a variable of type `Parent`, but then create a `SubClass` object instead. This is perfectly acceptable, however – it is yet another way of implementing polymorphism. Since `SubClass` 'is-a' `Parent`, any `Parent` or `SubClass` variable can hold a reference to a `SubClass` object. This is true in general. When using inheritance, a variable of the parent type can always hold references to any child type created from the parent, even if we are multiple levels deep in the inheritance hierarchy.

What may be more surprising is the message that is displayed in our message box when this code is run. The message we see is Hello from SubClass.

How can this be? The variable is declared as type `Parent` – shouldn't the `Parent` implementation be called? The reason the `DoSomething()` implementation from the child class is called is that the method is **virtual**. The concept of a virtual method is such that the 'bottom-most' implementation of the method is always used rather than the parent implementation – regardless of the data type of the variable being used in the client code.

> **All `Overridable` methods in Visual Basic .NET are virtual.**

The term 'bottom-most' comes from the typical way a chain of inherited objects is diagrammed. Usually, the base class is displayed, with the subclasses underneath. If the subclasses are also subclassed, then those classes are shown even further down. This is illustrated by the following UML diagram:

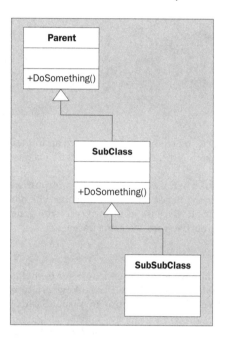

Regardless of the *variable* data type, the implementation of `DoSomething()` will be invoked based on the actual class we use to create the object. In our previous example, we created an object of type `SubClass`, thus ensuring that the `DoSomething()` implementation in that class would be invoked.

If we create an object from type `Parent` with the following code:

```
Dim obj As Parent

obj = New Parent()
obj.DoSomething()
```

the `DoSomething()` implementation in the `Parent` class will be invoked since that is the type of object we created. We might also create the object from the `SubSubClass` class:

```
Dim obj As Parent

obj = New SubSubClass()
obj.DoSomething()
```

In this case, the class doesn't directly implement `DoSomething()`, so we start looking back up the inheritance chain for an implementation of this method:

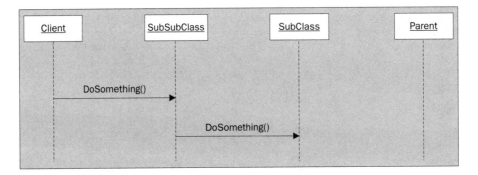

The next class up that chain is `SubClass`, which *does* have an implementation – so it is that implementation which is invoked. No code from the `Parent` class is invoked at all.

Virtual methods are very useful when we implement polymorphism using inheritance. A base class data type can hold a reference to any subclass object, but it is the type of that specific object that determines the implementation of the method. Because of this we can write generic routines that operate on many types of object as long as they derive from the same base class.

Me Keyword

The `Me` keyword is used any time we want our code to refer to methods within the current object. This was used in VB6 – when we might have utilized the `Me` keyword to refer to the current form, or the current instance of an object – and the same is true in Visual Basic .NET.

> *The `Me` keyword is analogous to the `this` keyword in C++ and C# languages.*

The `Me` keyword is usually optional, since any method call is assumed to refer to the current object unless explicitly noted otherwise. It can be very useful when working with inheritance, however, since the `Me` keyword allows us to leverage IntelliSense to get a list of the methods and properties supported by our class – including those we have inherited.

The exception is when we are working with **shadowed** variables.

> *We can also shadow methods and properties. There's even a `Shadows` keyword to formalize the concept. We will discuss all of this later in the chapter.*

A shadowed variable is a procedure-level variable with the same name as a class-level variable. For instance:

```
Public Class TheClass
   Private strName As String

   Public Sub DoSomething()
     Dim strName As String
```

```
        strName = "Fred"
    End Sub
End Class
```

Here the variable strName is declared at the class level *and* within the DoSomething() method. Within that method only the local, or shadowed, variable is used unless we explicitly reference the class-level variable with the Me keyword:

```
Public Sub DoSomething()
  Dim strName As String

  strName = "Fred"       ' sets the local variable's value
  Me.strName = "Mary"    ' sets the class level variable's value
End Sub
```

Here we can see that strName can be used to reference the local variable, while Me.strName can be used to reference the class-level variable.

As useful as the Me keyword can be for referring to the current object, when we start working with inheritance, it isn't enough to do everything we want. There are two issues we need to deal with:

❑   We may want to explicitly call into our *base* class

❑   We may want to ensure that the code in *our* class is being called, rather than the code in some subclass that has inherited our code

The second point is particularly important. Although we have said that we can use the Me keyword to refer to members within the current object, more precisely this keyword will reference the bottom-most member (with this name) of the current inheritance chain.

Therefore, say we created a virtual (overridable) method called OtherStuff(). Then we created a subclass of TheClass, and implemented an override of OtherStuff() in this subclass. In this case, calling OtherStuff() from within TheClass will actually call the overriding implementation of OtherStuff() in the subclass, which is probably not what we want. We will see a way around this problem, via the MyClass keyword, a little later.

MyBase Keyword

At times we might want to explicitly call methods in our base class. Remember that when we override a method it is virtual – so the method call will invoke the 'bottom-most' implementation – not the parent implementation. However, sometimes we might need that parent implementation.

To invoke the base class from within our subclass we can use the MyBase keyword. For instance:

```
Public Class SubClass
  Inherits Parent

  Public Overrides Sub DoSomething()
    MsgBox("Hello from subclass")
    MyBase.DoSomething()
  End Sub
End Class
```

If we run our client code now, we will get two message boxes. First, we will get the message from the subclass, followed by the one from the base class. This is illustrated by the following diagram:

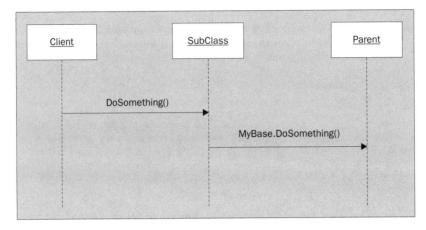

The `MyBase` keyword can be used to invoke or use any `Public`, `Friend`, or `Protected` element from the base class. This includes all of those elements directly on the base class, and also any elements the base class inherited from other classes higher in the inheritance chain.

`MyBase` *only* refers to the immediate parent of the current class. If we create a `SubSubClass` that inherits from `SubClass`, the `MyBase` keyword would refer to the `SubClass` code, not the `Parent` code. There is no direct way to navigate more than one level up the inheritance chain.

MyClass Keyword

A more complex scenario is one where the code in our class might end up invoking code from other classes subclassed *from* our class.

When we create a class, we'll frequently make calls from within our class to other methods within that same class. This occurs in the following code:

```
Public Class Parent
  Public Sub DoSomething()
    OtherStuff()
  End Sub

  Public Overridable Sub OtherStuff()
    MsgBox("Parent other stuff")
  End Sub
End Class
```

In this case, the `DoSomething()` method calls the `OtherStuff()` method to do some work. Notice however, that `OtherStuff()` is marked as `Overridable`, so a subclass might provide a different implementation for the method. For example:

```
Public Class SubClass
  Inherits Parent
```

```
      Public Overrides Sub OtherStuff()
         MsgBox("SubClass other stuff")
      End Sub
   End Class
```

As we discussed earlier, Visual Basic .NET methods are virtual – which means that an object of type `SubClass` will always invoke `OtherStuff()` from `SubClass` rather than from the `Parent` class. This is true even for code in the `Parent` class itself – so when the `DoSomething()` method calls the `OtherStuff()` method it will invoke the overridden implementation in `SubClass`. This can be illustrated by the following client code:

```
   Dim obj As New SubClass()

   obj.DoSomething()
```

We will see a dialog displaying **SubClass other stuff**.

Here we can see that the client calls `DoSomething()`, which is actually invoked from the `Parent` class. The `Parent` class then calls `OtherStuff()`, but since it is implemented in `SubClass`, that is the implementation that is invoked.

If we don't want this behavior – if we want the code in the `Parent` class to know for certain that it is calling the `OtherStuff()` implementation in `Parent` – we need to use the `MyClass` keyword:

```
   Public Class Parent
      Public Sub DoSomething()
         MyClass.OtherStuff()
      End Sub

      Public Overridable Sub OtherStuff()
         MsgBox("Parent other stuff")
      End Sub
   End Class
```

We shouldn't use the `Me` keyword, because the `OtherStuff()` method is virtual so we can't be sure the `Parent` class's implementation will be called. `MyClass`, on the other hand, forces the call to be handled by the code in the same class as the call – in this case the `Parent` class.

By using the `MyClass` keyword we get the behavior shown in the following diagram:

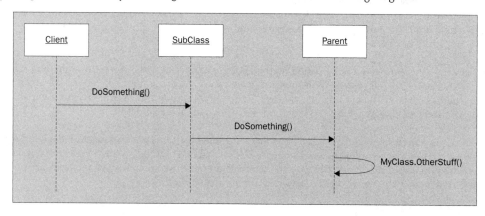

Overriding the Constructor Method

We have already seen how we can override methods, and how to use the Me, MyBase, and MyClass keywords to interact with the various overridden methods in our inheritance chain. However, there are special rules that govern the process of overriding the New() constructor method.

New() methods aren't automatically carried from a base class to a subclass like normal methods. Each subclass must define its own constructors, though those constructors may call into the base class using the MyBase keyword:

```
Public Class SubClass
  Inherits Parent

  Public Sub New()
    MyBase.New()
    ' other initialization code goes here
  End Sub
End Class
```

When calling the base class constructor, that call *must* be the first line in our constructor code – anything else is an error. This is totally optional, however, since the (parameterless) constructor of the base class is automatically called on our behalf before our constructor code begins to run, unless we make that call manually.

> If all constructor methods of the base class require parameters then we must implement at least one constructor in our subclass and we *must* explicitly call **MyBase.New()** from within our constructors.

As we discussed earlier, the New() method can be overloaded, providing various implementations. If our base class provides alternative implementations of New(), we may want to manually make the call in order to cause the correct implementation to be called, based on our requirements.

Shadowing Methods

Overloading allows us to extend the base class by adding new versions of existing methods as long as the method signatures are different. Overriding allows us to replace existing methods on the base class with a new implementation – given the permission of the base class through the use of the Overridable keyword.

Shadowing allows us to replace existing methods of the base class without regard to method signatures or the Overridable keyword. With shadowing we can replace any method, property or even variable from the base class with anything else that we desire – another method, a property, or a variable. In fact, we can even change a base class method into a variable if we so desire.

To override a method with the Overrides keyword, the base class method must be declared with the Overridable keyword. This makes the method into a virtual method – which means that it can be overridden in a subclass. Normally we can't override a non-virtual method. All methods are non-virtual unless they have the Overridable keyword in their declaration.

The `Shadows` keyword, on the other hand, allows us to override a base class method whether it was declared as `Overridable` or not.

> **Overriding a method not marked with `Overridable` is very dangerous, as the base class developer obviously didn't *intend* that the method be overridden. Use this capability with extreme caution.**

This means that we could have a base class such as:

```
Public Class Parent
  Public Sub DoWork()
    MsgBox("Base class DoWork")
  End Sub
End Class
```

Normally we could not override the `DoWork()` method, since it is not declared as `Overridable`, and the default is `NotOverridable`. However, by using the `Shadows` keyword we *can* override it in a subclass:

```
Public Class SubClass
  Inherits Parent

  Public Shadows Sub DoWork()
    MsgBox("Subclass DoWork")
  End Sub
End Class
```

We can now write client code such as:

```
Dim obj As New SubClass()

obj.DoWork()
```

The result is a message box displaying the text Subclass DoWork – indicating that we have called the shadowed version of the method.

The rules governing how shadowed methods are invoked are different from the rules for overridden methods. When we call a method that has been overridden, we always get the implementation of the method that is furthest down the inheritance chain, as we discussed earlier in this chapter. This occurs regardless of the data type of the *variable* referencing the object.

With shadowing, however, the data type of the object itself doesn't matter – it is the data type of the *variable* holding a reference to the object that dictates which version of the shadowed method will be invoked.

This means that we can change our client code to create an object of type `SubClass`, and reference it from a variable of type `Parent` and get different results:

```
Dim obj As Parent
obj = New SubClass()

obj.DoWork()
```

When this code is run we'll see a message box showing the text **Base class DoWork** – even though the object is of type `SubClass`. This is exactly opposite to the behavior we'd get from an overridden method.

In most cases the behavior we'll want for our methods is accomplished by the `Overrides` keyword and virtual methods. However, in those cases where we want to implement non-virtual methods, the `Shadows` keyword provides us with the needed functionality.

Arbitrary Shadowing

As though it wasn't dangerous enough to override a base class method that was not intended to be overridden, we can also use the `Shadows` keyword to entirely alter the nature of a method. This means we can change a `Sub` into a `Function` or a `Property` – or even a regular variable. However, this type of extreme change can make our subclass entirely incompatible with the base class or other classes derived from the base class, and so it is not a recommended practice.

Using this capability, we could have a `Parent` base class, and then we could then create a subclass that changes `DoWork()` from a method into a variable:

```
Public Class SubClass
    Private Shadows DoWork As Boolean
End Class
```

Notice that we've not only changed `DoWork()` from a `Sub` into a `Boolean` variable, but we've also changed its scope to `Private`. Shadowing allows us to totally recreate the element – ignoring whatever it might have been in the original base class.

At this point we cannot use the `DoWork()` method when interacting with an object of type `SubClass` through a variable of type `SubClass`. This means the following code will *not* work:

```
Dim obj As New SubClass()

obj.DoWork()
```

As with shadowing methods, however, it is the data type of the *variable* that counts, not the data type of the actual object. As a result of this, the following code *will* work:

```
Dim obj As Parent
obj = New SubClass()

obj.DoWork()
```

When run, this code will display a message box showing the text **Base class DoWork**. Because the variable's data type is `Parent`, we are invoking the version of `DoWork()` from the base class rather than attempting to invoke the shadowed variable provided by `SubClass`.

Abstract Base Classes and Methods

So far, we have seen how to inherit from a class, how to overload and override methods, and how virtual methods work. In all of our examples so far, the base classes have been useful in their own right. Sometimes, however, we want to create a class such that it can only be used as a base class for inheritance.

MustInherit Keyword

Returning to our original sales order line item example, it may make little sense for anyone to create an object based on the generic `LineItem` class. In fact, we may want to ensure that only more specific subclasses derived from `LineItem` can be created. This is done using the `MustInherit` keyword in the class declaration:

```
Public MustInherit Class LineItem
```

Typically, no other change is required in our class. The result of this keyword is that it is no longer possible to write client code that creates an instance of the `LineItem` class, so the following would cause a syntax error:

```
Dim obj As New LineItem()
```

Instead, to use the code in the `LineItem` class, we *must* create subclasses and use those throughout our application.

MustOverride Keyword

Another option we have is to create a method that must be overridden by a subclass. We might want to do this when we create a base class that defines a method, but relies on subclasses to provide the proper implementation of this method. This is accomplished by using the `MustOverride` keyword on a method declaration:

```
Public MustOverride Sub CalcPrice()
```

Notice that there is no `End Sub` or any other code associated with the method.

When using `MustOverride`, we *cannot* provide any implementation for the method in our class. Such a method is called an **abstract method** or **pure virtual function**, since it only defines the interface and no implementation.

Methods declared in this manner *must* be overridden in any subclass that inherits from our base class. If we don't override one of these methods, we will generate a syntax error in the subclass and it won't compile.

Creating Abstract Base Classes

We can combine the previous two concepts – using both `MustInherit` and `MustOverride` – to create something called an **abstract base class**. This is a class that provides no implementation, only the interface definitions from which a subclass can be created. An example might be as follows:

```
Public MustInherit Class Parent
  Public MustOverride Sub DoSomething()
  Public MustOverride Sub DoOtherStuff()
End Class
```

This technique can be very useful when creating frameworks or the high-level conceptual elements of a system. Any class that inherits `Parent` must implement (override) both `DoSomething()` and `DoOtherStuff()` or a syntax error will result.

In some ways an abstract base class is very comparable to defining an interface using the `Interface` keyword. We'll discuss the `Interface` keyword in detail later in this chapter. For now, be aware that the `Interface` keyword is used to formally declare an interface that can be implemented using the `Implements` keyword as in VB6.

We could define the same interface as shown in this example with the following code:

```
Public Interface IParent
  Sub DoSomething()
  Sub DoOtherStuff()
End Interface
```

Any class that implements the `IParent` interface must implement both `DoSomething()` and `DoOtherStuff()` or a syntax error will result – and in that regard this technique is similar to an abstract base class. There are differences, however.

In particular, when we create a new class by subclassing the `Parent` class, that class will directly contain the methods, properties, and events defined by the abstract base class as part of its interface. Any subclasses we create further down the inheritance hierarchy will also have these methods as part of their interface. This is illustrated by the following diagram:

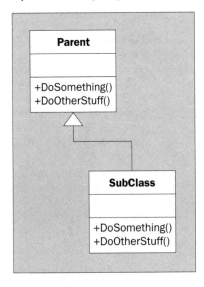

This UML diagram shows the abstract `Parent` base class, and a new `SubClass` that inherits from it, providing implementations for the two methods.

With the interface approach, the new class must provide implementation for the defined methods, just as it would with inheritance. However, these methods are not part of the interface of the class, nor will they be part of the interface of any subsequently created subclasses. Instead, this class and any of its subclasses now have a secondary interface that contains these methods. This is illustrated by the following diagram:

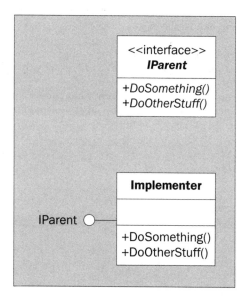

Notice that there is no inheritance relationship between the interface and the class. The class implements the interface, and inside the class are a couple of `Private` methods that are used to provide that implementation. The interface of the class itself has no methods at all – to use these methods we need to make use of the secondary interface.

We will discuss multiple interfaces later in the chapter, at which point it will become even more clear how inheritance differs from the ability to implement multiple interfaces.

The Effect of Inheritance on Events

Inheritance has some interesting effects on the way events work. Subclasses can receive events from their base classes, and with some extra work, a subclass can even raise a base class's event.

To explore how events work, assume we have the following base class:

```
Public Class Parent
   Public Event ParentEvent()
Public Sub DoSomething()
   RaiseEvent ParentEvent()
   End Sub
End Class
```

It is no surprise that code in this class can raise the `ParentEvent` event. Any subclasses derived from this class will also have the event as part of their interface, so client code can declare the subclass using the `WithEvents` keyword and handle the event.

Note that `Shared` events are not inherited by subclasses. `Shared` events are raised from a specific class, and so to handle those events we are required to work with exactly that class.

However, the subclasses cannot directly raise the event using the `RaiseEvent` keyword. This may pose a challenge, since there are times when actions of the subclass should raise the event. To handle this, we can add a new method to the base class:

```
Public Class Parent
   Public Event ParentEvent()

   Public Sub DoSomething()
     RaiseEvent ParentEvent()
   End Sub

   Protected Sub RaiseParentEvent()
     RaiseEvent ParentEvent()
   End Sub
End Class
```

Since this is a `Protected` method it is only available to subclasses, and they can use it to raise the event when needed. For instance, we might create a subclass like this:

```
Public Class SubClass
   Inherits Parent

   Public Sub DoOtherStuff()
     RaiseParentEvent()
   End Sub
End Class
```

This class is derived from `Parent` through the use of the `Inherits` keyword, gaining not only properties and methods, but also events from the base class. It then uses the `Protected` method to raise the event.

Events can be declared with any scope. Those `Private` in scope can only be received by the sending object, while those `Public` in scope can be received by any object. `Protected` events can only be received by objects created by the defining class or subclasses, while events declared as `Friend` can be received by any object within the Visual Basic .NET project.

To handle an event raised by the base class, we use the `MyBase` keyword in the `Handles` clause:

```
Public Class SubClass
   Inherits Parent

   Public Sub DoOtherStuff()
     RaiseParentEvent()
   End Sub

   Private Sub SubClass_ParentEvent() Handles MyBase.ParentEvent

   End Sub
End Class
```

This allows a subclass to receive any events raised by its base class.

Unlike methods, events cannot be overloaded using the `Overloads` keyword. A class can only define one event with any given name. Since any subclass will automatically gain the event from its base class, the `Overrides` keyword makes no sense and cannot be used with events.

Interfaces

VB has, for some time, allowed us to create objects with more than one interface. This was done using the `Implements` keyword. Any time our class implemented a new interface we were required to write code to implement each method on the interface. While inheritance provides a preferable alternative to this in many cases, there are still occasions when we may want to have our objects implement multiple interfaces.

Multiple interfaces remain very valuable when designing frameworks or building generic code that can act against any object that implements a specific interface. We can also use secondary interfaces to simulate the concept of multiple inheritance.

Where inheritance allows us to implement an 'is-a' relationship, multiple interfaces allow us to implement an 'act-as' relationship. When we inherit from a base class, our new subclass 'is-a' more specific type of that base class. Contrast this with interfaces, where implementing an interface doesn't mean our new class *is* of that type, it simply means it can 'act-as' that type.

Visual Basic .NET preserves the `Implements` keyword, and in fact the entire concept of interfaces is enhanced and made simpler as compared to VB6. However, Visual Basic .NET introduces a formalized structure for declaring interfaces. It also changes the syntax used in classes that implement an interface, making our code much more intuitive and clear.

Interface Declaration

The most visible enhancement is the introduction of a formal syntax for declaring an interface. This is done by using the `Interface` keyword, which we met before in an earlier section:

```
Public Interface MyInterface
   Event MyEvent()
   Sub MyMethod()
   Function MyFunction(ByVal Param1 As Integer) As Integer
   Property MyProperty() As String
End Interface
```

This approach is much more formal than the approaches available in VB6. It is also more powerful – notice that not only can we declare Sub, Function, and Property methods, but also declare events as a formal part of an interface. All of the elements described in this interface must be implemented by any class that chooses to implement the interface.

The scope of all methods and events in the interface is controlled by the scope of the interface itself. In this example all the interface elements are Public.

Overloading Interface Methods

As with methods in a class, methods in an interface can be overloaded. The rules for overloading are the same as we discussed earlier in the chapter – each overloaded declaration must have a unique method signature based on the data types of the parameters. Here's an example of an interface that contains overloads for the methods MyMethod() and MyFunction():

```
Public Interface MyInterface
   Sub MyMethod()
   Sub MyMethod(Data As String)
   Function MyFunction(ByVal Param1 As Integer) As Integer
   Function MyFunction(ByVal Param1 As Single) As Integer
End Interface
```

When a class implements an interface with overloaded methods, the class must implement each of the overloaded method declarations.

Implementing an Interface

As with VB6, implementing an interface is done through the use of the Implements keyword:

```
Public Class TheClass
   Implements MyInterface
End Class
```

In VB6, we would implement the various interface elements as a set of specially named Private methods, like this:

```
Private Sub MyInterface_MyMethod()
   ' implementation goes here
End Sub
```

The fact that this method implements part of the interface is only shown by its naming – a pretty obscure approach. We could declare this as Public and make it available for external use, but the name of the method couldn't change. Visual Basic .NET addresses this issue by providing a clear, concise syntax for implementing the interface – again through the application of the Implements keyword.

We can simply mark a method in our class as being the implementation of a specific method from the interface:

```
Public Sub MyMethod() Implements MyInterface.MyMethod
```

So, to implement our example interface, we'd have code such as:

```
Public Class Implementer
   Implements MyInterface

   Public Event MyEvent() Implements MyInterface.MyEvent

   Public Function MyFunction(ByVal Param1 As Integer) As Integer _
     Implements MyInterface.MyFunction

   End Function

   Public Sub MyMethod() Implements MyInterface.MyMethod

   End Sub

   Public Property MyProperty() As String _
       Implements MyInterface.MyProperty
     Get

     End Get
     Set(ByVal Value As String)

     End Set
   End Property
End Class
```

As with VB6, when we implement an interface, we must implement *all* of the elements in that interface – including events, methods, and properties.

We can now create client code that interacts with our object via this interface, in addition to the object's normal interface:

```
Dim obj As MyInterface

obj = New Implementer()
obj.MyMethod
```

Implementing Multiple Interfaces

A class can have more than one `Implements` statement – thus implementing more than one interface. Suppose we have the following interfaces:

```
Public Interface MyInterface
   Sub DoSomething()
End Interface

Public Interface OtherInterface
   Sub DoWork()
End Interface
```

235

We can construct a class that implements both interfaces:

```
Public Class TheClass
  Implements MyInterface
  Implements OtherInterface

End Class
```

Now we have a choice. We can implement separate methods to handle DoSomething and DoWork:

```
Private Sub DoSomething() Implements MyInterface.DoSomething
  ' implementation goes here
End Sub

Private Overloads Sub DoWork() Implements OtherInterface.DoWork
  ' implementation goes here
End Sub
```

Or, if they do the same thing, we can have a single method implement both methods:

```
Private Sub DoSomething() _
    Implements MyInterface.DoSomething, OtherInterface.DoWork
  ' implementation goes here
End Sub
```

As you can see, this is done by combining the list of implemented methods into a comma-separated list following the Implements keyword.

Cross-Language Inheritance

Visual Basic .NET is compiled to managed code – code that runs within the .NET Framework as discussed in Chapter 2. All managed code can interact with other managed code, regardless of the original language the managed code was compiled from. This means that we can create a class in one language and make use of it in another – in any way, including through inheritance.

In fact, we do this all the time. Much of the .NET system class library is written in C#, but we interact with and even inherit from those classes on a regular basis as we program in Visual Basic .NET.

Creating the Visual Basic .NET Base Class

For instance, we can create a Class Library project in Visual Basic .NET named vblib and add a simple class named Parent such as:

```
Public Class Parent
  Public Sub DoSomething()
    MsgBox("Parent DoSomething")
  End Sub
End Class
```

This will act as the base class from which we will create a subclass in C#.

Creating the C# Subclass

We can then add a new C# **Class Library** project to the solution (using **File | Add Project | New Project**) and name it **cslib**. Add a reference to our **vblib** project by using the **Project | Add Reference...** menu option. Also add a reference to `System.Windows.Forms.dll` so we can use Windows Forms classes.

> *While we are referencing this project directly within the IDE, we wouldn't need the Visual Basic .NET source code. Instead, we could have built the* `vblib` *project, thus creating an assembly, and then referenced that assembly from within the C# project to gain access to the base class.*

In the `Class1.cs` file change the code to appear as follows:

```
using System.Windows.Forms;
using vblib;

namespace cslib
{
  public class CsClass : Parent
  {
    public CsClass()
    {
      MessageBox.Show("csclass constructor");
    }
  }
}
```

This C# code shares common concepts with the Visual Basic .NET code we have seen so far in the book. However, C# is largely derived from C and C++ language syntax so things are a bit different. All lines of code must end with a semicolon to denote the end of the statement. Also, left and right brackets are used to form block structures. In Visual Basic .NET we might have a `Sub...End Sub` block, while in C# we will have { and }.

Let's walk through it to make everything clear. In C# the `using` keyword is equivalent to the `Imports` keyword in Visual Basic .NET. Since we are using both the `Systems.Windows.Forms` namespace and the namespace from our `vblib` project, we have `using` statements to make those namespaces easy to use:

```
using System.Windows.Forms;
using vblib;
```

In C#, we need to manually define the namespace for the file – Visual Studio .NET doesn't provide any automatic support for root namespaces when we are programming in C#. This is explicitly declared in each code module by using the `namespace` keyword:

```
namespace cslib
```

The next line of code declares the class we're creating and indicates that it is a subclass of `Parent`:

```
public class CsClass : Parent
```

In C# a subclass is declared by declaring a class, followed by a colon and then the name of the base class.

In Visual Basic .NET constructor methods are created using the reserved method name `New()`. In C#, constructors are created by using the name of the class itself as the method name:

```
public CsClass()
{
   MessageBox.Show("csclass constructor");
}
```

The brackets ({ and }) form a block structure within which we place the code for the method. In this case the method simply displays a dialog box indicating that the constructor method was invoked.

Now we can create client code to work with this new object.

Creating a Client Application

Use File | Add Project | New Project to add a new Visual Basic .NET Windows Application project to the solution.

In this new project add a reference to the cslib project by using the Project | Add Reference... menu option.

We also need to add a reference to the vblib project. Since cslib uses vblib, we need to reference both from our client application to ensure it has access to all the code needed for the solution. However, this can *not* be done by simply referencing the vblib project. We must use the Browse button on the .NET tab of the references dialog and navigate to the directory where the DLL is located. If we try to just reference the vblib project the references don't tie together properly and we will be unable to use CsClass in our code.

> *Presumably this is not intended behavior. Normally, it is perfectly acceptable to reference projects rather than directly referencing the DLL. The problem appears to be related to the fact that Visual Basic .NET and Visual C# .NET use slightly different directory structures as they compile and this is confusing Visual Studio .NET as it tries to find the DLLs to reference.*

Right-click on the project and choose the Set As Startup Project option so this project will be run when we press *F5*. Now add a button to Form1 and write the following code behind that button:

```
Private Sub Button1_Click(ByVal sender As System.Object, _
   ByVal e As System.EventArgs) Handles Button1.Click

   Dim obj As New cslib.CsClass()

   obj.DoSomething()

End Sub
```

This is really no different from if we'd created a Visual Basic .NET subclass – but in this case our subclass is actually written in a different language.

When we run this application and click the button, we should see a dialog box with a message indicating the constructor from the `csclass` was called, then another dialog indicating that the `DoSomething()` method from our Visual Basic .NET base class was called.

Visual Inheritance

So far, we have been discussing the new OO features of the Visual Basic .NET language, with a large focus on inheritance.

However, Visual Basic .NET also supports **visual inheritance** for Windows Forms. This means that we can create a Windows form, and then inherit from that form to create other forms that have the same layout, controls, and behaviors. This topic was covered in more detail in Chapter 5.

We can also use inheritance to create our own versions of Windows Forms controls. For instance, we may want to create an enhanced `TextBox` control that performs some specialized validation of the input data. This can be accomplished through inheritance by creating a subclass of the original `TextBox` control class and enhancing it as needed. This was also covered in Chapter 5.

The same is true of Web Forms controls, where we can take an existing Web Forms control and create a subclass. Our subclass can override existing functionality or add new functionality as required. See Chapter 7 for more on this.

Summary

Of all the features requested for the new version of VB, perhaps the most common was true class inheritance. As we have seen in this chapter, not only does Visual Basic .NET provide us with full class inheritance, but we also gain a number of other important new features and enhancements. These include constructor methods, overloading, overriding, and shadowing of methods.

Visual Basic .NET dramatically enhances the way we create and work with multiple interfaces, making them far easier to use than in the past. Additionally, because support for events is now a formal part of an interface, we can now express all the elements of an interface through this mechanism – methods, properties, and events.

For most people, the elimination of reference counting in favor of a garbage collection scheme for object termination will be a non-issue. However, it is important to be aware of this change, since an object that maintains a reference to expensive system resources will need some mechanism other than its termination to release those valuable resources.

Overall, Visual Basic .NET dramatically enhances our ability to create object-oriented applications with VB, while preserving the vast majority of the features we have become used to in previous versions of the language.

7

Web Capabilities

As we have previously seen in Chapter 2, the top layer of .NET provides three ways to render and manage user interfaces:

- ❏ Windows Forms
- ❏ Web Forms
- ❏ Console applications

and one way to handle interfaces with remote components:

- ❏ Web Services

Two of these, Web Forms and Web Services, are part of the new framework for Internet functionality in .NET, called **ASP.NET**.

It is easy to get a wrong first impression about ASP.NET just from the name. It is far more than just a replacement for Active Server Pages (ASP). It encompasses a completely new programming model for Internet user interfaces, and a new interfacing technology for remote component interaction in Web Services. It replaces existing WebClasses and DHTML Pages in VB6 with a much more consistent and easier-to-use programming model called Web Forms.

This chapter will look at these technologies from a VB developer's perspective. Web Forms and the server controls that are used on them will be compared to their closest equivalents in VB6. Web Services will be discussed as a new mechanism for building applications that are more distributed and Internet-dependent than older Windows DNA applications.

Unfortunately, a fast track chapter on web technologies in Visual Basic .NET cannot include coverage of general Internet development concepts. There have been many entire books written about Internet development, and it certainly cannot be done justice in a few pages. We will begin by noting a few of the Internet concepts that VB developers should know before doing Internet development.

For general coverage on Internet development concepts, the following resources are a good starting point:

- *Fast Track ASP.NET*, ISBN *1861007-19-1*
- *Professional ASP.NET 1.0 Special Edition*, *ISBN 1861007-03-5*
- *Professional ASP.NET Web Services*, ISBN 1-861005-45-8
- http://www.asptoday.com
- http://www.webservicesarchitect.com

Web development with Visual Basic .NET and ASP.NET is far simpler than working with earlier tools, such as ASP pages. However, some knowledge of Internet concepts and technologies is essential for effective web development in ASP.NET. You can develop simple pages without any significant knowledge of these technologies, but for production applications, you will need to be conversant with them.

This chapter assumes you have at least a general understanding of the following:

- HTTP as the standard, stateless protocol used on the Internet
- HTML and DHTML markup languages, and how they are used in web pages
- XML
- The general structure of ASP pages

You don't have to be a guru in all these concepts to use ASP.NET, but the more you know about them, the more effective you will be as an ASP.NET developer.

Why Replace Active Server Pages?

ASP pages are what some developers call 'dancing bear' software. That comes from an old quotation:

> *"The amazing thing about a dancing bear is not how well it dances, but that it dances at all."*

The amazing thing about ASP pages is not how well they do Internet interfaces, but that they do them at all.

ASP pages were Microsoft's first major attempt at a technology to develop web interfaces. Microsoft did a good job at getting something out fast that at least made it possible to do such development. Certainly, many successful applications have been developed with ASP pages. Alternatives such as developing straight to the ISAPI interface of Internet Information Server (IIS) are relegated to niche roles, for example when high performance is absolutely paramount.

Internet development with ASP pages has some major limitations, though, including:

- ❑ **Non-structured 'spaghetti' code** – Code in ASP pages is not created in a structured programming environment. It is all dumped into the ASP page. This makes it more difficult to structure code and encapsulate functionality. Include statements can be used to ameliorate this, but it takes discipline and skill.

- ❑ **Mixture of presentation and logic** – ASP script code is intermingled with HTML for layout, making construction, debugging, and maintenance of the code all more difficult.

- ❑ **Interpreted code** – Code in ASP is interpreted script, which has performance problems in high-volume situations. Interpreted script in ASP also lacks strong typing, which means additional data marshaling when talking to components (converting Variants to and from other types), and lack of early binding.

- ❑ **Weaker user interfaces** – HTML interfaces are very difficult to make as rich as typical VB interfaces. The native set of HTML controls is limited, and there is no programming model in ASP to extend them.

- ❑ **No state management** – HTML controls have no state management, forcing developers to write reams of code just to maintain state from page to page. The capabilities that are built into ASP that do preserve state, such as the Application object and the Session object, cause severe problems when scaling to multiple machines.

- ❑ **Need for multiple browser support in code** – Developers must be aware of browser differences and choose one of two bad options, which are:

  - ❑ Develop to a 'lowest-common denominator' standard, which seriously limits available interface technologies such as DHTML

  - ❑ Write extra code for whatever classes of browsers need to be supported

- ❑ **Poor support for visual tools** – While Visual InterDev makes a stab at allowing visual layout of web pages, its functionality is so limited that few developers routinely develop pages that way.

As we will see in this chapter, ASP.NET and Web Forms address all of these limitations to one extent or another. While Web Forms do not offer the panacea of making web development as easy as forms development in VB, they do make enormous strides in that direction.

Overview of Web Forms

The objective of Web Forms is to bring VB-style drag-and-drop design to the development of Internet interfaces. This programming model is much easier to use than typical existing web development technologies, and has the added advantage of being familiar to the huge existing base of VB developers.

It is important to understand that Web Forms is a significant extension over the idea of HTML forms. The <form> section of a typical HTML page can contain a limited number of controls, and the implementation of these controls is completely client-side. As we will see, Web Forms extends this idea to a much richer set of controls that also have server-side functionality.

We will start this section with an example of constructing a simple Web Form page. This page will look conceptually very similar to a form in VB6 or a Windows Form. While there are many differences in ASP.NET that we will be discussing in this chapter, this example highlights just how advanced Web Forms are over ASP pages.

To run this example, you will need access to a web server. For a development system, that typically means that IIS must be installed on the system. Some operating system installations do not install IIS by default. If your system does not have IIS installed, you will get an error message when you attempt to start an ASP.NET project. In that case, you must either install IIS locally from your operating system CD-ROM, or get access to a web server on your network.

It is a good idea to go through this example step by step in Visual Studio .NET. It will set a context for much of the following discussion.

A Web Form in Action

In this example, we will create a Web Form with four controls:

❑   A label that contains some text for us to change

❑   A button to change the text in the label and submit the page

❑   A textbox to enter information

❑   A validation control to check that if the textbox has something in it

First of all, create a new Visual Basic .NET and select the ASP.NET Web Application option. In ASP.NET, you name a project by specifying a directory location for it. This directory must be on a web server – for development this is typically localhost. The directory you specify for a new project normally does not yet exist.

If you are using localhost, your root web directory is probably `C:\Inetpub\wwwroot`, so if you want to navigate to the physical directory for your ASP.NET project, that's where you start. If you accepted the default name when you created the web project above, the project's physical folder would be `C:\Inetpub\wwwroot\WebApplication1`.

After clicking the OK button, Visual Studio .NET will create the directory (unless it already exists) and set up the web project. An ASP.NET project includes a lot more files than are created for a typical Visual Basic .NET forms project, as you can see on the following screen, which is the first screen you will get after starting a new ASP.NET Web Application.

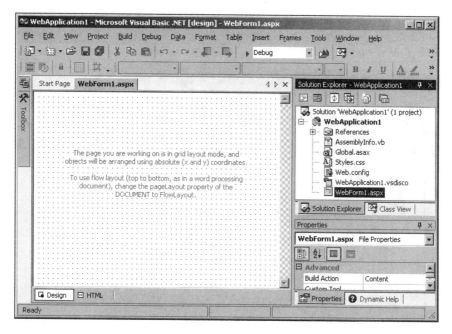

You can see the extra files created for the project, shown in the Solution Explorer in the upper right portion of the screen. Also notice a few differences in the development environment from working with Windows Forms. The design surface is all white, simulating a blank web page, and there is a note about layout options for Web Forms controls. Below that design surface are two tabs that will be familiar to Visual InterDev users. One shows the visual layout of the form (the Design tab), and the other shows the HTML that actually generates the layout and which can be directly edited (the HTML tab).

There are other differences that are not immediately apparent. The toolbars are slightly different, since Web Forms don't have all the layout options for controls that Windows Forms have and the Toolbox contains a different set of controls. But overall, the environment acts very similarly with Web Forms to the way it acts when creating Windows Forms.

We will be discussing layout options for Web Forms later in the chapter, but for now, you need to know that in the default layout format, the page is conceptually similar to an old-style Visual Basic Windows Form. You can position controls on a grid, and advanced browsers will display the page as you lay it out on the grid. Later, we will discuss the other layout option, which is more like a traditional HTML page.

From the Toolbox and Web Forms tab, click and drag a Label control onto the design surface and release it. (You can also just click on the Label control and then 'draw' it on the surface the way you can with a control in a VB6 form or Windows Form.)

The control will appear on the form, and you can drag it around to position it. When the Label control is selected on the design surface, its properties will appear in the Properties window. In the Properties window, change the Text property for the control to Original Text.

Now drag over a Button control, and then drag over a TextBox control. Finally, drag over a RequiredFieldValidator control, which will be towards the bottom of the control list. Arrange these controls to be in a column. At this point, the screen should look roughly like this:

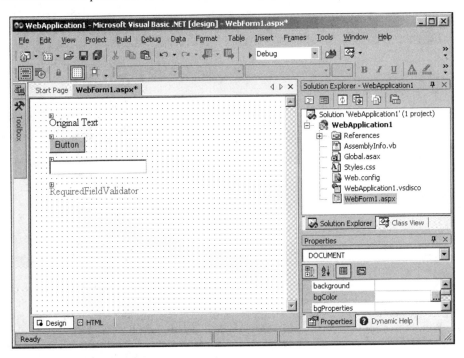

Next, we will set up the Button to change the text in the Label control. Double-click on the Button, and then its click event routine (named Button1_Click) will come up, just as with VB6 forms. In the event routine, type in the following code:

```
Label1.Text = "The text has changed!!"
```

Next, we will associate the RequiredFieldValidator control with the TextBox. Go back to the form view by clicking on the WebForm1.aspx tab. Then click on the RequiredFieldValidator control. In the Properties window for the RequiredFieldValidator control, find the ControlToValidate property. Click on the right of the property to set it. A drop down will show the controls that are available to validate, and in this case there is only one; TextBox1. Select it and press Enter. Also, change the error message to be displayed by changing the ErrorMessage property of the RequiredFieldValidator control to Textbox cannot be blank!!

We are now ready to test this Web Form. Press the Start icon (shaped like a play button) in the toolbar. It may take a while to see the resulting screen, especially if this is the first time you have shown a Web Form, because the page is being compiled. The screen that comes up is in Internet Explorer (unless your default browser has been set to something else), and it looks like this:

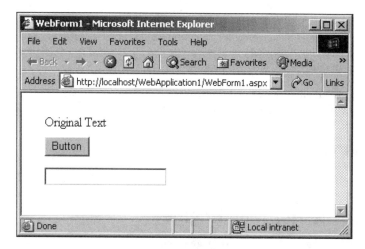

The RequiredFieldValidator is not visible because no validation has been done yet. To cause a validation to occur, press the button without placing anything in the textbox. The screen then displays a red error message (Textbox cannot be blank!!) in the position of the RequiredFieldValidator control, just under the textbox.

If your web server is on your local machine during development, it is hard to tell that the validation took place completely in the browser, with no server round trip. However, this would be obvious if the page was being accessed on a slow Internet connection.

Now type something into the textbox, and press the button. The label will change to say The text has changed!! and the error message from the RequiredFieldValidator will vanish. This operation caused a trip back to the server, because the button by default causes the browser to 'submit' the form to the server.

This very short exercise has demonstrated some key ideas about Web Forms:

❑   Laying out the form is much like it is for VB6 forms and Windows Forms.

❑   Controls in Web Forms act like VB6 controls, with properties to set behavior and event code behind them to take actions.

❑   Controls on Web Forms maintain their own state. Notice that when the button was pressed, the textbox did not lose its information.

❑   Validation is easy, and set through properties of a validator control. Different validator controls exist for various types of validation task.

Behind the Scenes

Unlike a Windows Form application, the page in the ASP.NET application came up in a browser. Since browsers can only understand HTML, the ASP.NET page had to be rendered as HTML.

If you click the HTML tab below the design surface for WebForm1.aspx, you will see the template used to create the HTML. This template can contain raw HTML, but it also has tags that refer to various elements on the page. You will see elements for each of the controls you dragged onto the page for example. (This template is discussed in more detail later in the chapter.)

These individual page elements are called **server controls**, and they generate additional HTML when the page is rendered. The template inserts their HTML at the appropriate place, and the result is a complete web page.

Since the end result is pure HTML, it can be displayed in the browser. It doesn't matter if the browser is on a system with the .NET Framework or not, because the client system only works with the received HTML, and not with any executable .NET code.

ASP.NET as the Runtime Engine

Execution of a Web Form to create an HTML page is more involved than execution of a Windows Form. A Windows Form is just another class module, which happens to inherit visual form capability. A Web Form consists of both code and layout, and the layout part is HTML-based. That template (which is a file with an .aspx extension) is executed by the ASP.NET runtime engine. Unlike compiled Windows Forms, which are executed directly by the CLR, Web Forms use the CLR indirectly.

As we discussed earlier, the .aspx file controls the page execution and serves as a template for the HTML stream. At various points, the template encounters page elements that are actually .NET components, and then it calls the CLR to execute those components. These components are compiled, not interpreted, offering a major advantage over the interpreted script of ASP.

ASP.NET pages can be edited directly in a text or HTML editor, and can have script code embedded directly in the page using any .NET language supported on the execution machine. This development model is similar to today's ASP pages. We will not discuss ASP.NET pages done this way, since that development model is unfamiliar to many Visual Basic developers. *Professional ASP.NET 1.0 Special Edition* by Wrox Press, ISBN *1-861007-03-5* is a good resource to learn more about that kind of development. We will concentrate on Web Forms, since this technique for creating web pages is likely to be most familiar and useful to Visual Basic developers.

System.Web.UI Namespace

The classes used for ASP.NET user interface constructs, including Web Forms, are in the System.Web.UI namespace. This namespace has many classes and a complex hierarchy. Unlike the discussion of Windows Forms, in which the appropriate namespace was extensively covered, this chapter will not detail the System.Web.UI namespace. We will only discuss some key classes in the namespace later in the chapter.

Anatomy of a Web Form

Earlier, we discussed the HTML-based template for layout of the web page. The other major part of a Web Form is a code module to contain code behind the page. When we typed in the code that changed the text in the label in our first example above, that code was placed in the page's code module. Let's look at each of these two pieces of a Web Form in some more detail.

The Template for Presentation

The HTML template for an `.aspx` page will look generally familiar to an ASP developer. It contains HTML header information, visual HTML elements, and can contain any valid HTML. Here is the template created by our example above (viewable by selecting the HTML tab for WebForm1.aspx):

```
<%@ Page Language="vb" AutoEventWireup="false" Codebehind="WebForm1.aspx.vb"
        Inherits="WebApplication1.WebForm1"%>
<!DOCTYPE HTML PUBLIC "-//W3C//DTD HTML 4.0 Transitional//EN">
<HTML>
  <HEAD>
    <title>WebForm1</title>
    <meta name="GENERATOR" content="Microsoft Visual Studio.NET 7.0">
    <meta name="CODE_LANGUAGE" content="Visual Basic 7.0">
    <meta name="vs_defaultClientScript" content="JavaScript">
    <meta name="vs_targetSchema"
      content="http://schemas.microsoft.com/intellisense/ie5">
  </HEAD>
  <body MS_POSITIONING="GridLayout">
    <form id="Form1" method="post" runat="server">
      <asp:Label id="Label1"
        style="Z-INDEX: 101; LEFT: 29px; POSITION: absolute; TOP: 26px"
        runat="server">Original Text</asp:Label>
      <asp:Button id="Button1"
        style="Z-INDEX: 102; LEFT: 29px; POSITION: absolute; TOP: 54px"
        runat="server" Text="Button"></asp:Button>
      <asp:TextBox id="TextBox1"
        style="Z-INDEX: 103; LEFT: 29px; POSITION: absolute; TOP: 92px"
        runat="server"></asp:TextBox>
      <asp:RequiredFieldValidator id="RequiredFieldValidator1"
        style="Z-INDEX: 104; LEFT: 29px; POSITION: absolute; TOP: 130px"
        runat="server" ErrorMessage="Textbox cannot be blank!!"
        ControlToValidate="TextBox1"></asp:RequiredFieldValidator>
    </form>
  </body>
</HTML>
```

When just starting out with Web Forms, it is not essential to know what all of this means. You can just create Web Forms with the form designer, and let the designer create this template code and modify it as necessary.

However, to take full advantage of what Web Forms can do, the traditional Visual Basic developer will need to become very familiar with the template (and with HTML and CSS), and have the ability to modify the template directly when necessary.

Here are a few things to notice about the template:

❑ The first line has attributes for the page. These include the language used, the location of the module containing the code behind the page, and the web form from which this page is inheriting its layout. The module containing the code behind the page (code connected to various page elements) is discussed later.

❑ The controls on the Web Form are all defined in the template with a line that begins `<asp:`. The tags used to identify controls that Microsoft provides for Web Forms all begin with the `asp:` prefix to differentiate them from everything else.

❑ Each defined control has an attribute of `runat="server"`. This indicates a server control. The concept of server controls is central to the operation of Web Forms, and they are discussed in more detail later.

❑ Each defined control has its properties set with attributes inside the definition line. For example, the `RequiredFieldValidator` control has properties set for `ErrorMessage` and `ControlToValidate`.

❑ All of the information about the form is inside the HTML block defined by the `<form>` and `</form>` tags. This allows encapsulation of the form information and provides the ability to put HTML elements such as page headers and footers in the page easily without disturbing the form.

The Code-Behind Module

If you look in the directory associated with our first example, you will see a file named `WebForm1.aspx`, which is the template file discussed above. You will also see `WebForm1.aspx.vb`. This is a .NET code module that contains the code behind the form. (You can look at this code by opening `WebForm1.aspx.vb`, but it is the same code that you would see by pressing the `WebForm1.aspx.vb` tab in Visual Studio. NET.)

This module is just a standard class module in Visual Basic .NET. When compiled, the class is placed in a DLL that is named for the project (along with any other code-behind modules in the project) in the `/bin` directory of the project. This DLL must be deployed as part of the web site if it is moved, because the template file must make calls into it to execute any code behind the form.

A Subclassed Instance of the Page Class

Each of these code-behind class modules inherits from the `System.Web.UI.Page` class. This class contains many properties, methods, and events that are useful in working with Web Forms. Some of the important properties of the `Page` class include:

Property	Description
Application	ASP developers are familiar with the `Application` object provided by the HTTP runtime, which manages state for an entire ASP-based application and provides global access to the state. The `Application` property of the `Page` class provides a reference to this object. Other HTTP objects are also available as properties, as indicated below.

Property	Description
ClientTarget	Indicates the capabilities of the requesting browser. Used during execution to see if the client is running on an up-level (advanced) browser, or a down-level (more primitive) browser. Allows code to deliver behavior appropriate to the current browser.
ErrorPage	Gets or sets the error page that will be the target of a redirection in the case of an unhandled exception in the page.
IsPostBack	If this is the first time a page is being rendered, this property will be False. Looking at this property in the Load event of the page allows you to take special action the first time a page is rendered. If the same page is being rendered again as a result of a submit, IsPostBack will be True.
IsValid	Indicates whether page validation succeeded.
Request Response Server Session	Provides a reference to the corresponding HTTP runtime objects. These objects will be familiar to ASP developers. While the objects do not need to be accessed manually as often in Web Forms as in ASP pages, there will still be situations where such access is needed.
User	Read-only property indicating the user making a page request.
Validators	The collection of validation controls on the page.

The important methods include:

Method	Description
LoadControl	Gets a UserControl object from the appropriate file and loads it. User controls are discussed later in the chapter.
Validate	Forces all the validation controls on the page to validate the data in their associated controls.

Web Forms Event Model

The template file shown above declares the page elements (server controls) that are needed on the page. However, it does not show any indication of the events associated with those server controls. The event code exists in the code-behind module, of course. Firing the events at the appropriate time, and tying them to the web page, is handled behind the scenes by the ASP.NET runtime engine.

The event model for Web Forms must take into account the fact that events are fired on the client, but must be executed on the server. Due to the way the Web works, this happens through an HTTP post. The ASP.NET runtime interprets the post, and if it finds an event, it calls the appropriate event handling routine in the code.

Since the ASP.NET runtime takes care of event management automatically, you don't have to do anything except put your code in the events you need. However there are some differences in the way events work in ASP.NET versus Windows Forms. Some of these differences can impact on the way you write your application.

Postback vs. Non-Postback Events

Some controls have events that do not immediately result in a post to the server. These events are captured and then delivered the next time the page is posted. The section on *Server Controls* below discusses the details of how these events are handled, and how to override the normal behavior to make such an event force a post.

A typical example of a non-postback event is the TextChanged event of a textbox. You don't want that event to cause a postback because there may be other textboxes that need to be filled out on the page. However, when the page is submitted, you may need to know that the text in the control has changed, so the event will be fired back on the server when the page is submitted.

Some server controls, such as a ListBox, have the ability to make their changed-type events (which are normally non-postback) into a postback event. Those controls have a property named AutoPostBack. Setting the property to True will make the event post back to the server immediately.

Order of Events

When a page is submitted, all the non-postback events are processed first, in no particular order. You should not write code in ASP.NET that depends on the events being fired in a particular order. When they are finished, the postback event (typically a click event) is fired.

Built-in Events are Limited

The biggest difference in event handling for Web Forms is performance. Most Web Form events require a server round trip. This limits the practicability of some types of events. Many of the mouse moving events that were practicable to handle with a VB6 forms client are not practicable in a web model. This means that server controls typically offer a more limited set of events than the equivalent Windows Forms controls. The bulk of these server control events are click-type and change-type events.

> *Mouse moving events in a browser can be handled in some cases using JavaScript on the client, but this is distinct from events that must tie into server code, so we will not discuss those techniques in detail.*

As mentioned earlier, most controls do offer an event to indicate that their contents or state have changed. The name varies with different controls. The CheckBox, for example has such an event, named CheckChanged. However, the TextBox server control does not have a change event for every character typed into it – it only generates a single TextChanged event when the page is posted back to the server.

Application and Session Events

Besides the events generated by the page, there are events that are raised by the ASP.NET Framework. These higher-level events include:

- ❑ **Application events** – `Application_OnStart` for initialization of resources used throughout the application, such as file locations, and `Application_OnEnd`, which provides an opportunity to clean up and dispose of resources when a web application terminates.

- ❑ **Session events** – Similar to application events, but associated with a user session instead of the whole application. `Session_OnStart` fires when a user first starts a session of the application, and `Session_OnEnd` fires either when the application closes a session for a user, or when the session times out.

In creating ASP pages, these events would need to be coded in the `Global.asa` page. With ASP.NET and Web Forms, the events are coded in the replacement for `Global.asa`, which is called `Global.asax`. If this module is selected in the **Solution Explorer**, it will be displayed in the code window, and the right-hand drop-down list at the top of the window will list the available events.

State Management and the Life Cycle of a Web Forms Page

The life cycle for a Web Forms page is dictated by the necessities of any web application. Most of the code defining the application runs on the server, but the user interface for the code displays on the remote client. Information must be passed between server and client through HTTP, which is a stateless protocol.

Since HTTP is stateless, web pages are created from scratch with every round trip. As soon as the server finishes processing a page and sends it to the browser, it is finished with the page and maintains no further connection to the client. The next time the page is posted, the server starts all over in creating and processing it. At their most fundamental level, web pages are **stateless** – that is, the values of a page's variables and controls are not preserved on the server.

In fact when a web page is recreated, even for the same user, it may not be the same server doing the work as the last time the page was created. In most server farms, each web page request is routed to one of a group of similar servers, and there is no assurance that a user will get the same server that served the last page to the user. This makes it literally impossible for a single server to maintain the state of a user's web page in a multiple web server environment.

The ASP.NET Framework manages to get around many of these limitations. Web Forms behave as if the server were maintaining state. In reality, the state information is transmitted with the page, and returned when a page is posted. You can see where the state information is stored on the page by selecting View | Source in the browser. For our earlier example, here are the some lines that appear about ten lines into the HTML that runs in the client browser:

```
<input type="hidden" name="__VIEWSTATE"
value="dDwtMTQyNDkyMjMzMjs7PjzWpT/wwsNdqOsle1ESmdMUhanR" />
```

These lines declare a hidden field on the page, with a `value` attribute. The `value` attribute contains what looks like a meaningless string of numbers and letters, but that string actually contains the state of all the server controls on the page. The state information is said to be **tokenized**, which means it is translated into a compressed form. The compressed form has to be in text, because the HTTP protocol does not allow a web page to contain binary information.

The tokenized state information can be rather long for a complex web page. It might be expected that this would result in a performance problem as the information is continually transmitted back and forth, and decoded and re-encoded on the server. However, tests at Microsoft have indicated that this technique for state management yields acceptable performance that is comparable to performance for other state management techniques.

The Web Forms controls' state information stored in the hidden field, plus any information entered by the user, is handled during the posting of the page by the ASP.NET framework. The controls get their state refreshed, and then updated with any new information on the page. All the state information is then automatically available in object properties of the controls on a Web Form, making their programming similar to controls on a VB6 form. This insulates the developer from needing to manage many of the details in the lifecycle of a web page.

Nevertheless, it is helpful to understand the sequence of events that occurs when a Web Forms page is processed. You can program your Web Forms pages more effectively if you understand some of what is going on behind the scenes. Here is a typical sequence of events that take place during the use of a Web Form:

1. A page based on the Web Form is created on the server and transmitted to the browser. It is in HTML, and any server controls have rendered their interface in HTML as part of the page.

2. The user views the page in the browser and responds to the page.

3. The user performs some action that causes the page to be posted back to the server (this can happen in a variety of ways, the most common being the pressing of a button).

4. The server processes the returned page. Server controls have their state restored from the tokenized state information and then updated with any new information from the user. The events that caused the post of the page are processed.

5. If the page needs to be updated on the client, the server prepares a new version on the page and transmits it to the browser, and the cycle starts over.

This cycle continues until a user is finished with a page, which may happen when a user goes to another page, when the user's session times out, or when the user just shuts down the browser.

It is possible for the page to contain client script for validation of user input or limited user interface programming, for example DHTML for sorting a short list of data items into a different order. However, client script does not interact with server components, and so does not affect the above sequence.

Disabling State Management

ASP.NET controls have a property called `EnableViewState`. This property is `True` by default, and when it is `True`, the state management for the control works as described above.

However, there are some occasions when it makes sense to turn off state management for a control to get better performance. An example is a large, read-only grid. If the grid is reloaded every time the page is rendered, then it makes no sense to use the automatic state management. This would just result in a lot of extra data being embedded into the page unnecessarily.

The Page class itself has an EnableViewState property as well. If it is set to False, the page uses no automatic state management at all, no matter what the EnableViewState property is set to for the controls on the page.

Layout of Web Forms

There are two quite different ways of laying out Web Forms. Both involve selecting controls in the Toolbox and placing them on the design surface. Where they differ is in where the controls end up on the design surface and the way controls are positioned in the underlying HTML. The two different techniques are called **Flow Layout** and **Grid Layout**. Grid Layout is the default. Which of these is applied to a given Web Form is determined by the pageLayout property of the form:

❑   In Flow Layout, the design surface is similar to a word-processing document. The user can insert text and paragraph marks, and the result is translated into HTML. When a control is dropped onto the design surface, it is placed in the middle of the text that was previously entered, where the cursor is currently positioned.

❑   In Grid Layout, the controls are actually placed on a grid on the design surface. They are not interspersed with the underlying text. This allows for a WYSIWYG style display similar to FrontPage and is a big improvement over the original layout editor included with InterDev. However, only advanced browsers are capable of properly positioning the controls in the displayed page.

Here are sample screens of both layout options. Flow Layout is on the left, and Grid Layout is on the right. Note how the controls in Flow Layout proceed linearly down the page while controls in Grid Layout have absolute positioning on the page:

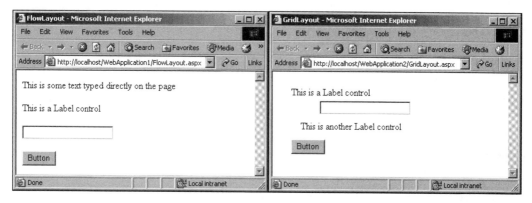

The differences between these layout techniques show up dramatically in the underlying HTML template. In Web Forms, any control that is placed on the design surface has code generated for it in the underlying HTML template. For example, placing a button on the Web Form in Flow Layout mode will cause the following code to be inserted into the HTML template:

```
<asp:button id="Button1" runat="server" Text="Button"></asp:button>
```

This declaration for the control includes no positioning information at all. The control is merely rendered in the Web Form at whatever point it is encountered when running the form.

If a button is dropped in a Grid Layout form, however, the inserted code is more complex. It looks something like this:

```
<asp:Button id="Button1"
    style="Z-INDEX: 102; LEFT: 32px; POSITION: absolute; TOP: 52px"
    runat="server" Text="Button"></asp:Button>
```

You can see the positioning information in this code. It tells ASP.NET what the position needs to be, and ASP.NET creates appropriate HTML to perform that positioning.

Each layout type is suitable for certain applications. Flow Layout is preferred if you need to support a lot of browsers, or you want a more conventional look to the browser page. Grid Layout gives you more control over the exact layout of the page, and acts a lot more like traditional forms, but you have to make sure the users for the pages have advanced browsers such as recent versions of Internet Explorer.

Server Controls

The ASP.NET framework depends heavily on server controls to get around the classic limitations of Internet development. Server controls provide a concrete layout element, very similar to the classic VB form control, and they also provide the capability to project a user interface for this UI element via standard HTTP to a browser. Along the way, server controls manage state, provide properties to be manipulated in code, and provide events to hook actions into logic.

Why Are Server Controls Needed?

Web pages usually project a user interface with HTML client controls, which are a part of standard HTML. Each client control is created on a page with a standard HTML tag.

HTML client controls are by far the most frequently used interface elements for current web applications. Alternatives such as Java applets and ActiveX controls are far less common.

The reason these controls are used so much is that they work in just about any browser, and they are so lightweight that their performance is acceptable. They have some big drawbacks though. For the purposes of our current discussion, the two main drawbacks are:

❑ HTML client controls require totally manual state management

❑ It's hard to create rich, sophisticated user interfaces with HTML client controls because the set of available controls is limited

Server controls do an excellent job of addressing both of these limitations. In many respects, server controls are the best of both worlds. The developer can program against server controls on the server just as if they were any other component, but the server controls project a user interface in standard HTML, using many of the old-style HTML client controls as necessary to create that client-side user interface.

Standard HTML client controls have server-based counterparts in ASP.NET, created by placing a `runat="server"` attribute in the standard HTML tag for the control. However, these are mostly for converting older pages, and not for doing visual design on new pages, so we will not discuss them in this chapter.

ASP.NET Server Controls

We have already seen server controls in action – the Label, TextBox, Button, and Validator control that we used in our first example. ASP.NET server controls are well-suited to visual layout of web pages, and have other characteristics to simplify web page development, including:

❑ Having a flexible object model, and one that is consistent and familiar to VB developers

❑ Creating appropriate HTML to render their user interface, combining various client-side HTML controls if necessary

❑ Performing automatic browser detection, and customizing their output to the current browser

❑ Being able to use data binding

These capabilities help dramatically cut development time for web pages. For example, you can place a fully functional calendar on a page with just a drag-and-drop, or you can cause a field on a page to be validated without writing a single line of script code. Some early ASP.NET development projects have resulted in reductions in development time of 50 to 80 percent.

The capability of server controls to customize their output to different browsers is particularly important. The server controls in the initial release of .NET basically address two types of browsers. The first type is generic browsers that understand HTML 3.2. The second type consists of more advanced browsers that can handle DHTML and other more recent innovations.

However, the architecture of server controls permits more differentiation, and future server controls should be able to distinguish among more classes of browsers.

Some ASP.NET controls are very similar to standard Visual Basic forms controls, all of which have equivalents in Windows Forms. They include:

❑ Label

❑ TextBox

❑ CheckBox

❑ ListBox

❑ Button (called command buttons in VB6)

❑ Image (similar to Image controls or Picture Boxes in VB6

Here are the additional controls, and descriptions of their functions:

Control name	Function
DropDownList	Acts like a VB combo box with Drop Down style selected
CheckBoxList	Sequence or group of Checkbox controls (similar to a VB6 control array)
RadioButtonList	Set of mutually exclusive option buttons (similar to a VB6 control array)
LinkButton	Works just like a Button control, except it displays as a hyperlink
ImageButton	Graphical image used as a button – can provide x and y coordinates of user's click
Table, TableRow, TableCell	Create tables and tabular layouts
Hyperlink	Allows navigation to other URLs
Calendar	Date selections (including date ranges) – resembles calendar controls used in VB
Repeater	Used to generate lists of items, using a snippet of HTML as a template
DataList	Similar to the Repeater control, but more control over output
DataGrid	Similar to the VB6 data grid, but works with ADO.NET hierarchical datasets
Image	Similar to the Image control or Picture Box in VB6
AdRotator	A control that displays graphic ads, rotating the ads with each page refresh
Literal	Like a label control, but emits simpler output. In particular, a label control embeds its output into a <span> tag, but a literal control does not. Can still be manipulated like a label.
XML	A placeholder for an XML file that will be embedded into the web page

In addition to the ASP.NET controls packaged with Visual Studio .NET, many third parties are introducing packages of controls. Just as VB6's functionality has traditionally been enhanced with third party OCX controls, now Web Forms' web interface functionality can be enhanced with third party ASP.NET controls. In fact, third party server controls for web interface functionality make even more sense, because there is no client install. A server control only needs to exist on the server, lowering the support and deployment costs for third party controls.

Validation Controls

Another general class of server controls for Web Forms are **validation controls**. These controls are used specifically to do various kinds of validation of user data in other controls. We saw an example in our first exercise – the RequiredFieldValidator.

For browsers that support client-side scripting, these controls will actually emit the JavaScript (ECMAScript) code to do validation on the client. If the target browser does not support client-side validation, then controls fall back and perform validation on the server.

How to Use Validation Controls

Validation controls must be attached to user input controls. A property called `ControlToValidate` provides the reference to the control that needs validation. You may recall that we used this property in our first Web Forms example to use a RequiredFieldValidator, which was attached to the textbox that was already on the Web Form.

Summary of Available Validation Controls

The controls that are available to do validation include:

Control	Validation action
RequiredFieldValidator	Ensures that the user fills in an input control, such as a textbox.
RangeValidator	Checks that a user's entry falls into a valid range of values. The limits on the range can be declared as preset values, or declared as values in other controls.
CompareValidator	Checks user's entry in one control against that in another control.
RegularExpressionValidator	Checks user input against a regular expression (there is a short discussion below about regular expressions, in case you are not familiar with them).
CustomValidator	Allows programmer to specify custom logic for validation (client-side and/or server-side).
ValidationSummary	Provides a text display summary of error messages produced by all validation controls.

Note that all validation controls consider a blank entry to be valid, except for the RequiredFieldValidator. So a RangeValidator, for example, will accept blank input as valid, even if an empty value is outside the validation range. If blank input is not desired, a RequiredFieldValidator should be used in addition to any other validation controls desired. You can attach more than one validation control to a single user input control.

Regular Expressions

The concept of regular expressions may be unfamiliar to some Visual Basic developers. The RegularExpressionValidator takes a string that expresses how the validation should be done. This string is called a **regular expression**. A string containing a regular expression can be used in a RegularExpressionValidator (and in functions accepting regular expressions) to check for predictable sequences of characters, such as a Social Security number, or a phone number. Here is an example of a regular expression that validates a string as a US Social Security number (having 3 digits, then a dash, then 2 digits, then another dash, and finishing with 4 digits):

```
"\d{3}-\d{2}-\d{4}"
```

These expressions have become a commonly used way to express formatting requirements, and they are used in many web applications today. You can consult your MSDN documentation for information on how to construct regular expressions if you are unfamiliar with them.

Laying Out Error Messages on the Page

Each error validation control has a property that determines how the error message displays. The property is called `Display`, and here are the values it can take and the effect of each value:

- **Static** – The validation control takes up space on the page even when no error message is displayed. This allows the page to have a fixed layout. Note that two validation controls with `Display` set to `Static` cannot occupy the same space on the page, so each control must be given its own location.

- **Dynamic** – The validation control takes up no space on the page until an error message is displayed for it. In this case, multiple validation controls can share the same location. The drawback to using dynamic display is that the layout of the page changes when an error is displayed, which may cause controls on the page to jump around.

- **None** – For validation controls except for the ValidationSummary, this turns off error message display by the individual control, and allows errors to be displayed by the ValidationSummary control only.

If the target browser supports DHTML, there is another option for displaying error messages by the ValidationSummary control. Such messages can go in a pop-up message box. To enable this behavior, set the `ShowMessageBox` property of the ValidationSummary control to `True`.

If there is a ValidationSummary control on the page, but the individual validation controls are set to `Static` or `Dynamic` display, then their output is duplicated, once for their own display, and once for the ValidationSummary.

Disabling Validation

Each of the validation controls has an `Enabled` property. Setting this property to `False` causes the control to cease to be rendered into the HTML that the web page creates, and turns off all validation that the control would perform (both on the client side and on the server side).

Custom Web Form Server Controls

In addition to the built-in server controls that can be placed on Web Forms, you can develop your own controls. There are two basic types of custom server controls that can be developed:

- A new server control that inherits from an existing server control and gives it new capabilities

- A new server control written from scratch

We will cover the second type in detail, with a step-by-step example, and then comment on differences in creating the other type.

The process of creating a new server control encompasses these steps:

1. Create a new project of type **Web Control Library**.

2. In the class created for the project, place code in the `Render()` method to make the control do anything necessary. This typically involves creating appropriate HTML to render the control's interface.

3. If the control needs any additional properties or methods besides the standard ones inherited from the `System.Web.UI.WebControls.WebControl` class, then these members should be coded as necessary.

4. Build the project to create a `.DLL` for the control.

5. Create a project to test the control. Reference the control in that project and drag the control onto a page for testing.

Our simple example will build a control that behaves as a label, but converts its text to uppercase or lowercase before displaying it. We will implement a property that can take on values of upper case or lower case, and the setting of this property will determine whether the control displays in all uppercase or all lowercase.

This example has a number of steps that must be performed precisely, so follow the instructions closely:

1. Start a new project from **File | New | Project**. Select the project type of **Web Control Library**. Name the project **MyNewServerControl**. In the project that comes up, the code window will appear.

2. In the definition line for the class (the line with `Public Class`), change the class name to `UpperLowerLabel`. Also change both places in the attribute list that say `WebCustomControl1` to `UpperLowerLabel`. Take care to spell all these changes correctly and exactly the same way. The resulting class declaration will then look like this (with some line breaks inserted for legibility):

```
<DefaultProperty("Text"),
  ToolboxData("<{0}:UpperLowerLabel runat=server></{0}:UpperLowerLabel>")>
  Public Class UpperLowerLabel
    Inherits System.Web.UI.WebControls.WebControl
```

3. Add the following code just under the declaration for the `_text` variable:

```
Dim _text As String
```

```
Public Enum enuCaseType
  caseUpper = 0
  caseLower = 1
End Enum
Dim mCase As enuCaseType
```

4. Create a new property called `Case` with the following code (note that the easiest way to type this is to cut and paste the `Text` property which is already in the code, and then alter that):

```
<Bindable(True), Category("Appearance"), DefaultValue("")> _
  Property [Case]() As enuCaseType
  Get
    Return mCase
  End Get

  Set(ByVal Value As enuCaseType)
    mCase = Value
  End Set
End Property
```

5. Place this code in the `Render()` method, replacing the single line of code that the designer previously placed in there:

```
Select Case mCase
  Case enuCaseType.caseLower
    output.Write(LCase([Text]))
  Case enuCaseType.caseUpper
    output.Write(UCase([Text]))
  Case Else
    output.Write([Text])
End Select
```

The `output.Write()` method sends the text into the HTML stream without any formatting. `output` is actually a method of the `HTTPResponse` class, which the environment makes available for writing of HTML output.

6. Build the web control by selecting **Build Solution** from the **Build** menu.

7. Start a new **ASP.NET Web Application** project using **File | Add Project | New Project...** and name the project **TestUpperLowerLabel**.

8. Right-click on the **Web Forms** tab in the **Toolbox**, and select **Customize Toolbox....**

9. Select the **.NET Framework Components** tab, click the **Browse** button and navigate to the **MyNewServerControl** directory. Go to the **bin** directory and select **MyNewServerControl.dll** and press the **Open** button.

10. Scroll down to the **UpperLowerLabel** control and ensure the box next to it is checked (it should already be checked). Click the **OK** button. The **UpperLowerLabel** control should now be in the **Toolbox**.

11. Now drag and drop an **UpperLowerLabel** control onto the Web Form design surface, and set the **Text** property in the new control to some value.

12. Set the Case property to caseLower. Note that the text in the label goes to all lowercase. The Render() method is called whenever a property is changed.

13. Set the Case property to caseUpper. Note that the text goes back to uppercase on the form.

14. Make the ASP.NET Web Form application the startup for the solution by right-clicking on the solution at the top of the Solution Explorer and selecting Properties. On the Properties dialog, change the value in the dropdown under Single Startup Solution to TestUpperLowerLabel.

15. Add other controls to the Web Form as desired and test. For example, you can add a button to the form, and in the button's Click event add code to change the text in the control, or change the Case property. Here is some typical code:

```
UpperLowerLabel1.Case = MyNewServerControl.UpperLowerLabel.enuCaseType.caseUpper
UpperLowerLabel1.Text = "SoMe MiXeD CaSe TeXt"
```

This exercise demonstrates that constructing a Web Form control is not difficult. The challenge is creating an appropriate Render() method. The more you know about HTML, the more sophisticated you can make the Render() method. For example, the method can check the browser level, and render different HTML based on what browser is currently being used.

The output.write() method used in our example does not add anything to the rendered output. The string that is sent to output.write() is sent straight into the HTML stream for the page. If your code inserts HTML tags into the string, those tags are sent into the stream as well.

There is another option to reformat the output string with HTML, and that is to use the System.Web.UI.HtmlTextWriter class. This class has shared properties (fields) for all the common HTML formatting options. Appropriate HTML options can be set on the class, and then the Write() method can be used to output a string with all HTML tags automatically added.

Differences for Extending an Existing Web Control

To extend an existing control, start a Web Control Library as before, and make your web control class inherit from the existing control instead of inheriting from the System.Web.UI.WebControls.WebControl class (which is the default when a new web control is created). Then, the existing controls, properties, and methods will be inherited, and can be overridden if necessary. Additional properties, methods, and events can also be added to the extended control as necessary.

Then, create a Render() method that overrides the Render() method of the base class. Place any logic there for your control to do special rendering. Part of that logic will typically be to call the parent class's Render() method also, to allow it to insert HTML into the stream.

Data Binding in Web Forms

Displaying data in Web Forms can be done with **data binding**, and the implementation of data binding in the .NET Framework allows more flexibility than data binding in VB6 and earlier. For example, grids can bind to arrays in Web Forms.

We must understand how data is handled in .NET before discussing data binding, so details on data binding in Web Forms, including examples, are in Chapter 8.

A Final Example – A Small Application Using Web Forms

We will conclude our discussion of Web Forms' capabilities by constructing a small application with a Web Form. The application will be a loan calculator. It will take in the amount of the loan, the number of payments, and the interest rate. It will validate each of these to acceptable values using validation controls. If all values are valid, it will calculate and display the payment amount.

All of this will be done without any work in HTML at all. The work will strongly resemble normal VB forms programming.

Step One – Initialize the Project

Start a new ASP.NET Web Application, and give it an appropriate name such as WebLoanCalculator.

Step Two – Place the Controls on the Web Form

Drag-and-drop the following controls onto the form, and set the properties as specified below in the Properties window with the control highlighted. Move the controls so they match the sample screen opposite. If you have trouble positioning the controls exactly the way you want, you may want to select Format | Snap to Grid from the menu.

Control	Location	Properties
Label	At top of screen	Text = Loan calculator
		Font	Size = Large
Label	To left of screen	Text = Loan Amount
Label	To left of screen	Text = No. of Months
Label	To left of screen	Text = Interest Rate (%)
TextBox	Beside Loan Amount label	(ID) = txtLoanAmount
TextBox	Beside No. of Months	(ID) = txtMonths
TextBox	Beside Interest Rate (%)	(ID) = txtInterestRate
Button	Below all the above controls	(ID) = btnCalculatePayment
		Text = Calculate Payment

The controls should be laid out so that the design surface looks roughly like this:

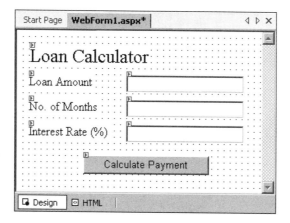

Step Three – Place a Label for the Result on the Form

Now drag-and-drop a Label control and place it just under the Button and to the left. Give the Label control an (ID) of lblPaymentAmount and change its Visible property to False. Change its Text property to Payment amount goes here.

Step Four – Place the Validator Controls on the Form

Drag-and-drop the following validator controls onto the form, and set their properties as indicated. Position them below the label inserted in *Step Three*:

Control	Properties
RangeValidator	(ID) = vldLoanAmount
	ControlToValidate = txtLoanAmount
	MaximumValue = 500000
	MinimumValue = 100
	ErrorMessage = Loan amount must be between 100 and 500000!
	Display = Dynamic
	Type = Double

Table continued on following page

Control	Properties
RangeValidator	(ID) = vldMonths
	ControlToValidate = txtMonths
	MaximumValue = 360
	MinimumValue = 3
	ErrorMessage = No. of months must be between 3 and 360!
	Display = Dynamic
	Type = Integer
RegularExpressionValidator	(ID) = vldInterestRate
	ControlToValidate = txtInterestRate
	ValidationExpression = \d*[.]{0,1}\d*
	ErrorMessage = Interest rate must be numeric!
	Display = Dynamic
ValidationSummary	(no properties need to be set)

Setting the Type property to Double for the RangeValidator controls ensures that the range checking is done numerically instead of with an ASCII compare. If you place a MaximumValue of 1000 and a MinimumValue of 100 in the control, but leave the Type property set to the default (which is String), then an entry of 500 would be considered invalid because the ASCII string 500 does not come between the ASCII strings 100 and 1000. Setting the property to Double takes cares of this, and the number 500 would then be considered valid because it is between the numbers 100 and 1000.

The regular expression used by the RegularExpressionValidator in this example requires the user to enter zero or more digits, then optionally a period, then zero or more digits again.

Actually, in a real application, it would probably be better to validate the interest rate in the same way as the other items, with a RangeValidator, but a RegularExpressionValidator is used in our examples for some variety.

Once all of these are placed on the form, the layout should look roughly like this:

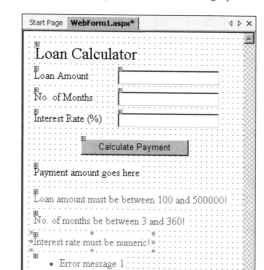

Step Five – Insert Code in the Button's Click Event

Double-click the button to get to its `Click` event in the code editor, and insert the following code:

```
Private Sub btnCalculatePayment_Click(ByVal sender As System.Object, _
    ByVal e As System.EventArgs) Handles btnCalculatePayment.Click

    Dim dblLoanAmount As Double
    Dim intMonths As Integer
    Dim dblInterestRate As Double

    ' Get values from user
    dblLoanAmount = CDbl(txtLoanAmount.Text)
    intMonths = CInt(txtMonths.Text)
    dblInterestRate = CDbl(txtInterestRate.Text) / 1200

    ' Calculate payment using standard function
    Dim dblPaymentAmount As Double
    dblPaymentAmount = -Pmt(dblInterestRate, intMonths, dblLoanAmount)

    ' Make payment amount label visible and display payment
    lblPaymentAmount.Visible = True
    lblPaymentAmount.Text = "Payment is " & FormatCurrency(dblPaymentAmount)

End Sub
```

The function that calculates the payment amount (Pmt) is from a standard library in the .NET Framework. It returns amounts to be paid as negative, so it is necessary to put a minus sign in front to reverse the sign before display.

Notice that the above code would look completely at home in any Visual Basic project. It is literally impossible to tell from the code that it is working with controls in a Web Form.

Now run the program and test it. It should allow calculation of loan amounts and display the result. It should also handle validation of the amounts input for the various parameters.

Notice that all validation controls except the ValidationSummary display their amounts as soon as the user leaves a field. The ValidationSummary control only rolls up the amounts when a post is attempted, such as by pressing the button.

Here is a view of the payment calculator in action:

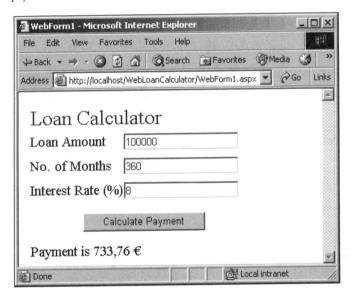

Remember that the displayed size of text in a browser can vary with the browser settings. The text in the sample screen above is somewhat larger than the text in design mode because the browser was set to Larger with the View | Text Size option in Internet Explorer.

The sample screen above shows the payment amount in euros instead of dollars because the system that generated it was set for European defaults. The actual formatting on your screen will reflect your defaults.

Configuring Your Application with Web.config

Despite the fact that the examples we have just seen worked in a manner superficially similar to Windows Forms, there are many aspects of a web-based application that are different. Web-based applications need different types of configurability, and certain aspects need to be configurable at run-time rather than during development.

Many of the configuration settings for a Web Forms application reside in a file named `Web.config`. This file is automatically created as part of an ASP.NET Web Application, so it will show up in the Solution Explorer for any of the examples we have done so far.

Explaining all the options that you can configure in `Web.config` would take far longer than we can discuss in this chapter. Resources like *Professional ASP.NET 1.0 Special Edition* from Wrox Press, ISBN *1-86100-703-5* go into detail on various configuration options.

It is however, helpful for you to know about a few key configuration settings, because using them is very common.

Securing an ASP.NET Web Site

Many web sites are only supposed to be available to certain users. In such sites, it is necessary to authenticate the user, that is, to make sure the user is one who is recognized by the site. Normally this is done with a login page, on which a user is required to enter an account and a password.

In a traditional ASP application, all security for authentication is managed in the code for the ASP pages. Each page must have logic to make sure the user is authenticated, and redirect to a login page if not. Typically this logic for an ASP page is in an INCLUDE file, so that it is not duplicated from page to page. If a particular page leaves off the security code, that page is unsecured and can be fetched without authentication of the user, if someone knows the URL of the page.

In ASP.NET, by default, web applications are unsecured. However, you can create a login screen, and set an option in `Web.config` to force all users of all pages in the site to be authenticated using that login screen. That is, if a user hits a page without being authenticated, the user will automatically be routed to the login screen.

The individual pages do not need any logic to do this. Once the option is set in `Web.config`, all `.aspx` pages on the site are secured, and cannot be accessed without the user being authenticated. (Static pages and old-style ASP pages with an `asp` extension are not secured because they are not processed by the ASP.NET engine.)

The section of `Web.config` that deals with this option is called `<Authentication>`. A related section allows more control over what individual users can do, and this is called `<Authorization>`.

Here's a quick example. The `Web.config` file for our earlier loan calculator example has `<Authentication>` and `<Authorization>` sections that look like this:

```
<!-- AUTHENTICATION
     This section sets the authentication policies of the application.
     Possible modes are "Windows", "Forms", "Passport" and "None"
-->
<authentication mode="Windows" />


<!-- AUTHORIZATION
     This section sets the authorization policies of the application. You
     can allow or deny access to application resources by user_or role.
     Wildcards: "*" mean everyone, "?" means anonymous (unauthenticated)
     users.
```

```
   -->
<authorization>
  <allow users="*" /> <!-- Allow all users -->

   <!--   <allow    users="[comma separated list of users]"
                     roles="[comma_separated list of roles]"/>
           <deny     users="[comma_separated list of users]"
                     roles="[comma_separated list of roles]"/>
   -->
</authorization>
```

The <Authentication> section is set to use Windows security, but the <Authorization> section is set to allow anyone to access the site, so that renders the <Authentication> section irrelevant.

Suppose we change these two sections to look like this:

```
<authentication mode="Forms">
  <forms name=".LOANCLC" loginUrl="login.aspx"
         protection="All" timeout="60" />
</authentication>

<authorization>
  <deny users="?"
</authorization>
```

Also, assume we create a page named login.aspx that handles user authentication. On this page, when you have assured yourself that the user is valid, the logic in that page should execute this line, where sUserName is the string with the user's account name:

```
FormsAuthentication.RedirectFromLoginPage(sUserName, True)
```

This line uses the FormsAuthentication object. The RedirectFromLoginPage sets a cookie to indicate authentication, and then redirects back to the page that was originally requested by the user.

Now when you attempt to access WebForm1.aspx, you will be redirected to login.aspx. Once login.aspx is satisfied that the user is valid and executes the line above, you will be redirected back to WebForm1.aspx.

There is a lot more to learn about settings for authentication and authorization in Web.config. However, this should give you a feeling for how much easier it is to handle such issues in ASP.NET.

State Management Options

In Active Server Pages, it was considered bad practice to use the Application and Session objects to store state, because doing so restricted the web site to running on just one server.

In ASP.NET, the Application and Session objects look mostly the same, but they work differently. By default, they still store state on the local web server, which causes the same constraints as in Active Server Pages. However, there are options in ASP.NET to store the state in two other places:

❑ On a Windows Service running on some machine on your network

❑ In a SQL Server database

Either of these options makes the state information independent of a particular web server. That means it is fine to use the `Application` and `Session` objects to store state in your ASP.NET applications. If the site needs to be deployed to more than one server, none of your code needs to change. The setting for the location where state is stored is configurable in `Web.config`. The section that deals with state management is called `<sessionState>`.

We will not go into how you change that section because the details will vary from site to site, but it is not difficult. If you need that capability, the .NET documentation has a good walkthrough to show you how to use it.

Overview of Web Services

Chapter 2 briefly discussed the concept of **Web Services** as one of the interfaces available in the .NET Framework. That chapter talked about the vision of Web Services, and future possibilities of globally distributed applications. Web Services is one of the key concepts in .NET, and they are expected to radically change the way applications are designed. The idea of applications being run on discrete, controlled sets of servers is expected to give way to the idea of applications wrapping up, processing, and presenting data from a widely distributed set of resources. These resources could potentially come from a multitude of different servers of different types and operating systems, and the universal interface of Web Services would allow them all to be treated as if they were generated by the same kind of system.

Keep in mind that a Web Service has no user interface. It is for program-to-program communication. We will see a technique in this section where a developer can 'peek' at the results from a Web Service, but this is just for convenience during development. Web Services will normally talk to other programs, not to users.

In this section, we will look at how to actually program Web Services in Visual Basic .NET. This section will be shorter than you might think, because programming a Web Service is functionally very similar to programming any other kind of component.

What are Web Services Used For?

Web Services provide a mechanism for programs to communicate over the Internet, using the **SOAP protocol** (discussed in more detail below). Conceptually, this is similar to DCOM in that it enables distributed environments, but Web Services work in a much broader context; that is, SOAP (and the client) no longer care what technology is at the target of the call.

Today, almost all data sent across the Web is embedded in a web page. With Web Services, data can be sent across the Web and then used by the consumer in any way desired. It might be folded into part of a page or screen, consumed by an 'agent' program that watches and analyzes the data looking for certain events or trends, or received and stored into a database for future use.

Here are a number of examples of services that might be exposed on the Internet as Web Services:

❑   Product status information

❑   Shipping and tracking information

❑   Current interest rates

❑   Stock quotes

❑   Current weather

❑   Latest items on sale from a retail site

❑   Best sellers on a retail site

❑   New upcoming items on a retail site available for pre-order

❑   Employee benefit information

❑   Data sets of real estate properties meeting a certain set of criteria

❑   Reminders, tasks, and to-do items

This is just a random sampling of items that are obvious candidates. Web Services could potentially be used for almost any web application that is data-centric.

In this section, we will discuss how Web Services work, starting with an overview of the XML-based SOAP protocol used for communication with Web Services. Then, after describing how to create a Web Service, and how to consume a Web Service in another application, we will cover a step-by-step example.

Understanding the SOAP Protocol

The **S**imple **O**bject **A**ccess **P**rotocol, usually abbreviated to **SOAP**, is an XML-based standard for component communication through HTTP. Since it is based on XML, it is text-based, and can go through firewalls.

Part of SOAP describes how Web Services initially establish communication with one another. The first phase of communications is called the **discovery phase**. During this phase, the Web Services transmit information about the component interface that is available. That information is transmitted in a sub-protocol called **W**eb **S**ervices **D**escription **L**anguage or **WSDL**.

Then, once the discovery phase is complete, the stage is set for normal **component interface calls**. These calls look and act a lot like calls to a local component, except that the information in the calls is being transmitted and received between the components as specified by the SOAP protocol.

The final response of a Web Service component is an **XML document** containing all the information returned by the Web Service. The consumer of the Web Service then interprets this XML document and extracts the information needed.

Here is a diagram showing the steps in this process:

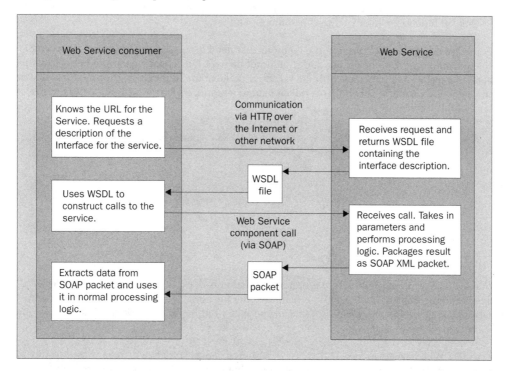

In Visual Basic .NET, it is not really necessary to know what is going on under the surface. The information sent to a Web Service is translated into the proper format by the .NET Framework automatically. The .NET Framework then manages the process, receives the returning XML document, and places the returned data into component interfaces as necessary.

The end result is that once you have referred to a Web Service by entering its address as a Web Reference in your project, you work with the Web Service in code as if it were a local component. This transparency in using Web Services is one of the more impressive advances in Visual Studio .NET. No other tools currently available to work with Web Services offer anywhere near this level of ease of use.

Creating a Web Service in Visual Basic .NET

Web Service components are created by selecting the appropriate option when starting a new project – ASP.NET Web Service. Once selected, it sets up the project parameters for a class library that will be Web Service-enabled.

The first view of the Web Service is similar to other component designer interfaces. There is a design surface onto which pre-packaged and system components, such as message queues, can be dragged. However, it is not required to use any such resources to create a Web Service. It is only necessary to produce a Web-enabled component interface.

Double-clicking on the component design surface will bring up the code editor for the Web Service code module. It will have all the necessary declarations already in it, and also includes a Hello World Web Service-enabled function, which you can uncomment and test.

A Web Service component will have some methods that need to be exposed as part of the Web Service, and others that are just for internal use and should not be exposed. Those that are to be a visible part of the Web Service interface are indicated with the WebMethod attribute. Otherwise, they look just like other methods. Here is an example of a Web Service-enabled method, which we will implement in our example at the end of this topic:

```
<WebMethod()> Public Function Color(iIndex as Integer) As String
  Select Case iIndex
    Case 1
      Color = "Red"
    Case 2
      Color = "Blue"
    Case Else
      Color = "No Color"
  End Select
End Function
```

Note that the only way this differs from a standard function is the <WebMethod()> in the declaration line. A declaration done this way adds a .NET attribute to the function. The attribute is stored as part of the metadata for the function, and the CLR treats all routines with the WebMethod attribute as appropriate to expose through Web Services.

If you create a Web Service in Visual Basic.NET and then run it, you get a browser-based testing interface for the Web Service. Here is a typical browser screen that comes up when activating a Web Service with the Color function shown above:

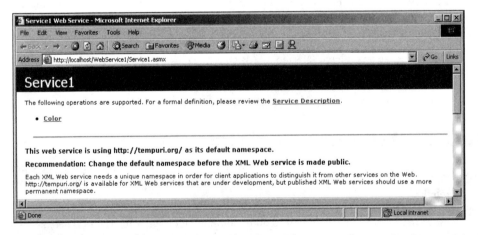

This very useful test bed uses the discovery capabilities of Web Services to query the interface of the Web Service and display information about it. It also lets you activate the web service for testing. You do that by selecting the operation you want to test (for example, Color in the screen above).

The activation screen that you get for an operation provides an input area to feed parameters directly to the Web Service. Once the Invoke button is pressed in this screen, the parameters are passed into the Web Service and the browser displays the XML packet that is returned with the output of the Web Service.

If a value for iIndex of 2 were entered, and the Invoke button pressed, the simplest possible version of the returned XML packet would look like this:

```
<?xml version="1.0" encoding="utf-8" ?>
<string xmlns="http://tempuri.org/">Blue</string>
```

Any consumer of this Web Service would get back such an XML packet. If the consumer is integrated into the .NET Framework, the values in the XML will be parsed and placed into a normal component interface. That is, a Web Service component accessed from within a .NET Framework program looks very much like any other component. The next section discusses such Web Service consumers.

Consuming a Web Service in Visual Basic .NET

Any Visual Basic .NET application may need to integrate a Web Service. That could include Windows Forms applications as well as Web Forms applications. It could also include a middle-tier component.

To integrate a Web Service into a Visual Basic .NET project, it is necessary to reference the service. This is done with the Project | Add Web Reference menu option. When that option is chosen, a screen like the following comes up:

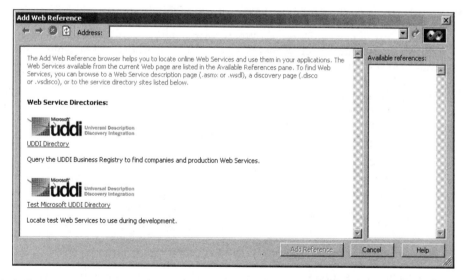

This dialog allows referencing of both local and remote Web Services by entering a URL for the service. It might be appropriate to reference a local Web Service for testing, but in most production situations, the Web Service will be remote. You also have the option of using a lookup service called UDDI to find a Web Service that does what you want.

A remote Web Service can be referenced with its URL. Microsoft includes some Web Service directories on its own servers to provide examples.

Entering the URL for a Web Service displays information about it, including an XML document that details its interface. The Add Reference button becomes enabled, and pressing that button adds the Web Service to the project.

Once a Web Service (local or remote) is referenced, it shows up in the Solution Explorer, and is treated locally just like any other component. The Web Service's interface even shows up in IntelliSense.

To reference a Web Service component, the following syntax is used:

```
Dim objWebService As New servername.servicename
```

Referencing a Web Service this way actually creates a local proxy object with the appropriate interface, and that's what your code is accessing. Behind the scenes, the proxy object is communicating with the actual Web Service using SOAP. The .NET Framework creates and manages the proxy object automatically.

Creating and Consuming a Web Service

In this final example, we will see how we can integrate the Web Service, created earlier with a Color function, into a Windows Form example:

1. Start a new Windows Application and add a reference to the Web Service created earlier using Project | Add Web Reference.... Enter the URL for the service with the Color function. If you named the project WebService1, then the URL would typically be http://localhost/WebService1/service1.asmx. After a short delay, XML information associated with Service1 will display and you can click the Add Reference button.

2. Go to the blank form that is created for the Windows Application (Form1), and place a Label, a TextBox, and a Button side by side, and another Label under all three of them. Change the text in the first Label to read Color Index and change the Text in the Button to Get Color. The form should now look like this:

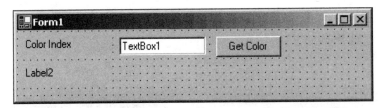

3. Double-click the Button to get to its event handling routine and in that Button1_Click routine, place the following code:

```
Private Sub Button1_Click(ByVal sender As System.Object, _
    ByVal e As System.EventArgs) Handles Button1.Click

    Dim objColor As New localhost.Service1()
```

```
    Dim sColor As String
    Dim iIndex As Integer
    iIndex = CInt(TextBox1.Text)
    sColor = objColor.Color(iIndex)
    Label2.Text = "Color is " & sColor

End Sub
```

In the first line of this code, `localhost` refers to the fact that the Web Service is on the local web server. `Service1` refers to the name of the service when it was compiled. Recall that the Web Service project created earlier included a service with the default name `Service1`.

Note that, after the declaration of `objColor` as a Web Service, there is no further indication in the code that a Web Service is being used. `objColor` looks just like a locally created object, as far as the rest of the code is concerned.

4. Run the project, type in 2 in the textbox and press the button. The second label will change to say Color is Blue.

Notice that after the Web Service object was declared in the first line of code in Step 3, the Web Service object is treated no differently from any other object in code. For example, you may have noticed that IntelliSense was available when typing the fifth line. This is just as true of remote Web Services as local Web Services. Once they are referenced into a project, they are used in code just like any other component. The work behind the scenes (discovering the interface, and transmitting information to and from the Web Service in XML) is handled transparently by the .NET Framework.

This example used Windows Forms, but the exact same procedure will work for a Web Forms version.

Security in Web Services

By default, Web Services are available to any caller that can get to the URL representing the service. By default, they also transmit their information in clear HTML. There are obviously situations where one or both of these are undesirable.

Normal Web-based methods of authentication and authorization, such as those used in ASP pages, can be used for Web Services as well. Doing such authentication for Web Services has some differences though. We cannot cover this process in detail, but you can find out more in *Professional ASP.NET Web Services* published by Wrox Press, ISBN *1-861005-45-8*).

For securing the information while in transit, Secure Sockets Layer (SSL) can be used, just as it can be for web pages. The resource mentioned above also covers this topic.

Summary

With Visual Basic .NET and ASP.NET, Web-based user interfaces can be designed quickly and easily with high-productivity visual tools. Services can be exposed to the Web as easily as writing a function.

That does not mean, however, that VB developers who have only worked on forms-based applications can become instant web developers. The learning curve has been shortened, but not eliminated. It is still necessary to become proficient in the basics of HTML, DHTML, and XML, and to have a general understanding of Web technologies and concepts such as state management. It is also helpful to know such client technologies as JavaScript.

With Visual Basic .NET though, the days of needing to know all the vagaries of Active Server Pages just to do a simple web application are gone – Web-enabling business applications has just become dramatically easier.

8

Data Access

Visual Basic was around for a couple of years before it became popular for corporate development projects. The reason is obvious – version 3.0 added built-in capabilities to extract data from relational databases. Today, most systems written in VB access relational data stores of some kind, the most common being **SQL Server** and **Oracle**.

However, the way data is accessed in VB has changed a lot since version 3.0. We have gone from local access to client-server access to Internet access, all in about seven years. This has forced evolution of the data access models programmers use to work with data.

That original data access model in Version 3.0 was called **Data Access Objects**, or **DAO**. It was created for access to *local databases* in the Access Jet format. It could be used to access databases on a central server, but lacked the performance and features that such access needed.

The successors to DAO were **Remote Data Objects** (**RDO**) and **ActiveX Data Objects** (**ADO**). Both were designed primarily for *client-server* use. RDO didn't hang around too long, but ADO is still widely used. It has been extended to the Internet world, with capabilities such as **Remote Data Services** (**RDS**) and with minimal XML capabilities. ADO is still the easiest data access model to use for client-server projects, but is more cumbersome for the highly distributed environment of the Internet.

For the .NET Framework, a new data access model has been created that is optimized for *distributed* use. It is called **ADO.NET**. It uses the same access methods for local, client-server, or Internet access. It also allows data to be easily passed around to the place it is needed. This makes ADO.NET a good model for many different types of applications (though not for all applications, as we will discuss later.)

Despite the name, ADO.NET is not really a new generation of ADO. ADO.NET does have some significant similarities to ADO, especially in the way it connects to databases, but it also has some major differences, including the way code is written to access tables, records, and fields.

ADO.NET can be used for accessing many kinds of data stores. This is a continuation of a trend begun by ADO. In ADO, data is accessed through an **OLE DB provider**, and such a provider can be written for all kinds of data sources, such as file systems and flat files, in addition to traditional relational stores. ADO.NET goes even further by converting just about any data fed into it into XML, and then accessing that. This makes it even easier to write a provider for ADO.NET because it simply has to translate data into XML format.

Most data access involves traditional relational databases, and the examples in this chapter emphasize that type of data access. However, with XML as its internal data format, ADO.NET can naturally be used to access native XML, with no relational database engine involved at all. This makes it far easier to do access to simple XML for routine purposes.

However, it is still necessary in some cases to work with XML at a very detailed level. .NET also includes classes that allow reading, writing, and manipulation of XML. These are the replacements for the MSXML classes that were sometimes used in VB6. However, we will not cover that type of access in this book because it would take a lot explanation of the basic XML concepts involved, although you can learn more about this type of access in *Professional XML for .NET Developers* published Wrox Press, ISBN *1-861005-31-8*.

> *The examples in this chapter that require a database all use the* **Northwind** *sample database in SQL Server. Only the* Customers *and* Orders *tables are used, because these are sufficient to do examples with a master file (*Customers*) and a related detail file (*Orders*). If you have a database with two other tables that have a master-detail relationship, it is relatively easy to translate the examples to use your data.*

> *Most of the examples in this chapter use SQL statements to access the database, in order to keep them as simple as possible. In production applications, it is more typical to use stored procedures for these operations. Later in the chapter, we will discuss how to use stored procedures in ADO.NET instead of SQL statements.*

ADO.NET vs. ADO

Traditional ADO was designed for tightly coupled, connected architectures and, by default, passes data around in a binary, proprietary format through COM interfaces. It has therefore needed to evolve quickly to be usable in Internet applications. The history of ADO has led to several issues for today's Internet-based development:

❑ Maintaining a connection to a database, as done in vanilla ADO, is resource intensive and limits scalability of applications. Such architecture is unsuitable/unworkable for most Internet applications.

❑ The main alternative for disconnected access is Remote Data Services (RDS). This exposes new Internet functionality, but introduces additional complexity. Developers have a tough learning curve before being able to use the right features of RDS for a given application architecture.

❑ XML support is very limited, so accessing XML typically means going through the MSXML libraries and accessing the XML DOM.

❑ Multiple versions of ADO exist, and some versions are mutually incompatible.

ADO.NET and the .NET Framework together solve these limitations:

❑ A set of data in ADO.NET can be passed to any appropriate application tier in XML, so no continuous connection to the database is necessary.

❑ The same access techniques in ADO.NET can work for local, network, or Internet access.

❑ XML support is built in. This makes ADO.NET a flexible alternative, suitable for many different kinds of data access in VB.NET, including access to local data without using a database engine.

❑ The .NET Framework allows side-by-side access to multiple versions of the same components. Applications in .NET will always use the correct ADO.NET installation.

The .NET Framework also includes support for traditional ADO, using COM interoperability on the standard ADO libraries. Besides providing backward compatibility, this also gives access to capabilities of ADO that ADO.NET does not have. For example, ADO.NET has no function for record locking, so applications that need the ability to lock records must use ADO.

The syntax for using ADO in Visual Basic .NET is quite similar to equivalent syntax in VB6, so this chapter will not discuss coding syntax for doing data access in Visual Basic .NET using ADO. If you are interested in more information about using ADO in .NET, you should refer to *Professional ADO.NET*, ISBN 1-861005-27-X, or *Professional Visual Basic Interoperability: COM and VB6 to .NET*, ISBN 1-861005-65-2, both published by Wrox Press.

ADO.NET Demands New Architectures

The programming model for ADO.NET will not look too alien to developers accustomed to ADO, once a couple of key new concepts are understood. The logic for getting a connection is similar, for example. Both models manipulate collections of rows and fields. Both models have support for transactions through the connection object, and both models can be bound to controls for automatic data handling.

However, the architectures that use ADO.NET in an optimal way are quite different from the architectures appropriate for ADO-based applications. ADO.NET is designed for loosely coupled, highly distributed applications. Developers moving to Visual Basic .NET and ADO.NET will need to learn new variations on classic multi-tier architectures, and we will consider how best to use ADO.NET in more depth toward the end of the chapter.

ADO.NET – Important Concepts

This section will introduce some of the most important concepts in ADO.NET in a way that should be fairly easy to digest. Then, the rest of the chapter will get into more details about these concepts.

Location of the ADO.NET Classes

The classes for ADO.NET are all in the System.Data namespace, or in namespaces beneath it such as System.Data.SQLClient (which contains classes specific to SQL Server) and System.Data.OleDb (which contains classes for data access using OLE DB). Almost all of the examples in this chapter presume that the System.Data and System.Data.OleDb namespaces have been referenced in a code module with these lines:

```
Imports System.Data
Imports System.Data.OleDb
```

Replacing Recordsets

A major difference between ADO and ADO.NET is that the new functionality in ADO.NET does not support a Recordset class. However, as we mentioned earlier, existing ADO capabilities including Recordsets are available for compatibility and for some application designs where traditional ADO is still superior.

For many data access purposes, the Recordset concept has been replaced in the new ADO.NET syntax by the more flexible DataSet. Especially for those functions related to changing, manipulating, and randomly accessing data, DataSets are a good improvement, and much of the chapter discusses how to use them.

In addition to the DataSet, there is another data class available in ADO.NET for read-only access to data. It is called a DataReader, and it is similar to a read-only Recordset with a forward-only cursor. It has the advantage of much higher performance for such sequential, read-only situations. This chapter also includes an example of creating and using a DataReader.

Datasets are a bit more difficult to understand than DataReaders, so we begin by getting a better idea of what a Dataset is.

What is a DataSet?

A DataSet is a collection of mini-tables or recordsets, and the relationships between them. Perhaps the best way to picture a DataSet is a miniature relational database, in which the data is kept in memory.

This 'virtual' local relational database is totally disconnected from the original source of the data, yet it has very useful relational capabilities. The DataSet contains a local copy of the data, and is used for local processing, whether on a client workstation, a web server, or a remote Internet client. All operations that need to be carried out on the data are done on this local copy, with no continuous connection to the original data store. This is a major advantage over classic ADO, which does require such a connection.

When all processing operations have been completed on the local DataSet, it is submitted to be resolved with the original store. Any changed records in the DataSet can be updated in the source database, new records that were added to the DataSet can be added to the tables in the database, and so forth.

> *We will examine the* DataSet *– its object model, the process of getting data into it, operating on the data, and returning it back to the original data store – later in the chapter. We will also discuss issues relating to data concurrency – that is, what to do if data in the original store was changed while the local* DataSet *was being manipulated.*

While DataSets are typically manipulated in memory, they are passed between application tiers as XML. The XML document for a DataSet contains both the schema and the data. However, you don't have to know anything about XML to use a DataSet. When you are using it in your code from the in-memory representation, or sending the DataSet between tiers, you don't see XML at all.

As befits an XML-based technology, once the data has been placed in a DataSet, the original source does not matter. The data is operated on identically regardless of how it came to be in the DataSet.

This design for DataSets fixes a lot of the drawbacks of using Recordsets in VB6. In particular, Recordsets do not handle hierarchical data structures very well, but DataSets are designed to work with hierarchical data. Later in the chapter, we will see how DataSets in ADO.NET facilitate access to master-detail data such as customers and their orders. Such capabilities are a major improvement over ADO.

A DataSet with just one table in it can fill the same conceptual role as a Recordset. Such a DataSet needs no relationships set up within it and might not use any of the other advanced features of DataSets. However, it is not a good idea to simply port old designs to ADO.NET by substituting one-table DataSets for Recordsets. DataSets open up new design possibilities, such as the master-detail example shown later in the chapter, that will work better in most typical data-processing applications.

Data Flow Overview for a DataSet

Data used in ADO.NET usually starts in a traditional relational data store such as SQL Server or Oracle. From there, it is extracted for use by a part of ADO.NET called a **data provider** (sometimes called a **managed provider**). This is conceptually similar to the role played in ADO by an OLE DB provider. A data provider is the interface technology that knows how to connect to a database and get data into and out of it. We discuss data providers in more detail below.

Once the data has been extracted by a data provider and placed in a DataSet, there is no longer a need to continue a connection to the database. The data can then be operated on in a variety of ways.

One of the most common operations is to specify relationships in the DataSet so that the data can be treated relationally. Then code and/or bound controls can change the data in the DataSet, adding in new rows, changing or deleting old ones, and so on. When those changes are finished, the data provider then resolves the changes. It looks through the DataSet, finds the changed or added data, and attempts to place the changes or additions into the original data store. If there are concurrency problems, or other problems such as having the database go off-line, then the data provider can raise appropriate errors.

Here is a diagrammatic representation of the steps described above. The process starts in the upper left with data being extracted from the original data store:

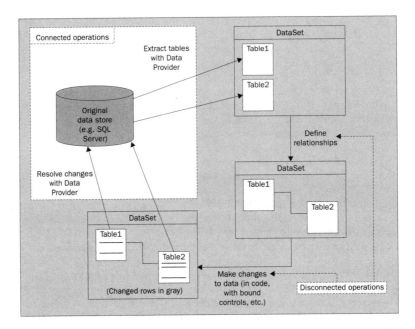

The diagram illustrates the parts of the cycle that take place in a connected fashion, all of which involve the data provider. Other operations take place disconnected from the main data store.

This diagram does not explicitly state where the DataSet resides. That's because the cycle is the same no matter where the DataSet gets manipulated. It could be on the same system as the data store, or on a client workstation on the same network, or in a browser on an Internet client. Even if the DataSet is on the local machine with the database, manipulation of the DataSet takes place without a connection to the database being necessary.

There are additional operations that are not included in the above example. Some of the possibilities include:

❑   Adding constraints to the relational structure in the DataSet.

❑   Attaching a schema to the DataSet to help with operations such as data validation.

❑   Defining and adding new columns to the tables in the DataSet, such as derived columns that are calculated from other columns for reporting purposes. (Since these columns are not in the original data store, they are not part of the operation to place changes back in the database.)

These operations will be discussed below in the section describing the DataSet in more detail. That section will cover DataSet-related elements in the ADO.NET namespace and classes.

However, before going into some more details on DataSets, it is helpful to understand how the data gets into them, via data providers.

Data Providers for Connected Operations

Data providers were mentioned above as the part of ADO.NET that provides an interface to the original data store. Data providers take care of functions like the following:

- ❏ Making a connection to a database

- ❏ Getting a stream of data from the database to place into a read-only set of query results (called a DataReader)

- ❏ Getting a stream of data from the database to place into a table in a DataSet for manipulation

- ❏ Interfacing to stored procedures in the database

- ❏ Examining changed DataSets for differences that need to be recorded in the source database

- ❏ Raising errors during data resolution

All these operations are carried out by the data providers while connected to the original data store. Data providers carry out all of the database interaction in ADO.NET that needs to be done with an active connection to the database.

Providers Included with .NET

The .NET Framework currently includes two data providers. They are:

Type of provider	Namespace	Additional information
OLE DB	System.Data.OleDb	A generic provider that talks to a variety of OLE DB providers through COM interoperability. It takes care of the interface to the COM-based OLE DB provider, and exposes the functionality of the OLE DB provider in the .NET Framework.
SQL Server	System.Data.SQLClient	Specifically for SQL Server, versions 7.0 and 2000. Implemented completely in managed code, and provides the fastest performance when talking to SQL Server.

All of the classes in the OLE DB .NET data provider are prefixed with OleDb and all of the classes in the SQL Server .NET data provider are prefixed with Sql.

An additional provider for ODBC (namespace Microsoft.Data.ODBC) can be downloaded from Microsoft, and more are expected from Microsoft or third parties. For example, at publication time, a data provider specifically for Oracle (namespace System.Data.OracleClient) is in beta test, and the beta version is available on Microsoft's web site.

The OLE DB Data Provider

The OLE DB .NET data provider is a generic provider that should work with most OLE DB providers. It has been tested with the following:

- ❑ SQLOLEDB – SQL OLE DB provider
- ❑ MSDAORA – Oracle OLE DB provider
- ❑ JOLT – Jet OLE DB provider

The OLE DB .NET data provider does not work with the OLE DB Provider for ODBC (MSDASQL). As mentioned above, a separate provider for ODBC can be downloaded from Microsoft's web site.

The OLE DB .NET data provider also does not work with OLE DB providers that require support for OLE DB 2.5 interfaces. This includes the OLE DB provider for Microsoft Exchange and OLE DB provider for Internet Publishing (both from Microsoft).

The SQL Server Data Provider

The SQL Server .NET data provider provides access only to Microsoft SQL Server (versions 7 and 2000). It is implemented totally in the .NET Framework and does not go through a COM-based OLE DB provider. As a result of this design, the SQL Server .NET data provider yields better performance than the OLE DB .NET data provider going through SQLOLEDB.

For consistency, all the examples in this chapter use the OLE DB .NET data provider. The interface of both data providers is the same except for the different prefixes in the class names (as mentioned previously, and covered in more detail below), so there should be no problem in translating examples for use with the SQL Server .NET Data provider if you wish.

Classes Implemented by Data Providers

The classes available in the two data providers installed with the .NET Framework are:

Type of Class	Name in OLE DB .NET Data provider	Name in SQL Server .NET Data provider	Function
Connection	OleDbConnection	SqlConnection	Establishes a connection to the database. Similar to the Connection object in ADO.
Command	OleDbCommand	SqlCommand	Carries out an operation while connected to the database. Conceptually similar to the Command object in ADO, but contains substantial new features.

Type of Class	Name in OLE DB .NET Data provider	Name in SQL Server .NET Data provider	Function
DataReader	OleDbDataReader	SqlDataReader	Holds a stream of data from the database for a query operation. Loosely corresponds to a forward-only, read-only Recordset.
DataAdapter	OleDbDataAdapter	SqlDataAdapter	Transfers data back and forth between the database and a DataSet.

Working with Data Provider Classes Using Wizards

In most cases, the fastest way to integrate data provider classes into a project is to use the Data tab of the Toolbox. This tab contains versions of all the classes listed above except the DataReader classes, with each class wrapped up as a 'control' that you can drag and drop into your project.

For the connection and command ADO.NET classes, this just gives you an alternative way to do your configuration, namely, with the Properties window. However, when you drag over one of the DataAdapter controls, a wizard will begin. Once the wizard has been completed, you have a DataAdapter control configured and ready to use throughout your project. The wizard also creates the connection and command objects needed by the DataAdapter, so you don't have to configure them manually either (although you do have to supply the connection information).

If you have used the Data Environment in VB6, you may be skeptical of this approach. The Data Environment hid most of its operations, so you didn't always know what it was doing. The controls on the Data tab are quite different. The wizard that configures the DataAdapter control produces code to implement the operations, so you can always see exactly what it is doing, and even use that code as a template for your own operations.

The automated approach is not the ideal way to learn about these classes, however. To help you understand how the data provider classes work, we will first examine how they are used in code. After we have discussed using the classes at this in-depth level, we will return to an example that uses a wizard to do much of the work.

Combining Classes from Different Data Providers

If you wish to use a class in one data provider, you are not allowed to combine it with a class from another data provider. For example, you can't create your connection with a SqlConnection object, and then switch namespaces to use an OleDbCommand object to generate queries against the database. If you begin using a SQLConnection object, then you must only use classes in the SQL Server data provider set. And if you begin using an OleDbConnection, you must stick to other classes in the System.Data.OleDb namespace to interact with it.

This limitation does not apply to the classes in `System.Data`, such as the `DataSet` class. These classes can work with either type of data provider. In fact, as we will discuss later, a `DataSet` can contain data from different data sources, so it can work with any number of `DataAdapters` from different data providers.

Working with Data Providers in Code

Data provider classes can be manipulated in code like any other .NET class. You can also take advantage of options in code that the wizards and dialog boxes discussed above do not include.

In the next few sections, we will take a closer look at specific data provider classes, illustrating their use with code examples.

We will do two brief code examples, one for constructing a `DataReader` and another for creating a `DataSet` and placing a table within it. Both of these examples also include code to instantiate and configure the other data provider classes needed, such as the `OleDbConnection` and `OleDbCommand` classes. However, first we will look at how the connection and command classes are created and configured.

Connection Classes

To create one of the connection classes (`OleDbConnection` or `SqlConnection`), you must supply all the information need to establish a connection to the database. This is typically done with a connection string, and the string is close to identical to a connection string in ADO. Here is an example of a connection string for an `OleDbConnection` object:

```
Dim sConnectionString As String = _
    "Provider=SQLOLEDB.1; User ID=sa; " & _
    "Initial Catalog=Northwind; Data Source=MYSERVER"
```

The only difference for a connection string for a `SqlConnection` object is that the `Provider` clause is left out. It's not needed since that provider only works with SQL Server.

You can also configure several other parameters of the connection class, such as a connection timeout period. You can do that in the connect string, or you can use properties of the connection object.

Once a connection string is created, a connection object can be instantiated and opened. Here is code to do that, assuming the connection string was set as above:

```
Dim myConnection As New OleDbConnection(sConnectionString)
myConnection.Open()
```

As with the ADO `Connection` object, the primary methods needed to work with connection classes are the `Open()` method and the `Close()` method. A connection object must be explicitly opened before it can be used. The `Close()` method should be called as soon as you are finished with a connection object to release the resources used by the object.

> Note that you can't set parameters on a connection object when it is open. If you need to set properties on a connection object after it is instantiated, you must do so before you call the **Open()** method.

Command Classes

Once a connection is established, you will need classes to interact with and manipulate data. The classes that provide a gateway for this are the `OleDBCommand` and `SqlCommand` classes, which we refer to generically as the **command classes**.

As we mentioned earlier, ADO.NET command classes are conceptually similar to the `Command` object in ADO, but the methods and properties are different. There are also more ways to create a command object in ADO.NET.

There are two properties for a command object that must be set before the command object can be used. One is the connection that will be associated with the command object. The other is the SQL statement or stored procedure to carry out some desired operation.

You can include this information when you instantiate a command object, using code like this:

```
sSQL = "SELECT * FROM Customers"
Dim myCommand As New OleDbCommand(sSQL, myConnection)
```

You also have the option of leaving off one or both of these parameters at instantiation, and then setting them with properties after the command object is instantiated. Here is some code that illustrates that option:

```
sSQL = "SELECT * FROM Customers"
Dim myCommand As New OleDbCommand()
myCommand.CommandText = sSQL
myCommand.Connection = myConnection
```

The resulting command object behaves the same way, regardless of the technique you use to create it.

There is more to setting up the `Command` object to use a stored procedure. That operation is discussed later in the chapter in the section called *Using Stored Procedures in ADO.NET*.

Methods of the Command Classes

Classic ADO command objects only have one method, `Execute()`, which executes a SQL statement, and returns a result set if there is one. The ADO.NET command classes don't have a single `Execute()` method. In its place are several `Execute()` methods, each used for a different purpose. These include:

Method	Description
ExecuteNonQuery()	Used to execute a SQL statement that does not return any results, such as INSERT, UPDATE, and DELETE statements.
ExecuteReader()	Returns a reference to a DataReader object. We will cover the DataReader below.
ExecuteScalar()	Executes a SQL statement, and returns only the first field in the first row of the result. This is often helpful when accessing aggregate SQL functions such as COUNT.

Table continued on following page

Method	Description
ExecuteXMLReader() (only available for SQLCommand class)	Like ExecuteReader(), but returns rows in XML format as an XMLReader. This is an easy way to get XML straight out of a SQL Server database.

None of these are used to fill up a DataSet – this requires a DataAdapter, which we will discuss later, but these methods are useful for several other data access scenarios.

Later in the chapter, we will see the ExecuteReader() method in action. Using ExecuteNonQuery() is as easy as constructing a SQL statement that doesn't return anything, and then calling the method.

ExecuteScalar() is almost as easy. Suppose we want to find how many customers in the Northwind database are in the UK. We could get that count into a variable named nCustomersInUK using this code:

```
Dim sConnectionString As String = _
  "Provider=SQLOLEDB.1; User ID=sa; " & _
  "Initial Catalog=Northwind;Data Source=MYSERVER"
Dim myConnection As New OleDbConnection(sConnectionString)

Dim sSQL As String
sSQL = "SELECT COUNT(CustomerID) AS CustomersInUK " & _
  "FROM Customers WHERE (Country = 'UK')"
Dim myCommand As New OleDbCommand(sSQL, myConnection)

Dim nCustomersInUK As Integer
myConnection.Open()
nCustomersInUK = CInt(myCommand.ExecuteScalar)
MsgBox(nCustomersInUK)
```

Obviously, you would need to change the connection string to point to your SQL Server, and to use a different account and password if necessary.

If you have the standard Northwind sample database loaded, this code should display a message box with the value 7 in it. Obviously, if the database has been changed since SQL Server was installed, the count might be different.

The Importance of Connected Operations

Even though ADO.NET is designed to support distributed data architectures, the capabilities of the command classes allow many data-related tasks to be done in a connected mode with ADO.NET. There are scenarios in which this mode of operation is preferred over the disconnected use of DataSets.

For example, when rendering a web page that displays data from a database, the fastest way to get the data is to use a DataReader, which operates in a connected mode. Or, if you need to make bulk updates to a database, it can be done faster, and with less code, by constructing an appropriate SQL statement, and using the ExecuteNonQuery() method of a command class.

The DataReader Class

We have previously referred to the `DataReader` class as similar to a forward-only, read-only recordset. A `DataReader` is created using the `ExecuteReader()` method of a command object, and then its rows are accessed using a `Read()` method. (The `DataReader` classes do not have a public constructor, so they can't be directly instantiated.) A detailed example below shows how to create a `DataReader` and access the data it exposes.

Creating a DataReader

The following code uses the Northwind database in SQL Server, creating a connection object and a command object, and then using them to initialize a `DataReader`. The `DataReader` is then placed in a loop to display some of the information placed into it.

You will need to refer to the namespaces needed with `Imports` statements. The following code should go at the top of your code module:

```
Imports System.Data
Imports System.Data.OleDb
```

This code will work fine in just about any circumstances, as long as the server (*MYSERVER*) is changed to the correct name, and any other necessary login information is entered into the connection string. For example, the code could be placed in a button event on a Windows form (which is actually where I tested it):

```
' Code to create and use a DataReader

' Create connection and command objects
Dim sConnectionString As String = _
  "Provider=SQLOLEDB.1; User ID=sa; " & _
  "Initial Catalog=Northwind;Data Source=MYSERVER"
Dim myConnection As New System.Data.OLEDB.OleDbConnection(sConnectionString)
Dim myCommand As New OleDbCommand("SELECT * FROM Customers", myConnection)

' Declare the DataReader
Dim myReader As OleDbDataReader

' Open the connection and stream data into the reader
Try
  myConnection.Open()
  myReader = myCommand.ExecuteReader

  ' Check the data in the reader
  While (myReader.Read)
    Console.WriteLine("customer name: " & myReader("CompanyName"))
  End While

Catch myException As Exception
  MsgBox(myException.ToString())

Finally
  ' Close the connection and flush the reader
```

```
      If myConnection.State = System.Data.ConnectionState.Open Then
        myConnection.Close()
      End If
      If Not myReader Is Nothing Then
        myReader = Nothing
      End If
   End Try
```

> **A special note on SQL Server 2000 logins. If you have trouble making the code above work with a SQL Server 2000 installation, and the exception indicates an invalid login, you should check to make sure that your SQL Server is configured to accept SQL Server logins such as the sa login above. It may be set to accept Windows logins only, because that is the default setting at installation. So, if you are on a freshly installed test machine, go to SQL Enterprise Manager, right-click on the server name and select Properties. On the dialog that appears, click the Security tab. If the Windows only option is selected under Authentication, you will have to either (1) change the option to SQL Server and Windows; or (2) change your connection string to use a Windows login.**

Let's do a short walkthrough of the code. First, the connection and command objects are declared and initialized. Notice that the code uses the new ability in Visual Basic .NET to pass parameters to a class at instantiation. The equivalent code to declare a connection object in VB6, for example, would require separate lines to declare the object and then pass in an initialization string.

After the connection and command objects are created and initialized, the DataReader is declared (but not instantiated). Then the connection is opened and data is streamed into the reader. This code also shows how exceptions generated during database operations are typically coded. More extensive discussion on handling exceptions is included later in the chapter.

Then, a While loop is used to display the data in the DataReader to the console, which is accessed in Visual Studio .NET as the Output window:

```
Output                                                              ₽ ×
Debug
  customer name: Alfreds Futterkiste
  customer name: Ana Trujillo Emparedados y helados
  customer name: Antonio Moreno Taquería
  customer name: Around the Horn
  customer name: Berglunds snabbköp
  customer name: Blauer See Delikatessen
  customer name: Blondesddsl père et fils
```

Since the DataReader is forward-only, once the data is read in a loop like this, the DataReader has no more data in it to access. It must be reinitialized before being used again.

Using a DataReader is a lot like using a forward-only, read-only Recordset in ADO. However, the code has one significant difference. A new DataReader is positioned to a null record until the Read() method is executed for the first time. This contrasts with ADO logic, in which a new Recordset is positioned at the first record by default. The main difference that this causes in code is that the Read() method for the DataReader is accessed at the top of the While loop, where typical ADO logic would use a MoveNext() just prior to the end of the loop.

After looping through all of the records with the DataReader, the Catch structure takes care of exceptions, in this case by just displaying the error message in a message box. Then, the Finally structure closes the database, if it is still open, and makes sure that the DataReader object is set to Nothing.

The DataAdapter Class

The last type of class in a data provider is the DataAdapter class. It is an interface between the data provider and a DataSet.

A DataAdapter is easy to create in code. It requires a command object that is configured to execute a SELECT operation (through a SQL statement or a stored procedure). The command object is created as we covered above. Putting that code together with one new line allows us to create a DataAdapter:

```
Dim sConnectionString As String = _
  "Provider=SQLOLEDB.1; User ID=sa; " & _
  "Initial Catalog=Northwind;Data Source=MYSERVER"
Dim myConnection As New OleDbConnection(sConnectionString)

Dim sSQL As String
sSQL = "SELECT * FROM Customers"
Dim myCommand As New OleDbCommand(sSQL, myConnection)

Dim myDataAdapter As New OleDbDataAdapter(myCommand)
```

Once you have a DataAdapter created, it can be used to build a DataTable in a DataSet. It extracts data using the SQL statement in the associated command object. Each DataAdapter can fill up one DataTable in the DataSet, so a DataSet with more than one DataTable will also need more than one DataAdapter to transfer the data from the database.

DataAdapters transfer data to a DataTable with the Fill() method. We could extend the code above to fill a DataTable named Customers inside a DataSet with this code:

```
Dim myDataSet As New DataSet("MyNewDataset")
myDataAdapter.Fill(myDataSet, "Customers")
```

Creating a DataSet

The code for creating a DataSet is similar in some respects to the DataReader code above, particularly in the section that creates the ADO connection and command objects. Here's the code:

```
' Code to create and use a DataSet
' Module must also have the following lines in the declarations section:
'   Imports System.Data
'   Imports System.Data.OleDb

' Create connection and command objects
Dim sConnectionString As String = _
  "Provider=SQLOLEDB.1; User ID=sa; " & _
  "Initial Catalog=Northwind;Data Source=MYSERVER"
Dim myConnection As New System.Data.OLEDB.OleDbConnection(sConnectionString)
Dim myCommand As New OleDbCommand("SELECT * FROM Customers", myConnection)
```

```
' Here's where the code is different from the previous example:
Dim myDataAdapter As New OleDbDataAdapter(myCommand)

' Declare the DataSet named Example1
Dim myDataSet As New DataSet("Example1")

' Open the connection and put customer data
' into the DataSet as a table named Customers
Try
   myConnection.Open()
   myDataAdapter.Fill(myDataSet, "Customers")

   ' Check the data in the DataSet
   Dim rowCustomer As System.Data.DataRow
   For Each rowCustomer In myDataSet.Tables("Customers").Rows
      Console.WriteLine("customer name: " & rowCustomer("CompanyName"))
   Next

Catch myException As Exception
   MessageBox.Show(myException.ToString())

Finally
   ' Close the connection and destroy the DataSet
   If myConnection.State = Data.ConnectionState.Open Then
      myConnection.Close()
   End If
   If Not myDataSet Is Nothing Then
      myDataSet = Nothing
   End If
End Try
```

The code doesn't really show any differences until after the connection and command objects are created. To build a DataSet, there is a new step at this point. It is necessary to create a DataAdapter object. This object is associated with the OleDbCommand object created earlier. The DataAdapter object has a Fill() method that is used a few lines later.

Next, the DataSet is instantiated, and a name for the DataSet is supplied as part of that operation. Then, the connection is opened and the DataSet is filled with a table. The name of the table is specified in the Fill() method as Customers, but that designation is for the use of the programmer, and does not indicate the source of the data. The actual source of the data was established when the OleDbCommand object was initialized (with a SQL statement selecting all the customers). The DataAdapter object is associated with that OleDbCommand object, so any operation done by the DataAdapter object takes place on that customer data.

This example was constructed to be as similar as possible to the earlier DataReader example. This allows you to easily see the difference in constructing these two objects for accessing data. If you were writing a real application similar to this, the DataReader would give superior performance. However, DataSets give a lot more flexibility, as we will see in later examples.

The section below contains more details on manipulating DataSets and also includes coverage of the process of using the DataAdapter object to place data back in the original database.

How the ADO.NET Classes Work Together

Now that we have covered the main classes in ADO.NET, including the data provider classes and the DataSet, we can see how they fit together to give access to data. The following diagram shows how the classes work together:

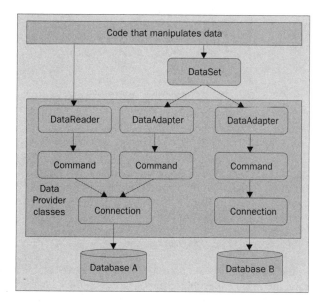

This diagram emphasizes that:

❑   The classes in the data provider are essential for getting connections to a database

❑   The DataSet is not part of a data provider, but can be used by any data provider

❑   The DataSet can get data from multiple data sources

❑   The DataReader can be used to get data into code, but it is a data provider class, and therefore requires a connection

Structure of a DataSet

The relational capabilities of a `DataSet` are implemented in the following object model:

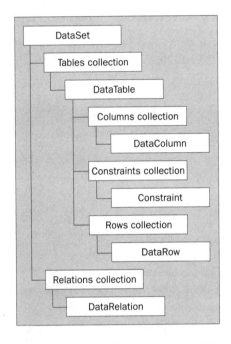

For a `DataSet` to be functional it must contain at least one `DataTable` object in its `Tables` collection and, to contain any data, the `Rows` collection of the `DataTable` must have some rows whose layout is described by the `Columns` collection. All the other elements of the object model are optional.

The relational structure and capabilities of the `DataSet` are described in the `Tables`, `Columns`, `Constraints`, and `Relations` collections. The layout of the tables, including information such as data types, is in `Tables` and `Columns`, the constraints for a particular table are in `Constraints`, and the relationships between tables are in `Relations`.

It is worth mentioning a potential point of confusion in comparison to previous data access models, such as DAO and ADO. With these models, no explicit `Rows` collection existed. Instead, a `Recordset` was positioned to a row (sometimes referred to as a record) using various methods of the `Recordset` (`MoveNext()`, `MoveFirst()`, `Seek()`, and so on). Then the `Fields` collection (in DAO or ADO) or the `Columns` collection (in RDO) of the `Recordset` could be used to access data in that row.

In ADO.NET, each `DataTable` contains both a `Columns` collection and a `Rows` collection. The `Columns` collection is accessed to get or set schema information about the fields in each row. The `Rows` collection contains individual `DataRow` objects representing a row or data record in the table. Each `DataRow` has an `Item` property, indexed with column names from the `Columns` collection, to get to individual fields in the row. The syntax for getting information out of tables and rows is discussed in the section later called *Working with a DataSet*.

Let's go through the classes in the object model and gain a better understanding of what each one does.

DataTable

A `DataTable` object contains one table of in-memory data. It has a collection of columns that contain the schema for the table; the `DataColumn` class for columns is described in the next section. A `DataTable` also contains a `Rows` collection of `DataRow` objects. Each `DataRow` represents an individual data record. `DataRows` are also discussed below.

As we saw in the first code example on creating a `DataSet`, the `OleDbCommand` object can create a `DataTable`'s schema from a database automatically, and then add in the appropriate data into the table. Alternatively, a schema for the `DataSet` can be created in code, and then data added manually. To create the schema in code, the `Columns` collection is created (described below).

To add new rows to a `DataTable`, the `NewRow()` method returns an object reference to a new row. Then each field (column) in the row can have data inserted. As we will see below, the `NewRow()` method does not automatically insert the row – it just returns a row of the appropriate structure. It's also necessary to add the new row to the `DataTable`'s `Rows` collection using the `Add()` method.

A `DataTable` can also contain a `Constraints` collection. The capabilities of constraints are discussed below.

`DataTables` have several useful properties and methods. Here are some examples of the properties:

Property	Description
HasErrors	Indicates if there are errors in any of the rows in any of the tables in the `DataSet` to which the `DataTable` belongs (because of violation of constraints, for example)
PrimaryKey	Gets or sets an array of columns that make up a primary key for the `DataTable`

and some examples of useful methods:

Method	Description
AcceptChanges()	Accepts all changes made to the table since the last call of `AcceptChanges` (or since the table was loaded if this is the first call to `AcceptChanges`). You have to be careful when using this method, because it marks the changes as 'accepted', and they will not be included on updates to the original data source. This method is more useful for situations where there is no back-end data store except an XML file. The `DataSet` also has an `AcceptChanges()` method, which carries out the operation on every `DataTable` in the `DataSet`. In a general sense, `AcceptChanges()` is like a commit operation. To continue that comparison, the `RejectChanges()` method (covered below) is the analog of a rollback operation. The comparison is not exact because we are not in a strict transactional mode, but it is helpful for thinking about how you would use the operations.

Table continued on following page

Method	Description
Clear()	Clears the table of all data, while leaving the data schema of the table intact. This operation effectively removes all rows from the Rows collection of the DataTable. There is also a Clear() method of the DataSet, which clears all DataTables in the DataSet.
GetErrors()	Returns a collection of any DataRow objects that contain errors.
NewRow()	Creates a new, empty DataRow with an appropriate structure for holding data from this DataTable, and returns a reference to it. This method does not insert the DataRow into the DataTable's Rows collection. This must be done in code.
RejectChanges()	Throws away all changes made to the table since it was loaded, or since the last time AcceptChanges() was called.

DataColumn

The DataColumn represents a schema element for a field in a DataTable. A DataColumn object has a DataType property to hold the data type for the column. Behavior of the column can be set with properties such as AllowDBNull, Unique, and ReadOnly.

If a DataSet is created with a DataAdapter, the DataColumns objects are automatically created to hold the schema of the data in the database. However, it can still be helpful to set some additional properties of individual columns in the DataTable, or to add new columns such as calculated columns (discussed below). Also, in some situations you may be building a DataTable or DataSet from scratch, and in that case you will need to create DataTables and set many of their properties to appropriate settings.

A DataColumn can be set to automatically insert an incremented value for the column in new rows, similar to an Identity column in SQL Server or an AutoNumber field in Access. The AutoIncrement property turns this feature on, and the AutoIncrementSeed and AutoIncrementStep properties control where the value starts and how it is incremented.

Most columns will hold simple data values, but a column can also be set to hold an expression that calculates a value for the column based on other columns in the same row. For example, a column could be created in a Recordset to hold WholeSalePrice, which is calculated from a SuggestedRetailPrice column and a WholeSaleDiscount column. The code would look like this:

```
MyTable.Columns("WholeSalePrice").Expression = _
    "SuggestedRetailPrice * (WholeSaleDiscount / 100)"
```

DataRow

As previously discussed, the `DataRow` contains actual data values (in contrast to the `DataColumn` which contains only schema information). The `Item` property of the `DataRow` class is indexed on the column name (which is taken from the `DataColumn` object for a column). So, if we have a `DataColumn` object named `FirstName`, then, for a particular `DataRow`, the value in the `FirstName` column can be fetched with code like this:

```
sFirstName = MyDataRow.Item("FirstName")
```

However, the `Item` property is the default property for a `DataRow`, and it is an indexed property, so the following syntax is also permitted:

```
sFirstName = MyDataRow("FirstName")
```

The columns can also be accessed by their numerical index. If the `DataColumn` for `FirstName` had a numerical index of 4 in the `DataTable` (it was the fifth column) then the following code would also work:

```
sFirstName = MyDataRow(4)
```

This type of access is marginally faster, but makes the code more difficult to read. Also remember that numeric indexes to a `DataColumn` object can change if you add or delete columns in the `DataTable`.

Changing Data in a Row

`DataRows` can be changed by simply accessing the columns and setting values. For small, routine changes, this is the simplest way to get changes into a `DataTable`. The code is just the reverse of the example above:

```
MyDataRow("FirstName") = sFirstName
```

However, each of these changes generates an event and this may be undesirable. Besides the performance problems, if the event performs some validation that depends on other columns, and the other columns have not been set yet, the validation will fail.

To take care of this, the row can be placed in an editing mode. While in the editing mode, no events or validation will be performed. Events and validation will only take place when the editing mode is exited. Here are the methods that control the editing mode of a `DataRow`:

Method	Description
`BeginEdit()`	Starts editing the row. (Not present in ADO – a row is available for edit when it becomes the current row in an ADO `Recordset`.)
`CancelEdit()`	Cancels editing the row and throws away any changes made. Similar to `CancelUpdate()` in ADO. (Also cancels any pending events related to the changes.)

Table continued on following page

Method	Description
EndEdit()	Commits the changes to the row and ends editing on it. Similar to the Update() method in ADO. (Before the commit is done, any pending events are fired.)

There is a big difference in the way these changes work compared to a Recordset in ADO. In a Recordset, the comparable methods are executed for the current row in the Recordset. This means that, in traditional ADO, only one row at a time can be in an edit state. In an ADO.NET DataTable, each row is a separate entity and can be treated separately from any other rows. That means it is possible to have several rows in an editing state at once.

Besides this technique for managing changes to a DataRow, there are also AcceptChanges() and RejectChanges() methods for individual DataRows. These methods work similarly to the AcceptChanges() and RejectChanges() methods for the DataTable, which we discussed earlier, except that they are only for an individual row. These methods do not have any effects on the events generated by changing data.

The AcceptChanges() method of a DataTable does have one side effect related to the editing methods in the table above. Executing the AcceptChanges() method of a DataTable does an implicit EndEdit() on any row in the DataTable that is in an editing mode.

Examining Different Versions of Data in a Row

One of the most important capabilities of the DataRow class is to expose various versions for the data in a row. This allows considerable latitude in the logic that edits or commits changes for rows. Versions of data in a DataRow can include:

Version	Description
Current	The current data in the row, as of the last time changes to the row were accepted or rejected.
Default	The original default values in the row. These are the values that would be in a row when it had just been created by a NewRow() method on the DataTable.
Original	The data in the row when the table was first added to the DataSet, or the data in the row after the last time an AcceptChanges() was done on the DataTable. (Note that an AcceptChanges() on the DataRow does not affect the Original version of the data – it just puts the Proposed value into the Current value.)
Proposed	The row has some new data that has not been committed with an AcceptChanges() method on the DataTable or the individual DataRow. Such data can be rolled back with a RejectChanges() method on the DataTable or DataRow and returned to its previous value.

At any given time, a particular row may have data in more than one of these versions. That is, a given row may simultaneously have an Original version of its data, a Current version, and a Proposed version. The Default version for a row is always available.

For a column in the row, the value for each version is obtained using an optional parameter of the `Item` property. To get the proposed value in a `FirstName` column for example, the line of code would look like this:

```
sFirstName = MyDataRow("FirstName", DataRowVersion.Proposed)
```

However, this will generate an error if the data version requested does not exist in the row. To check the versions that are available for the row, the `DataRow`'s `HasVersion()` method is used. There are various circumstances under which a data version may not exist. For example, the `Proposed` version of data only exists in a row after changes to the row have been made but not accepted with an `AcceptChanges()` method.

Here is code to look at a row and check for new, proposed data within it. If the row has proposed data that is different from the original data in the row in the `FirstName` field, then the changes will be accepted. But if the proposed data in `FirstName` is the same as the original data in `FirstName`, the editing will be canceled.

```
If MyRow.HasVersion(DataRowVersion.Proposed)
  Then
    If MyRow("FirstName", DataRowVersion.Current) = _
    MyRow("FirstName", DataRowVersion.Proposed)
    Then
      MsgBox("FirstName is unchanged - edit cancelled")
      MyRow.CancelEdit
    Else
      MyRow.AcceptChanges
    End If
  Else
    MsgBox("Row has no proposed data")
End If
```

Constraints

The `Constraints` collection of a `DataTable` contains a set of objects that describe constraints for working with data in the `DataTable`. There are two constraint classes, `ForeignKeyConstraint` and `UniqueConstraint`.

A `ForeignKeyConstraint` object must be set with:

❑   The related `DataTable` that the foreign key points to

❑   The column(s) containing the foreign keys in the `DataTable` that contains this constraint

❑   What action is to be taken if the constraint is violated

The other type of constraint class is `UniqueConstraint`. It is much simpler. It is only necessary to set the columns in the `DataTable` that must contain unique values by associating them to a `UniqueConstraint`.

Constraints are not automatically added to `DataTables` when `DataSets` are filled with a `DataAdapter`. Even primary keys in the database do not get a `UniqueConstraint` applied. If you wish to have constraints on the `DataTables` you manipulate, you must create and manage the constraints in code.

Here is an example. Suppose you have a `DataSet` with a `DataTable` named `Customers`. The column `CustomerID` in the `DataTable` corresponds to the primary key in the database, and you would like to place a `UniqueConstraint` on it. Here is code to do that:

```
Dim CustomersTable As DataTable
CustomersTable = DataSet1.Tables("Customers")
Dim myConstraint As New UniqueConstraint("PrimaryKey", _
   CustomersTable.Columns("CustomerID"))
CustomersTable.Constraints.Add(myConstraint)
```

Now `DataRows` in the `CustomerTable` object will not accept any duplicate values in the `CustomerID` field. If you try to insert a duplicate value in that field for a row, you will get an exception.

DataRelation

Relations are associated with the `DataSet` as a whole. Each `DataRelation` object in the `Relations` collection contains information linking two `DataTables` in the `DataSet`'s `Tables` collection. The `DataTables` are linked by specifying a column in each table for the link, very much like associating a primary and foreign key when specifying a relationship in a relational database.

The relationship is a parent-child relationship. A typical example would be a parent `Customers` table related to a child `Orders` table. That is, for each row in the `Customers` table, there would be zero, one, or many related records in the `Orders` table for that particular customer. In this case, the `Customers` table has a primary key named `CustomerID`, and the `Orders` table has a foreign key with the same name. Here is a code example to specify such a relationship for a `DataSet`, including the code to create and fill the `DataSet`. This is our first example that demonstrates the ability to have more than one `DataTable` in a `DataSet`.

```
Dim sConnectionString As String = _
   "Provider=SQLOLEDB.1; User ID=sa; " & _
   "Initial Catalog=Northwind;Data Source=MYSERVER"
Dim myConnection As New OleDbConnection(sConnectionString)
Dim myCustomerCommand As New OleDbCommand( _
   "SELECT * FROM Customers", myConnection)
Dim myOrdersCommand As New OleDbCommand( _
   "SELECT * FROM Orders", myConnection)

Dim myCustomerDataAdapter As New OleDbDataAdapter(myCustomerCommand)
Dim myOrderDataAdapter As New OleDbDataAdapter(myOrdersCommand)

Dim myDataSet As New DataSet("CustomersAndOrders")

' Open the connection and put customer data
' into the DataSet as a table named Customers
Try
```

```
      myConnection.Open()
      myCustomerDataAdapter.Fill(myDataSet, "Customers")
      myOrderDataAdapter.Fill(myDataSet, "Orders")

   Catch myException As Exception
      MessageBox.Show(myException.ToString())

   Finally
      ' Close the connection - we don't need it while working on the DataSet
      If myConnection.State = Data.ConnectionState.Open Then
        myConnection.Close()
      End If
   End Try

   ' Establish a DataRelation between Customers and Orders
   Dim ParentColumn As DataColumn
   Dim ChildColumn As DataColumn
   ParentColumn = myDataSet.Tables("Customers").Columns("CustomerID")
   ChildColumn = myDataSet.Tables("Orders").Columns("CustomerID")

   ' Ready to create the DataRelation object
   ' and add it to the Relations collection
   Dim relCustomerToOrders As New DataRelation("CustomersToOrders", _
      ParentColumn, ChildColumn)
   myDataSet.Relations.Add(relCustomerToOrders)
```

Notice that the parameters used to create the relation are the name of the relation (which can be anything desired by the programmer), the correct column reference in the parent table, and the correct column reference in the child table. Both columns must have the same data type.

Using DataRelations for Master-Detail Data

Master-detail or parent-child data structures, such as the Customers-Orders example discussed above, are common in business applications. The ideal way to access such records is to use code with the following structure (written in pseudo-code – real code comes a bit later):

```
   ' This is pseudo-code, not real code!!
   For Each Customer In Customers
      Print Header Information for Customer
      For Each Order In This Customer's Orders
         Print Information on the Order
      Next Order
   Next Customer
```

Unlike ADO, ADO.NET supports syntax for such code structures. Once a relationship between Customers and Orders is specified, it is possible to get individual orders associated with a particular customer record by using the GetChildRows() method of a customer DataRow. This method returns a collection of all the rows in the Orders table that are related to that row in the Customers table. Here is the code to demonstrate. This code will work when placed just below the code in the DataRelations example above:

```
Dim rowCustomer As System.Data.DataRow
Dim rowOrder As System.Data.DataRow

For Each rowCustomer In myDataSet.Tables("Customers").Rows
  ' Work with header information for customer, like this
  Console.WriteLine(rowCustomer("CompanyName"))

  ' Now get orders associated with the customer
  For Each rowOrder In rowCustomer.GetChildRows("CustomersToOrders")
    Console.WriteLine(rowOrder("OrderDate"))
  Next

Next
```

This kind of logic is significantly cleaner than any equivalent functionality in traditional ADO. The sections for dealing with customer header information and for dealing with individual order information are cleanly separated, and easy to manage.

Note that the DataSet could have another relationship defined to connect a parent Orders table to a child OrderDetails table. Then a For Each loop for order details could be nested inside the For Each loop for orders.

Working with a DataSet

We have discussed the fact that accessing data with a DataSet is simpler and more consistent than accessing Recordsets in ADO. In this section, we will look at how to work with DataSets to accomplish common programming tasks.

The simpler model of ADO.NET removes a lot of the concepts that experienced ADO developers might expect. The idea of different types of cursor (forward-only versus client versus server) is missing in the DataSet object, eliminating confusion over which cursor to choose for a given situation. And regardless of the location of the DataSet (local, remote, in a client browser, and so on), the full object model of the DataSet is available.

Adding Rows to a DataTable

We previously noted that the DataTable class has a NewRow() method for constructing a new row. Here is an example of adding a new customer to our Customers DataTable that was created in earlier DataSet examples:

```
Dim rowNewCustomer As DataRow
rowNewCustomer = myDataSet.Tables("Customers").NewRow
rowNewCustomer("CustomerID") = "CYBER"
rowNewCustomer("CompanyName") = "Cyberdyne Systems"
rowNewCustomer("ContactName") = "Miles Dyson"
' Set values for all customer fields...

' New row is now complete. Add it to the DataTable
myDataSet.Tables("Customers").Rows.Add(rowNewCustomer)
```

This syntax follows the basic OO idea of creating an object, and then adding it to a collection. In this case, we create the `DataRow`, configure it, and then add it to the `DataTable`'s rows collection. We also have the option of adding the newly created `DataRow` to the `Rows` collection before configuring it. That would mean moving the last line in the example above to become the third line instead.

Finding a Particular Row in a DataTable

The `DataTable` class has a `Select()` method that is used to get a particular row or set of rows that you are interested in. For example, here is code to get a reference to the row for our new customer above (`CustomerID` of CYBER):

```
Dim rowsSelected() As DataRow
rowsSelected = myDataSet.Tables("Customers").Select("CustomerID = 'CYBER'")
```

The `Select()` method always returns an array of rows, even if there is only one element in the array. The code above would return such a one-element array.

The array contains references to the rows in the `DataSet`, so those rows can now be manipulated. If we want to change the `ContactName` for the row selected above, this line would do it:

```
rowsSelected(0).Item("ContactName") = "John Connor"
```

Of course, the select may not match any rows, in which case the array will not have any elements. You can check that using the `Length` property of the array. If the array is empty, it will return a value of 0.

Deleting Rows from a DataTable

There are two ways to get rid of rows in a `DataTable`. First, the rows can be removed from the `Rows` collection with the collection's `Remove()` method. In that case, they're gone for good. Second, the rows can be marked for deletion, but not actually removed from the `Rows` collection.

For both techniques, you need a reference to the row or rows you want to delete, of course. The selection technique discussed above will work fine for that.

Here is an example of using the first technique, in which rows are removed from the `Rows` collection. Suppose we have done a selection process to get a set of rows representing customers we no longer want in our `DataSet`. We have placed that set of rows in the array `rowsToDelete`. We can remove them all with this code:

```
Dim i As Integer
For i = 0 to rowsToDelete.Length - 1
  myDataSet.Tables("Customers").Rows.Remove(rowsToDelete(i))
Next i
```

However, you should note that this is not usually the appropriate way to deal with deleted records, because it does not work properly with data that will be restored to a database.

The `DataRow` class has a `Delete()` method, which is preferable any time you are working with data that will be restored to a database. For rows that were originally added from the database, this method marks the `RowState` property to indicate deletion, but it does actually remove the row from the `Rows` collection. That leaves open the possibility of restoring the row by manipulating the `RowState` property.

For rows that were added since the data was loaded from the database, the `Delete()` method will remove the rows from the `Rows` collection. This simplifies the resolution of the changes in the data back to the database.

Here is how the code above would be changed to use this technique:

```
Dim i As Integer
For i = 0 to rowsToDelete.Length - 1
    rowsToDelete(i).Delete()
Next i
```

Now, when the `DataSet` is updated to the database, the `DataAdapter` can use the `RowState` property to know which rows to delete in the database.

Creating a DataSet Manually

Since the entire object model of ADO.NET is exposed, it is possible to create and work with a `DataSet` manually, totally divorced from any database server. Here is a code example that creates a simple `DataSet`, adds a single table to it, and adds a couple of columns for the table:

```
' Create DataSet
Dim MyDataSet As New DataSet("ManualDataSet")

' Create a new DataTable and add it to the DataSet
Dim tblDataTable As New DataTable("SampleTable")
MyDataSet.Tables.Add(tblDataTable)

' Create two columns for the table, set their properties
' and add them to the Columns collection for the table
Dim colDataColumn As New DataColumn("FirstColumn")
colDataColumn.DataType = System.Type.GetType("System.String")
colDataColumn.DefaultValue = "Default"
tblDataTable.Columns.Add(colDataColumn)

Dim colDataColumn2 As New DataColumn("SecondColumn")
colDataColumn2.DataType = System.Type.GetType("System.Int32")
tblDataTable.Columns.Add(colDataColumn2)

' Create a DataRow, add it to the table, and set its values
Dim rowMyDataRow As DataRow
rowMyDataRow = MyDataSet.Tables("SampleTable").NewRow
MyDataSet.Tables("SampleTable").Rows.Add(rowMyDataRow)
rowMyDataRow("FirstColumn") = "New text"
rowMyDataRow("SecondColumn") = 10000
MyDataSet.AcceptChanges()
```

```
' Loop through the rows and display values
Dim rowDataRow As DataRow
For Each rowDataRow In MyDataSet.Tables("SampleTable").Rows
  MsgBox(rowDataRow.Item("FirstColumn").ToString & " - " & _
    CStr(rowDataRow("SecondColumn")),,"Show data")
Next
```

Walking through the code, we begin by creating a new DataSet with the name ManualDataSet. Then we create a new DataTable named SampleTable and add it to the DataSet. At this point the table has no columns.

The next section creates two columns for the DataTable and sets their properties. Setting the Default property for the first column is actually optional, but is included as an example of the possibilities. Actually, the only property that must be set for a column is DataType. After each column is created and initialized, it is added to the Columns collection of the DataTable named SampleTable.

Then a single DataRow is created. Notice that it is necessary to create the DataRow with the NewRow() method of the DataTable to get the proper structure (schema) of the row. However, the NewRow() method *does not* add the row automatically to the Rows collection. This must be done explicitly.

Finally, code is included to loop through the Rows collection (in which there is only one row at this point) and display the values of the two columns in each row. If this code is run, the result should be a message box that displays the string **New text – 10000**.

At this point, any manipulation of the DataSet can be carried out. For example, one of the columns in the table could be set to be a primary key, or a constraint could be added to make a column only accept unique values.

Creating a DataSet Using the DataAdapter Wizard

While it will sometimes be useful to construct a DataSet manually, as in the above example, the typical way is to extract the data from a database with a data provider. We covered a brief example of this operation early in the chapter, and another example in the section on DataRelations above. Those examples included code to manually create a connection to the database, create an ADO.NET command object, and use it to copy tables from the database into a DataSet.

Earlier in the chapter, we mentioned that Visual Studio .NET offers a wizard that can handle a lot of the routine coding for filling up a DataSet. Let's step through an exercise that uses the automated capabilities of Visual Studio .NET extensively to create a DataSet for manipulation. We will create basically the same DataSet as in the DataRelations example, which was constructed with the Customers and Orders tables in the Northwind sample database in SQL Server. The DataSet will contain a set of customers and their related orders.

Windows Form Example

For simplicity, this exercise will use a bound `DataGrid` in a Windows Form to allow access to the `DataSet` for viewing and changing data. However, we will place the data code in a component, which will allow us to reuse it for the equivalent Web Forms example later. Follow these steps to complete the example:

1. Create a new Windows Application project in Visual Studio .NET. Select Project | Add Component... to add a new Component Class to the project, and name it CustomerOrders.vb.

2. In the Toolbox, select the Data tab. Drag an OleDbDataAdapter onto the design surface of the component. A wizard to configure the OleDbDataAdapter will begin. Press the Next button on the introductory screen.

3. You will be asked to select a connection. The connection you need probably does not exist yet, so press the New Connection button. Then, a dialog to configure a connection will appear. Enter information as appropriate on the Connection tab.

Press the Test Connection button to see if you have correctly configured the connection. If you are having trouble getting a connection to work, take care of this before proceeding with the exercise. If the connection is configured correctly, press OK to create it.

4. Next, press the Next button to proceed to the next step, which is to Choose a Query Type. There are three options. The default is to Use SQL statements and we will take this option to keep the exercise simple. (The other options allow the component to work through stored procedures, either by having the wizard create new ones or by specifying ones that already exist.)

Press the Next button. The following screen allows you to choose the SQL that will be used to specify the data to be fetched by the OleDbDataAdapter. The SQL can be typed in manually, but it's easier to use the SQL builder. Press the Query Builder... button, and on the first dialog that appears, select the Customers table, press the Add button, and then press Close.

The resulting screen looks like the screenshot opposite. You have almost certainly worked with query construction screens like this before, probably in Access. In the box at the top, containing the listing of columns in the Customers table, check the following: CustomerID, CompanyName, and Phone. Notice that the SQL to get these fields is automatically generated. After selecting these columns, press the OK button:

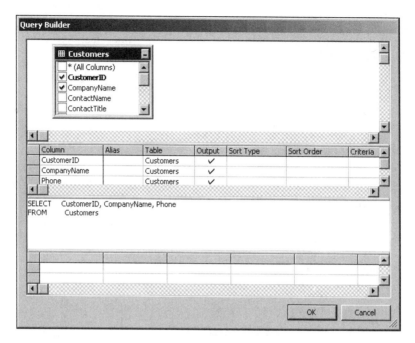

The following screen displays a summary of the generated SQL. Confirm this by pressing Next and then the Finish button. Looking at Visual Studio .NET's design surface now, you can see that the OleDbDataAdapter has been initialized in the component as OleDbDataAdapter1, and the connection has been initialized as OleDbConnection1. We do not have an OleDbCommand object, because one is created automatically by the OleDbDataAdapter (this is an optional capability of the DataAdapter classes).

The Advanced Options button contains some additional capabilities that we will not use in this exercise. For example, if you know that you will only not be updating the DataSet back to the database with this DataAdapter, you can uncheck the advanced option that creates Insert, Delete, and Update statements for those unnecessary operations.

5. Drag another OleDbDataAdapter onto the component design surface. Go through the wizard again for this OleDbDataAdapter, with the following differences:

❑ There is no need to define the connection – just select the existing Northwind connection

❑ In the Query Builder, select the following columns from the Orders table: OrderID, CustomerID, and OrderDate.

Now OleDbDataAdapter2 is defined for the component class. You may wish to look at the code generated by the wizard for both DataAdapters. This can give a better idea of how they are configured in code, and you can be assured that there are no 'hidden' operations going on the way there were with the Data Environment in VB6.

6. We are ready to place a method in the component to fill a `DataSet` with customers and orders. Right-click on the component design surface and select View Code. Then, type the following method into the `CustomerOrders` class:

```
Public Function FillPurchaseOrdersDataSet() As DataSet

    ' Declare a new DataSet
    Dim myDataSet As New DataSet()

    ' Open a connection and use the DataAdapter
    ' objects to put two tables in the DataSet.
    ' Close the connection when done.
    Try
        OleDbConnection1.Open()
        OleDbDataAdapter1.Fill(myDataSet, "Customers")
        OleDbDataAdapter2.Fill(myDataSet, "Orders")
    Catch eFillException As System.Exception
        MsgBox(eFillException.ToString)
        'TODO: Handle errors here
    Finally
        OleDbConnection1.Close()
    End Try

    ' Add a relation between the tables
    Try
        myDataSet.Relations.Add("CustomersToOrders", _
        myDataSet.Tables("Customers").Columns("CustomerID"), _
        myDataSet.Tables("Orders").Columns("CustomerID"))
    Catch eException As System.Exception
        Throw eException
        'TODO: Handle errors here
    End Try

    ' We're done - return the DataSet
    Return (myDataSet)
End Function
```

7. Go to the design surface for Form1, select the Windows Forms tab in the Toolbox and drag a Button and a DataGrid onto the form. Set the Text property of the Button to Get Data. Position the DataGrid at the bottom of the form and set its Anchor property to Bottom, Left, Right. The layout of the form should now look something like this:

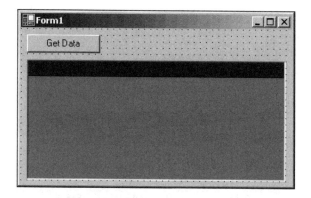

8. Right-click on the form and select **View Code**. Add the following two `Imports` statements above the class declaration:

```
Imports System.Data
Imports System.Data.OleDb
```

Then add the following line:

```
Inherits System.Windows.Forms.Form
```

```
Dim MyDataSet As DataSet
```

9. Go back to the form's design surface and double-click the button to get to its `Click` event code. Then insert the following:

```
Private Sub Button1_Click(ByVal sender As System.Object, _
    ByVal e As System.EventArgs) Handles Button1.Click

    Dim objCustomerOrders As New CustomerOrders()
    MyDataSet = objCustomerOrders.FillPurchaseOrdersDataSet()

    DataGrid1.DataSource = MyDataSet
    DataGrid1.DataMember = "Customers"

End Sub
```

10. Now run the project and the form will appear. Press the button and after a delay to access the data, the DataGrid will show customers, with a screen like this:

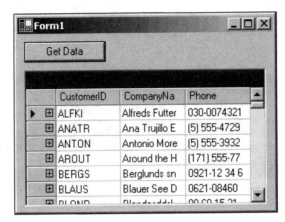

Press the plus sign in the DataGrid next to the third customer (the one with CustomerID of ANTON). Then select the CustomersToOrders relation, and the grid will show the orders associated with that customer. To get back to the list of customers, press the left arrow in the upper right corner of the grid. From that point, you can play around with the DataGrid, trying different displays of customers and their orders.

At this point, the DataSet has been created and placed in the grid. Since the DataGrid is bound to the DataSet, any changes typed into the grid are placed into the DataSet.

However, at this stage, there is no code to move the changes from the DataSet back into the database. Let's do that next.

11. Close the running project by closing the form. Go to the code window for the CustomerOrders component and add the following method to the class:

```
Public Sub UpdateDataSet(ByVal updatedDataSet As DataSet)

    Try
        ' This updates the customers table
        OleDbDataAdapter1.Update(updatedDataSet)

        ' This updates the orders table
        OleDbDataAdapter2.Update(updatedDataSet)

    Catch eException As System.Exception
        Throw eException
    End Try
End Sub
```

We don't really expect any errors, either here or in the calling routine, but it is good practice to catch errors in a component like this and throw them to the calling application if an error, such as a concurrency problem, does occur. Place another button on the form beside the existing one and set its **Text** property to **Update Data**. Double-click the new button to get to its `Click` event. Then place the following code inside:

```
Private Sub Button2_Click(ByVal sender As System.Object, _
    ByVal e As System.EventArgs) Handles Button2.Click

    Dim objCustomerOrders As New CustomerOrders()
    MyDataSet = DataGrid1.DataSource
    objCustomerOrders.UpdateDataSet(MyDataSet)

End Sub
```

Run the program and as before, press the **Get Data** button. When the data is loaded into the **DataGrid**, go to **Orders** and change the first **OrderDate**. Then press the **Update Data** button. The changed data will be saved to the database. (You can test to see that the changes in the grid are only saved if the **Update Data** button is pressed.)

There is an important item to note about the code used in this example. The component is completely stateless. It is created when needed, and can be destroyed as soon as it has carried out its operation. This makes the component completely suitable for use in a web application as well as with a Windows Form. Creating such stateless components is easy with ADO.NET because the `DataSet` contains all the data information needed, rendering it unnecessary for a data component to hold any state or maintain any connections.

Web Forms Example

Creating a Web Forms version of this example is straightforward, although there are minor differences because the Web Forms **DataGrid** is not as flexible as the Windows Form **DataGrid**. The Web Forms **DataGrid** handles in-place editing differently, so this example is read-only. Also, the Web Forms **DataGrid** can only be bound to one table at a time, and cannot be hierarchical.

To make a Web Forms version, follow the same steps as above, except for the following differences:

1. Open a new **ASP.NET Web Application** project instead of a **Windows Application** this time.

2. Place one **Button** (instead of two) and a **DataGrid** control on the designer, dragging them off the **Web Forms** tab in the **Toolbox**. Right-click on the **DataGrid** control, click on **Auto Format...** in the **Properties** window, and choose **Professional 1** style.

3. Again, initializing `MyDataSet` is required:

```
Inherits System.Web.UI.Page
Protected WithEvents Button1 As System.Web.UI.WebControls.Button
Protected WithEvents DataGrid1 As System.Web.UI.WebControls.DataGrid

Dim MyDataSet As DataSet
```

4. In the `Click` event for the button, the code needs to change a little. It should look like this:

```
Dim objCustomerOrders As New CustomerOrders()
MyDataSet = objCustomerOrders.FillPurchaseOrdersDataSet()

DataGrid1.DataSource = MyDataSet

' Need an additional line to explicitly bind the control to the data
DataGrid1.DataBind()
```

Rather than rebuilding the component from scratch, you can copy and paste it from the Windows Form example.

The running application will look like this in Internet Explorer:

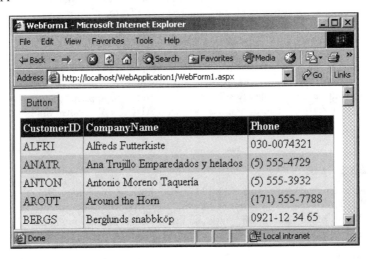

Note that you can change the `DataTable` that is used for data binding on the ASP.NET `DataGrid` with the `DataMember` property. If the following line of code is placed just above the line of code that sets the `DataSource` for the `DataGrid`, then the `DataGrid` will bind to the `Orders` `DataTable` in the `DataSet`, instead of the `Customers` `DataTable`:

```
DataGrid1.DataMember = "Orders"
```

The reason that the Customers `DataTable` was selected in the example above is that the default (if the `DataMember` property is not set) is to use the first `DataTable` in the `DataTables` collection in the `DataSet`.

Using DataViews

We have already seen that DataSets are very flexible. The concept of **DataViews** adds another layer of flexibility in ADO.NET.

A DataView is a DataTable with filtering and/or sorting applied. The DataView can be set to return subsets of the rows in the original DataTable and to specify the sorting order for the rows.

One common use of DataViews is to provide for data binding to controls, particularly in Web Forms. A DataView can be used to set the particular table in a DataSet to use for binding, for example.

Another use of DataViews is to provide multiple, simultaneous views of the same data in different controls. For example, one grid on a form could hold all rows in a table, while another grid simultaneously displays only deleted rows or only changed rows. Editing the rows in either control would cause the underlying data in the DataTable to be changed, and would then affect the data in the other control when it was refreshed.

Creating a new DataView for a given DataTable is done by declaring the DataView and passing a reference to the desired DataTable into the DataView constructor – like this:

```
Dim MyNewDataView As New DataView(MyDataSet.Tables("Customers"))
```

When first created like this, the DataView defaults to all the rows in the specified table of the DataSet. Properties are available for getting a subset of the rows into the DataView, or for sorting it, and these are covered below. These properties can be changed on the fly to dynamically alter the output of a DataSet.

Getting a Subset of Data into a DataView

Getting a subset of data is done with the RowFilter property and/or the RowStateFilter property of the DataView class. The RowFilter property is used by supplying an expression (similar to a SQL WHERE clause) to use for filtering. For example, for our DataView defined just above for the Customers table, we could set the DataView to only return customers with company names beginning with the letter 'A' by using this code:

```
MyNewDataView.RowFilter = "CompanyName Like 'A*'"
```

RowFilter expressions can be quite complex, and may include arithmetic computations and comparisons involving various columns in the data and constants.

The RowStateFilter works differently. It has defined values that fetch specific subsets of the data in the DataTable. Here are the available settings for RowStateFilter:

Setting	Description
CurrentRows	Shows current rows, including unchanged, new, and modified rows, but leaving out deleted rows.
Deleted	Shows deleted rows. Note that a row is only considered deleted if the Delete() method of a DataRow was used to delete it. Removing rows from the Rows collection will not mark them as deleted.
ModifiedCurrent	Shows rows with a current version of data that is different from the original data in the row.
ModifiedOriginal	Shows modified rows, but displays them with the original version of the data (even if the rows have been changed and have another current version of the data in them). Note that the current version of data in these same rows is available with the ModifiedCurrent setting.
Added	Shows new rows. These are rows added with the AddNew() method of the DataView.
None	Shows no rows at all. Could be used initially on a DataView for a control before the user has chosen viewing options.
OriginalRows	Shows all rows with their original data version, including unchanged and deleted rows.
Unchanged	Shows rows that have not been changed.

These settings can be used in various combinations by adding them together when setting the RowStateFilter property. For example, this line of code causes the DataView to expose only new rows and deleted rows:

```
MyNewDataView.RowStateFilter = DataViewRowState.New + _
                             DataViewRowState.Deleted
```

Sorting a DataView

The Sort property of a DataView takes a string that describes the desired sorting. Sorting can be done on one or more columns, and each column can be sorted in ascending or descending order. The string to specify the sorting should contain a column name, optionally followed by the letters ASC for ascending or DESC for descending. The default is ascending.

For multiple column sorting, the string should have a comma after the first column, and then another column name followed by ASC or DESC. This can be repeated for as many columns as needed. Here is an example:

```
MyNewDataView.Sort = "PostalCode DESC, CompanyName ASC"
```

This would sort the rows in the `DataView` first by `PostalCode` (called zip code in the US) in descending order. Then, within a given `PostalCode`, the rows would be sorted in ascending order of `CompanyName`.

Typed DataSets

Data is normally accessed in traditional ADO using indexes on collections in the object model. All of the examples in ADO.NET that we have covered up to now also use this syntax. Here is an example from earlier in the chapter illustrating the syntax, with some lines removed to simplify it:

```
Dim rowCustomer As System.Data.DataRow

For Each rowCustomer In DataSet.Tables("Customers").Rows
  Console.WriteLine(rowCustomer("CompanyName"))
Next
```

This syntax works well but it has a couple of drawbacks. It is a bit difficult to read, and it does not check the index values used in the collections for misspellings at compile-time. If the second line of code here were to have `Customers` misspelled as `Cutsomers`, it would generate a run-time error, not a compile-time error.

There is an alternative syntax that can be used with ADO.NET that is more intuitive. With this syntax, the above code would look like the following:

```
Dim rowCustomer As System.Data.DataRow

For Each rowCustomer In DataSet.Customers.Rows
  Console.WriteLine(rowCustomer.CompanyName)
Next
```

However, you must create a special kind of `DataSet` to support such syntax. Such a `DataSet` is called a **typed DataSet**. These are specially sub-classed `DataSets` generated by the data designer tool in Visual Studio .NET, and they have a schema attached to provide the information to do the typing. The schema can be automatically generated from the source database, or can be attached from an existing XML schema document.

Typed `DataSets` support the easier, more intuitive syntax above (called strongly-typed syntax). Errors in the syntax caused by misspellings are detected at compile time rather than run time. The syntax support includes IntelliSense and auto-completion on the syntax elements. This means that when you access a collection of tables in a `DataSet`, you get a pop-up list of all the available tables, rather than struggling to remember the table name that you created a few days ago. However, since creating such a `DataSet` requires a special operation, typed `DataSets` should be based on schemas that you know to be stable.

Let's step through an example creating such a `DataSet`, and then go through some code that uses strongly typed syntax:

1. In Visual Studio .NET, bring up the project that you created for the *Windows Form Example* in the *Creating a DataSet Using the DataAdapter Wizard* section earlier.

2. Bring up the design surface for the component (`CustomerOrders.vb`), right-click on the design surface and select the **Generate DataSet** menu option **Generate DataSet....** A dialog box will appear that requests the name of the `DataSet` class, and a checkbox for each `DataTable` available from the **DataAdapter**s currently available in the component (**Customers** and **Orders**). Enter the name **TypedCustomerOrders** in the **New** textbox and leave both tables checked. Also, check the option that says **Add this dataset to the designer** and press **OK**.

3. The Solution Explorer will have a new element named **TypedCustomerOrders1**. The `.xsd` file is the XML template file (sometimes called an XSD template) for the typed dataset. You can open it up if you wish and examine the XML created to define the template.

4. Right-click on the design surface for the component, and select **View Code**. Enter the following code into the component's code module:

```
Public Sub TestTypedDataSet()

  Try
    OleDbConnection1.Open()
    OleDbDataAdapter1.Fill(TypedCustomerOrders1, "Customers")
    OleDbDataAdapter1.Fill(TypedCustomerOrders1, "Orders")
  Catch eFillException As System.Exception
    MsgBox(eFillException.ToString)
    'TODO: Handle errors here
  Finally
    OleDbConnection1.Close()
  End Try

    Dim rowDataRow As TypedCustomerOrders.CustomersRow
    For Each rowDataRow In TypedCustomerOrders1.Customers.Rows
      Console.WriteLine("customer name: " & rowDataRow.CompanyName)
  Next

End Sub
```

5. On the Windows Form, place a new **Button** and change its text to **Test Typed DataSet**. Double-click the **Button** and enter the following code in the button's `Click` event:

```
Private Sub Button3_Click(ByVal sender As System.Object, _
  ByVal e As System.EventArgs) Handles Button3.Click

  Dim objCustomerOrders As New CustomerOrders()
  objCustomerOrders.TestTypedDataSet()

End Sub
```

6. Run the project and press the **Test Typed DataSet** button. You will see the customer names listed in the **Output** window, just as in some previous examples.

The important thing to note about this example is the last four lines of code in the `TestTypedDataSet` subroutine. These lines used strongly typed syntax instead of indexed collections in the object model. All of the tables and columns of the `DataSet` are similarly available using strongly-typed object syntax.

Using Stored Procedures in ADO.NET

All of the examples shown so far have used SQL statements to get access to data in databases. This was done to keep the examples as simple as possible. However, in real-world applications, it is common to use stored procedures for most operations that interact with the database.

ADO.NET can work with stored procedures instead of SQL statements. As with ADO, there is a bit more work required to interface to a stored procedure. In particular the calling code must set up the parameters for the stored procedure.

The two classes that work with stored procedures in ADO.NET are the `Command` classes and the `DataAdapter` classes. Let's look at using stored procedures in `Command` classes first.

Stored Procedures with Command Classes

To configure a command object to use a stored procedure, first supply the name of the stored procedure instead of a SQL statement when the command object is instantiated. Then, set the `CommandType` property of the command object to `CommandType.StoredProcedure`.

The next step is to build a collection of parameters needed by the stored procedure. For each parameter, a parameter object must be instantiated, configured, and added to the command object's `Parameters` collection. The information that must be supplied for each parameter is the name, the data type, the length, and the value.

Here is an example that configures a command object to use the `CustOrderHist` stored procedure that comes with the Northwind sample database. This stored procedure takes a customer ID, and returns a set of products ordered by that customer. The result set of the stored procedure only includes the `Product Name` and `Total` fields.

To construct the example, create a new Windows Forms project. On the blank `Form1`, place a button that says **Get Data** and a **DataGrid**. In the button's `Click` event, add the following code:

```
Private Sub Button1_Click(ByVal sender As System.Object, _
    ByVal e As System.EventArgs) Handles Button1.Click

    Dim sConnectionString As String = _
        "Provider=SQLOLEDB.1; User ID=sa; " & _
        "Initial Catalog=Northwind;Data Source=MYSERVER"

    Dim MyConnection As OleDbConnection = _
        New OleDbConnection(sConnectionString)
```

```
Dim StoredProcCommand As OleDbCommand = _
   New OleDbCommand("CustOrderHist", MyConnection)
StoredProcCommand.CommandType = CommandType.StoredProcedure

Dim myParm As OleDbParameter = _
   StoredProcCommand.Parameters.Add( _
   "@CustomerID", OleDbType.VarChar, 5)
myParm.Value = "ALFKI"

MyConnection.Open()

Dim MyDataSet As New DataSet("CustOrderHist")
Dim MyDataAdapter As New OleDbDataAdapter(StoredProcCommand)
MyDataAdapter.Fill(MyDataSet, "OrderHistory")

MyConnection.Close()

DataGrid1.DataSource = MyDataSet.Tables(0)

    End Sub
```

Don't forget to add the two Imports statements at the top of the class!

Now run the program and press the button. The grid will contain all of the products ordered by the customer with ID ALFKI.

We used a DataSet in this example, but once the command object is configured to use a stored procedure that selects data, the ExecuteReader() method of the command object can also be used to create a DataReader. This allows the results of a stored procedure to be exposed through a DataReader instead of a DataSet. The other methods of the command object, ExecuteNonQuery() and ExecuteScalar(), can also work with a stored procedure, using the same general syntax as the example above.

Using Stored Procedures with DataAdapters

The example above used a DataAdapter to fill up a DataTable in a DataSet with data returned by a stored procedure. However, if a DataSet changes, and the changes need to be resolved to the database, a different set of stored procedures is needed to update, delete, or add rows in the database.

Each such stored procedure requires its own command object to be created and configured, using the same syntax as the example above. The command objects are then hooked to the DataAdapter using the following properties:

❑ InsertCommand property – Points to the command object that is configured with a stored procedure to insert new rows into the database

❑ DeleteCommand property – Points to the command object that is configured with a stored procedure to delete rows from the database

❑ `UpdateCommand` property – Points to the command object that is configured with a stored procedure to change existing rows in the database

❑ `SelectCommand` property – Points to the command object that is configured with a stored procedure to select rows form the database when filling up a `DataTable` in a `DataSet`

The earlier example took care of the `SelectCommand`. If you are only fetching data from the database and will not be writing any changes back, the `SelectCommand` configuration is all you need. But if you are going to use the `Update()` method of the `DataAdapter`, then the other command objects must be set up as well.

If you use a wizard to configure a `DataAdapter`, there is an option to use stored procedures instead of SQL statements in the `DataAdapter`. If you select that option, the wizard will include a screen to choose the stored procedures you want to use. The code to configure the necessary command objects is then generated for you.

We will not show an example of using stored procedures for these operations because the sample Northwind database doesn't contain the appropriate stored procedures to use. However, since we understand how the example worked to do selection of data with a stored procedure, changing the code to use update, delete, and insert stored procedures should be straightforward.

Exception Classes for ADO.NET

The .NET Framework includes a base class for exceptions – the `System.Exception` class. It has some general features for containing error information. The .NET Framework also includes a number of classes derived from `System.Exception` that have additional capabilities for special circumstances.

ADO.NET includes two of these exception classes. The `OleDbException` class contains exceptions resulting from use of the OLE DB .NET Data provider, and the `SQLException` class contains exceptions resulting from use of the SQL Server .NET Data provider. In addition to the capabilities supported by the generic `Exception` class, these classes also have an `Errors` collection to hold multiple errors (whereas the generic `Exception` class only holds one error).

You can use the capabilities of these classes to gain more precise control over errors in a `Try...Catch...Finally` construct, and to print out error information. For example, instead of using the generic `Exception` class in the `Catch` statement (as we have done in examples throughout this chapter), you can use code with multiple `Catch` clauses instead. Each `Catch` clause checks for a different type of exception. The general structure of such a `Try...Catch...Finally` code block would look like this:

```
Try
   ' Some ADO.NET data handling logic goes here
Catch MyOleDbException As OleDbException
   ' Do error handling on OLE DB exceptions here
Catch MyGeneralException As Exception
   ' Do error handling on any other exceptions here
Finally
   ' Wrap up code goes here
End Try
```

You can also have special routines to log or print information from the ADO.NET exception classes, which are typically used in the `Catch` block. Here is a routine to print errors from an `OleDbException` instance:

```
Public Sub DisplayOleDbErrors(ByVal MyOleDbException As OleDbException)
  Dim iIndex As Integer
  Dim sErrorSummary As String
  Dim sCrLf As String = CStr(Chr(13)) & CStr(Chr(10))

  sErrorSummary = "Error generated by object " & _
                MyOleDbException.Source.ToString

  For iIndex = 0 To MyOleDbException.Errors.Count - 1
    sErrorSummary = sErrorSummary & sCrLf & "Index #" & iIndex & _
      " - Error: " + MyOleDbException.Errors(iIndex).ToString()
  Next iIndex

  MsgBox(sErrorSummary)
End Sub
```

It is recommended practice to use these exception classes in your code whenever doing database access through the ADO.NET Data providers.

Data Binding

We have already seen some simple data binding in earlier examples in this chapter. In particular, we have used data binding with grids in both Windows Forms and Web Forms.

The kind of data binding that was available in VB6 is also available in Visual Basic .NET. Textboxes can be bound to particular fields in a `DataSet`, for example. This is done, as in VB6, by setting the data binding properties of a control.

However, there is a lot more to data binding in .NET, especially in Windows Forms. Data binding is far more flexible and useful in .NET, so those developers who have given up on data binding in previous versions of VB should give it another chance in Visual Basic .NET.

Here are some of the new features of data binding that will be of interest to typical Visual Basic .NET developers.

Data Binding with Listboxes and Combo Boxes

In data-oriented applications, it is common to allow users to select from a list of names or descriptions, and then translate the name or description to some kind of ID value. The control typically used is a listbox or combo box. Since listboxes and combo boxes are not multi-column, handling this in VB6 requires a fair amount of manual work. It is much easier using data binding in .NET.

A listbox or combo box in a Windows Form can be bound to any data container. Available containers include the ADO.NET classes we have looked at in this chapter (DataSets, DataTables, DataViews), and also other classes such as arrays.

Most of these data containers have several fields. To indicate the field that needs to be exposed in the control, the listbox and combo box controls have a property called DisplayMember. If a DataTable contains fields for CustomerID, CustomerName, and PhoneNumber, setting the DisplayMember property of a bound listbox to CustomerName will cause the listbox to contain a list of customer names, with one for each row in the DataTable.

As we pointed out above though, a program may actually need the ID of the customer for further processing. That is, the field used by the user to select the record is not necessarily the field needed by the program's internal logic.

To indicate the field used for internal use, there is another property for listboxes and combo boxes named ValueMember. In our example above, we could set the ValueMember property to CustomerID. Then the listbox shows the customer name (because of the DisplayMember setting), but when you retrieve a selected item from the listbox in code, it returns the customer ID associated with the selected name.

To see this in action, let's go back to the Windows Forms example covered above under *Creating a DataSet Using the DataAdapter Wizard*. This example contained a grid on the form. Delete the grid, and add a listbox to the form in its place. Then change the code in the button's click event to look like this:

```
Dim objCustomerOrders as New CustomerOrders()
MyDataSet = objCustomerOrders.FillPurchaseOrdersDataSet()

ListBox1.DataSource = MyDataSet.Tables(0)
ListBox1.DisplayMember = "CompanyName"
ListBox1.ValueMember = "CustomerID"
```

Add another button to the form with a Text property that says Select, and place this code in its click event:

```
MsgBox(lstBox.SelectedValue.ToString)
```

Now run the program. When the Get Data button is pressed, the listbox will contain a list of company names. Select an item in the listbox and press the Select button. You will see a message box with the CustomerID of the selected company name.

Data Binding to a Collection of Objects

Another data container that can be bound to listboxes and combo boxes is a collection of objects. If you have a collection of customer objects in your application, for example, you can have a listbox bound to that collection.

The `DisplayMember` and `ValueMember` properties are still used to determine what is shown in the listbox or combo box, and what is returned as a selected item in your code. In this case, `DisplayMember` and `ValueMember` are set to the names of properties of your object. If you are using customer objects, and those objects have properties named `CustomerID` and `CustomerName`, then the syntax to data-bind to the collection would look the same as the syntax to data-bind to a `DataTable`.

Data Binding to any Property

In VB6, data binding was restricted to only particular properties of certain controls, but in .NET, any property of any control can be data-bound. This can be very useful for creating a responsive user interface. For example, you could data bind the background color of a textbox to a calculated field in a `DataSet`, while simultaneously data binding the `Text` property of the text box to some other field.

Such data binding is accomplished using the `DataBindings` collection of a form or control. Suppose we want to data bind the background color of a textbox named `TextBox1`. It is to be bound to a field named `BackGround` in a `DataTable` named `Customers`, in a `DataSet` named `MyDataSet`. The following line of code, which would typically be placed in the `Form_Load` event, would accomplish the binding:

```
TextBox1.DataBindings.Add _
    (New Binding("BackColor", MyDataset, "Customers.BackGround"))
```

There is a more to this process because the data binding operation must track the current row that will be used for the binding. The entire process is beyond the scope of this chapter, but there are several articles on Microsoft's MSDN web site to go into more depth. You can search on that web site with the search terms 'Windows Forms data binding' to find them.

Accessing XML through ADO.NET

Since `DataSets` are based internally on XML, it is relatively straightforward to create a `DataSet` from a valid XML document. The `DataSet` method to do this is `ReadXML()`. Here is an exercise that uses an XML document to create a `DataSet`. It is similar to a part of the previous exercise that created a `DataSet` from a database, emphasizing the commonality of these situations.

1. Open your favorite text editor or XML editor, and enter the following XML document. If you have a small, valid XML document with hierarchical data in it, you can use that instead. Save the document as `xmltest.xml`.

```
<root>
<Customer>
  <CompanyName>Northern Access, Ltd</CompanyName>
  <Order>
    <OrderDate>12-19-2000</OrderDate>
    <ShipVia>UPS</ShipVia>
  </Order>
  <Order>
    <OrderDate>01-07-2001</OrderDate>
    <ShipVia>FedEx</ShipVia>
```

```
    </Order>
  </Customer>
  <Customer>
    <CompanyName>Southern Access, Inc.</CompanyName>
    <Order>
      <OrderDate>12-22-2000</OrderDate>
      <ShipVia>UPS</ShipVia>
    </Order>
  </Customer>
</root>
```

2. Start a new **Windows Application** in Visual Studio .NET. Go to the design surface for `Form1`. Drag a Windows Forms **Button** and a **DataGrid** onto the form.

3. Set the `Text` property of the button to **Get Data**. Position the **DataGrid** at the bottom of the form, and set its **Anchor** property to **Bottom, Left, Right**.

4. Right-click on the form, and select **View Code**. Place the following two lines at the top of the code for the form:

```
Imports System.Data
Imports System.Data.OleDb
```

5. Go back to the form's design surface. Double-click the **Button** to get to its `Click` event code. Insert the following logic in the `Click` event, substituting your own location for your XML file created in Step 1:

```
Private Sub Button1_Click(ByVal sender As System.Object, _
    ByVal e As System.EventArgs) Handles Button1.Click

    Dim MyXMLDataSet As New DataSet("XMLDataSet")
    ' substitute your path here
    MyXMLDataSet.ReadXml("C:\TEMP\xmltest.xml")
    DataGrid1.DataSource = MyXMLDataSet
    DataGrid1.DataMember = "Customer"

End Sub
```

Now run the project and the form will come up. Press the button. At this point, the `DataGrid` is loaded with the two customers that appear in the XML file. As before, you can now navigate through the hierarchical `DataSet` in the `DataGrid`.

Saving Changes to the Data

As the `DataSet` has been created and placed in the grid, and since the `DataGrid` is bound to the `DataSet`, any changes typed into the grid are placed into the `DataSet`. As with the earlier example, those changes are not automatically placed back in the XML file. However, you can create another button with the following code in it to save the data:

```
Private Sub Button2_Click(ByVal sender As System.Object, _
    ByVal e As System.EventArgs) Handles Button2.Click

    Dim MyXmlDataSet As DataSet
    MyXmlDataSet = CType(DataGrid1.DataSource, DataSet)
    ' Change path as necessary
    MyXmlDataSet.WriteXml("C:\TEMP\xmltest.xml")

End Sub
```

Of course, you can save the XML data to any file, not just the one that you originally got it from.

Note that, while the data is in the DataSet, you can manipulate it with any of the DataSet syntax covered earlier in the chapter. You can add rows, add columns, change data items, and so on. The saved XML will then contain all of these changes.

Persisting a DataSet in XML

The WriteXML() method is available for any dataset, regardless of how it was created. That means you can always save the current state of a DataSet by writing it to disk with the WriteXML() method. When you are ready to work with it again, you can re-create it in your code using the ReadXML() method.

Accessing XML through the DOM

Manipulating XML data through ADO.NET (as in the example just seen) is quite a bit simpler than many of the alternatives, such as using the XML Document Object Model (DOM). The ADO.NET syntax is consistent with other data manipulation code, making it unnecessary to learn a different, more complex object model for routine manipulation of XML data.

However, XML is used for a lot of different purposes other than simple ADO-like data manipulation, and not all XML data is easily accessed through the relational model used in a DataSet. So the .NET Framework also includes the ability to work with XML through the DOM.

The System.XML Namespace

All of the classes to work with XML outside ADO.NET are in the System.XML namespace. The technology in System.XML is the replacement for (and descended from) the MSXML libraries that are distributed with recent versions of Internet Explorer.

Manipulating XML through the DOM is beyond the scope of this book. Complete books have been written on how to do it. It requires you to understand general XML concepts such as nodes, entities, attributes, and so on, plus the concept of character streams. A good resource to get started in this area is *Professional XML for .NET Developers*, ISBN *1-861005-31-8*, published by Wrox Press.

Some General Guidelines for Using ADO.NET

ADO.NET provides a different model for accessing and manipulating data compared to older data access technologies. This means that you must learn different data architectures to use it. You also need to understand how to apply the different technologies in ADO.NET in the right circumstances.

When to Use DataReaders

DataReaders are the fastest way to get to data in .NET. If you are doing read-only, forward-only access to data, then DataReaders are the obvious choice.

Less obvious is the usage of DataReaders when constructing ASP.NET web pages. Complex data pages in ASP.NET are often created with data binding, and DataReaders can be used for that purpose (as can DataSets). If you are creating an ASP.NET page that displays a grid containing a lot of data, you'll usually want to use DataReaders to get the best performance.

You cannot use DataReaders for binding in Windows Forms. The controls used in Windows Forms require an in-memory representation of the data, and a DataReader does not provide one.

When to Use DataSets

DataSets are useful for more design scenarios than DataReaders. For any of the following situations, you should first consider a DataSet as the likeliest candidate for a solution:

❑ You want to manipulate data, and then return the changes to the database. If you want to do it without maintaining a connection, a DataSet is particularly appropriate. (For some connected data manipulation scenarios, classic ADO is a better solution. That is discussed later in the chapter.)

❑ You need to pass data around among different tiers in some sort of data container (the way you would pass a Recordset object around in Visual Basic .NET). The DataSet can be that container.

❑ You need to expose a complex set of data with a Web Service. Again, the DataSet can be the container to use. It can even be read by non-.NET clients as XML.

❑ You have data with a master-detail relationship that you need to work with in code. Working with master-detail data in DataSets is much easier than working with such data via DataReaders or via classic ADO.

❑ You want to do data binding in Windows Forms. This includes situations where you need to filter or sort the data in data-bound controls on the client.

❑ You want to expose data from multiple data sources. DataReaders and ADO Recordsets can only work with a single connection, but different DataTables in a DataSet can originate in different data sources through different DataAdapters that use different connections.

❑ You need to cache data on the server between calls to a web page. You can't cache a DataReader, but you can cache a DataSet.

Changes to the Business Tier with ADO.NET

Data-related objects in .NET projects look somewhat different from such objects in VB6. In particular, inheritance opens up some new design options.

For example, you may have data objects that work with various tables and views in your database. However, all of these objects may need to share the same connection information. You may find it useful to create a base class for your objects that handles the connection to the database, and then inherit from that class to all of the objects that will use the connection.

Another possibility is to inherit directly from the ADO.NET classes. For example, you could have a `CustomerList` object that inherited from the `DataSet` class. The `CustomerList` object would immediately gain all the capabilities of a `DataSet`, which would allow it to be bound to controls, or to have `DataViews` imposed on it. It could then have a custom method to add a new customer to the list, and this method would manipulate the underlying `DataSet`.

There are also architectural considerations for applications that need to work with more than one type of database engine. It is possible to use generic interfaces in place of the classes in the various data providers. For example, instead of using a `SqlConnection` class or an `OleDbConnection` class, your code could work with the `IDbConnection` interface and be compatible with both. Chapter 5 talks more about using interfaces in Visual Basic .NET.

When is Classic ADO Still Needed?

We noted early in the chapter that ADO.NET is not a complete replacement for ADO. There are still design scenarios in which ADO is better, or even essential. Here are the most important examples.

Pessimistic Concurrency

ADO.NET implements an **optimistic concurrency** model. Data in a disconnected `DataSet` is checked for changes when updates are attempted. If the data has changed in the mean time, an exception is thrown and the developer must have code that decides what to do with the changes.

This makes complete sense in a disconnected environment. But some applications need to access certain records, and lock the records so that no other application can get to the record (except in a read-only mode). Locking a record while making a change – to make sure that no one else can alter it in the mean time – is called **pessimistic concurrency**.

There is no capability in ADO.NET to lock records in a database and maintain the lock until the application is through with the data. That is, ADO.NET does not support pessimistic concurrency. That means that those .NET applications that need pessimistic concurrency must either use ADO to get it, or do significant extra work to implement a custom locking scheme that will lock the records as they are being placed in an ADO.NET `DataSet`.

For example, if a client-server application for a credit card company supports operators that change credit card data for customers, normally such an application would use pessimistic concurrency. When one operator opens a customer record for changes, that operator does not want any other operator to be able to alter the record until it is released. If another operator attempts to access the record, that operator knows immediately that the data cannot be changed.

Applications that Need Server-Side Cursors

Cursors are a means of accessing a particular record in a set of records. They can be thought of as a 'pointer' to an active record in the set.

The only cursor available in ADO.NET is for the `DataReader`. A `DataSet` accesses rows by using indexes of row collections, so it has no cursor. Furthermore, the `DataSet` is always local to the running application because it is an in-memory representation of the data. There are situations in which this can be a problem. For example, working with large volumes of data is inadvisable in ADO.NET, because all the data is transferred to the client and stored in memory. In this case, using a server-side cursor (available in ADO) might offer better performance.

Other situations in which server-side cursors are helpful or essential are those in which the underlying data is changing a lot, and the changes must be reflected in the data immediately for all consuming clients. For example, a reservation system for airlines has constantly changing availability of seats, and an operator needs to know immediately if a seat becomes unavailable because another customer has just reserved it. ADO with a server-side cursor will handle this requirement, but there is no technology in ADO.NET that is suitable.

Summary

This chapter has covered the basics of data access using ADO.NET. The central idea of a `DataSet` has been extensively discussed. We have discussed the lifecycle of the `DataSet`, its constituent elements (such as `DataTables` and `DataRows`), and how to create a `DataSet` from various data sources. If you understand what a `DataSet` is, how to create one, how to manipulate one, and how to save the results, you are well on your way to being proficient at data access in Visual Basic .NET.

We have also covered the other classes in ADO.NET, including those that provide connected access to databases (`Connection`, `Command`, and `DataAdapter` classes). To adequately cover a variety of data applications, you particularly need to understand when the `DataReader` provides an alternative to `DataSets`.

We also discussed data-related topics such as data binding, and when to continue to use classic ADO. The general strategy recommendations towards the end of the chapter should help you in your initial decision making when designing data architectures in .NET.

However, there is obviously a lot more to ADO.NET than we can cover here. We have concentrated on what you need to know initially, but as you begin data-related development, you are certain to go beyond the techniques that this chapter includes. For more in-depth information on working with data in Visual Basic .NET, you can consult *Professional ADO.NET* from Wrox Press, ISBN *1-861005-27-X*.

9

Advanced Topics

So far in this book, we have been covering fairly mainstream features and capabilities of Visual Basic .NET – language changes and enhancements, Windows Forms, Web Forms, and data access. However, there are several more advanced features and capabilities that are important to consider as well. These are either provided directly by Visual Basic .NET, or flow from the .NET system class libraries but are of interest to VB developers.

The .NET Framework and Visual Basic .NET are tightly integrated. The .NET Framework was discussed in Chapter 2, and as we saw, it provides us with extensive capabilities, many of which were difficult to access in the past since they required calling Win32 APIs, or were impossible to access due to limitations of VB. Now, however, VB can make use of any of the capabilities provided by the .NET Framework, opening up a great many possibilities.

We won't try to cover all of them here, but there are some major features, or changes to existing functionality, available now that are worth quick exploration, including:

- ❑ Creating middle tier components
- ❑ Free-threading
- ❑ Creating console applications
- ❑ Printing with Visual Basic .NET
- ❑ Creating Windows NT/Windows 2000 services
- ❑ Monitoring the file system for changes
- ❑ Command line options and tools

Obviously, these topics are largely unrelated, so we have grouped them together in this chapter devoted to covering various advanced topics. As we mentioned way back in Chapter 1, the .NET Framework and Visual Basic .NET have so many features, that there is no way to do them all justice in a single book. This is certainly made clear in this chapter, where we will touch on the basics of a number of capabilities and features, each of which is very extensive.

Middle Tier Components

Over the past few years, VB has become used increasingly for the development of **middle tier components**. These components include those running on a web server for use by ASP pages and those running in MTS packages or COM+ applications. There are also times when these middle tier components are accessed directly via DCOM (Distributed COM), without using either MTS or COM+. In environments where queued messaging is employed, they also are typically the components that interact with MSMQ.

Visual Basic .NET supports these scenarios as well, though not always quite in the same manner.

We have already seen how ASP.NET and Visual Basic .NET work together to create applications that run on the web server itself. This is directly analogous to using COM components behind ASP, but with much tighter integration, better performance, and the elimination of the deployment issues presented by COM components in that environment.

What we will explore in this section is the creation of .NET assemblies that can be used in a middle tier scenario, much like COM components accessed via DCOM or running in a COM+ application. We will discuss three key middle tier technologies for .NET:

❑   .NET Remoting

❑   Enterprise Services, specifically 2-phase transactional support

❑   Queued messaging

Let's start by discussing the .NET equivalent to DCOM – .NET Remoting.

.NET Remoting

In VB6, any time you wanted to interact with an object across the network, you typically relied on DCOM. You might have also used MSMQ, Remote Data Services (RDS), or more recently, the SOAP Toolkit. However, most people have relied on DCOM. This is true whether the remote object was hosted in an ActiveX EXE, in MTS, or in COM+.

DCOM has its strengths and weaknesses. It is very simple to use, it provides location transparency in conjunction with COM, and it is integrated with the Windows security system. However, DCOM is very difficult to implement across a firewall since it makes use of many ports. It is also often considered a 'heavy' protocol, especially when compared to lightweight counterparts such as pure IP socket-based communication or HTTP.

We could also use RDS to access COM objects through port 80. This technology solved some of the problems, but used a proprietary communication scheme as opposed to .NET, which defaults to using the emerging SOAP standard.

The .NET Framework does not use DCOM for cross-process or cross-network communication, preferring instead to make use of some more Internet-friendly technologies. There are two options available for creating middle tier components in Visual Basic .NET:

❏ Use XML Web Services to create SOAP and XML-based methods that can be called from clients

❏ Use .NET Remoting to expose middle tier objects to clients for their use, using either XML or binary protocols

In Chapter 7, we discussed web development using ASP.NET. In that chapter, we also discussed XML Web Services and the role they play. In this chapter, we will focus on .NET Remoting, which is a faster and more powerful technology for working with middle tier components.

The built-in remoting technology offers more flexibility than DCOM, but does require a bit more effort to implement. It also requires more work than XML Web Services, but offers a much richer feature set by comparison.

Typically, we will want to use .NET Remoting for communication between a .NET client and a .NET server, but use XML Web Services if our server needs to expose its data to non-.NET clients. Remember that XML Web Services are all about exposing data for interoperability, while .NET Remoting is all about accessing objects *or* data between .NET applications.

Remoting separates the concept of calling an object from the underlying transport mechanism for the call. COM automatically invoked DCOM as a transport, but remoting allows us to specify the transport or connection mechanism via configuration files, outside of our program code. This means we can switch from one type of connection to another without recoding.

These transports or connections are called **channels** in remoting parlance. The currently supported channels include:

❏ HTTP

❏ Direct TCP sockets

Both the HTTP and direct TCP socket technologies create direct connections from the client application to the server over a specified port of our choice.

In the case of the HTTP channel, our host application acts as an HTTP listener, accepting requests and sending the response via HTTP. With this channel, it defaults to transferring the data back and forth using SOAP formatting, which is XML-based.

Similarly, a host using the direct TCP technology provides a socket listener, accepting and responding over that socket in a binary format by default – basically a binary derivative of SOAP.

Before we get too deep into the technical implementation of .NET Remoting, we need to have a discussion about how .NET works with classes in DLLs. The rules we are used to from VB6, COM, and DCOM are not always valid in .NET, so it is important to understand how .NET makes objects available to remote clients.

Rules for Remote Access to Objects

Visual Basic .NET allows us to easily create DLL files containing our application code. These are not the COM DLLs created by VB6, but rather, are .NET assemblies designed to run within the context of a .NET application. A Visual Basic .NET class library is like a conventional ActiveX DLL from VB6, in that it is a DLL containing a set of classes for use by our applications. In the case of both .NET and COM DLLs, a host application (EXE) is required for the code in the DLL to be run – but there the similarity largely stops.

> *In Chapter 11, we will see that these .NET DLLs **can** be used from COM clients just like a regular COM component – giving us the best of both worlds.*

When a .NET DLL is loaded directly into an application, we can use the classes and data types from that DLL directly. This is equivalent to the behavior we had in VB6 when an application made use of an ActiveX DLL.

Things are quite different, however, if the client application is running in a different process or on a different machine from that where the .NET DLL is hosted.

Default of No Remote Access

By default, a .NET class is set up for *direct* use by an application, *not* for use remotely across the network or even from another application on the same machine. To make a regular class work properly in a distributed environment where the DLL is in a separate process or on a separate machine from the client, we need to take some extra steps.

.NET objects are, by default, available only to other code running in the same process or host application. Within the host application, all the objects are passed by reference, just as objects are in VB6.

In VB6, we could make an object available to code running in other processes or host applications by creating an ActiveX EXE or running our ActiveX DLL in MTS or COM+. This required little or no change to our code at all. Client applications were able to get a reference to the object, communicating with it between processes or even across the network.

Outside of a single process or host application .NET objects are, by default, unavailable. They are not passed by reference like COM objects in VB6 – at least not without us making some code changes. In particular, we need to specifically indicate that our object can be passed by reference by inheriting from the correct base class – something we will discuss in detail shortly.

To summarize, when a DLL is used by a client in the *client's process*, then objects are passed by reference as a default behavior. When a DLL is used by a client and the DLL is in *another process* or on *another machine*, then by default the client has no access to the DLL unless we add some extra code to our classes in the DLL.

This extra code will define whether our objects are available to the client application *by value* or *by reference*. We'll discuss these two options next.

Passing Objects by Value

Remotely accessed .NET objects can do something that VB6 COM objects could not do, and that is be passed by value. In this case, the client application doesn't get a reference to our object, but rather, gets a *copy* of the object that runs in the client application's process rather than in the original process. By default, .NET objects cannot be passed by value; we need to specifically mark the class with an attribute to indicate that it should be passed by value.

Serialization is the process of converting an object's data into a simple stream of bytes, which can be easily moved from one process to another or from one machine to another. This stream of bytes can then be *deserialized* to create a copy of the original object within the new process or on the new machine. It is this technique that allows objects to be passed *by value* between processes or across the network.

> *There are two types of serialization in .NET – **deep** and **shallow**. What we are talking about here is deep serialization, where the actual variables within the object are being serialized. Shallow serialization is used by XML Web Services and merely copies the public read write property values, not the actual variable values. Both are valuable, but obviously only deep serialization can make a true and complete copy of an object.*

By default, .NET objects are not serializable – meaning that they can't be passed by value. To make an object serializable, we need to mark the class with the `Serializable` attribute.

If we mark a class as serializable, using the `<Serializable()>` attribute, and access it from across the network or from another process on the same machine, it will be passed *by value* rather than by reference. In COM, objects are always passed by reference – there isn't even a built-in provision to allow for passing objects by value. In .NET, by contrast, objects can be passed by value.

Keep in mind that this is deep serialization, so the actual variables, `Public` or `Private`, within our object will be transferred to the client, so the client application will have a full and complete clone of the original object. If we want to prevent a variable from being transferred we need to mark it with the `<NonSerializable()>` attribute.

> **To achieve a type of behavior comparable to that which we get with DCOM, MTS, or COM+, we need to pass our objects by reference.**

The `Object` class from which all other classes are ultimately derived (even without an explicit `Inherits` statement) is designed for passing by value. So, for us to pass an object by reference, we need to derive our class from some other base class designed to be passed by reference, as we cover in the next section.

Visual Basic .NET provides us with two types of class – a simple **class** and a **component**. The only real difference is that a component has a graphical designer associated with it, which comes from the fact that it is a subclass of `System.ComponentModel.Component` instead of being a direct subclass of the `Object` type.

We can also pass components by value. The default base class for a component is
`System.ComponentModel.Component`, which does not allow passing of the component by value.
However, we can inherit from `System.ComponentModel.MarshalByValueComponent` and mark
the component with the `<Serializable()>` attribute. This allows us to pass components by value just
as we can with regular objects.

So to make a regular class available to remote clients by value, we simply add the `<Serializable()>`
attribute to the class. To make a component available by value to remote clients, we need to mark it
with the `<Serializable()>` attribute *and* have it inherit from `MarshalByValueComponent`.

Passing Objects by Reference

In VB6, DCOM allowed us to access remote objects *by reference*. This meant that the COM object
remained on the server machine, and each method call from the client was sent across the network to
the object so it could be handled.

We can achieve the same behavior in Visual Basic .NET by specifying that our remote objects are to be
accessed by reference. This is done by inheriting from a special base class that handles all the details of
access by reference – `MarshalByRefObject`.

This base class is used to create objects for use by reference across the network or across process
boundaries. For our objects to be available across the network by reference, we must inherit from
`MarshalByRefObject` or subclass of this class.

In reality, we have two main options for creating objects that will be passed by reference. We can create
a simple class that inherits from `MarshalByRefObject`, or we can create a component class.
Components inherit from `System.ComponentModel.Component`, which in turn is a subclass of
`MarshalByRefObject`, and thus can be passed by reference. Both approaches allow us to easily create
objects that can be invoked by clients from across the network.

> *Either way, we can continue to use inheritance within our application designs as normal. By
> default, all classes inherit from the System.Object class and we work from there. All we are
> doing here is choosing our top-level class so it now inherits from one of the by reference bases rather
> than the by value System.Object base class.*

Directly inheriting from `MarshalByRefObject` allows us to create a class with the least amount of
code. However, the Visual Studio .NET IDE provides extra features to component classes, most notably
drag-and-drop capabilities within the component designer.

Create a new **Class Library** project in Visual Studio .NET, and name it **Chapter9Library**. The default
class created by the IDE is very simple:

```
Public Class Class1

End Class
```

To make this class available by reference we can simply change the `Inherits` statement:

```
Inherits MarshalByRefObject
```

Then add a method to be called remotely:

```
Public Function GetValue() As Integer
  Return CInt(AppDomain.GetCurrentThreadId)
End Function
```

This method returns the current thread ID – a number uniquely identifying the thread of execution that is running our code. This is a useful debugging technique, since we will be able to prove that our remote object is running on a different thread from the client, as the thread ID values will be different for the server and the client.

With that change, our class is now ready for use by reference from remote clients.

Implementing Remoting

.NET Remoting is the equivalent to DCOM in the VB6 world. It is, in fact, a superset of XML Web Services as well. .NET Remoting allows us to do everything XML Web Services can do, plus it allows us to have stateful server-side objects like DCOM and it also allows us to pass objects by value as well as by reference.

Setting up remoting involves a number of pieces. These are illustrated in the following diagram:

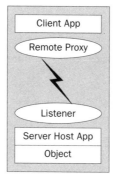

The remoting infrastructure sets up a proxy on the client that represents the object to the client, but actually makes any calls to the object's methods across the network to the real object. On the server side, our host application invokes the remoting infrastructure to set up a listener to receive those method calls. The host application also provides the process in which our server-side object will run.

For those familiar with DCOM, or any other type of object remoting technology, this diagram should seem familiar. Most major remoting technologies involve the same basic concepts of a client talking through a proxy object to a server where the object is hosted.

Any code that is run in Windows must run within a process, and all .NET code runs within an AppDomain that resides within a Windows process. A DLL relies on some other executable program to create the process and then load the DLL into that process. This is true in COM and VB6, and it remains true in .NET. We have seen how to create a .NET assembly in the form of a DLL, and how to subclass from MarshalByRefObject such that our object will be passed by reference rather than by value. Now we need to create a process to house that DLL so it can be used by other applications.

339

We will walk through the process using two techniques – IIS as the host, and a custom host we create ourselves.

Using IIS to Host Remoting

The easiest way to create a host for our server-side DLL is to use IIS. In this case, all we need to do is create an ASP.NET web application or Web Service application, reference our DLL, and make some entries in the web.config file. While very simple and straightforward, this approach does require that our server be running IIS 5.0 or higher, and it does force us to always use the HTTP protocol to communicate with our remote objects.

In Visual Studio .NET, add a new project to the solution using the File | Add Project | New Project menu option. Make this an ASP.NET Web Service project and name it Chapter9IIShost. While we won't actually create a Web Service, this project type does provide us with a good starting point when creating a remoting host.

We don't need Service1.asmx, the default module, since we are not creating a Web Service. Right-click on it in the Solution Explorer and delete it.

> *Technically, we don't need any of the files in this type of project other than the* Web.config *file and the* bin *directory that will hold our DLL. Instead of using Visual Studio .NET, we could manually create a virtual root, mark it as an application in the IIS management console, use a text editor to create the* Web.config *file and place our DLL in the* bin *directory under the virtual root.*

Now use the Project | Add Reference... dialog to add a reference to the Chapter9Library project. This will cause Visual Studio .NET to automatically copy the Chapter9Library.dll into the bin directory for our Web Service. For us to host a DLL for remoting, the DLL must reside in our web application's bin directory.

The dialog has three tabs, including a Projects tab that will allow us to reference other projects in our solution, including Chapter9Library:

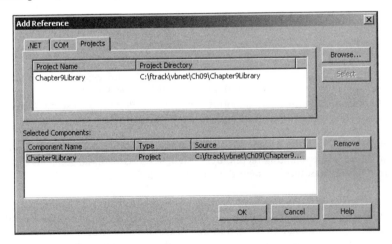

All we need to do now is update the `Web.config` file to indicate that the DLL should be exposed via remoting. Open the `Web.config` file for editing in Visual Studio .NET and add the following section to the document:

```xml
<?xml version="1.0" encoding="utf-8" ?>
<configuration>

  <system.runtime.remoting>
    <application>
      <service>
        <wellknown
          mode="SingleCall"
          objectUri="Chapter9.rem"
          type="Chapter9Library.Class1, Chapter9Library" />
      </service>
    </application>
  </system.runtime.remoting>
```

This section defines the settings for the remoting subsystem of .NET. It indicates that this is a remoting application and that we are defining a service.

Within the service, we are defining a well known class. The parts of this `<wellknown>` tag are the key information remoting needs to operate.

The `mode` indicates how clients will activate the server-side object. There are two options:

❑   `SingleCall` – An object is created for each method call

❑   `Singleton` – All method calls from all clients are sent to the same instance of the object

The `objectUri` specifies how clients will address the object. Remote objects are accessed via a URI, or universal resource indicator. Note that the `objectUri` doesn't point to a physical file – it points to a virtual entity corresponding to our DLL. ASP.NET uses this entry in the `Web.config` file to intercept the inbound request and routes it to our DLL to be handled.

When a remote object is hosted by IIS, the URI is the server name, the virtual root of the host application, and this `objectUri` value. Thus, we are specifying that the URI for this object is:

```
http://myserver/Chapter9IIShost/Chapter9.rem
```

Finally, the `type` specifies two things – the full class name of the class being exposed, and the name of the assembly or DLL in which it can be found. In our case, the full class name is `Chapter9Library.Class1` and the name of the assembly is `Chapter9Library`.

With this information, the remoting subsystem has enough information to make `Class1` available for use by remote client applications.

Creating a Host Application

Any application can act as a remoting host. We have just seen how IIS can be used as a host, but there are many times where we may want to use an existing application as a host, or where we may not want to incur the overhead of requiring IIS just to make an object available remotely. Additionally, there are cases where the HTTP protocol may not be ideal and we want to use the lower-level TCP socket channel. In these cases, we need to know how to create our own host application. This is very easy to do and requires little code. We have two options when creating a host application. The host application can be configured based on a config file, with a format similar to the `Web.config` file we just edited, or we can configure the host application via code.

The host application can be virtually any type of executable program, including Windows Forms, console applications, and Web Forms. It may also be a Windows service. We will discuss these later in this chapter.

For this example, we will create a simple Windows Forms application since that style of program is quite familiar to most VB developers.

Simply add a new **Windows Application** project in the IDE, and call it **Chapter9Host**.

Use the **Project | Add Reference...** menu option to add a reference to the **Chapter9Library** project just as we did in the IIS host project. The host application needs access to the DLL containing the class we want to expose for remote access, and adding a reference ensures that it will have access.

Next, open the code window for the `Form1.vb` file. We need to add an `Imports` statement at the top of this file to make it easier to work with the `Remoting` namespace:

```
Imports System.Runtime.Remoting
```

The `System.Runtime.Remoting` namespace contains the basic classes needed for remoting to work. Importing this namespace makes the namespace available to our code. However, we also need to add a reference to the actual `System.Runtime.Remoting` assembly by using the **Project | Add Reference...** dialog.

Finally, we need to simply add a line of code to invoke the remoting functionality. This is added in the load event for the form, thus ensuring it is run as the application is loaded:

```
Private Sub Form1_Load(ByVal sender As System.Object, _
    ByVal e As System.EventArgs) Handles MyBase.Load

    RemotingConfiguration.Configure("Chapter9Host.exe.config")

End Sub
```

Notice that we are simply invoking the `Configure` procedure contained within the remoting namespace, passing it a path to a configuration file. It is this configuration file that defines how our host will receive requests from clients. We will discuss the configuration file shortly.

Now we build the solution. This will build both the library containing our class and the host application. It will also cause the DLL containing our server-side object to be automatically copied by the IDE into the same directory as the host application's EXE. At this point, all we need is the configuration file and we are ready to host.

Setting Up the Host Configuration File

A nice feature of the Visual Studio .NET IDE is that it allows us to attach arbitrary files to our project, including simple text files such as the configuration file required to set up a remoting host.

In our host application project, Chapter9Host, choose the Project | Add New Item... menu option. In the resulting dialog, choose the Application Configuration File option and name the file Chapter9Host.exe.config:

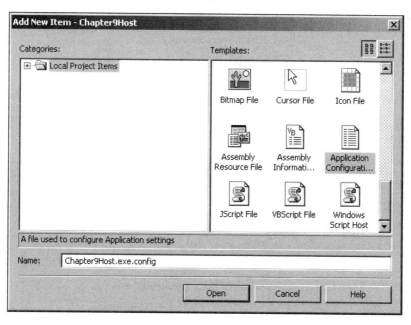

The normal name for application configuration files is the name of the final EXE followed by .config, which is what we are doing here.

This file can contain a number of different entries to configure our application, including information to configure the remoting subsystem. The file *should* reside in the same directory as our final EXE. This means it should be in the bin directory for our project. Normally the bin directory is not visible within the Solution Explorer window, but we can make it visible by clicking on the show all files button in the Solution Explorer's toolbar. Do this, then drag-and-drop the config file into the bin directory:

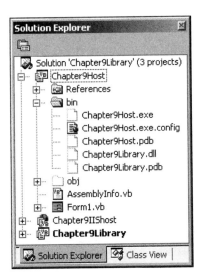

This will make the config file available to our application.

Now double-click the config file to open it for editing. We will add a section to the file that is very similar to that we created to configure IIS for hosting:

```xml
<?xml version="1.0" encoding="utf-8" ?>
<configuration>

  <system.runtime.remoting>
    <application name="Chapter9Host">
      <service>
        <wellknown
          mode="SingleCall"
          objectUri="Chapter9.rem"
          type="Chapter9Library.Class1, Chapter9Library" />
      </service>
      <channels>
        <channel port="8080" ref="http" />
        <channel port="8081" ref="tcp" />
      </channels>
    </application>
  </system.runtime.remoting>

</configuration>
```

There are some differences in the configuration compared to the IIS host.

First, notice that the `<application>` element has a name attribute. This specifies the name of our application and it also acts as the name of the virtual root for the URI that will be used to address our class.

Remember that virtual roots are, in fact, *virtual*. We often lose sight of this when working with web servers such as IIS where a virtual root points to a physical directory, but in reality, a virtual root doesn't need to point to any physical location at all. That is what is happening here – we are creating a virtual root that simply points to our application running in memory, not to any specific location on a disk at all.

We are specifying that the URI for our class is:

```
http://myserver/Chapter9Host/Chapter9.rem
```

The `<wellknown>` element is the same as it was in IIS. Notice the new `<channels>` element, however:

```
<channels>
  <channel port="8080" ref="http" />
  <channel port="8081" ref="tcp" />
</channels>
```

This element defines the channel or channels on which our host application will listen for inbound requests. When we host in IIS, this is taken care of automatically, since IIS itself is configured to listen only for HTTP requests on the port defined for the web site. When we create our own host, however, we need to define the details ourselves.

In this case, we are defining both the `http` and `tcp` channels, each with its own port.

When creating a host, we need to specify the ports on which it will listen for requests. When choosing a port, keep the following port ranges in mind:

- ❑ **0-1023** – Well known ports reserved for specific applications such as web servers, mail servers, and so on

- ❑ **1024-49151** – Registered ports that are reserved for various widely used protocols such as DirectPlay

- ❑ **49152-65535** – Intended for dynamic or private use, such as for applications that might be performing Remoting with .NET

With the host created and the configuration file set up, we are ready to create a client application that will use our object, either from the same machine or from another application on the same machine.

Programmatically Configuring the Host

Configuration of the host application can be done programmatically as well – thus avoiding the process of creating a config file. The advantage is that we avoid creating the configuration file, but the drawback is that the configuration is hard-coded into our application instead of being defined externally.

Before we write the configuration code, we need to add a couple of new `Imports` statements to the form:

```
Imports System.Runtime.Remoting
Imports System.Runtime.Remoting.Channels
Imports System.Runtime.Remoting.Channels.Http
Imports System.Runtime.Remoting.Channels.Tcp
```

345

To configure our host application through code, we would change form's load event as follows:

```
Private Sub Form1_Load(ByVal sender As System.Object, _
    ByVal e As System.EventArgs) Handles MyBase.Load

    RemotingConfiguration.ApplicationName = "Chapter9Host"

    RemotingConfiguration.RegisterWellKnownServiceType( _
        GetType(Chapter9Library.Class1), "Chapter9.rem", _
            WellKnownObjectMode.SingleCall)

    ChannelServices.RegisterChannel(New HttpChannel(8080))
    ChannelServices.RegisterChannel(New TcpChannel(8081))

End Sub
```

Instead of calling the Configure() method to get information from the config file, we are now calling a series of methods that do the same work.

First we set the application's name to Chapter9Host. As before, this defines the virtual root by which we will address any classes available through this host. Then, we call the RegisterWellKnownServiceType method to make Chapter9Library.Class1 available to remote clients. Finally, we create and register both the http and tcp channels, specifying the ports on which each protocol will listen for inbound requests.

This code accomplishes the same end result as the config file – making our server-side class available for use by remote client applications.

Testing the Host via a Browser

We can now quickly test the host by using the browser.

To use IIS as the host, use Internet Explorer and navigate to the URI specified in the config file:

http://localhost/Chapter9IIShost/Chapter9.rem?wsdl

To use our custom host application, we need to first run the host application. Once it is running, use Internet Explorer to navigate to the URI for the custom host:

http://localhost:8080/Chapter9Host/Chapter9.rem?wsdl

Either way, the result should be a display of XML within the browser. This is the definition of our component from a SOAP perspective. If nothing is displayed or the browser returns an error, then we know immediately that something is not configured correctly in our host application or its config file.

Creating a Client Application

Client applications also use the System.Runtime.Remoting namespace and either a configuration file or programmatic configuration. These are used in concert to allow the client application to locate and invoke the remote object. A client application can be easily created by making new Windows Application project in Visual Basic .NET, calling it Chapter9Client.

As with the host application we created earlier, we need to add a reference to the class library project that contains the object we want to call. This can be done using the **Project | Add Reference...** menu option, then browsing to the `Chapter9Library.dll` file in the **Chapter9Library** project directory.

Once the class library is referenced, we need to add a couple of `Imports` statements to the top of the `Form1` module:

```
Imports System.Runtime.Remoting
Imports Chapter9Library
```

Also, make sure to use **Project | Add Reference** to add a reference to the `System.Runtime.Remoting` assembly or it won't be available to our application.

At this point, our **Chapter9Client** application is ready to make use of our object, which is nice since we will get full Intellisense and type checking capabilities as we code. We still need to initialize the remoting system, which is done in the same way as we initialized it in the host application.

Within `Form1`'s load event we can simply make a call to initialize remoting:

```
Private Sub Form1_Load(ByVal sender As System.Object, _
  ByVal e As System.EventArgs) Handles MyBase.Load

  RemotingConfiguration.Configure("Chapter9Client.exe.config")

End Sub
```

As with the host application, our client application will require a configuration file, which is referenced in this code and which we will discuss shortly. The configuration can also be done programmatically – which we will also cover.

We can now write code within our application to make use of the remote object, just as if it were local to our program. Remember that our server-side class returns its thread ID as a value. In our client application, we will display both the client's thread ID and the value returned from the server. They should be different, thus proving that the object was run in a separate process on a separate thread.

Add a button to the form and the following code:

```
Private Sub Button1_Click(ByVal sender As System.Object, _
  ByVal e As System.EventArgs) Handles Button1.Click

  Dim obj As Class1

  MsgBox(CStr(AppDomain.GetCurrentThreadId), _
    MsgBoxStyle.Information, "My thread")

  obj = New Class1()

  MsgBox(CStr(obj.GetValue), _
    MsgBoxStyle.Information, "Remote thread")

End Sub
```

After we build the client application, all that remains is to create the configuration file so the remoting system can locate the server-side object.

Setting Up the Client Config File

Now we need to add an application configuration file to the project as we did earlier for the host application. As before, make sure to click the show all files button on the **Solution Explorer**'s toolbar and drag the file into the `bin` directory. Then, double-click on it to edit it and add the following:

```xml
<?xml version="1.0" encoding="utf-8" ?>
<configuration>

  <system.runtime.remoting>
    <application>
      <client>
        <wellknown
           type="Chapter9Library.Class1, Chapter9Library"
           url="http://localhost/Chapter9IIShost/Chapter9.rem" />
      </client>
    </application>
  </system.runtime.remoting>

</configuration>
```

This configures the application to use the IIS host. Alternatively we could use our custom host application by just changing the URL for the object:

```xml
<wellknown
   type="Chapter9Library.Class1, Chapter9Library"
   url="http://localhost:8080/Chapter9Host/Chapter9.rem" />
```

With the config file set up, we should be able to run the client application and have it call our server-side object, whether in a separate process on the same machine or across the network to another machine that is hosting the object.

Setting Up the Client Programmatically

As with the remote host, we can also skip the config file for the client and configure the client programmatically. This has the advantage of avoiding the creation and maintenance of the config file, but it does hard-code the configuration into the application.

Change the form's load event as follows:

```vb
Private Sub Form1_Load(ByVal sender As System.Object, _
    ByVal e As System.EventArgs) Handles MyBase.Load

  RemotingConfiguration.RegisterWellKnownClientType( _
    GetType(Chapter9Library.Class1), _
    "http://localhost/Chapter9IIShost/Chapter9.rem")

End Sub
```

Now, instead of configuring remoting from a file, we are directly calling the `RegisterWellKnownClientType()` method to register the remote class. Again, the URL may point to either the IIS host as shown, or to our custom host.

The end result is the same as using the config file. We can now run the application and it will communicate with the remote object.

Enterprise Services

The .NET runtime provides support for a set of powerful services collectively known as **Enterprise Services**. These provide important capabilities that we may want to use in our applications, and in the world of VB6, they were collectively known as COM+. Behind the scenes, the .NET runtime still actually uses COM+ to provide these services, though their use from within Visual Basic .NET is typically simpler than in VB6.

> *Since Enterprise Services use COM+ behind the scenes, code that uses any Enterprise Services will only run where COM+ is present, meaning Windows 2000 or higher.*

Any class that will make use of Enterprise Services will derive from a base class named `ServicedComponent`. This comes from the `System.EnterpriseServices` namespace, and requires that the project have a reference to the `System.EnterpriseServices.dll` assembly.

The specific Enterprise Services used in any given class are controlled by the use of attributes on the class or method involved. For instance, to make a method transactional, we would apply the `<Transactional()>` attribute to the method. There are a number of services available to our classes. The most useful include:

Service	Description
2-phase transactions	Provides transactional protection to our code so it can update two or more different databases within the context of a single transaction
Object pooling	Causes the creation of a specific number of objects that are kept in memory for use by clients
Queued components	Allows us to write code that appears to be talking to an object, when in reality all our method calls are recorded, the series of calls is queued, and later replayed against the real object

Other services exist as well, though some are less useful in the .NET platform than they were in the COM environment.

Transactional Processing

One of the strengths of the Microsoft Windows DNA platform has long been its strong and highly integrated support for transactional processing. This was first accomplished through the Distributed Transaction Coordinator (DTC), but the DTC was rather hard to work with. Microsoft then created Microsoft Transaction Server (MTS), which automatically invoked the DTC on our behalf, making transactional processing a practical reality for most developers. More recently, Windows 2000 introduced COM+, which further refines the MTS environment by making it easier to use, more powerful, and faster.

Microsoft continues to support transactional processing in the .NET environment through Enterprise Services, relying on COM+ to take care of the details behind the scenes.

The transactions we are talking about here are distributed, 2-phase commit transactions. Simpler transactions that can be handled directly through ADO.NET were discussed in Chapter 8.

Since the underlying transactional support for .NET is provided by COM+, the overall process should be quite familiar to those who have created MTS or COM+ components in VB6.

Transactional components are typically running on a server and are often accessed from client workstations or web server machines. In VB6, we used DCOM to communicate from the client machine to the server. In .NET we will typically use either XML Web Services or .NET Remoting for this communication.

In this section, we will show how to use XML Web Services to create an assembly that uses the transactional capabilities provided by Enterprise Services to protect the updates to two different databases. If you were simply updating a single database, you would almost certainly avoid the use of Enterprise Services in favor of the much faster transactional support provided directly by ADO.NET.

Creating a Transacted Web Service

Making a Web Service class transactional is very straightforward. Start by creating a new ASP.NET Web Service project in the Visual Studio .NET IDE named Chapter9Service. This will start us with a project that has a Web Service code module named Service1.asmx. Creating a web service was covered in Chapter 7, so we will assume you can set up a basic Web Service project.

Upon opening the code window for the Service1.asmx file, you will see the code for the underlying Web Service class. To this code we can easily add some methods that update data elements in the pubs database on a couple different database servers.

As we discussed in Chapter 8, when working with data, we need to reference and import the ADO.NET assemblies. The Visual Studio .NET IDE automatically adds a reference to the System.Data.dll assembly for the ASP.NET Web Service type project. However, since this code will use SQL Server, we will want to add another Imports statement to the top of the Service1.asmx file:

```
Imports System.Data.SqlClient
```

We can then add a couple of methods within the Service1 class:

```
<WebMethod(False)> _
    Public Sub UpdateLName(ByVal au_id As String, ByVal au_lname As String)

    UpdateDB1(au_id, au_lname)
    UpdateDB2(au_id, au_lname)

End Sub
```

This method updates the last name of an author in the pubs database in two different databases. We provide it with the au_id value and the new last name and it updates the databases by calling the UpdateDB1() and UpdateDB2() methods. By passing False to the <WebMethod()> attribute, we are indicating that we don't need session support for this method, which is a faster approach.

For this to work, you will need two SQL Server database servers. If you don't have two servers available, this example could be altered to update two different tables in two different databases on the same server. Either way, the point is to prove that we have 2-phase transactional support as we do updates across multiple databases. If any update fails, the updates to all the databases should be rolled back.

These two methods are essentially identical, each one opening a specific database and updating the indicated record:

```
Private Sub UpdateDB1(ByVal au_id As String, ByVal au_lname As String)
  Const dbConn As String = "server=server1;uid=sa;pwd=;database=pubs"
  Dim cn As SQLConnection
  Dim cm As SQLCommand
  Dim SQL As String

  SQL = "update authors set au_lname='" & au_lname & _
        "' where au_id='" & au_id & "'"
  cn = New SQLConnection(dbConn)
  cn.Open()
  cm = New SQLCommand(SQL, cn)
  cm.ExecuteNonQuery()
End Sub

Private Sub UpdateDB2(ByVal au_id As String, ByVal au_lname As String)
  Const dbConn As String = "server=server2;uid=sa;pwd=;database=pubs"
  Dim cn As SQLConnection
  Dim cm As SQLCommand
  Dim SQL As String

  SQL = "update authors set au_lname='" & au_lname & _
        "' where au_id='" & au_id & "'"
  cn = New SQLConnection(dbConn)
  cn.Open()
  cm = New SQLCommand(SQL, cn)
  cm.ExecuteNonQuery()
End Sub
```

This simple code accepts a record ID and new last name value, and updates that row on two different database servers. Nothing complex, but enough to illustrate how we might use the transactional capabilities of .NET Enterprise Services (and thus COM+) to transactionally protect the operation.

Were we using VB6, we would mark the class module with a `RequiresTransaction` property. Then, when we put the DLL into COM+, it would pick up that attribute and automatically set up the component to require a transaction. The concept in .NET is comparable, but the process is actually easier.

To use Enterprise Services, we must first use the Project | Add Reference... dialog to add a reference to the `System.EnterpriseServices.dll` assembly. With that done, we can add an `Imports` statement to the top of our module:

```
Imports System.EnterpriseServices
```

Now, to make our code transactionally protected, we simply alter the `WebMethod` attribute for our method:

```
<WebMethod(False, TransactionOption:=TransactionOption.Required)> _
Public Sub UpdateLName(ByVal au_id As String, ByVal au_lname As String)
```

Rebuild the Web Service project and we are all done. At this point, if an error occurs anywhere during the update process, neither database will be updated – we have full 2-phase commit transactional protection.

To prove this, change the `UpdateDB2()` method so it intentionally causes an error by adding the following:

```
Private Sub UpdateDB2(ByVal au_id As String, ByVal au_lname As String)
  Const dbConn As String = "server=server2;uid=sa;pwd=;database=pubs"
  Dim cn As SqlConnection
  Dim cm As SqlCommand
  Dim SQL As String

  ' force an error to prove the rollback occurs
  Err.Raise(1, "Chapter9Service", "Our forced error")

  SQL = "update authors set au_lname='" & au_lname & _
        "' where au_id='" & au_id & "'"
  cn = New SqlConnection(dbConn)
  cn.Open()
  cm = New SqlCommand(SQL, cn)
  cm.ExecuteNonQuery()
End Sub
```

Now when we invoke the Web Service it will fail – *after* updating the first database. That update should be automatically rolled back due to the error, thus proving that we have the desired transactional protection.

This functionality uses the automatic complete feature of COM+ by default, so if our code doesn't raise an error, the transaction will be committed.

Using Explicit Transactional Control

We can opt to take more explicit control if we like – just as we could with COM+ and VB6. We do this by explicitly calling `SetComplete` or `SetAbort` depending on whether our code completes. Here too, our task is a bit easier than it was in VB6 with COM+ or MTS.

Since we have already imported the `System.EnterpriseServices` namespace, we have everything we need within our code. Our code has access to quite a few classes from this namespace, including `ContextUtil`. This class provides access to the COM+ object context. To use this in VB6, we needed to call the `GetObjectContext` function, but in Visual Basic .NET, we can just use the `ContextUtil` object to get at the same context information. This is another example of now Visual Basic .NET just simplifies many of the same tasks we did in VB6.

To indicate our code completed successfully, we can call the `SetComplete()` method:

```
ContextUtil.SetComplete()
```

Alternatively, if our code didn't succeed, we can cause a rollback by calling `SetAbort()`:

```
ContextUtil.SetAbort()
```

This gives us the same level of control available to us in VB6, with a bit less coding on our part. We will explore transactions some more in Chapter 11 when we discuss COM interoperability.

Using Microsoft Message Queue (MSMQ)

Another key middle tier technology is the ability to use **asynchronous queued messaging**. **MSMQ** provides us with a powerful set of services to fill this need, and the .NET system class library includes the `System.Messaging` namespace to give us access to MSMQ.

> To make use of the **System.Messaging** functionality you will need to have MSMQ installed on your machine.

In addition, the **Server Explorer** window in the Visual Studio .NET IDE can be used to further simplify our use of MSMQ by providing queue management options, including the ability to add or remove queues from within the development environment. Better still, we can actually drag-and-drop a queue from the **Server Explorer** directly onto a form or component designer.

Installation of MSMQ varies by the version of Windows. In Windows 98 or Windows NT 4, we need to install MSMQ as an additional piece of software, just as we do with MTS. It is available on the same CDs as MTS in fact.

On Windows 2000 or Windows XP MSMQ is an additional server component that can be installed during the operating system installation, or by using Add/Remove Programs in the Control Panel to add the Message Queuing system component.

Another way to drag-and-drop a queue is from the **Toolbox** under the **Components** tab, where we find a **MessageQueue** entry. If you take this approach, however, you need to manually set the properties on the object such that it references the queue you want to use.

Either way, we will need to do some coding to make use of the queue, requiring us to gain some familiarity with the `System.Messaging` namespace.

The System.Messaging Namespace

The `System.Messaging` namespace provides us with access to the messaging assembly. If you use the **Server Explorer** or **Toolbox** to drag-and-drop a queue onto our form or component, this assembly is automatically referenced. Otherwise, before using the `System.Messaging` namespace you need to use **Project | Add Reference...** to add a reference to `System.Messaging.dll`.

With this done, we can add an `Imports` statement to the top of our code module:

```
Imports System.Messaging
```

at which point we are all ready to make use of the MSMQ subsystem.

In this book we will keep things relatively simple, so we will see how to send and receive a basic `String` containing some text.

> *Of course 'simple' is relative. The MSMQ support in .NET is largely geared toward the transmission and reception of objects that are passed by value. Receiving a simple text value is a bit trickier than one might expect.*

First, create a new Windows Application project in Visual Studio .NET and name it Chapter9MSMQ.

Referencing the Queue

Make sure to first reference and import the `System.Messaging` assembly as described earlier, then add a button to the form. We will write our code in the button's click event.

We can declare a `MessageQueue` object variable as:

```
Dim q As MessageQueue
```

At this point, we can either open an existing queue or create a new one. To open an existing queue, we can provide the queue's path to the constructor:

```
q = New MessageQueue(".\private$\test")
```

In this case, we are opening a private local queue named `test`. We would use this same syntax to open any queue – public or private – as long as we know the queue's path. If the queue doesn't exist, this will result in a trappable error.

To create a new queue, we can use the shared `Create()` method:

```
q = MessageQueue.Create(".\private$\test")
```

Again, this code demonstrates the creation of a private queue named `test`. If the queue already exists, this will result in a trappable error. However, we may want to use the shared `Exists()` method to see if the queue exists, as follows:

```
Private Sub Button1_Click(ByVal sender As System.Object, _
  ByVal e As System.EventArgs) Handles Button1.Click

  Dim q As MessageQueue

  If MessageQueue.Exists(".\private$\test") Then
    q = New MessageQueue(".\private$\test")
```

```
        Else
            q = MessageQueue.Create(".\private$\test")

        End If

        q.Close()

    End Sub
```

In the end, assuming no errors, our code will have a reference to a queue.

Also notice that we are closing the queue at the end of the method. This is important, as we want to make sure that the queue resource is released as soon as we are done with it, rather than waiting an indeterminate period of time before the garbage collector reclaims our object.

Sending a Text Message

Sending a text message is quite simple. As with VB6 and MSMQ, we simply set a `Message` object's `Body` property to a `String` value:

```
    Private Sub Button1_Click(ByVal sender As System.Object, _
        ByVal e As System.EventArgs) Handles Button1.Click

        Dim q As MessageQueue

        If MessageQueue.Exists(".\private$\test") Then
            q = New MessageQueue(".\private$\test")

        Else
            q = MessageQueue.Create(".\private$\test")

        End If

        q.Send(".NET rocks")

        q.Close()

    End Sub
```

The `Send()` method will wrap the `String` value in XML using SOAP encoding automatically on our behalf. While we think we are sending a simple bit of text, it is important to realize that the message in the queue is actually a SOAP-formatted message containing some text marked as type `String`. This makes it consistent with other messaging within .NET, but may not be ideal for communicating with non-.NET code that isn't as well versed in SOAP.

Receiving a Text Message

Receiving a message involves opening the queue and calling its `Receive()` method to retrieve a `Message` object. Given that `Message` object, we can retrieve the data from the `Body` property.

Here is where things get a bit more complex than we might expect. Remember that the text we sent was actually wrapped up as a SOAP-formatted XML message on our behalf. As a result of this, we need to provide .NET with some extra information as we read the message so it knows how to properly unpack the data.

Add another button to the form to receive the message, and write the following code:

```
Private Sub Button2_Click(ByVal sender As System.Object, _
   ByVal e As System.EventArgs) Handles Button2.Click

   Dim q As MessageQueue
   q = New MessageQueue(".\private$\test")

   Dim formatter As XmlMessageFormatter = CType(q.Formatter, _
      XmlMessageFormatter)
   formatter.TargetTypeNames = New String() {"System.String"}

   Dim m As Message = q.Receive(New TimeSpan(0, 0, 3))

   MsgBox(CStr(m.Body))

   q.Close()

End Sub
```

Again, we have the lines to open the queue. The next couple lines define the expected format of the message we are receiving, indicating that what we expect to get is a single String value:

```
Dim formatter As XmlMessageFormatter = CType(q.Formatter, _
   XmlMessageFormatter)
formatter.TargetTypeNames = New String() {"System.String"}
```

The XmlMessageFormatter is a piece of software from the .NET Framework that understands how to decode the SOAP-formatted XML. Its TargetTypeNames property represents an array of data types we expect to find in the message. In this case, we are setting it to an array containing a single entry of type System.String. This indicates that we are expecting just a single String value in the message and are instructing the XmlMessageFormatter to decode the message accordingly.

With this defined, we can now receive a message from the queue and display it:

```
Dim m As Message = q.Receive(New TimeSpan(0, 0, 3))

MsgBox(CStr(m.Body))
```

Of course, we close the queue object at the end of the method, ensuring the resource is released, now that we are done with it.

Support for MSMQ in the .NET Framework is much more capable and sophisticated than that which we have seen here, but these examples demonstrate how to use MSMQ in a fashion similar to how we typically used it in VB6.

.NET Threading

One of the most anticipated features of Visual Basic .NET is the ability to create full multi-threaded or free-threaded applications. VB6 had some serious limitations in its design that prevented the use of free-threading, unless you were willing to jump through some tricky hoops.

With free-threading, we can now create applications that do their work in the background while still allowing the user to interact with the user interface. In VB6, for instance, it was difficult to create a dialog box with a Cancel button to stop a long-running task since the long-running task consumed the application's thread. In Visual Basic .NET, we can have the task run on a separate thread, leaving the UI fully responsive and able to accept user input.

In Visual Basic .NET, using threads is quite easy due to the threading support built into the .NET system class library. In fact, we can not only create multi-threaded applications in VB, but the `System.Threading` namespace also provides facilities for thread pooling and other advanced features. In this section, we will focus on basic multi-threading within Visual Basic .NET applications.

> **Before we get too far into this discussion, it is important to realize the dangers and difficulties involved in writing free-threaded applications. When we create more than one thread in a single process, all the threads share the same memory, the same variables, and the same environment. It is *very* easy to create complex bugs in free-threaded code.**

We can easily tell which thread our code is using by calling the `AppDomain.GetCurrentThreadID()` method. This method returns an `Integer` value indicating the ID for the current thread. We will use this method in our examples to prove to ourselves that our code is, in fact, running on various threads.

Working with Threads

.NET applications always run within an AppDomain. An AppDomain is always contained within a Windows process. Every AppDomain has at least one thread. Typically, our applications run in AppDomains that have just one. Unless some code explicitly creates another, our code will always run on this thread. This is illustrated by the following diagram, showing how our typical single thread of execution runs within an AppDomain contained in a Win32 process:

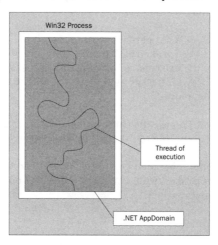

All AppDomains have the *potential* to run multiple threads, even though they only start with one. New threads can be created directly by our code and threads can also be created by other classes, including those in the .NET system class library. Often, these threads are started because we requested an asynchronous operation – something we will discuss briefly after we get through basic thread creation.

First, create a new **Windows Application** project named **Chapter9Threads**.

To simplify our use of threads we can use the `Imports` statement at the top of our form's code:

```
Imports System.Threading
```

Before we create a thread, we will need some code for the thread to execute. In Visual Basic .NET, we use the `AddressOf` operator to find the address of any routine or method that is to be called in such a manner. So, as we create a thread, we will pass it the address of a method that is to be run.

It is important to realize that much of the .NET Framework itself is not **threadsafe**. This means that much of the code in the Framework was not written to be automatically safe when used by more than one thread at a time within a single application. Proper handling of multiple threads requires synchronization and exquisite attention to detail to avoid very nasty bugs.

This synchronization often combines to make multi-threaded code run slower when used by a single thread. Any time our code uses variables or other data that is shared by multiple threads, we need to add extra code to ensure that only one thread can access the data at a time. Any other threads trying to access the data are simply blocked and unable to move until the current thread is complete. Even if two threads *don't* try to use the same data at the same time, just the fact that we have to establish cross-thread locking mechanisms decreases performance. To avoid this slowdown, most of the code in the Framework is not designed for use by multiple threads.

Updating Windows Forms Controls

This includes the Windows Forms components of the Framework. They are not designed to have multiple threads concurrently updating the display or working with forms or controls. Instead, they provide an `Invoke()` method that we can use from background threads to formally request that the primary UI thread update the display.

The use of the `Invoke()` method is not particularly intuitive. It is a totally generic method that accepts two parameters – the method to be invoked and an array of parameter values to be passed to that method. This is late-binding in the extreme, with no IntelliSense and very little design-time debugging. However, this is the only safe way for background threads to interact with any Windows Forms components such as controls on a form.

Add a **ListBox** control to `Form1` and use the **Dock** property in the **Properties** window to make it fill the entire form. We will display output from our threads in this control.

To do this display safely in a multi-threaded environment, we need to use the listbox's `Invoke()` method. The `Invoke()` method takes two parameters, a delegate pointer to the method that should be invoked and an array of parameter values.

Unfortunately, we can't simply pass the address of the method to be invoked. The `Invoke()` method requires a formal `Delegate` object as a parameter, and so we are required to formally define a `Delegate` to represent the method we want to invoke. This `Delegate` must have an identical method signature to the target method.

Since we want to call the `Items.Add()` method on the listbox, we need a delegate that matches that method. Declare this at the top of the code module:

```
Imports System.Threading

Public Delegate Function theMethod(ByVal item As Object) As Integer

Public Class Form1
```

Now we can create a thread-safe method that uses this delegate to invoke the `Items.Add()` method on the listbox. Add this to the form's code:

```
Private Sub Display(ByVal Text As String)

    Dim d As New theMethod(AddressOf ListBox1.Items.Add)
    Dim p() As Object = {Text}
    ListBox1.Invoke(d, p)

End Sub
```

This method creates an instance of the delegate by using the address of the `Items.Add()` method on the control. The resulting variable, d, contains a type-safe formal pointer to the method we want to invoke, and so it can be passed to the `Invoke()` method.

We then declare an array to contain our parameter value, which, in this case, is the text we want to display. Finally the code calls the `Invoke()` method on the listbox to safely call the method by passing our formal delegate pointer and the array of parameter values.

Though this code may run on a background thread, the actual method call itself will always be safely handled by the UI thread, avoiding any threading issues that might otherwise occur.

SyncLock

When working with multiple threads, any code we call must be written so as to be threadsafe, otherwise we risk introducing unforeseen bugs, very possibly causing our application to crash entirely. Threadsafe code is code that will operate properly when more than one thread is running within that same code. Without extra effort, most code is not threadsafe.

If you are working with code that is *not* threadsafe (or code that you don't *know* is threadsafe) you can use various synchronization methods to ensure that only one thread uses that code at any one time.

To make this easier, Visual Basic .NET includes the `SyncLock` keyword – a block structure that protects all the code in that block. `SyncLock` accepts an object as a parameter, and that object is used as the lock key. Any object can be used to synchronize our code, but keep in mind that each instance of the same *class* is a different *object*. It is a singular instance of an object that is used here – not the class. Any time we are within a `SyncLock` block based on a given object, we know that no other code in our application can also be in a `SyncLock` block using that *same object*. `SyncLock` blocks based on other objects are another matter.

If we want to ensure that all updates to an object are done by one thread at a time we can use
SyncLock. For instance, we might write code such as:

```
Dim obj As New Customer()

SyncLock obj
  obj.Name = "Fredrico Armon"
  obj.Sales = 12345.32
End SyncLock
```

As long as *all* code that interacts with the object is contained within a SyncLock block, we know that
only one thread can use it at a time – all other threads will be blocked until the current thread exits the
block. At that point, one of the blocked threads will be allowed into the code, while any others will
remain blocked.

Many of the .NET Framework objects have a SyncRoot property, which is a reference to an object that
can be used by the SyncLock statement. When an object exposes this property, all of our code should
use that SyncRoot object to do any synchronization with the object. By following this convention, we
help ensure that any other code that is also using that object will synchronize against the same
SyncRoot. If some code synchronizes against one object and some against another object, we will likely
end up with multiple threads simultaneously executing code meant only for access by a single thread.

The System.Threading namespace also provides other synchronization mechanisms we can use.
These include:

Mechanism	Description
Interlocked	Safe atomic updates of variables
Monitor	Synchronizes access to objects
Mutex	Synchronization primitive that works across processes as well as across threads
ReaderWriterLock	Provides the ability to allow multiple readers or one single writer for an object

Typically, SyncLock is the easiest to use, but these other options are often useful when creating multi-
threaded applications.

A Worker Method

When we create a background thread, it needs some work to do. Threads are always created to run a
method that does the work. Add the following worker method to the form:

```
Private Sub Worker()

  Display("Running on thread " & CStr(AppDomain.GetCurrentThreadId))

End Sub
```

We can call this routine ten times from within a regular program, for instance:

```
Private Sub Form1_Load(ByVal sender As System.Object, _
  ByVal e As System.EventArgs) Handles MyBase.Load

  Dim Index As Integer

  For Index = 1 To 10
    Worker()
  Next

End Sub
```

The **ListBox1** control will display exactly the same text over and over, since there's only one thread involved here:

Creating Threads

However, we can alter the code so that it creates multiple threads:

```
Private Sub Form1_Load(ByVal sender As System.Object, _
  ByVal e As System.EventArgs) Handles MyBase.Load

  Dim Index As Integer
  Dim t As Thread

  For Index = 1 To 10
    t = New Thread(AddressOf Worker)
    t.Start()
  Next

End Sub
```

This code declares a `Thread` variable, then creates ten threads in a loop – each one calling `Form1`'s `Worker()` method.

The result will be a display with a different thread ID for each line, something like this:

As you can see, each time the Worker() method was invoked, it ran on a different thread.

Thread Lifetimes

We have code to start our threads, but how do they stop? A thread will continue running until one of the following occurs:

❑   The method it is running completes

❑   The process containing the thread terminates

❑   We call the Abort() method on the thread object itself

In our example, as is typically the case, each thread stops when its method is complete. As soon as the code in the Worker() method is done, the thread running that code becomes available for termination. Keep in mind that the thread is controlled by a Thread object, which won't actually go away until .NET garbage collection reclaims the object.

If we run a method on a background thread that goes into an infinite loop, then that thread will not terminate, but will continue running within that loop until either that thread's Abort() method is called or the containing process terminates.

Interacting with the Current Thread

Throughout our code, we can use the Thread.CurrentThread property to get a reference to the current Thread object. This allows us to interact with our thread. This object has a number of methods that allow us to retrieve information about the thread and manipulate the thread in various ways, including altering the thread's priority and putting the thread to sleep for a time.

Using the Sleep() method is very nice, since it stops the thread from processing without consuming any CPU time as a busy wait in a loop would. For instance, the following line of code will cause the current thread to sleep for 42 milliseconds:

```
Thread.CurrentThread.Sleep(42)
```

This method can be used even on the main thread created in a process, so we can use it in any application, even if we aren't creating our own threads.

There is also a shortcut for the `Sleep()` *method, since it is exposed as a shared method of the* `Thread` *class itself – we can call* `Thread.Sleep()` *instead of referring explicitly to the* `CurrentThread` *property.*

Passing Data to a Thread

In our `Worker()` method example, we didn't pass any data to the method as it was started. In fact, it is not possible to directly pass parameters to a method that is being invoked in this manner. If we need our new thread to have specific data we will have to take a different approach.

It is important to remember that all our threads share the same memory. They all have equal access to any global variables or objects within our process. If two or more threads interact with the *same* variables or objects at the same time, we need to worry about synchronization. To keep things simple, it is ideal to provide each thread with its own individual set of variables on which it can operate.

The easiest technique is to create a class that has properties for the data we will need, and then place the worker method into that class. For each thread we want to create, we can create a new instance of the class and start the thread within that instance. In this way, each thread has its own object – each object containing the data specific to that thread.

To illustrate this, we will need to change `Form1` and also create a new class. In the form, change the `Display()` method's scope so it can be called from other code in our project:

```
Friend Sub Display(ByVal Text As String)

   Dim d As New theMethod(AddressOf ListBox1.Items.Add)
   Dim p() As Object = {Text}
   ListBox1.Invoke(d, p)

End Sub
```

Then, create a class with the following code:

```
Public Class ThreadObj
  Private theForm As Form1
  Private Count As Integer

  Public Sub New (ByVal Frm As Form1, ByVal ID As Integer)
    theForm = Frm
    Count = ID
  End Sub

  Public Sub Worker()

    theForm.Display(CStr(Count) & " starting on thread " & _
      CStr(AppDomain.GetCurrentThreadId))

  End Sub
End Class
```

So that we can continue to display the output in `Form1`, we are passing a reference to the form into this object. Additionally, this object will contain a numeric ID value, provided by the calling code via the object's constructor method. We have also created a method similar to the `Worker()` method from `Form1`.

Finally, we can update the form's `Load()` method to make use of this new class to provide information to each thread as it is created. In this case, we are providing the ID value so each thread has a numeric value we are assigning, along with a reference to the form so that the background thread can update the display:

```
Private Sub Form1_Load(ByVal sender As System.Object, _
   ByVal e As System.EventArgs) Handles MyBase.Load

   Dim Index As Integer
   Dim t As Thread
   Dim obj As ThreadObj

   For Index = 1 To 10
      obj = New ThreadObj(Me, Index)
      t = New Thread(AddressOf obj.Worker)
      t.Start()
   Next

End Sub
```

For an ID value, the loop index is passed as a parameter. Now, when we run the code, we will get a similar result to before, but the index value of the thread will also be displayed:

Notice that the threads don't necessarily display in straight numeric order. This directly illustrates how the threads are running concurrently – each being run according to the operating system thread scheduler.

*The Windows operating systems all give us the illusion of doing multiple things at once by using a preemptive thread scheduler. This scheduler allows any given thread to run for a small period of time known as a **quantum**. Typically, a quantum is about 20 ms, after which time the current thread is suspended and the scheduler starts another thread. Also, threads may do something that blocks the thread – like asking for data from a file or database, in which case the thread becomes temporarily suspended and the scheduler will start another thread. Since any thread only runs for 20 ms or less, we get the illusion that several things are happing at once even though only one is running at a time.*

Of course, if we have a multi-CPU machine, then the scheduler does this for each CPU and so we'll have as many threads running at any given time as we have CPUs to run them.

While using individual objects to provide data to each thread is the easiest approach, it is also possible to use global variables to provide such data. Keep in mind, however, that all the threads have equal access to those global variables and if more than one thread interacts with the variables at the same time the results can be very unpredictable. Make sure to use some synchronization technique, such as SyncLock, to ensure that only one thread interacts with the global variables at any one time.

Asynchronous Processing

Now that we have seen how to explicitly start threads through the use of the Thread object, let's take a look at **asynchronous processing** – a concept frequently used within the .NET system class libraries that can also cause threads to be started.

Asynchronous processing is the idea that we can start a process, and then we get to continue while that process runs in the background or maybe even sometime in the future. The process we have initiated becomes largely independent of our current process; they are not synchronized to each other.

When we call a method in our code, such as the Open() method on an ADO.NET database connection object, we expect that our application will wait until that method completes before continuing. This is an example of synchronous processing.

If we opened the database connection *asynchronously*, then our application would continue to run its code *at the same time* as the connection was being opened. Obviously, we would have to take extra steps to ensure that we didn't try to use the connection until it was actually open – illustrating how asynchronous programming is often much more complex than the normal synchronous programming we're used to.

Asynchronous processing is used in a number of places within the system class libraries. These include:

- ❏ XML Web Services
- ❏ .NET Remoting
- ❏ File I/O
- ❏ IP sockets
- ❏ Sending and receiving MSMQ messages
- ❏ HTTP processing
- ❏ Data access

The .NET system class libraries follow a general pattern for each of these by providing us with a BeginXXX() method to start the process, and an EndXXX() method that can be called when the process is complete. The EndXXX() method will typically provide us with information about the process that just completed, like how many bytes of data were received, or whether the process succeeded or failed.

The .NET Framework supports the concept of a **thread pool**. This is a pool of background threads maintained by .NET on our behalf. Methods can be queued up to be run by the pool, and as soon as one of the threads in the pool becomes idle, that method will be run on the idle thread. This is a powerful concept that is nicely abstracted by the .NET Framework.

The BeginXXX() method runs on our current thread, and starts the background process as appropriate for whatever we are trying to do. Later, when the process is complete we will get a callback or event telling us it is complete. This callback will run on a different thread – and that thread comes from the thread pool.

> *We can use the thread pool directly as well. It is the* ThreadPool *class in the* System.Threading *namespace.*

We know when a process is complete because the class library will call back into our application using a delegate that we provide, and that call will run on a thread from the thread pool.

In most cases, there is no way to cancel an asynchronous process. The .NET Framework objects typically don't provide a CancelXXX() method to cancel the background process. Review the help topics for the specific framework objects to see how to cancel the operations of each technology.

To start an asynchronous process, we might have code something along these lines:

```
Public Sub Start()
  Dim obj As New SomeLibraryObject ()

  AddHandler obj.XXXCompleted, _
    New XXXCompletedEventHandler(AddressOf OnXXXCompleted)

  obj.BeginXXX()
End Sub
```

The code creates an instance of the class (such as a FileStream, MessageQueue, or Socket), and then uses the AddHandler statement to add an event handler (or delegate) to that object so it knows how to call back into our code. This statement accepts the address of a method within our code that will receive the completed event when the operation is done.

The specific BeginXXX() and EndXXX() method names vary depending on the specific operation being performed. For instance, if we are dealing with MSMQ, we will have BeginReceive() and EndReceive() methods to receive a message, while the IP socket classes have BeginConnect() and EndConnect() to handle making a connection to another machine.

> **In some cases, the BeginXXX() method accepts the address of the callback delegate as a parameter. Consult the documentation for each individual function to see how it works.**

Finally, this code calls the BeginXXX() method to start the process. The code in our application will continue to run normally, with the newly started operation running on another thread in the background, which is created automatically. Our application can continue to do other processing, interact with the user, or whatever is required.

When the background task is complete, it will call back into our code by calling the method we indicated with the `AddHandler` statement. That method may look like this:

```
Private Sub OnXXXCompleted(ByVal sender As Object, _
                           ByVal e As AsyncEventArgs)
  Dim obj As LibraryObject = CType(sender, LibraryObject)

  obj.EndXXX()

  ' process the results here

  obj.BeginXXX()
End Sub
```

> The callback will typically occur on a different thread from that which our main application is using, so multi-threading and synchronization issues are important when using this type of technique.

The parameters passed to this method are the same as for any standard event – a reference to the sending object and the event arguments. Typically, the event arguments are of a type specific for the operation we are performing, but they are always derived from `AsyncEventArgs`.

> Of course, as with any good rule, there are always exceptions. Some events will not follow this pattern, so we need to consult the documentation appropriate to the operation we are trying to perform.

Since we often want to interact with the calling object, it can be beneficial to declare an object of the appropriate type and cast the `sender` parameter into the appropriate data type using the `CType()` method.

Typically, there will be an `EndXXX()` method that we can call to tell the sending object that we are processing the result. Often, this method is a function that will return some value. For instance, when reading from an IP socket, the return value is the number of bytes read from the socket.

Next we would have code to do any work we need to do as a result of the task being complete.

Finally, we will want to call the `BeginXXX()` method to restart the asynchronous processing. If we don't make this call, no further asynchronous processing will occur.

The location where we place the code to process the event is important. As shown in the example, the processing will occur before the next asynchronous task is started. This design ensures that we will only ever be processing the results from one task at a time.

We can put our processing code *after* the call to BeginXXX(), thus allowing the asynchronous task to run in the background as we process the current result. This design will allow multiple completed tasks to occur at once, since this event could be called again before we are done with the first call:

```
Private Sub OnXXXCompleted(ByVal sender As Object, _
                           ByVal e As AsyncEventArgs)
  Dim obj As LibraryObject = CType(sender, LibraryObject)

  obj.EndXXX()

  obj.BeginXXX()

  ' process the results here
End Sub
```

As soon as we call BeginXXX(), we indicate that we are ready to receive another event, so if any are pending, we will get one right away, even if our current thread isn't done processing the first event. In such a case, we need to be very sensitive to the fact that multiple threads may be running through the same routine at the same time.

IP Socket Example

As a quick example of asynchronous coding, let's take a look at some simple code to read data from an IP socket.

> *When planning to do a lot of work with sockets, make sure to look at the other classes available in the* System.Net.Sockets *namespace, as there are often simpler ways to interact with sockets than the one shown here.*

Create a new Windows Application named Chapter9IP.

To simulate a client application coming in to talk to our IP server, we will create a new class module named IPClient. Here is the code:

```
Imports System.IO
Imports System.Net
Imports System.Net.Sockets

Public Class IPClient
  Private s As Socket
  Private b(4096) As Byte    ' bytes just received

  Public Sub New(ByVal Host As String, ByVal Port As Integer)
    Connect(Host, Port)

    s.BeginReceive(b, 0, b.Length, SocketFlags.None, _
      AddressOf Me.ReceiveData, Nothing)
  End Sub

  Private Sub ReceiveData(ByVal ar As System.IAsyncResult)
    Dim cnt As Integer
    Dim idx As Integer
```

```
            Dim d() As Char
            Dim txt As String

            cnt = s.EndReceive(ar)

            ReDim d(cnt)
            For idx = 0 To cnt - 1
              d(idx) = ChrW(b(idx))
            Next
            txt = New String(d)

            ' do something with the data in txt
            MsgBox(txt, MsgBoxStyle.OKOnly, "Text")    ' for example

            s.BeginReceive(b, 0, b.Length, SocketFlags.None, _
                AddressOf Me.ReceiveData, Nothing)
        End Sub

        Private Sub Connect(ByVal Host As String, ByVal Port As Integer)

            s = New Socket(AddressFamily.InterNetwork, _
                SocketType.Stream, ProtocolType.Tcp)
            Dim host_addr As Integer = Dns.Resolve(Host).AddressList(0).Address
            s.Connect(New IPEndPoint(host_addr, Port))

        End Sub
    End Class
End Class
```

The constructor method accepts the host and port indicating the server to which we want to connect. The `Connect()` method creates a `Socket` object and binds it to the host and port we provided. We won't get into detail here, since our focus is on the asynchronous reads. The online help provides more information about the `Socket` object and how it can be used.

The call to `BeginReceive()` starts the read process. This method accepts the address of the callback delegate method as a parameter, so we provide it with the address of our `ReceiveData()` method:

```
    s.BeginReceive(b, 0, b.Length, SocketFlags.None, _
        AddressOf Me.ReceiveData, Nothing)
```

The method also accepts a `Byte` array (b) into which to put the data, the position within the array to start writing the data, and the maximum number of bytes to be read and a state object – which we pass as `Nothing`.

The `Byte` array is available not only to our main thread, but will also be used by the background thread during the receive process. We need to be very careful about how this variable is used to avoid threading conflicts. In this code, the variable isn't used by the main thread at all, other than to pass it to the background thread for its use. This avoids any conflicts, since only the background thread uses the array.

As with any socket programming, the array provides a buffer into which the received data will be written. To this end, it is reinitialized to a reasonably large size so we can get a decent amount of data from each receive event.

Our application will continue to run, allowing the user to interact with our form or anything else. In the meantime, in the background, we have a task waiting for input from the socket. As soon as the socket has data, our `ReceiveData()` method will be called to process that data.

The first thing the `ReceiveData()` method does is call the socket's `EndReceive()` method. This method returns the actual number of bytes read from the socket:

```
cnt = s.EndReceive(ar)
```

Of course, this value will never be larger than the size of our `Byte` array, because we provided that size to the `BeginReceive()` method as the maximum number of bytes we were prepared to read. This means that there could be more data waiting to be read right away when we next call `BeginReceive()`.

The next section of code converts the `Byte` array into a `String` so we can more easily work with the data:

```
ReDim d(cnt)
For idx = 0 To cnt - 1
  d(idx) = ChrW(b(idx))
Next
txt = New String(d)
```

At this point, we can work with the data as required. In the example, we are displaying the data in a message box. Even though we are on a background thread, it is perfectly acceptable to invoke a message box – it is only when working with pre-existing UI elements such as a form or control that threading issues are complex as we discussed earlier.

Finally, the `BeginReceive()` method is called again – restarting the background task to listen for further incoming data via the socket:

```
s.BeginReceive(b, 0, b.Length, SocketFlags.None, _
    AddressOf Me.ReceiveData, Nothing)
```

This illustrates the basic flow of an asynchronous process. By using this process, we are implicitly creating a multi-threaded application, since the .NET system class libraries can, and will, create threads for us in the background in order to service the asynchronous tasks we request.

To finish our test application, open up the designer for `Form1`. We will create a quick IP host application that will send some text when a client such as `IPClient` connects.

First let's add a button to the form so we can activate our 'client' when we are ready. Add the following code:

```
Private Sub Button1_Click(ByVal sender As System.Object, _
    ByVal e As System.EventArgs) Handles Button1.Click

    Dim objReader As IPClient
    objReader = New IPClient("localhost", 5000)

End Sub
```

This will instantiate an `IPClient` object – having it connect to the local machine on port 5000. Our code to process the result is a `MsgBox`, so we will see any returned text displayed in a dialog.

Now let's build the listener part of the application. Add a couple `Imports` statements to `Form1`:

```
Imports System.Net
Imports System.Net.Sockets
```

Next, let's add a method to send some text to a socket:

```
Private Sub Send(ByVal s As Socket)

  Dim txt As String = "Hello world"
  Dim c() As Char
  Dim b(Len(txt)) As Byte
  Dim idx As Integer

  ' convert the string to an array of char
  c = txt.ToCharArray

  ' convert the char array to a byte array
  For idx = 0 To c.Length - 1
    b(idx) = AscW(c(idx))
  Next

  ' send the byte array to the socket
  s.Send(b, b.Length, 0)

End Sub
```

This method accepts a socket as a parameter and then sends some text to that socket. The text is a `String` to start with, and so much of the code is consumed with converting that text into a `Byte` array for transmission. Unfortunately there's no direct way to convert a `String` to an array of type `Byte`.

We have to convert the `String` to an array of type `Char` first, which is easy. We can then convert each `Char` in the array into a `Byte` in the target array. This obviously only works for ASCII text – if your text was in some other Unicode character set, you would also have to put the second byte in each `Char` into the `Byte` array and also alter the client accordingly.

Now add a method to listen for incoming IP socket requests:

```
Private Sub DoListen()

  Dim myListener As TcpListener = New TcpListener(5000)

  myListener.Start()

  ' Program blocks on AcceptSocket() until a client connects
  Send(myListener.AcceptSocket)

  myListener.Stop()

End Sub
```

This code makes use of a helper class in the `System.Net.Sockets` namespace – the `TCPListener`. This class listens on the specified port and returns a new socket as the result of the `AcceptSocket()` method. This socket is connected to the new client.

Finally, update `Form1`'s `Load` event so the listener is running on a separate thread:

```
Private Sub Form1_Load(ByVal sender As System.Object, _
  ByVal e As System.EventArgs) Handles MyBase.Load

  Dim t As New System.Threading.Thread(AddressOf DoListen)
  t.Start()

End Sub
```

Now when the application starts it will start listening for incoming socket requests on a background thread, leaving the main thread available so the UI will be responsive to the user. If the user clicks our button, it will run the code to create an `IPClient` object – which will connect to our listener via a socket and get our text.

Console Applications

VB has always been about creating Windows GUI applications. More recently it has become a commonly used tool for the development of middle tier objects, typically allowing ASP code to generate the user interface. Another type of user interface that can be very useful, but has always been off-limits to VB developers, is the console application.

Console applications accept input and display output via a Windows text console, often called a DOS window. Visual Basic .NET allows us to easily create applications for this environment, including directly reading from and writing to the standard input and output streams.

In fact, in the Visual Studio .NET IDE, Console Application is one of the standard project types available to Visual Basic .NET developers. When we create a new Console Application project, we are presented with a `Module` that contains an empty `Sub Main` routine:

```
Module Module1

    Sub Main()

    End Sub

End Module
```

The first code run in such an application is always a `Sub Main` routine. From there, we can either directly write our code as a set of procedures, or invoke objects as needed.

Use of the System.Console Namespace

Console applications get their input from the console and write their output back to the console window. The objects that support these, and other useful operations for console applications, come from the `System.Console` namespace. When creating console applications, it is often useful, though not always necessary, to import that namespace:

```
Imports System.Console
```

Writing Text to the Console

To write a line of text to the standard output stream, we can use the `WriteLine()` method:

```
Sub Main()
   WriteLine("This is a test")
End Sub
```

Without importing the namespace, we can write this code as:

```
Sub Main()
   Console.WriteLine("This is a test")
End Sub
```

The `WriteLine()` method can take different forms, including various control characters and replaceable parameters. For instance, we can print out a couple of values in the text as follows:

```
WriteLine("The number {0} is {1}", 5, "five")
```

This will print out the following:

```
The number 5 is five
```

The `WriteLine()` method always sends a carriage return and line feed at the end, causing the cursor to move to a new line. If you want to continue to append to the same line, you can use the `Write()` method:

```
Write("Hello ")
Write("World")
WriteLine("!")
```

This will result in the following single line of output:

```
Hello World!
```

The `Write()` method also supports control characters and replaceable parameters.

Reading from the Console

Likewise, we can read from the console by using the `ReadLine()` method. This method accepts input from the console, returning it to our application when the user presses *Enter*.

```
Dim txt As String

txt = ReadLine()
```

If you want to read character-by-character, you can use the `Read()` method:

```
Dim txt As Char

txt = Chr(Read())
' type conversion because Read is Integer and txt is Char
```

The `Read()` method returns an `Integer` value corresponding to the numeric value of the character entered by the user. This method supports both ASCI and Unicode, and we can use the `Chr()` function to convert the numeric value to a character value.

Keep in mind that even with the `Read()` method, our application won't get access to the input until the user presses *Enter*. The `Read()` method will return each character the user entered – one at a time.

Asynchronous Support

We can also perform asynchronous reading and writing in a console application. This is accomplished through the `OpenStandardInput()`, `OpenStandardOutput()`, and `OpenStandardError()` methods, each of which provides access to the corresponding underlying `Stream` object. These `Stream` objects have methods that enable asynchronous reading and writing, as discussed earlier in the section on threading in Visual Basic .NET. For instance, the `OpenStandardInput` object has a `BeginRead()` method that starts an asynchronous read operation:

```
Sub Main()
    OpenStandardInput.BeginRead(b, 0, b.length, AddressOf OnRead, Nothing)
End Sub
```

Of course, this assumes we declare a module-level array:

```
Private b(4096) As Byte
```

and implement an `OnRead()` method to accept the callback:

```
Sub OnRead(ByVal e As IAsyncResult)
  Dim cnt As Integer

  cnt = OpenStandardInput.EndRead(e)

  ' process input

  OpenStandardInput.BeginRead(b, 0, b.length, AddressOf OnRead, Nothing)
End Sub
```

We can implement similar code against other stream objects such as `NetworkStream` and `MemoryStream`.

New Printing Model

Visual Basic .NET relies on a set of objects from the .NET system class library to provide printing support. Visual Studio .NET also includes a new version of the Crystal Reports system for report generation, but our focus here will be on the more native printing functionality available to us as developers.

PrintDocument and Related Objects

In VB6, we had a `Printer` object that we could use to create output that would be sent to the printer. The .NET system class libraries include a `PrintDocument` class that provides relatively comparable functionality. This class is found in the `System.Drawing.Printing` namespace, and provides more comprehensive support than the venerable `Printer` object available in the past.

There are some other key objects we will probably use when printing, since we may want to control the layout of the page, the printer we are printing to, and other aspects of the process. These objects include:

Object	Description
PrinterSettings	Object containing the printing settings, including the printer on which the document will be printed.
PageSettings	Object containing the printing settings for a particular page.
PrintDialog	Object providing access to the Windows printer selection dialog.
PrintPageEventArgs	This object is the parameter to the delegate method we must create to print a page. It contains information about the current page, including margins, and the very surface on which we'll print.

Additionally, we are likely to use some common dialogs from the `System.Windows.Forms.CommonDialog` namespace, including:

Dialog	Description
PageSetupDialog	Object providing access to the Windows page properties dialog
PrintPreviewDialog	Object providing access to a standard print preview dialog
PrintPreviewControl	The control that displays a print preview

With these dialogs, we can provide our user with the typical printing experience they expect from any application.

Implementing Printing

Printing in .NET is done using asynchronous callbacks, one for each page to be generated. This is quite different from the approach taken in previous versions of VB, where printing was a relatively linear process. Instead, in Visual Basic .NET, we set up the details of the printing process, tell the printing engine the address of our delegate method that will render each page, and then call the Print() method to start the process.

This means that our 'real' printing code will be contained in a method that is called by the print engine when it is ready for more information.

Basic Code Structure

This provides us with a lot of flexibility. The basic structure of code to handle printing to a printer is as follows:

```
Private WithEvents MyDoc As PrintDocument

Public Sub StartPrint()
  MyDoc = New PrintDocument()
  MyDoc.Print()
End Sub

Private Sub PrintPage (ByVal sender As Object, _
  ByVal ev As System.Drawing.Printing.PrintPageEventArgs) _
  Handles MyDoc.PrintPage

End Sub
```

To start the printing process, we simply call the Print() method on the document. This will cause the document to automatically fire the PrintPage event for each page that is to be printed. Notice the use of the Handles keyword to link our PrintPage() method to the appropriate event from the document.

Implementing Print Preview

The code we have just seen would cause the printing to occur on the default printer when the StartPrint() method is called. If you want to do a print preview instead of printing to the printer, you merely change the code that invokes the print process:

```
Public Sub StartPrint()
  Dim PPdlg As PrintPreviewDialog = New PrintPreviewDialog()

  PPdlg.Document = MyDoc
  PPdlg.ShowDialog()
End Sub
```

Again, the PrintPage event will fire for each page that is to be printed, but this time the output will be displayed in a print preview window instead of being printed to the printer. This requires no change to the PrintPage code that actually renders the output.

Creating an Example

Let's create a simple test application. Open a new **Windows Application** named **Chapter9Printing**. Add an `Imports` statement to the top of `Form1`:

```
Imports System.Drawing.Printing
```

This namespace includes some important classes that we will be using. We also need to add some class-level variables:

```
Public Class Form1
    Inherits System.Windows.Forms.Form

    Private Data() As String
    Private CurrentLine As Integer
```

The array will contain the text we are printing, while the `CurrentLine` variable will act as a line counter as we index through the array of text.

Using `Form1`'s designer, add a `PrintDocument` control from the **Toolbox**. This control is an instance of the `System.Drawing.Printing.PrintDocument` class.

> *We could also create this class by hand, declaring it using the `WithEvents` keyword, and get the same effect.*

Then, add a button to the form, along with the following code:

```
Private Sub Button1_Click(ByVal sender As System.Object, _
    ByVal e As System.EventArgs) Handles Button1.Click
    ReDim Data(4)
    Data(0) = "This is line 1"
    Data(1) = "This is line 2"
    Data(2) = "This is line 3"
    Data(3) = "This is line 4"
    Data(4) = "This is line 5"

    PrintDocument1.Print()
End Sub
```

This simple code just populates the array from which we will get our data, and then uses the `PrintDocument1` control's `Print()` method to start the printing process.

Rendering the Output

To actually render our text to the printer, we need to implement a method to handle the `PrintDocument1.PrintPage` event. This code can draw virtually anything onto the 'surface' of the current page, including text or graphics. Such flexibility is powerful, but has its drawbacks. It also means that we need to keep track of our own X and Y coordinates so we can draw our text where we want it to be.

This implementation will vary depending on the source of the data to be printed. The data could come from virtually anywhere – an ADO.NET DataSet, an ADO Recordset, a String variable, a text file or, as in our simple example, from an array.

Add the PrintPage() method to Form1:

```
Private Sub PrintPage(ByVal sender As Object, _
    ByVal ev As System.Drawing.Printing.PrintPageEventArgs) _
    Handles PrintDocument1.PrintPage

    Dim yMax As Single
    Dim LineHeight As Single
    Dim yPos As Single
    Dim LeftMargin As Single = ev.MarginBounds.Left
    Dim PrintFont As Font

    PrintFont = New Font("Arial", 10)

    LineHeight = PrintFont.GetHeight(ev.Graphics)

    yPos = ev.MarginBounds.Top

    Do

        yPos += LineHeight

        ev.Graphics.DrawString(Data(CurrentLine), PrintFont, _
            Brushes.Black, LeftMargin, yPos, New StringFormat())

        CurrentLine += 1

    Loop Until ypos >= ev.MarginBounds.Bottom Or _
        CurrentLine = UBound(Data) + 1

    If CurrentLine < UBound(Data) + 1 Then
        ev.HasMorePages = True
    Else
        ev.HasMorePages = False
    End If
End Sub
```

Let's take a closer look at this code. It makes heavy use of the PrintPageEventArgs object that we receive as a parameter. This object provides us with some key information about the print margins, as well as providing the surface on which we will render the output.

The operative line of code in this routine is the one that draws our text onto the print surface:

```
ev.Graphics.DrawString(Data(CurrentLine), PrintFont, _
    Brushes.Black, LeftMargin, yPos, New StringFormat())
```

The `DrawString()` method renders text onto the drawing surface. The first parameter is the text to be rendered, which, in our case, is coming from the array. If the data were coming from some other source then this would vary.

The other two key parameters worth noting are the `LeftMargin` and `yPos` values. These specify the X and Y coordinates on the print surface where the text will start. Earlier in the method, we retrieved the left margin value from the `PrintPageEventArgs` object:

```
Dim LeftMargin As Single = ev.MarginBounds.Left
```

The `yPos` variable is a bit more complex, since it will change as we continue to print lines on the page. As each line is printed we recalculate the Y position, in pixels, by adding the height of the font being used – in this case a 10 point Arial. First we calculated the line height:

```
LineHeight = PrintFont.GetHeight(ev.Graphics)
```

Then, as each line is printed, we increment the `yPos` variable:

```
yPos += LineHeight
```

This causes the print to move down the page as appropriate. There are two conditions where we need to stop printing on this page. We could run out of space or data for the particular page. These conditions are checked in the `Loop` statement:

```
Loop Until ypos >= ev.MarginBounds.Bottom OrElse _
    CurrentLine = UBound(Data) + 1
```

Once we fall out of the loop, we need to determine if there is more data to be printed. This is important, since we need to tell the print engine whether it should raise the `PrintPage` event again to render another page. This implies that we are responsible for keeping track of how far we are through our total data, using member variables or some other technique to monitor how much we have printed and whether there is any data left to go.

The final code in the routine does this check, setting the `HasMorePages` property as appropriate:

```
If CurrentLine < UBound(Data) + 1 Then
    ev.HasMorePages = True
Else
    ev.HasMorePages = False
End If
```

This simple routine illustrates the basis for printing to a printer or to a print preview window. However, we can provide more options to the user by displaying the print and page dialogs and utilizing the choices made by the user.

We should now be able to run our application and have the text print out on the printer. Alternatively, we could generate a print preview of the text by changing the code behind our button to:

```
Private Sub Button1_Click(ByVal sender As System.Object, _
   ByVal e As System.EventArgs) Handles Button1.Click

   ReDim Data(4)
   Data(0) = "This is line 1"
   Data(1) = "This is line 2"
   Data(2) = "This is line 3"
   Data(3) = "This is line 4"
   Data(4) = "This is line 5"

   Dim PPdlg As PrintPreviewDialog = New PrintPreviewDialog()

   PPdlg.Document = PrintDocument1
   PPdlg.ShowDialog()
End Sub
```

No change is required to the code that renders our page, just to the routine that invokes the print process.

Invoking the Print Dialog

The Print dialog allows the user to select the printer and set any properties of the printer that they require. This dialog is easily invoked through the use of the `PrintDialog` class. In our sample application we could alter the code behind our button:

```
Private Sub Button1_Click(ByVal sender As System.Object, _
   ByVal e As System.EventArgs) Handles Button1.Click

   ReDim Data(4)
   Data(0) = "This is line 1"
   Data(1) = "This is line 2"
   Data(2) = "This is line 3"
   Data(3) = "This is line 4"
   Data(4) = "This is line 5"

   Dim Pdlg As New PrintDialog()
   Pdlg.Document = PrintDocument1

   Dim result As DialogResult = Pdlg.ShowDialog()

   If result = DialogResult.OK Then
      PrintDocument1.Print()
   End If
End Sub
```

The first couple of lines in this routine create the `PrintDialog` object and associates it with the `PrintDocument` object we are using, `PrintDocument1`. These objects take care of working together by themselves, so we don't have to worry about those details.

Next, we call the `ShowDialog()` method, capturing the result in a `DialogResult` object. The result will indicate which button was clicked by the user to exit the dialog, and we only want to invoke the print process if the user clicked the **OK** button. Finally, if the user did click **OK**, we call the `Print()` method of the document.

The printer selected by the user will be automatically provided to the document by the dialog, so the printing will go to the selected location.

Invoking the Page Dialog

The other major print dialog users often expect to see is the page dialog, allowing them to specify details such as portrait and landscape, and other print settings. This dialog basically acts as an editor for a `PageSettings` object. We need to maintain this object within our application and supply it to the `PrintDocument` before calling the final `Print()` method.

In `Form1`, declare a module-level `PageSettings` object as:

```
Private Data() As String
Private CurrentLine As Integer
Private MyPageSettings As PageSettings
```

Then, we can use this object when we invoke the page setup dialog. In our button code, do the following:

```
Private Sub Button1_Click(ByVal sender As System.Object, _
  ByVal e As System.EventArgs) Handles Button1.Click

  ReDim Data(4)
  Data(0) = "This is line 1"
  Data(1) = "This is line 2"
  Data(2) = "This is line 3"
  Data(3) = "This is line 4"
  Data(4) = "This is line 5"

  Dim Pdlg As New PageSetupDialog()

  If MyPageSettings Is Nothing Then
    MyPageSettings = New PageSettings()
  End If

  Pdlg.PageSettings = MyPageSettings

  Pdlg.ShowDialog()

  PrintDocument1.DefaultPageSettings = MyPageSettings

  PrintDocument1.Print()
End Sub
```

This code creates a new `PageSetupDialog` object. We then check to see if we already have a `PageSettings` object – which would indicate that the user has already used this dialog once before. If there is such an object, we will use it so that the user sees their previous selections, otherwise we create a new object to use.

Either way, the `PageSettings` object is provided to the page setup dialog so it can store its data in our object, and the `ShowDialog()` method is called to display the dialog for the user.

When the dialog returns, we can apply the `PageSettings` object to our document, which will cause the document to be printed according to those settings. What this really controls is the layout of the graphics object we'll be provided when we go to paint each page – its margins, height, and width for instance.

Creating a Windows NT/2K Service with VB

When developing complex systems, it is often desirable to have some of our code always running on a server, even when no one is logged onto the server machine. In the Windows environment, this typically translates to the use of a Windows NT or Windows 2000 service. A **service** is a program that can be automatically started as the operating system boots up, having nothing to do with whether a user is logged into the machine or not.

Creating a Windows Service

Services typically also provide other administrative functionality, including the ability to start, stop, pause, and continue the service while it is running. In addition, services have no guarantee of an actual user interface, since they start as the system is booted, when no user may be logged into the system at all. As a result, they typically utilize the system's Application Log if they need to output any informational data or error messages.

Historically, VB has had no native support for the creation of a Windows service. Various 'hacks' have been created over the years, including programs that host another program as a service, an ActiveX control that makes a VB program into a service, and frameworks that load an ActiveX DLL as a service.

The Windows Service Project

With Visual Basic .NET however, we have full native support within VB for the creation of Windows services. Windows Service is a project type available to us within the IDE. Create a Window Service project and name it Chapter9WinSvc. This project type starts us out with a `Service1` code module containing a class. Use the property dialog for the service to change its name to TestService. Also change the ServiceName property to TestService in the Properties window.

Unfortunately this won't automatically change everything that needs to be changed. We must also manually edit the autogenerated code in the service by opening the Component Designer generated code region and making the following change in the `Main()` method:

```
<MTAThread()> _
Shared Sub Main()
  Dim ServicesToRun() As System.ServiceProcess.ServiceBase

  ' More than one NT Service may run within the same process. To add
  ' another service to this process, change the following line to
  ' create a second service object. For example,
  '
  '   ServicesToRun = New System.ServiceProcess.ServiceBase () _
```

```
'        {New TestService, New MySecondUserService}
'
    ServicesToRun = New System.ServiceProcess.ServiceBase() _
      {New TestService()}

    System.ServiceProcess.ServiceBase.Run(ServicesToRun)
  End Sub
```

Then, we need to use the project's **Properties** dialog to configure the **Startup object** to be Sub Main. Access the **Properties** dialog by right-clicking on the project in the **Solution Explorer** window and choosing the **Properties** menu option.

The service class is derived from the ServiceBase class:

```
  Public Class TestService
    Inherits System.ServiceProcess.ServiceBase
```

The base class also provides us with the general capabilities needed when creating a Windows service application, including overridable methods in which we can place our code to start and stop the service's process as appropriate:

```
    Protected Overrides Sub OnStart(ByVal args() As String)
      ' Add code here to start your service. This method should set things
      ' in motion so your service can do its work.
    End Sub

    Protected Overrides Sub OnStop()
      ' Add code here to perform any tear-down necessary to stop your service.
    End Sub
```

Similarly, we can implement OnPause() and OnContinue() methods, if appropriate, for our service. If you choose to implement these methods, you will want to set the CanPauseAndContinue property to True in the property dialog for the service object. This will enable the pause and continue operations in the service management console, and will route those requests to our methods appropriately.

Writing to the Application Log

At a minimum, we will probably want to log the fact that our service has started. We can do this by using the System.Diagnostics.EventLog class:

```
    Protected Overrides Sub OnStart(ByVal args() As String)
      ' Add code here to start your service. This method should set things
      ' in motion so your service can do its work.
      EventLog.WriteEntry("TestService", "Starting", _
        EventLogEntryType.Information)
    End Sub
```

This will write a message to the system's **Application Log**, which we can view using the **Event Viewer** tool available in Windows.

Creating Worker Threads

When creating a service, it is strongly recommended that all actual work be done on threads other than the main application thread. The main application thread should be free to accept start, stop, and pause requests from the user or operating system. We discussed threads and the multi-threaded capabilities of .NET earlier in this chapter.

It is also very important that our worker thread uses as few system resources as possible when it is not actively working, since a service is always running, from the time when the system boots up until the time it shuts down. If the service has busy wait loops or allocates huge amounts of memory, those resources will never be available to other applications on the machine. Instead, we need to use blocking waits and minimize the amount of memory or other resources we're consuming.

Services, by their very nature, are often designed to perform asynchronous tasks. Earlier in this chapter, we discussed asynchronous processing and how it relates to multi-threading. It is quite common for a service to start an asynchronous process in the `OnStart()` method, allowing each completed request to be processed on a separate thread automatically.

Another easy way to cause processing to occur on another thread is to use the `System.Timers.Timer` class. This timer fires its `Elapsed` event on a thread from the .NET thread pool rather than firing the event on our main thread like the normal Windows Forms timer. This means that our application's main thread remains idle and the `Elapsed` event will be running on a background thread with no extra work on our part.

Better still, we can make use of the Timer control under the Components tab in the Toolbox to work with this timer. Simply drag-and-drop this timer control onto the designer surface for `Service1` and we are ready to go.

> This is different from the **Timer** control under the **Windows Forms** tab in the toolbox.

Make sure to set the control's Interval property as appropriate (perhaps try 500), and set its Enabled property to False. As our service is loaded, we don't want the timer to fire. It shouldn't be enabled until the `OnStart` event occurs within the service.

Now we can change the `OnStart()` and `OnStop()` methods to start and stop the processing:

```
Protected Overrides Sub OnStart(ByVal args() As String)
  ' TODO: Add code here to start your service. This method should set
  ' things in motion so your service can do its work.
  EventLog.WriteEntry("TestService", "Starting", _
    EventLogEntryType.Information)
  Timer1.Enabled = True
End Sub

Protected Overrides Sub OnStop()
  ' TODO: Add code here to perform any tear-down
  ' necessary to stop your service.
  Timer1.Enabled = False
End Sub
```

The code to do any work will go in the `Elapsed` event handler for the timer control:

```
Private Sub Timer1_Elapsed(ByVal sender As System.Object, _
  ByVal e As System.Timers.ElapsedEventArgs) Handles Timer1.Elapsed

  EventLog.WriteEntry("TestService", _
    "Working on thread " & AppDomain.GetCurrentThreadId(), _
    EventLogEntryType.Information)

End Sub
```

In this case, we are simply writing an entry to the event log, but this routine could do any other work required by our application.

Installing the Service

Service applications can't be run from the Visual Studio .NET IDE or from the command line – they must be installed into the Windows environment so we can control them from the **Service Management Console**. To install the service, we can use the installation services described in Chapter 10, or we can use the `installutil.exe` command line utility.

Either way, however, we need to do some extra coding so the install process can properly install the service. In particular, we need to add a special class to our project that will interact with the installer during the install process. This class sets up the behaviors for our service, including what user account the service will run under, and its default startup mode (`Manual` or `Automatic`).

Add a new item to the project using the **Project | Add New Item...** menu option and select the **Installer Class** option.

This will add a new component named **Installer1** to the project. This component starts with some key code. First, it has the `<RunInstaller()>` attribute to indicate that this is an installer class. It also derives from `System.Configuration.Install.Installer` so it has the behaviors needed to act as an installer class.

The first thing we need to do is add an `Imports` statement to bring in the namespace that contains all the types we will be using to configure the installation:

```
Imports System.ServiceProcess
```

Next we need to declare a of couple variables:

```
Private mServiceInstaller As New ServiceInstaller()
Private mProcessInstaller As New ServiceProcessInstaller()
```

These two objects will contain the information needed to drive the installation process. They need to be initialized appropriately, so let's add a method to take care of that:

```
Private Sub InitInstaller()
  mProcessInstaller.Account = ServiceAccount.LocalSystem
```

```
        mServiceInstaller.StartType = ServiceStartMode.Manual
        mServiceInstaller.ServiceName = "Chapter9WinSvc"
        Installers.Add(mServiceInstaller)
        Installers.Add(mProcessInstaller)
    End Sub
```

Here, we are specifying that the service should run under the local system account. This account has no password and is used primarily to run services, but it may have security access greater than the typical user. We may choose to set this to `ServiceAccount.User`, in which case we would need to specify a username and password under which the service will run. This will still allow the server to start as the system boots up (when no user is logged in interactively), but also allows us to control the security privileges of the user account that will be running the service. If we do not set the `Username` and `Password` properties, we will be prompted for account information as the service is installed and can provide the information at that time.

Next, we are specifying that the service should have a `Manual` start type. If we specified `Automatic`, the service would automatically start every time the system was booted. Finally, we provide the service with a name for display in the management console.

Now we need to ensure that this method is called when appropriate events occur during the installation process. There are three events that can occur during installation or uninstallation where we need to initialize these settings:

❑ Begin installation

❑ Rolling back installation

❑ Uninstalling

The following code handles these events by calling our initialization routine:

```
    Private Sub Installer1_BeforeInstall(ByVal sender As Object, _
      ByVal e As System.Configuration.Install.InstallEventArgs) _
      Handles MyBase.BeforeInstall

      InitInstaller()

    End Sub

    Private Sub Installer1_BeforeRollback(ByVal sender As Object, _
      ByVal e As System.Configuration.Install.InstallEventArgs) _
      Handles MyBase.BeforeRollback

      InitInstaller()

    End Sub

    Private Sub Installer1_BeforeUninstall(ByVal sender As Object, _
      ByVal e As System.Configuration.Install.InstallEventArgs) _
      Handles MyBase.BeforeUninstall

      InitInstaller()

    End Sub
```

At this point, we can build the project and use the `installutil.exe` utility to install the service. This utility is run from a console window, when in the project's `bin` directory, as follows:

```
> installutil windowsservice.exe
```

To uninstall the service use the `/u` switch:

```
> installutil windowsservice.exe /u
```

> *Note that the uninstall won't actually complete while the Service Management Console is open. If the console is open, it must be closed and reopened to allow the uninstall to complete.*

At this point we can use the Service Management Console to start and stop the service:

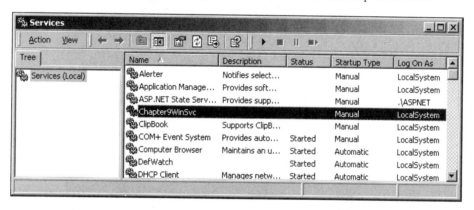

Upon starting and then stopping the service, we can go to the Event Viewer utility and view the Application Log:

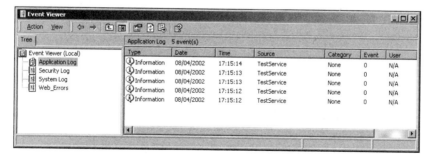

Each of the entries here was created by the service as it ran. They look something like this:

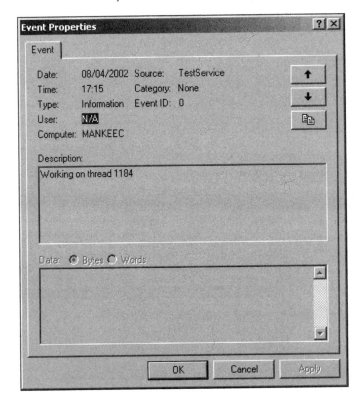

We can see the text written to the event log from our code, along with various other useful pieces of information.

The `ServiceBase` base class also automatically writes some entries on our behalf, noting when the service has started and stopped successfully. These entries are worded
The service has started successfully and The service has stopped successfully.

At this point we have a functioning service, ready for use.

Monitoring the File System

The Windows file system allows applications to be notified when a directory is changed. This capability can be easily illustrated by opening two explorer windows to display the same directory. Add or delete a file, and both windows automatically update to show the new status. Sometimes, it is nice to have this capability within our applications as well, perhaps when writing an application that acts on files as they are copied to our server via FTP.

The .NET Framework provides hooks that allow us to easily write an application that monitors the file system for changes. When a change occurs, we can react appropriately based on the requirements for our application. This capability can be combined with the ability to create a Windows service as discussed earlier, to create many interesting types of application.

This functionality is encapsulated within the FileSystemWatcher class, which is located in the System.IO namespace. We can create an instance through code or drag-and-drop the component from the Components tab of the Toolbox onto a form or component designer window.

The FileSystemWatcher allows us to easily watch a file, directory, or sub-directory for changes. It can also be used to watch network drives and remote directories.

There are some limitations when watching remote directories. Refer to the on-line help on the FileSystemWatcher class for further details.

We can watch for various events, including writes to the file or directory, file size changes, attribute changes, security changes, and file access.

Creating a Windows application to log when new files are added to or removed from a directory is quite straightforward. Create a new Windows Application project and add a ListBox control to the form, setting its Dock property to Fill. Also, add a FileSystemWatcher control from the Components tab of the toolbox. Set the Path property to the directory to be watched. In our example, we will use C:\.

Open the code window and add the following to the Form1 class:

```
Private Sub FileSystemWatcher1_Changed(ByVal sender As Object, _
    ByVal e As System.IO.FileSystemEventArgs) _
    Handles FileSystemWatcher1.Changed
  ListBox1.Items.Add("File: " & e.FullPath & " changed")
End Sub

Private Sub FileSystemWatcher1_Created(ByVal sender As Object, _
    ByVal e As System.IO.FileSystemEventArgs) _
    Handles FileSystemWatcher1.Created
  ListBox1.Items.Add("File: " & e.FullPath & " created")
End Sub

Private Sub FileSystemWatcher1_Deleted(ByVal sender As Object, _
    ByVal e As System.IO.FileSystemEventArgs) _
    Handles FileSystemWatcher1.Deleted
  ListBox1.Items.Add("File: " & e.FullPath & " deleted")
End Sub

Private Sub FileSystemWatcher1_Renamed(ByVal sender As Object, _
    ByVal e As System.IO.RenamedEventArgs) _
    Handles FileSystemWatcher1.Renamed
ListBox1.Items.Add("File: " & e.OldFullPath & " renamed to " & e.FullPath)
End Sub
```

These methods handle the `Created`, `Changed`, `Deleted`, and `Renamed` events generated by the `FileSystemWatcher` component, and log the resulting changes to the **ListBox1** control on the form. When we run this program, any changes to the directory or its files will be logged to our form.

The `Created`, `Deleted`, and `Renamed` events are pretty straightforward. The `Changed` event covers a lot of ground however, including changes to file size, attributes, security permissions, and last accessed and created dates. Using these events we can detect pretty much any change to a file or directory.

Command Line Options

VB has always been primarily a graphical development tool. While Visual Studio .NET continues to provide us with a powerful graphical IDE for development, there are times when we may want to do some operations from a console window, command line, or batch file.

Visual Basic .NET has a compiler that can be invoked from the command line, and the .NET Framework SDK provides us with a number of command line tools and utilities that we may find useful in some circumstances.

> In fact, using a text editor, the command line compiler for Visual Basic .NET, and the .NET utilities, it is technically possible to create any Visual Basic .NET application without using Visual Studio .NET.

Obviously this would require us to write all the code that is automatically generated by the IDE, and so this approach is rarely ideal, but the fact that it is possible illustrates the power at our disposal through the command line compiler and the various other tools.

vbc Command Line Parameters

The Visual Basic .NET compiler is named `vbc.exe` and can be invoked from within a console window. Try typing `vbc` with no parameters at the prompt and you will see help information on how to use the command.

Using the command line compiler is a bit trickier than allowing the Visual Studio .NET IDE to do the work for us. In particular, all the references we add to a project need to be explicitly added to the command line. For instance, even the simplest console application is compiled using the following command:

```
> vbc /t:exe /r:system.dll mysource.vb
```

We don't always need to explicitly reference `System.dll`. In fact, we wouldn't need to in this example. However, there are times when not referencing the `System.dll` will cause applications to fail, so it is best to always reference this DLL.

The `/t:exe` flag indicates that the target type for the application is a console application. An application that makes use of Windows Forms functionality would also reference that assembly, and might look like this:

```
> vbc /t:winexe /r:system.dll /r:system.windows.forms.dll mysource.vb
```

Basically, any references to assemblies that we would have added within the Visual Studio .NET IDE need to be added to the command line using /r flags.

The /t:winexe flag indicates that the application is a Windows application, but we also need to explicitly add the reference to the system.windows.forms.dll for the application to compile.

A key to success in deployment and management of .NET applications is the proper use of versioning. When doing command line compilation, we must handle versioning on the command line by using the /version switch:

```
> vbc /t:exe /r:system.dll /version:1.0.0.1 mysource.vb
```

The four parts of /version's value refer to major version, minor version, revision, and build.

Obviously, there are many other options available for our use, but these are the most commonly used when building applications by hand.

Compiling is only half the story though. For instance, Windows services must be installed on the machine and Web Services must be advertised for discovery by clients. These operations are provided either by the Visual Studio .NET IDE, or by using various other command line tools and utilities included in the .NET Framework SDK.

Description of Tools in the bin Directory

When the .NET Framework SDK is installed, it includes a set of important tools and utilities for our use. These are located in a couple places on the hard drive. The .NET Framework SDK, which is automatically installed as part of the Visual Studio .NET installation, uses one directory, and Visual Studio .NET itself puts files in a separate directory. The files can be found in directories similar to:

❑   C:\Program Files\Microsoft Visual Studio .NET\FrameworkSDK\Bin

❑   C:\WINNT\Microsoft.NET\Framework\v1.0.3705

The former is the location for the Visual Studio .NET files, the latter for the .NET Framework SDK installation.

The Visual Studio .NET installation adds a menu option we can use to open a command prompt fully initialized with these directories as part of the path. This is the simplest way to gain access to the command line utilities. This menu is located at Start | Programs | Microsoft Visual Studio .NET | Visual Studio .NET Tools | Visual Studio .NET Command Prompt.

The majority of these tools are run from the command line, though some are graphical Windows applications. The Visual Studio .NET IDE has most of the functionality provided by these tools built in, so most applications can be created without any need to use them.

Configuration and Deployment Tools and Utilities

The first group of tools is used to configure and deploy .NET applications of all sorts:

Tool	Description
Assembly Generation Utility `al.exe`	Accepts as input one or more files that are either MSIL format or resource files, and outputs a file with an assembly manifest.
Global Assembly Cache Utility `gacutil.exe`	Used to view and manipulate the contents of the global assembly cache. This utility can be used from build scripts, make files, and batch files.
Installer Utility `InstallUtil.exe`	This tool works in conjunction with the Installer Framework. It allows you to install and uninstall server resources with an assembly, by executing the installer components of that assembly.
Assembly Registration Tool `RegAsm.exe`	Enables classic COM clients to call managed classes. `RegAsm` reads the metadata within an assembly, then adds the necessary entries to the registry so classic COM clients can create the managed classes transparently.
Services Registration Tool `RegSvcs.exe`	Adds managed classes to Windows 2000 Component Services by performing several tasks within a single utility. These tasks include loading and registering the assembly, and generating, registering, and installing the type library into an existing COM+ 1.0 application.
Assembly Cache Viewer `shfusion.dll`	Windows shell extension for viewing and manipulating the contents of the global assembly cache using the Windows Explorer. This cache is in an `ASSEMBLY` directory under the system root directory – often something like `C:\WINNT\ASSEMBLY`.
Assembly Binding Log Viewer `fuslogvw.exe`	Helps diagnose why the .NET Framework cannot locate an assembly at run-time.
Native Image Generator Tool `Ngen.exe`	Creates a native image from a managed assembly and installs it into the native image cache on the local machine.
Isolated Storage Utility `storeadm.exe`	Used to manage isolated storage for the currently logged in user. Isolated storage is a mechanism within .NET that allows our applications to store user files without possibility of naming collisions with other users or viewing other user's files.

Tool	Description
Type Library Exporter `TlbExp.exe`	Using a managed assembly as input, generates a type library containing COM definitions of the public types defined in that assembly.
Type Library Importer `Tlbimp.exe`	Converts the type definitions found within a COM type library into equivalent definitions in managed metadata format.
Common Language Runtime XML Schema Definition Tool `xsd.exe`	Used for working with XML schemas that follow the XML Schema Definition (XSD) language proposed by the W3C.

Windows Forms Design Tools and Utilities

These tools are primarily used when building and designing Windows applications:

Tool	Description
Windows Forms ActiveX Control Importer `aximp.exe`	Using an ActiveX control's type library as input, generates a wrapper control that allows the ActiveX control to be hosted by a Windows Forms form.
Resource File Generator Utility `ResGen.exe`	Reads text files containing name-value pairs and produces a managed binary `.resources` file. The utility can also be used to decompile the binary `.resources` file.
Windows Forms Resource Editor `Winres.exe`	Allows you to quickly and easily localize Windows Forms forms.

Security Tools and Utilities

These utilities are used to configure and alter security settings, create security certificates, and to sign our code:

Tool	Description
.NET Framework Configuration Tool `mscorcfg.msc`	This is a plug-in for the Windows management console (MMC) that allows us to manage .NET Framework security policy and applications that use remoting services.
Code Access Security Policy Utility `caspol.exe`	Used to examine and modify machine and user code access security policies.
Certificate Manager Utility `certmgr.exe`	Used to manage certificates, certificate trust lists (CTLs), and certificate revocation lists (CRLs).

Table continued on following page

Tool	Description
Certificate Verification Utility `chktrust.exe`	Checks the validity of an Authenticode signed file.
Certificate Creation Utility `makecert.exe`	Creates, for test purposes only, X.509 certificates. These may be used as input to the `cert2spc.exe` utility.
Software Publisher Certificate Test Utility `cert2spc.exe`	Creates, for test purposes only, a Software Publisher's Certificate (SPC) from one or more X.509 certificates.
Permissions View Utility `permview.exe`	Used to view the permission sets requested by an assembly.
SecUtil Utility `SecUtil.exe`	Extracts Strong Name public key information or Authenticode publisher certificates from an assembly, in a format that can be incorporated directly into code.
Set Registry Utility `setreg.exe`	Changes registry settings related to test certificates.
File Signing Utility `signcode.exe`	Signs a PE file with requested permissions to give developers more detailed control over the security restrictions placed on their component.
Strong Name Utility `Sn.exe`	Creates and verifies assemblies with strong names.
PEVerify Tool `PEverify.exe`	Assists in validating the type safety of code prior to release. Also assists in generating IL, and in determining if IL code and associated metadata meets type-safety verification requirements.

General Tools and Utilities

The following are a set of assorted tools and utilities that are useful in various situations:

Tool	Description
Common Language Runtime Debugger `cordbg.exe`	A command line utility that can help tools vendors and application developers find and fix bugs in programs that target the CLR.
Microsoft CLR Debugger `DbgCLR.exe`	Provides debugging services with a graphical interface to help application developers find and fix bugs in programs that target the run-time.

Tool	Description
Common Language Runtime IL Assembler `ilasm.exe`	Using IL as input, generates a PE file containing the IL and the required metadata. The resulting executable can be run to determine whether the IL performs as expected.
Microsoft .NET Framework IL Disassembler `ildasm.exe`	Used to disassemble and inspect the IL code in a PE file.
Soapsuds `soapsuds.exe`	Converts CLR metadata to and from an XML schema. Fully represents the full CLR type system needed for CLR remoting.
Web Services Description Language Tool `Wsdl.exe`	Generates code for ASP.NET Web Services and Web Services clients from Web Services Description Language (WSDL) contract files, XML Schema Definition (XSD) schema files, and `.discomap` discovery documents.
Web Services Discovery Tool `Disco.exe`	Discovers the URLs of Web Services located on a web server, and saves documents related to those Web Services on a local disk.
Common Language Runtime Minidump Tool `Mscordmp.exe`	Creates a file containing information that is useful for analyzing system issues in the runtime.
Management Strongly Typed Class Generator `Mgmtclassgen.exe`	Allows you to quickly generate an early-bound class in C#, Visual Basic, or JScript for a specified Windows Management Instrumentation (WMI) class.
Windows Forms Class Viewer `wincv.exe`	Finds the managed classes matching a specified search pattern, and then uses the Reflection API to display information about those classes.

The tools and utilities provided with the .NET Framework SDK provide a powerful set of capabilities for our use. While particularly useful when developing applications outside of the Visual Studio .NET IDE, some of these tools may be useful when configuring, deploying, securing, and debugging any application.

Summary

Along with all the exciting advances in the VB language and the Visual Studio .NET IDE, we also gain a lot of powerful capabilities from the .NET Framework and the .NET system class libraries. As we have seen in this chapter, many things that were impossible or very difficult in the past have now become quite easy.

Obviously, this chapter merely scratches the surface of the capabilities available to VB developers within the .NET environment. The system class libraries contain many more features and capabilities that go far beyond what we could show here, and also provide capabilities in areas we haven't even discussed.

10

Installation and Deployment

One of the biggest challenges we have faced over the past many years in Visual Basic has been deployment of our applications. In the early days of VB we were faced with the nightmare of VBX and DLL conflicts as well as all the issues surrounding INI files. Later, when VB moved into the 32-bit world of Win32 and COM, we were faced with 'DLL Hell', as the continuing plague of DLL version conflicts, registry corruptions, and a host of related problems became pervasive.

At first glance, it appeared that web technologies would solve this problem, and they do in terms of client deployment. Unfortunately, due to the way IIS and COM components interact, deployment of a COM-based solution on a web server was not easy either. Not only might we run into DLL Hell issues on the web server, but IIS locks any COM components it uses – requiring that we restart the IIS process any time we want to update a DLL.

Even if we put our COM DLLs in an MTS Server Package or COM+ Server Application things weren't perfect. While we could stop the package to update a DLL, it still meant stopping all users from making use of our application during the update process.

The .NET Framework takes DLL Hell head on, making it much easier to deploy and update applications to our client workstations and to our web servers. Visual Basic .NET provides us with this entire range of deployment options, relying on the underlying .NET Framework to ensure our components don't conflict with other components during the installation or update process. We can use:

❑ XCOPY deployment – the user simply copies application files onto a target machine

❑ Formal installation programs – the user walks through a series of dialogs to configure the deployment process

❑ Auto-deployment – no user intervention is required

We will discuss all of these options in this chapter.

Build Configurations

Before we discuss installing applications, we should quickly discuss the difference between **Debug** and **Release** configurations within Visual Studio .NET.

By default, when we build our applications in Visual Studio .NET we are building them using the Debug Configuration. This means that our applications are compiled with extra information required for the debugger to operate properly.

If we intend to install our applications to client workstations or production web servers, we will typically want to build the application using the Release Configuration. This configuration doesn't include the information necessary to drive the debugger, which means that our application files are smaller and faster.

Many of the project's properties are set *per configuration*. This means that we can have different project properties for debug mode from those for release. It also means we need to be very careful to ensure that key properties are the same in both configurations. Most notably, if we are exposing our assembly for use by COM, we need to make sure to check the appropriate box in the release configuration as well as in the debug configuration.

In any project's properties dialog we can see a dropdown for configuration:

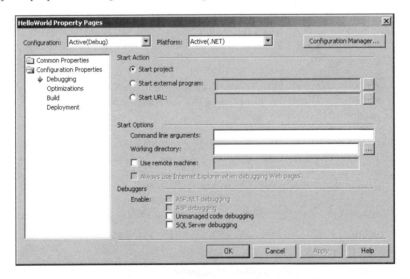

All of the properties under the Configuration Properties section in this dialog are *per configuration*. Notice the dropdown in the upper-left of the window, where we can select the configuration to edit.

We can also create custom configurations if needed. By default we start with Debug and Release defined, but if we also want a Test configuration we could create it.

To change between configurations, or to create new ones, we use the Configuration Manager dialog. This is available by choosing the Build | Configuration Manager... menu option in Visual Studio .NET:

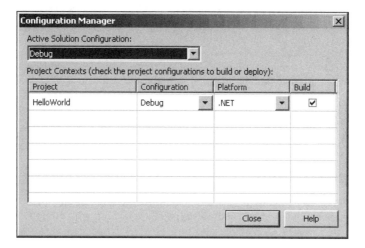

We will typically use this dialog to switch our active configuration from Debug to Release before building the application for final deployment.

The .NET Framework Redistributable

It is important to recognize that any machine that needs to run .NET applications must first have the .NET runtime installed. The **.NET Framework Redistributable** is not installed automatically on any shipping operating system, including Windows XP Personal or Windows XP Professional. All client workstations and servers must have the .NET Framework Redistributable installed before .NET applications will run on that machine.

The .NET runtime can be freely downloaded from the MSDN downloads web site at http://msdn.microsoft.com/. Look for the .NET runtime redistributable download.

The .NET runtime is also located on the Component Update CD provided with Visual Studio .NET. The file is:

```
cddrive:\dotNetFramework\dotnetfx.exe
```

The .NET runtime requires that MDAC 2.6 or higher be installed on the client machine as well.

The installation of the .NET runtime and MDAC 2.6 can be incorporated into our setup project, ensuring that the required components are automatically deployed to the client workstation before our application is installed. MSDN includes coverage of this process in an online article titled *Using Visual Studio .NET to Redistribute the .NET Framework*, which is available at http://msdn.microsoft.com/.

XCOPY Deployment

One of the primary design goals of .NET was to enable what is called **XCOPY deployment**. The idea is that an application can be deployed by simply copying a directory tree to the client machine and running the program, much like the venerable DOS XCOPY command.

.NET comes very close to this ideal, though there are some extra steps required to set up icons for a Windows application, or create and configure a virtual root for a web application.

XCOPY deployment is a very powerful option. For web applications XCOPY deployment is often the preferred installation approach. The ability to update a web site by simply copying the new files into a directory on the web server is very compelling.

Windows Applications

Windows applications are typically installed on client workstations so that the user can run the program. XCOPY deployment can be used to install this type of application with the following basic steps:

1. Install the .NET Framework Redistributable on the workstation

2. Copy the application's directory tree to the workstation

3. Set up icons for the user to invoke the application

Steps 1 and 3 are only required the first time the application is installed. Subsequent updates to the application typically only require copying the new files into the directory on the client workstation.

Take our Hello World application from Chapter 1 for instance. We can deploy this to a client workstation by first ensuring that the client workstation has the .NET Framework Redistributable installed. Next we can copy the files from the `bin` directory to the client workstation. In our case, this is just one file, `HelloWorld.exe`. This file can be copied to the client workstation directly, via a network drive, a floppy disk, a CD, a DVD, or via any other mechanism at our disposal.

In reality, most applications have a number of files, including the EXE, some DLLs and probably an XML configuration file. This is where the XCOPY concept comes into play. What we actually need to do is copy the entire directory tree containing all these files to the client workstation.

Once the application directory is on the client workstation's hard drive, all that remains is to set up an icon so that the user can invoke the application. This step is obviously optional, since we could require that the user navigate to the directory where the EXE resides using the Windows Explorer and then double-clicks the program. Typically this is not acceptable, however, so we need to create an icon.

To do this, we can right-click on the desktop and select the New | Shortcut menu option. This brings up a brief wizard that walks us through the process of creating the icon. It requires that we specify the path to the EXE file and then provide a user-friendly name for the shortcut to display. The result is an icon on the desktop that allows the user to invoke the application.

Subsequent updates to the application won't require that we install the .NET Framework Redistributable, nor will we need to recreate the icon – all we will need to do is copy the updated application directory to the client workstation.

Web Applications

Web applications can also be installed using XCOPY-style deployment. In fact, web applications are perhaps where this concept shines the most, since most web applications are deployed by IT professionals rather than end users, and so expecting them to be able to copy files, create virtual roots, and so on, is quite reasonable.

The basic steps for installing an ASP.NET web application by copying files are:

1. Install the .NET Framework Redistributable on the web server

2. Create the application directory

3. Set up a virtual root to point to the directory

4. Make the virtual root an application

5. Copy the files into the directory

After the initial installation, steps one through four are no longer required. Subsequent updates to the web site merely require copying the new application files into the directory on the web server.

As with any .NET application, before the application can be run on a machine, that machine must have the .NET Framework Redistributable installed. This redistributable requires MDAC 2.6 or higher, so that may need to be installed as well.

> *This is true for web servers running Windows 2000 and Windows XP. Microsoft has indicated that the Windows .NET Server products will come with the .NET Framework Redistributable pre-installed on the servers.*

Visual Studio .NET creates a virtual root and associated directory tree for our development purposes. It is this directory tree, in its entirety and keeping its structure, that needs to be copied. To do this we can use XCOPY from the command line with the /e switch:

```
> xcopy /e sourcedirectory targetdirectory
```

or we can just use the Windows Explorer to drag and drop the directory, since that too will preserve the directory structure.

On the target server, we can create the application directory by simply creating a directory on the hard drive of the server in a location where IIS has security rights to access the directory. One such location is the inetpub\wwwroot directory tree, though any directory tree with sufficient security rights for IIS will work.

To create the virtual root, we can use the Internet Services Manager tool, which is in the Control Panel under Administrative Tools.

Let's assume we've created a directory for our application named:

```
C:\MySites\TestApp
```

We can then use the Internet Services Manager to set up a virtual root pointing to that directory. Expand the tree on the left so it displays the Default Web Site entry, then right-click on that entry and choose New | Virtual Directory. This will bring up a wizard that walks us through the process of setting up the virtual directory and virtual root.

We need to specify an alias for the directory. This is the name of the virtual root, and so defines the name of the web site on the server. In other words, if we put foo here, our web site will be http://myserver/foo.

Enter TestApp as the alias and move to the next panel in the wizard. In this panel, we are prompted for the physical directory where the web site's files will reside. Here we need to enter C:\MySites\TestApp.

The next panel allows us to specify the permissions for the web site. This is different from the permissions on the *directory* itself, which are set using the Windows Explorer. These permissions are used by IIS to control how users can access the web site. The default permissions are fine to run an ASP.NET site, so just click Next.

At this point the wizard is complete and we have a virtual directory pointing at our physical directory on disk.

In this scenario, we are all set. However, there are cases where the virtual directory is not created as an *application* from the IIS perspective. For ASP.NET to operate properly, a virtual directory containing an ASP.NET application must be marked as an *Application* in IIS.

> **The virtual directory must be an *Application* for ASP.NET to operate properly.**

To make the virtual directory an application, right-click on its entry in the Internet Services Manager and select Properties. In the resulting properties dialog, click the Create button to make the virtual directory into an application:

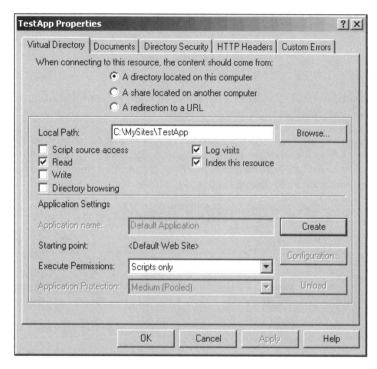

With this complete, all that remains is to copy the files from our development virtual directory location into the new directory on the target web server. Subsequent updates to the web site merely require copying the new files from the development directory into the web server's directory.

Formal Installers

For Windows applications, end users often expect a more polished installation process than having to manually copy files and set up icons in an XCOPY-style deployment. End users tend to prefer simple, graphical install and uninstall options for Windows applications, much like we have today with formal installer products such as InstallShield, Wise Installer, and the VB Package and Deployment Wizard.

Indeed, this is true for some web applications as well. Increasingly, business applications are being designed to run from a web server, and in more and more cases there is an end user installing the web application on the server. In such scenarios it is often preferable to use a more polished formal installer so the user can avoid having to manually create virtual roots and copy files to the right locations.

In today's world, a good installer interacts closely with the Windows Installer, helping to avoid file conflicts and to ensure that uninstalls of an application are complete and don't accidentally remove files shared with other applications.

The Visual Studio .NET tool provides us with powerful formal installation options, including:

❑ Self-installing CAB file

❑ Setup via an `msi` file (Windows System Installer)

❑ Deployment to a web server

Visual Studio .NET will also create a merge module, which is a pre-built installation component that can be used by another install option at a later time.

We also have a Setup Wizard to assist us in creating setup applications that will install our application when run on the target machine

The installation options available in Visual Basic .NET are displayed in the
Visual Studio Setup and Deployment Projects menu choice, which is available via the
File | New | Project... or File | Add Project | New Project... menu options. Upon selecting this project category, we are presented with a dialog similar to the following:

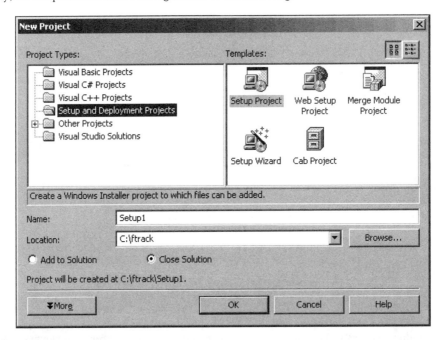

Typically, a setup project is added to an existing solution using the File | Add Project menu option, thus allowing the wizards to automatically run against the other project or projects in the solution.

Remember that any machine where we want to install .NET applications will need the .NET Framework Redistributable installed first. Obviously this doesn't apply to client machines that are accessing ASP.NET applications via a browser unless those applications download .NET components to the client workstation.

The Setup Wizard automatically adds a check at the beginning of the install to ensure that the client machine has the .NET runtime installed. If it does not, a warning dialog will be displayed and the installation will terminate.

We won't cover all the options in detail in this book, focusing instead on the high-level steps needed to create installations for a rich client a and web server.

The Setup Wizard option can be used to walk us through the process of selecting the appropriate setup project type and creating that project. If we already know which type of setup project we need, and are comfortable configuring that project manually we can simply add the appropriate type of project to our solution. In many cases, however, it is easier to allow the Setup Wizard to walk us through the process, as it does a lot of steps for us behind the scenes.

Windows Applications

The Setup Wizard provides the simplest way to create an installation package for our Windows applications. The wizard is typically run by adding it to a solution that contains the application we want to deploy.

To see how it works with a Windows Forms application, let's start by creating a simple application.

Creating a Test Application

Open Visual Studio .NET and create a new Windows Application named Chapter10Test and then add a new Class Library project to the same solution and name it Chapter10Objects. This will provide us with the foundation for testing the deployment of not only an EXE, but also an associated DLL.

Open the code window for Class1 and add the following code:

```
Public Class Class1

    Private mName As String

    Public Property Name() As String
      Get
        Return mName
      End Get
      Set(ByVal Value As String)
        mName = Value
      End Set
    End Property

End Class
```

Now, in the Chapter10Test project, add a reference to the Chapter10Objects project. Add a button to the form and double-click on it to open the code window and add the following code:

```
Private Sub Button1_Click(ByVal sender As System.Object, _
    ByVal e As System.EventArgs) Handles Button1.Click

    Dim obj As New Chapter10Objects.Class1()
```

```
    obj.Name = "Arron Molanski"
    MsgBox(obj.Name)

End Sub
```

This gives us a good test solution to deploy. We should run the application at this point to make sure that it is all set up and working properly before we try to install it.

Running the Setup Wizard

Add a new project to the existing solution. Choose Setup and Deployment Projects, then select the Setup Wizard option in the dialog and name it Chapter10WinSetup. When you click OK, the wizard will be launched and will walk us through the process of creating the appropriate deployment package for our application.

The first panel of the wizard is simple introduction and instructions. Step 2 is more interesting, as we have a number of options:

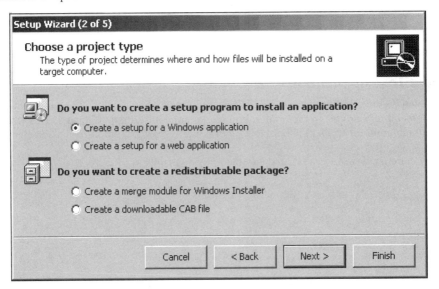

We can choose from the four options listed:

Create a setup for a Windows application	This will create a standard setup application that will install a Windows application on a client machine.
Create a setup for a web application	This will create a standard setup application that can be run on a web server to deploy a web application.
Create a merge module for Windows Installer	This will create a merge module, which can be used by other setup applications to deploy dependent components.
Create a downloadable CAB file	This will create a CAB file that can be downloaded via the web as part of an installation process.

In our case, we are deploying a Windows Application, so the first option is the one to choose.

The next panel allows us to control the files that are included in the installation. At a minimum, we will want to choose the primary output from the EXE project in our solution, though we may also choose some of the other options if they are appropriate.

Since Chapter10Test has a dependency on Chapter10Objects, we don't need to explicitly check the Chapter10Objects project. That DLL will automatically be added to the setup.

As we can see, we can not only include the EXE and DLL files, but we can also choose to include any resource files containing localized resources such as our text in various languages. We can also install debugger information, and even the source code for our project.

Select the Primary output from Chapter10Test option and click Next.

The next panel allows us to include any other arbitrary files we may want to include as part of the installation. These may include configuration files, images or anything else needed by our application. Remember that the Setup Wizard only includes the core application files by default – any extra files that the application requires must be added manually here in this window.

The fifth and final panel merely confirms our selections and allows us to Finish the wizard. The setup project has a graphical designer that is now displayed:

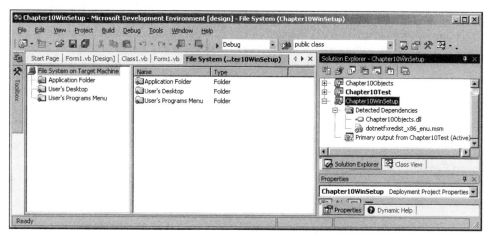

In fact, the setup project has a number of graphical designers, which can be activated by right-clicking on the project in the Solution Explorer and choosing the View menu. These include:

❑ File System

❑ Registry

❑ File Types

❑ User Interface

❑ Custom Actions

❑ Launch Conditions

These various designers allow us to control the setup and installation process to a reasonably fine degree.

Project Properties

We will typically want to set a few properties in the setup project to make the display more professional during the installation process.

Specifically we will want to change both the ProductName and Manufacturer properties of the setup project to be more friendly. Change ProductName to Chapter 10 Test and Manufacturer to Wrox Press by using the Properties window. This will make the setup process more human-readable and friendly for the end user, since these values are displayed as part of the setup process.

More importantly, they are used to specify the default path for the installation of the files on the client workstation, as we will see later when we run the setup program.

We may also want to change other properties such as the Title, Author, and Description values.

Adding an Icon to the Desktop

Additionally, we can use the main designer, shown in the previous screenshot, to add and remove files from the installation process. For instance, we may want to include an icon on the desktop to launch our application.

To do this, click on the Application Folder in the left-hand pane. The right-hand pane should now display our project and the Chapter10Objects.dll file. Right-click on the Primary output from Chapter10Test (Active) entry in the right-hand pane and select the first option – to create a shortcut. Rename the shortcut to Chapter10Test, then drag-and-drop it onto the User's Desktop entry in the left-hand pane. The User's Desktop folder now has a shortcut. We can use the same technique to add other shortcuts, or add shortcuts to the user's Programs menu as well.

Building the Setup Project

By default a setup project will not be built when we build the solution. There are two ways to deal with this.

First, we can directly build the setup project. This is done by right-clicking on the setup project in the Solution Explorer and choosing Build from the menu.

Alternatively, we can update the solution's build configuration. This is done by selecting the Build | Configuration Manager... menu option to bring up the Configuration Manager dialog:

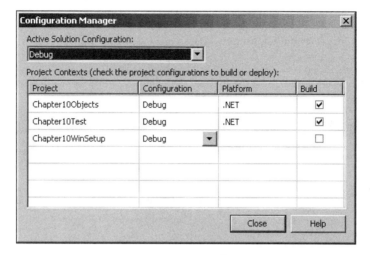

This dialog allows us to specify whether each project in our solution should be built when we build the solution. In the screenshot above, we are looking at the Debug configuration, and we can see that the Chapter10WinSetup project is not checked to be built. If we check this box, then any time we build the solution the setup project will automatically be built as well.

Typically, we will want to manually build the setup project, as it can take some time to do this build, and we probably only want to rebuild the setup project when we are about to release our project for installation.

Either way, once we have built the project, we will have a group of typical setup files in the directory of the setup project under the current configuration name – Debug or Release. We can then place these files on a network share or a CD for installation. The files are:

InstMsiW.Exe	The installer for Windows Installer to make sure the client has the right version (Windows NT)
InstMsiA.Exe	The installer for Windows Installer to make sure the client has the right version (Windows 95/98)
Setup.Exe	The setup program that the user will run to launch the install process
Setup.Ini	The initialization file that controls the setup process
Chapter10WinSetup.msi	The Windows Installer package that will install our application

Running the Setup Program

After we have built the setup project, we can run the Setup.Exe program on a client machine to install the application. The setup program does some initial checks to ensure that the .NET runtime and the required version of the Windows System Installer are already on the machine, and then launches into the actual setup process for our application.

The first panel we will see is an introduction to the process. Then, we are prompted for the directory into which the application should be installed on the client machine. The default location is determined by the ProductName and Manufacturer properties we set for the setup project:

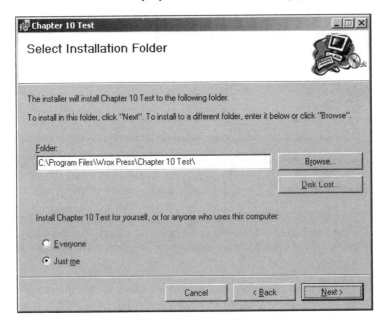

This panel also allows us to specify whether we are installing the application for a single user or system wide, and has a button labeled Disk Cost, which we can click to see how much disk space is required and how much is available per disk on our workstation.

The final panel of the wizard simply confirms that we want to proceed with the installation. When the installation is complete, we are presented with a dialog indicating the conclusion of the process. The application's icon will be available to our users to run the application and it will also appear in the Add/Remove Programs dialog in the Control Panel.

If you click the link for support information, you will be presented with a dialog of information based on the properties we set for the setup project:

The display and links shown in this dialog come from the Manufacturer, Author, SupportURL, and Description properties in the setup project.

Web Applications

The setup wizard can also be used to create formal setup programs for web applications. Most web applications are installed manually using techniques similar to those we discussed earlier in the section on XCOPY deployment. However, there may be times when an end user will need to install a web application and we will need to provide a friendlier installation experience.

Creating a Test Application

To see how the setup wizard works with web applications, let's create a simple ASP.NET application for test purposes. Create a new ASP.NET Web Application project in Visual Studio .NET and name it Chapter10Web.

Use the Add Reference... dialog to add a reference to the Chapter10Objects assembly we created earlier in the chapter. As with our Windows example, this will help demonstrate how the setup process handles dependencies on other assemblies.

Add a Button and Label to the Web Form, then double-click on the button to bring up the code window and add the following:

```
Private Sub Button1_Click(ByVal sender As System.Object, _
  ByVal e As System.EventArgs) Handles Button1.Click

  Dim obj As New Chapter10Objects.Class1()

  obj.Name = "Arron Molanski"
  Label1.Text = obj.Name

End Sub
```

411

Now build and test the application to make sure it works before we move on to create a setup program so that it can be installed on other web servers.

Running the Setup Wizard

As with our Windows application earlier, the easiest way to create a setup program for a web application is to add a **Setup and Deployment Project** to the current solution. Add a new **Setup and Deployment Project** of type **Setup Wizard**, just as we did before, and name it Chapter10WebSetup. Again this will launch the **Setup Wizard**. On the second panel, we need to specify that we want to create a setup for a web application.

Next, we need to indicate which files are to be included in the setup process. Since this is a web application, we will not only want the primary output files, but also the content files so that any images or other data files supporting our web site are also included:

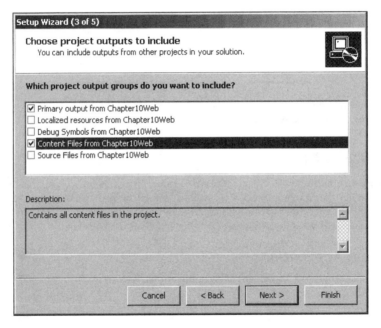

Again we are given the option to include any additional files. The web.config and any other required files are automatically included by the setup wizard, so we typically don't need to add anything here.

When the wizard is done we are presented with a setup project similar to that for our Windows application earlier. As before, the wizard detected the dependency on Chapter10Objects.dll and automatically included it.

Project Properties

As with the Windows setup, we will typically want to set several properties in the setup project to make the display more professional during the installation process.

Again we will want to change both the ProductName and Manufacturer properties of the setup project to be more friendly. Change ProductName to Chapter 10 Web Test and Manufacturer to Wrox Press by using the Properties window. Again, we may also want to change other properties such as the Title, Author, and Description values.

For a web application setup, we also need to specify the default name for the virtual root on the web server. To do this, open the File System Editor for the setup project by selecting the setup project in the Solution Explorer and clicking the File System Editor button in the Solution Explorer's toolbar.

In the left-hand pane of the display, select Web Application Folder, which will cause the properties dialog to display the properties for this folder. One of the properties is VirtualDirectory, which we should change to Chapter10Web.

Building the Setup Project

Use the Configuration Manager dialog to mark the setup project for building, and then rebuild the solution. The result will be the same set of files as for the Windows setup program contained in the setup project's directory under the name of the current configuration – Debug or Release.

Running the Setup Program

We can now take the setup files and distribute them to a web server using a CD, DVD, network drive, or any other means we feel appropriate. On the web server where the application is to be deployed we can then run `Setup.Exe`.

The setup program first checks to ensure the required version of the Windows System Installer and the .NET runtime are installed, and then launches into the setup of our web application. As with the Windows setup program, we get an introductory dialog first, but then the next panel of the wizard is quite different from the Windows setup counterpart. Rather than asking for an installation directory, we are prompted for the virtual root and port on which the web site should run:

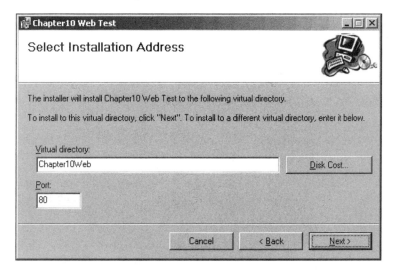

The dialog also includes the Disk Cost button, which we can use to see the required and available disk space on the system. The final dialog is simply a confirmation that we want to proceed with the installation. The installation will then run and we will be presented with a completion dialog just as we were with the Windows installation earlier.

The result is that our web application is installed into a directory the name of which is the same as the virtual root name under the `inetpub\wwwroot` directory on the server. At this point, users can use their browsers to interact with the web site.

As for the Windows installation, the web application is also visible in the Add/Remove Programs dialog in the Control Panel. This allows for easy uninstallation of the application by the end user. Again, the support information link will display information about the application based on the properties specified in the setup project. The Manufacturer, Author, SupportURL, and Description properties, if they have been set, are displayed.

Automatic Deployment

For enterprise applications, manual installation, whether via XCOPY or a formal installer, is typically unacceptable. If we need to update dozens of web servers in a web farm, or hundreds or thousands of desktops with a Windows application, we need some type of 'zero-touch' installation mechanism that will automatically deploy the client code to the target machine in the first place, and update components over time as needed – with no intervention from the user at all. Components are initially downloaded on demand from a central server, and are automatically updated on the client if a new version is placed on the central server.

One of the big advantages to building browser-based applications is that they have a zero incremental deployment cost. Once the browser is installed on the client machine, deployment of applications to the browser costs essentially nothing.

By using auto-deployment of .NET applications we can achieve this same zero increment cost deployment for Windows applications. This is certainly a huge step forward as compared to the overwhelming complexity and cost of deploying and updating a VB6 application and its associated DLLs.

There are security considerations involved here. Automatically downloaded assemblies run in a sandbox with restrictive default security. This is nice, because it means the downloaded code can't do anything dangerous, but it can be overly restrictive for normal business applications (which may need to interact with files on the local hard drive or establish network connections to other servers within our network). We will discuss how to configure security for our assemblies later in the chapter.

Automatic deployment does require a small bit of code to be installed on the client using conventional means. Typically this code is contained in a small EXE that the user launches, and the remainder of the application's components are then automatically downloaded from the central server on demand.

This 'bootstrap' EXE can take two general forms:

❑ If we are creating a large and complex application that has many types of functionality, then it may make a lot of sense to create a shell program that encapsulates the menuing for that application, but uses auto-deployment to download the DLLs that contain each bit of functionality. This type of large application is often created using an MDI interface to help keep the interface comprehensible to the end user, though MDI is certainly not required to use auto-deployment.

❑ As a more general solution, we can create one simple EXE that can be used to launch any other .NET EXE via a URL, causing the program's EXE and any required DLLs to be automatically downloaded to the client on demand. This general solution is often preferable because it allows us to create the business application just as we normally would – with virtually no consideration for the fact that it is running via a URL instead of directly from a hard drive.

We will discuss both of these options, starting with the more powerful and general solution that allows us to run any .NET Windows program via a URL.

Launching a .NET Program from a URL

We are used to running applications from a hard drive – we simply click on an icon and away we go. However, before that can happen we need to get the application to the hard drive. We've seen how to do this manually using the XCOPY approach, and how to do this with a setup program, which also requires manual intervention.

In this section, we will see how to create one simple program that, once manually deployed, allows us to run any other .NET program from a URL. That program's EXE and any required DLLs will be automatically downloaded to a cache on our machine and they will run from there.

Though this NetRun application has some complex code, none of the .NET programs we run via URL need to have any special code in them at all – they are just normal .NET programs.

However, there are two caveats to this scenario:

❑ **Security** – We will discuss security and how to configure it later in the chapter, but it is important to recognize that any .NET code that runs from a URL is running in a sandbox and thus will have, by default, limited capabilities.

❑ **Application configuration files** – The .NET Framework includes the System.Configuration namespace that automatically reads our application's configuration file and makes its values available to our code. When using the NetRun application, the configuration file that is loaded is the one for NetRun itself, not for our auto-deployed application. This means that application configuration files can't be used normally in applications that are auto-deployed using NetRun.

When we are done, the `NetRun` application will allow us to run any application using a command line or Windows shortcut similar to:

```
> NetRun http://myserver/myroot/myprogram.exe
```

The program and any DLLs it requires will automatically download and run on our client workstation. This truly provides the same zero-incremental cost deployment as we get for web applications, but with the rich user experience provided by a Windows application.

Creating the NetRun Application

Start off by creating a new Windows Application project and name it **NetRun**. Delete **Form1** from the project. This application won't have any graphical component, relying on the program we are launching to provide any UI.

Next, add a **Module** (using **File | Add New Item...**) to the project and name it **Main**. At the top, add an `Imports` statement:

```
Imports System.Reflection
```

In the module, add the `HandleAssemblyResolve()` method. This method will be used to resolve any assemblies that can't be found automatically, such as during the deserialization process:

```
Module Main

  Function HandleAssemblyResolve(ByVal sender As Object, _
    ByVal args As ResolveEventArgs) As [Assembly]

    Dim a() As [Assembly] = AppDomain.CurrentDomain.GetAssemblies()

    Dim asm As [Assembly]
    For Each asm In a
      If asm.FullName = args.Name Then
        Return asm
      End If
    Next
  End Function

End Module
```

Finally, add a `Main()` method to the module:

```
Public Sub Main()
  Dim Domain As AppDomain = AppDomain.CurrentDomain
  AddHandler Domain.AssemblyResolve, AddressOf HandleAssemblyResolve

  Try
    Dim a As [Assembly] = _
      [Assembly].LoadFrom(Microsoft.VisualBasic.Command)
    a.EntryPoint.Invoke(a.EntryPoint, Nothing)
```

```
      Catch
        MsgBox("Could not load remote application" & vbCrLf & _
          Err.GetException.ToString)
      End Try
    End Sub
```

The first couple of lines here are familiar, as they set up the event handler for the `AssemblyResolve` event of our current `AppDomain`. This is the same code we put in the form's `Load` event earlier.

We then load the remote assembly using the `LoadFrom()` method. In this case we're loading the assembly passed to us as a command line parameter:

```
    Dim a As [Assembly] = _
      [Assembly].LoadFrom(Microsoft.VisualBasic.Command)
```

The next line of code is new. Rather than creating an object based on a class in the assembly, we are finding the **entry point** of the assembly and we're invoking it. All applications have an entry point, which is the method that the runtime invokes to start the program. What we're doing here is simply invoking that same method, causing the application to be started:

```
    a.EntryPoint.Invoke(a.EntryPoint, Nothing)
```

Finally, use the project's **Properties** dialog to change the **Startup object** to **Sub Main**, and then build the application. At this point, any machine that has the .NET runtime and `NetRun.exe` installed can run other .NET programs from a URL.

Deploying an Application

To test `NetRun`, we need to have an application available to be run from a URL. The first step is to create a virtual root where we can place the EXE and any DLLs required by our application. This virtual root can be a simple directory under `inetpub\wwwroot` – name it `Chapter10UI`.

Copy the `Chapter10Test.exe` and `Chapter10Objects.dll` files from earlier in the chapter into the `Chapter10UI` directory. That's all we need to do in terms of deploying the application. It is now available for use by any client workstation that has `NetRun`.

At the command prompt we can type:

```
  > NetRun http://localhost/Chapter10UI/Chapter10Test.exe
```

This will cause `Chapter10Test.exe` to be downloaded into our local cache, from where it will be run. When we click on the button our code uses an object from `Chapter10Objects.dll`. When the button is clicked, the .NET runtime will notice this requirement and will automatically and transparently download `Chapter10Objects.dll` into our client-side cache from where it can be used.

Any subsequent updates to the program or DLL will be automatically and transparently downloaded to the client – providing us with zero incremental cost to deploy .NET Windows applications.

Adding NetRun to the Path

To make the use of `NetRun` as transparent as possible, it is beneficial to add it to our system's path variable. The steps to do this vary by operating system.

On Windows 2000 and Windows XP the path variable is set using the properties dialog for My Computer off the desktop. Under the Advanced tab is a button for Environment Variables. This button brings up another dialog, which contains an entry for the path system variable, along with the ability to edit it. Double-click on this entry and you will get an editor dialog:

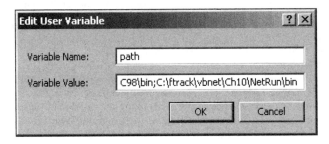

Just add a semicolon and the directory containing `NetRun.exe` to the end of the path. From this point forward, `NetRun` can be typed at any command prompt or in any Windows shortcut to launch applications via URL.

Creating a Windows Shortcut

To illustrate just how powerful `NetRun` can be, let's use it to create an icon on the desktop that the user can use to launch our test application via a URL.

Right-click on the desktop and choose New | Shortcut from the menu. This wizard allows us to create an icon that runs an application. The first panel asks us to indicate the path of the application. The path here will be the command line that uses `NetRun` to launch the application, so it may be similar to:

```
> NetRun http://localhost/Chapter10UI/Chapter10Test.exe
```

Since `NetRun` is in our system path variable, we don't need to worry about its location, so we can just use it like a simple command, passing it the URL of the application to be launched.

In the second panel we need to specify the name to go on the shortcut – probably something like Chapter 10 Test.

At this point the user has a simple icon on their desktop. When it is double-clicked, the application will be launched via URL – but transparently. To the user it will seem as though the application were run directly from the hard drive, not auto-downloaded and automatically updated from a central server location.

Using a Shell Program

Another approach to using auto-deployment is to create a more sophisticated shell program that is actually part of our overall application. This can be useful in the case that our application is large with many options. We may want to provide the user with a cohesive view of our overall application, possibly presenting them with an MDI interface or an interface similar that used by Microsoft Outlook.

By using configuration files or an XML Web Service, a shell application can dynamically generate its menu system, allowing us to add new functions, screens and capabilities to the application over time, without ever having to manually deploy any of these new capabilities to the client workstations.

This approach is more limited than the NetRun application we created earlier, but may offer a more controlled mechanism by which parts of a large application can be invoked. We are presenting it here to illustrate the different ways auto-deployment can be implemented in Visual Basic .NET.

Creating the Shell Application

There are many ways to create a shell application with a menu structure. One of the most obvious is to make the shell application consist of an MDI parent form with a menu that allows the user to launch child windows that are auto-downloaded from the central server. In this way, the shell application will merely provide the MDI container form and a launching mechanism and all the real work in the application will be done in the downloaded assemblies.

While it is possible to make the menu such that it is driven by metadata and thus fully configurable without updating the shell application, in this example we will keep the focus on the auto-deployment features and just hardcode the menu structure.

Start by creating a new Windows Application project and name it Chapter10Shell, and then change the form's IsMdiContainer property value to True, and drag a MainMenu control onto the form from the Toolbox.

Next, using the menu editor, create a top-level Run menu, with a menu item named Test:

Set the menu item's Name property to mnuRunTest.

The Automatic Download Method

Open the form's code window and add the following Imports statement at the top:

```
Imports System.Reflection
```

The System.Reflection namespace includes a great deal of functionality that allows us to write code that interacts directly with assemblies, classes, and other types. In our case, we will use it to dynamically load an assembly (DLL) from a URL and then to create an instance of a class from within that assembly.

Then add the following method to the form:

```
Private Sub LaunchWindow(ByVal AssemblyURL As String, _
  ByVal TypeName As String)

  Try
    Dim a As [Assembly] = [Assembly].LoadFrom(AssemblyURL)
    Dim w As Form = a.CreateInstance(TypeName)
    w.MdiParent = Me
    w.Show()

  Catch
    MsgBox("The functionality for this menu option could not be loaded", _
      MsgBoxStyle.Exclamation)

  End Try

End Sub
```

This method accepts a parameter to indicate the URL where the assembly (DLL) can be found, and the type name of the class we want to load. This type name will be the name of a form's class in that DLL. The method uses the LoadFrom() method of the Assembly class to load an assembly from a URL:

```
Dim a As [Assembly] = [Assembly].LoadFrom(AssemblyURL)
```

This line of code causes the DLL to be downloaded from the server into a client-side cache. To see which assemblies have been dynamically downloaded, we can use the following command line utility:

```
> gacutil /ldl
```

Now that we have an assembly object, representing the downloaded assembly, we can use it in the method to create an instance, or object, of any type contained within the assembly:

```
Dim w As Form = a.CreateInstance(TypeName)
```

Though the `CreateInstance()` method returns an `Object`, we are placing the return value directly into a variable of type `Form`. This ensures that only forms can be loaded by this code, as any other type of class would cause an error.

Now that we have a `Form` object, we can set its `MdiParent` property and show it, causing it to be displayed as a child of our MDI parent form.

Making Serialization Work

While the code we've just created will work in most cases, it turns out that it will fail to operate properly if our code uses .NET serialization. In other words, if we are serializing objects marked with the `<Serializable()>` attribute, the code will cause an error when deserialization is attempted.

The error that is raised comes from the fact that dynamically loaded assemblies are stored in a different list in memory from assemblies that are loaded directly from a design-time reference. The deserialization process only looks in the list of referenced assemblies, not in the list of dynamically loaded assemblies.

We can overcome this by adding just a bit more code. It turns out that an event is raised any time an assembly can't be found, and we can handle this event and supply a reference to the assembly.

Add the following method to the form. It will act as our event handler:

```
Private Function HandleAssemblyResolve(ByVal sender As Object, _
  ByVal args As ResolveEventArgs) As [Assembly]

  Dim a() As [Assembly] = AppDomain.CurrentDomain.GetAssemblies()

  Dim asm As [Assembly]

  For Each asm In a
    If asm.FullName = args.Name Then
      Return asm
    End If
  Next
End Function
```

It turns out that the dynamically loaded assembly *is* listed in our `AppDomain` as a valid assembly, so all we need to do is run through the `AppDomain`'s list of valid assemblies, find the one that we need and return a reference to it.

With that done, all that remains is to set it up so that this method handles the event. We will use the `AddHandler()` method to achieve this. Add the following to the form's `Load` event:

```
Private Sub Form1_Load(ByVal sender As System.Object, _
  ByVal e As System.EventArgs) Handles MyBase.Load

  Dim Domain As AppDomain = AppDomain.CurrentDomain
  AddHandler Domain.AssemblyResolve, AddressOf HandleAssemblyResolve

End Sub
```

421

This code simply gets a reference to the current AppDomain in which we are running, and then sets up our method to handle the AssemblyResolve event. This event will fire if an assembly can't be found automatically – such as when the deserialization process fails to find the assembly.

At this point, we have all the code we need to dynamically load a DLL and create and display any form contained in that DLL.

The Menu Code

Now we can make our Test menu come alive by adding the following code to the form:

```
Private Sub mnuRunTest_Click(ByVal sender As System.Object, _
  ByVal e As System.EventArgs) Handles mnuRunTest.Click

  LaunchWindow("http://localhost/Chapter10UI/Chapter10Child.dll", _
    "Chapter10Child.Test")

End Sub
```

Notice the call to LaunchWindow(). We are passing in a URL to a DLL (which we will create shortly), and the full class name of a form within that DLL. This will cause the Test form to be loaded and displayed as a child form in our application.

If we wanted to make this shell application totally dynamic, we'd probably make the menu list be driven by metadata from an XML file, a Web Service, or a database table. Each menu item merely needs to have the URL and class name in order to load a form into the application.

Creating a Child Form

Now we can create the DLL that does our application's work. Add a new Class Library project to the existing solution and name it Chapter10Child.

Remove Class1 from the project and add a new Windows Form named Test. Add a Button to the form and double-click to add the following code:

```
Private Sub Button1_Click(ByVal sender As System.Object, _
  ByVal e As System.EventArgs) Handles Button1.Click

  MsgBox("Hello from the child form")

End Sub
```

Now build the solution to create both the EXE and DLL.

Deploying the DLL to the Server

We need to put the DLL in a web-accessible location. We will use the Chapter10UI directory we created earlier in the chapter. Simply copy the Chapter10Child.dll file into this directory. It is now deployed and accessible to the shell application.

Run the shell application and click on the **Test** menu option. There may be a brief pause while the DLL is downloaded from the web server into the local cache, then the child window should be displayed. Any subsequent updates to the child DLL will be automatically updated on the client.

In this implementation the menu is hard-coded, but it could easily be generated from an XML file or data from an XML Web Service, allowing us to build a cohesive menuing structure for a large application, where adding new functionality is simply a matter of adding a new DLL to the virtual directory and updating some metadata so that the shell application makes it available to our users.

Security Considerations

Microsoft .NET provides a security mechanism based on where code 'came from'. By default, code comes from one of the Internet Explorer security zones, and code in each zone is granted only certain capabilities. The defaults are:

Security Zone	Code privileges
My_Computer_Zone	Code has full trust and can do anything.
LocalIntranet_Zone	This includes http://localhost, any file-base servers, and web servers in the IE Intranet zone.
	Code from this zone has access to the USERNAME environment variable, can bring up file dialogs, use isolated storage, has limited use of reflection, can display a user interface, has DNS access, can print to the printer, and has limited access to the event log.
Internet_Zone	This includes any web servers not in other zones.
	Code from this zone can bring up file dialogs, use isolated storage, can display a user interface, and can do simple printing.
	Note that in .NET SP1 this behavior changes to preclude any applications or DLL from running out of the Internet_Zone by default. If SP1 is installed on the client, we will have to update security for our specific URL to allow our code to run at all.
Restricted_Zone	Code from this zone is not allowed to execute at all.
Trusted_Zone	This zone has the same trust as the Internet_Zone.

Any code that is automatically deployed is coming from a server and is being run from a client-side cache. The .NET runtime is aware that the code originally came from a remote server, and so the code is run in a security context appropriate to that server. Therefore, in both of our earlier examples, we were running code from http://localhost, which is in the LocalIntranet_Zone and so provides a limited environment.

If we create an application that requires more security clearance than is available by the default, we will want to change the security settings for that application. We can change security at several levels, and the changes can apply at user, machine, or enterprise scope. We can open security for a specific virtual root, a specific file or a specific publisher rather than opening security for an entire zone.

When we broaden security, we should be careful to do it in such a way that only the code we intend gets the broader security clearance.

> **The default security for each zone should not be changed. Changing security for a zone may allow malicious code to gain access to our client machine in unforeseen and unpleasant ways.**

Security can be managed via a command line utility (which was listed in Chapter 9) or through a graphical interface. In this chapter, we will use the graphical interface to increase the security for our Chapter10UI virtual root.

The .NET Framework Configuration tool is a Microsoft Management Console (MMC) plug-in. It can be launched from an icon under the **Administrative Tools** folder on the machine. The following image shows the tool with the security tree expanded in the left-hand pane:

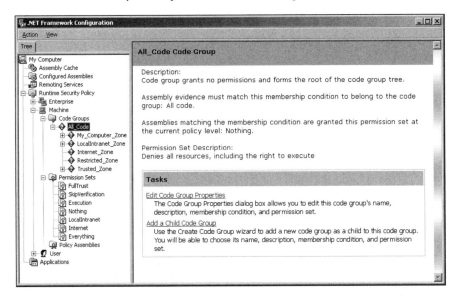

Here we can see the security zones for this machine – we can examine their default settings and alter them if desired. More importantly, we can add new entries under the zones to provide custom security as needed.

Right-click on LocalIntranet_Zone and choose New.... This will bring up a dialog that allows us to create a new security code group under the LocalIntranet zone. Enter a name and description for the group as shown:

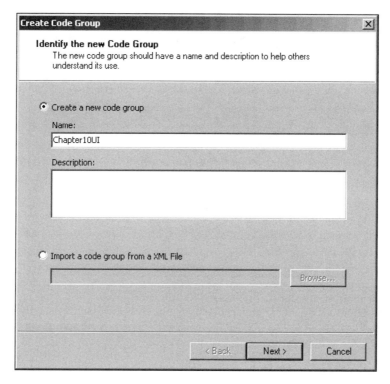

The next panel of the wizard allows us to specify the code to which this group will apply. There are many options here, allowing us to be very specific or very broad in our definition of what code should get the new security rating. In our case, we will select the URL option so we can specify security for any code coming from our virtual root:

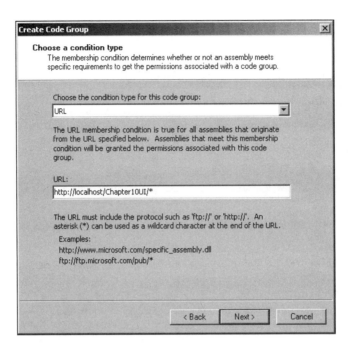

Finally, we are asked what security is to be used for this code group. We can use one of the existing default permission groups, or we might create our own that has the specific security needed by the application. In this case, we are running code we know to be safe so we will give it Full Trust.

At this point our machine is configured so that any code coming from our specific virtual root will be trusted as though it came directly from our C:\ drive.

Where possible, it is always best to just use the default security, but where that is not possible, this configuration tool can be used to provide extra permissions to applications as needed.

Summary

For many years, we have struggled with deployment and installation issues in Visual Basic. In the early days, there were DLL and INI file issues, followed in Win32 and COM by 'DLL hell' and the Windows Registry.

The .NET platform addresses these issues head-on, eliminating the need for the Windows Registry, providing a strong versioning scheme for our assemblies and making each assembly self-describing through metadata. Because of this, Visual Basic .NET applications can be deployed by simply copying an application's directory to the client machine and running the program – otherwise known as XCOPY deployment.

Typically, we will want a smoother, more polished deployment experience. The
Setup and Deployment Projects available in Visual Studio .NET help address this by allowing us to create standard Windows setup programs for both Windows and web applications. With a bit of extra work these can even install the .NET runtime on the client machine automatically.

Better still, we can use auto-deployment to automatically download our application's components from a central server to the client workstations. This provides a no-touch deployment mechanism so that Windows applications can be deployed to clients at zero incremental cost, just as web applications are in a browser.

11

Interoperability and Migration

By this point in the book, it has become apparent that .NET and Visual Basic .NET are quite different from COM and VB6 in many ways, yet most people have substantial investments in the COM and VB6 technologies, and it is unrealistic to expect that our .NET applications will exist independently in most cases. To meet this need, the .NET Framework has a mechanism for interoperating with COM and ActiveX components. This mechanism provides bi-directional capabilities, allowing .NET applications to call COM components, and also allowing COM components or applications to call .NET assemblies.

While .NET provides the new ADO.NET data access technology, there are times when we may want to use the original ADO for data access. This can be particularly useful in cases we need to interoperate with or quickly port existing code that uses ADO. Fortunately, ADO is represented as a set of COM components, and so we can use the COM interoperability support to access ADO when needed.

Additionally, though the .NET system class libraries are extensive, there are times, such as when calling specialized functionality like DirectX, when applications may need more direct access to the underlying operating system. Visual Basic .NET supports this concept, allowing us to call Win32 API functions when necessary.

There are also occasions when interoperability may not be sufficient and we will need to migrate existing VB6 code into Visual Basic .NET. Microsoft provides an **upgrade wizard** that helps move VB6 code into Visual Basic .NET. It doesn't take care of everything, but it certainly handles much of the drudgery that we would otherwise have to do by hand.

In this chapter, we are going to have a closer look at these COM/Win32 API interoperability and migration options.

COM/DCOM Interoperability

Since the release of version 4.0, VB developers have been developing applications based on ActiveX and COM. Many applications are designed to use ActiveX DLLs. Others are designed as ActiveX EXE projects, and many make use of user-created ActiveX controls. All of these are examples of COM components that are likely to be used within our existing applications.

The same is true for web applications. While some ASP applications are written entirely in scripting code within the ASP pages, a great many sites are designed to have the ASP script code call into COM components. These components are often written in VB as ActiveX DLL projects.

Given the tremendous use of COM for development, it comes as no surprise that Microsoft has included COM interoperability support in the .NET platform. For some time to come, it will be a rare .NET application that makes no use of COM components, since most of us will want to make use of our existing code when building new applications, regardless of whether they are COM or .NET.

The interoperability support is fairly extensive, although there are limitations. .NET applications can make calls into COM components – including ActiveX DLLs (both locally and though DCOM) and ActiveX controls. It is also possible to design .NET assemblies so that they are accessible from applications based on COM, so the support is bi-directional. Since there are substantial differences between the COM platform and the .NET platform, however, it is very important to test each individual component or control to ensure it works appropriately through interop.

You should also be aware that interoperability is not a panacea. There is a substantial amount of overhead involved when communicating between .NET and COM, which degrades application performance. In addition, interoperating with COM components can limit our ability to take full advantage of the features of the .NET platform. Perhaps most importantly, any time we use a COM component in our application, all the deployment and DLL Hell issues from the COM platform must be dealt with – something we avoid when building an application entirely in .NET.

Therefore, interoperability should really be viewed as a short-term solution as we migrate or rewrite our VB6 code to Visual Basic .NET over time.

> *For more extensive coverage of COM interoperability, please refer to Professional Visual Basic Interoperability: COM and VB6 to .NET published by Wrox Press, ISBN 1-861005-65-2.*

Invoking COM Components From .NET

The .NET Framework provides extensive support to allow managed code in .NET to call out to COM components. The Visual Studio .NET environment uses this support to make accessing a COM component as simple as adding a reference to the component from within the IDE.

Designing COM Components for .NET

There are some rules that must be followed by the designer of the COM component for this mechanism to work properly. Fortunately, these rules are automatically followed by virtually all COM components created with VB6, with no extra effort on our part.

However, for those developing COM components in other languages, the following is a summary of the best practices for success:

❑ Create a type library

❑ Provide version and locale information in the type library

❑ Use only data types supported by COM automation

❑ Use types common to both COM and .NET (isomorphic types)

❑ Avoid 'chatty' interfaces

❑ Name enums and structures clearly – these names carry through

❑ Explicitly free resources

❑ Do not use methods with the same method names as the `System.Object` class in .NET

❑ Use the `Binary Compatibility` setting in VB6

Let's look at some of these points in more detail now.

Data Types

It is important to use only data types that are OLE Automation-compliant. This includes all the basic data types in VB6, and so most VB6 components are automatically fine.

The exception is the `Variant` data type. The `Variant` data type can hold many types of data, including the common data types in VB6, but also including object references and user-defined types (UDTs). UDT data cannot be passed to or from .NET using a `Variant` – this is simply not supported by the default interoperability capabilities of .NET.

While there are workarounds to using a `Variant` to pass complex data between the platforms, it is better to simply avoid the use of `Variant`s when doing interop. For more details about the workaround, refer to *Professional Visual Basic Interoperability: COM and VB6 to .NET*.

The other major issue with data types – even OLE Automation-compliant ones – is to realize that they come in two flavors.

First, we have isomorphic data types that include the simple numeric types such as `Integer`, `Long`, and `Single`. Isomorphic data types have the same *internal* representation in COM as they do in .NET. In other words, they are stored in the computer's memory in exactly the same way on both platforms. This means that moving an isomorphic variable from COM to .NET is simply a matter of copying a few bytes of memory and so it is very fast. These are also known as **blittable data types**.

Then there are the non-isomorphic data types, which include `String`, `Boolean`, and most other data types. Non-isomorphic data types are stored in the computer's memory in different ways in COM from in .NET. Moving this type of data from one platform to the other requires some conversion effort and isn't a matter of simply copying some memory. They are also known as **non-blittable types**. This means that they are slower to work with than blittable data when doing interop.

Providing a Type Library

It is mandatory that we provide a type library otherwise .NET won't be able to determine how to call into the component. COM components created using VB6 automatically incorporate the type library directly into the component (DLL, EXE, or OCX), so we typically don't need to worry about this issue.

Ideally, the type library would include versioning and locale information, as that information is carried through into the .NET environment. Again, this work is done by VB6 by default, so we typically don't need to worry about it.

The caveat here is when we create our own type libraries using Visual C++ and then *implement* them in VB6. In that case, many of the automatic capabilities of VB6 are not present and it is the responsibility of the developer to create a type library that will work properly with .NET.

When a COM DLL is imported into .NET, a **runtime-callable wrapper** (**RCW**) is created within .NET by which we can reference the component. The RCW provides a .NET interface around the COM component, and includes all the code to handle the marshaling of data between the two platforms.

This wrapper class is derived from the base `System.Object` type in .NET, meaning that it will automatically have methods named `Equals()`, `Finalize()`, `GetHashCode()`, `GetType()`, `MemberwiseClone()`, and `ToString()`. To avoid conflicts, the COM component should not use any of these names as members of its interface.

Marshaling Between .NET and COM

Data is marshaled between the .NET and COM environments every time we make a method or property call. There are a couple of implications here.

First off, for the marshaling to work, the data types must be convertible between the two environments. The marshaling mechanism understands the OLE Automation types commonly used by COM components and the Common Language Interface (CLI) types from .NET. The best thing to do is to stick with types that are common to both environments (such as integer and floating-point numbers) as they marshal most easily. Other types (such as strings or dates) require conversion during the marshaling process, which can have a negative performance impact.

> **Remember that the integer data type sizes are different in Visual Basic .NET from those in VB6, as explained in Chapter 4.**

Strings are one of the most commonly passed data types. .NET strings are always Unicode, and can be efficiently marshaled to code that expects Unicode string data, while ANSI string data must be converted to and from Unicode. Fortunately the native VB6 `String` data type is Unicode, so conversion won't be required. However, there is still more overhead involved in working with `String` data as compared to isomorphic data types such as `Integer`.

Arrays are also of concern because all Visual Basic .NET arrays are now zero-based. If you are using anything other than zero-based arrays in your VB6 applications, you will need to compensate for the different array bounds in Visual Basic .NET.

Since data must be marshaled between the two environments, we should always strive to minimize the number of method calls from .NET into a COM component. Each call from one environment into the other will take time, so the more calls we make, the poorer our application will perform. Ideally, the COM components we call would have very few methods, each of which does quite a lot of work. We should avoid interacting with COM components that have a lot of small methods or properties, as this leads to 'chatty' interaction between the .NET code and the COM component.

> *If you must interact with a fine-grained COM component (one with many properties and methods), it may be beneficial to create a second COM component with just a few methods that can 'automate' or wrap your calls into the original component. This technique is described by the well-known design pattern named Façade. Refer to Design Patterns by Erich Gamma et al., published by Addison-Wesley ISBN 0-201-63361-2, for further details.*

The reality is that the performance impact depends on our environment. If you are creating a client application that is using a COM object or control, you will probably see no visible difference in performance. However, if you are creating a high volume server-side .NET application such as a web application or a Web Service, then this small performance hit is multiplied by the number of requests per second hitting the server: in this case a delay of a few extra milliseconds per method call can soon add up!

Component Termination and Garbage Collection

.NET makes the COM component available to our code via a .NET RCW object. It is the RCW that holds the actual reference to the COM object behind the scenes. Since the RCW is a .NET object, it will be destroyed by the .NET garbage collection mechanism as opposed to being destroyed when we de-reference the object. The COM component itself won't be released until the .NET wrapper object is terminated. See Chapter 6 for more information about garbage collection.

> **This means that the COM component may be retained in memory for an indeterminate period of time before it is released.**

To avoid resource reclamation problems, it is always wise to explicitly release the reference to the COM object when we are done with it. It isn't enough to simply set the object reference to Nothing, we must call a special method that releases the COM reference behind the scenes, `Marshal.ReleaseComObject()`. This directly decrements the COM reference count on the COM object, and it will be immediately destroyed when that hits zero – following normal COM rules.

The `Marshal` class comes from the `System.Runtime.InteropServices` namespace, so it is always wise to import that namespace at the top of any Visual Basic .NET file where we'll be using COM components.

VB6 and Binary Compatibility

While most of the major rules for making a .NET-friendly COM component are automatic when building the components with VB6, there is one key step that is unique to the VB environment – the use of **binary compatibility**.

The use of binary compatibility is not new or unique to interoperability. Using and understanding binary compatibility is key to the success for VB6 COM programming, and remains equally important when working with .NET through interoperability.

When a COM component is referenced by .NET, the reference is against the component's unique CLSID value. In VB6, by default, each time a component is recompiled it gets a new ID value – meaning that all .NET code will lose access to the component. .NET will see the newly compiled version as an entirely different DLL.

By using Binary Compatibility within the VB6 IDE (on the Component tab of the Properties window, reached via the Project | Properties menu) two things happen. Firstly, any time the component's interface is changed, we will be warned that it will be incompatible with the existing component. Secondly, as long as we *don't* change the interface such that it becomes incompatible with the existing component, the CLSID value will be preserved as we recompile. This means that .NET won't lose access to the component each time we recompile.

Remember that VB6 allows us to *add* new properties and methods to our classes without issuing the warning about incompatibility. This is dangerous however, because if we are set to be compatible with a copy of our component then subsequent compilation will regenerate ID values for these new methods – causing compatibility issues.

To avoid this, be sure to either set the compatible DLL to be the same as the DLL we are creating, or update the copy of the DLL with the new version any time new methods or properties are added.

Again, if we follow the best practices for binary capability that we have used in VB6 for years then we should be in good shape.

Calling a COM Component

Now that we have some background, let's take a look at how we can call a COM component from within Visual Basic .NET. First, we will create a simple ActiveX DLL using VB6, reference it from within Visual Basic .NET, and then write some code to interact with the object.

Creating the COM Component

We can easily create a simple COM component in VB6 by creating an ActiveX DLL project. Name the project COMServer and rename Class1 to be COMClass, and then add the following code:

```
Option Explicit

Public Function GetValue(Data As String) As String
  GetValue = "The data is " & Data
End Function

Public Function GetNumber() As Long
  GetNumber = 42
End Function

Public Function GetArray() As Integer()
  Dim a(5) As Integer

  a(0) = 0
```

```
    a(1) = 1
    a(2) = 2
    a(3) = 3
    a(4) = 4
    a(5) = 5
  GetArray = a
End Function

Public Function GetVar() As Variant
  GetVar = Now
End Function

Public Function GetDate() As Date
  GetDate = Now
End Function
```

With this code, our object will return a variety of data types, including text, numeric, date, Variant, and an array.

> It is worth quickly reviewing user-defined types (UDTs). A UDT can be returned from a VB6 method if it is an explicit result type. If we attempt to return a UDT via a Variant return type however, it will fail. This is one example of a wider scenario where complex data types can't be returned through generic return types such as Variant. While this can be solved, it is complex and involves direct editing of IL code and assorted other steps. This issue is discussed further in Professional Visual Basic Interoperability: COM and VB6 to .NET.

We can also make use of Public Enum declarations, since they will be made available within our Visual Basic .NET project. An Enum data type can be passed to and from a COM component as a parameter or return value without difficulty – interop services will handle the conversion for us automatically.

Once we compile this code to create the COMServer.DLL file, we are ready to switch into Visual Studio .NET and build a program that makes use of these methods. Again, remember to use **binary compatibility** to ensure that the component remains available to our .NET code.

Referencing the Component

In a Visual Studio .NET project we can gain access to the COM component by just adding a reference to the component. For instance, in a **Console Application** project, we could choose the **Project | Add Reference...** menu option and then select the **COM** tab within the dialog. After a short wait while all the COM components on the machine are cataloged, we will be presented with a list of available components. Scroll down to the **COMserver** entry and double-click:

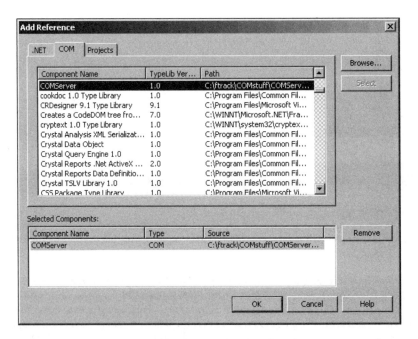

When we click the OK button, the Visual Studio .NET IDE will add a reference to this component to our project.

> *We can also use a command line utility named* `tlbimp.exe` *to create a .NET assembly that contains the RCW class for the component. Please refer to* Professional Visual Basic Interoperability: COM and VB6 to .NET *for more details.*

This reference is more complex than it might appear at first. The IDE will examine the component's type library – the information describing the component's interface – and will use that information to generate a .NET assembly that contains an RCW class. The RCW makes the component look and feel like a .NET assembly. We don't actually see any of this, including the wrapper. Instead, it appears to us that we have just added a new assembly to our project. The assembly containing the RCW class for the COM component is added to our project by Visual Studio .NET, but it is hidden from view by default. We can click the Show All Files button in the Solution Explorer to see the DLLs in the bin directory if desired.

The new reference is visible in the Solution Explorer window just like any other reference. At this point, we can write code to make use of the new 'assembly'.

> *The above procedure assumes that both the COM component and Visual Studio .NET are on the* **same** *machine. If this is not the case, then you will need to register the component on the .NET machine using* `regsvr32.exe`*.*

Using the Object

Once referenced, a COM component appears to our code just like any other .NET assembly. This includes having a namespace by which the component's elements are referenced. We can use the `Imports` statement to provide a shortcut to these elements, or we can use their full namespace name. An imports statement for our example component would appear as:

```
Imports COMServer
```

We should also import the interoperability services namespace:

```
Imports System.Runtime.InteropServices
```

We will use this almost any time we are working with COM objects – if for no other reason that to release the reference to the COM object when we are done with it.

In a Visual Basic .NET **Console Application** we could write the following code to use the component:

```
Imports System.Console
Imports COMServer
Imports System.Runtime.InteropServices

Module Module1

  Sub Main()
    Dim com As New COMClass()

    WriteLine(com.GetValue("sample data"))

    WriteLine(com.GetNumber())

    WriteLine("It is now {0}", com.GetDate)

    WriteLine("The array contains:")
    Dim num As Short
    Dim a() As Short = com.GetArray()
    For Each num In a
      WriteLine(num)
    Next

    WriteLine("It is now {0}", CDate(com.GetVar()))

    Marshal.ReleaseComObject(com)
    Set com = Nothing

    Read()
  End Sub

End Module
```

The `GetValue()` method accepts a `String` and returns a value as a `String`. It is pretty straightforward.

The `GetNumber()` method returns an `Integer` value. Remember that we declared it as type `Long` in VB6, which corresponds to the `Integer` data type in Visual Basic .NET as we discussed in Chapter 4.

The GetDate() method returns a Date data type. While the name of the data type is the same from VB6 to Visual Basic .NET, the underlying structure is not identical, but the marshaling process takes care of those details for us.

The GetArray() method returns an array of type Short rather than Integer. The VB6 Integer data type corresponds to the Visual Basic .NET Short type. This array can be treated like any other array, including looping through all the elements as shown. Note that the VB6 array was zero-based, and so it works fine. If it were a one-based array it would give us a runtime error as we attempt to retrieve the data from VB6, as it couldn't cast that into .NET automatically.

> **Use only zero-based arrays in VB6 when interoperating with Visual Basic .NET.**

The GetVar() method returns a value of type Object. In VB6 this method returned a Variant, which roughly corresponds to Object in Visual Basic .NET. Since we know that it is returning a Date we can use CDate() to convert the generic data type into a specific data type so that we can use it effectively.

Finally, notice the call to release the reference to the COM object, so that COM can clean it up:

```
Marshal.ReleaseComObject(com)
```

This is essentially the VB6 equivalent of setting the object reference to Nothing. Remember that in .NET all objects are garbage collected, including the RCW, so without this call, the underlying COM object won't be released until the RCW is destroyed sometime in the future. By calling ReleaseComObject() explicitly, we help preserve the expected behavior for the COM component by having it destroyed immediately. We also set the variable to Nothing. This prevents any accidental attempts at using the variable, which is important since its underlying COM object is probably already destroyed.

When we run this application we should get output similar to the following:

Accessing a COM component is virtually as easy and painless as using a native .NET assembly.

Using ADO from Visual Basic .NET

Given that we can easily access COM components from within .NET, and given that ADO is exposed as a set of COM components, it naturally follows that our .NET applications can make use of ADO for data access if needed.

Of course .NET provides us with the new ADO.NET data access technology, and that is the preferred mechanism for data access. However, there may be times when ADO is required – for instance, pessimistic locking is not supported by ADO.NET, so if we need that feature, we will need to use ADO.

Gaining access to ADO is as simple as adding a reference to the appropriate ADO library. We can do this in a couple ways. Microsoft provides a pre-built interop assembly that gives us access to the current version of ADO. This appears in the .NET tab of the **Add References** dialog, and is called **adodb**.

Adding this reference will give us access to the ADO COM component via the pre-built interop assembly. If we want to use a different version of ADO we can access it via the **COM** tab of the dialog:

Adding this second type of reference will cause Visual Studio .NET to create an interop assembly for us so we'll have an RCW for this particular version of ADO.

Either way, we will have a reference in place, so we will have access to ADO via the ADODB namespace. To use it most easily, add an Imports statement:

```
Imports ADODB
Imports System.Runtime.InteropServices
```

We have also imported the InteropServices namespace, since we are working with COM objects.

Then, in a **Windows Application** with a **ListBox** control on the form, we could write the following method:

```
Private Sub Form1_Load(ByVal sender As System.Object, _
  ByVal e As System.EventArgs) Handles MyBase.Load

  Dim rs As New ADODB.Recordset()
  Const dbConn As String = "PROVIDER=SQLOLEDB;Data Source=myserver;" & _
    "Initial Catalog=pubs;User id=sa;Password=;"

  rs.Open("SELECT au_lname, au_fname FROM authors", dbConn, _
    ADODB.CursorTypeEnum.adOpenForwardOnly, _
    ADODB.LockTypeEnum.adLockReadOnly)

  Do While Not rs.EOF
    ListBox1.Items.Add(CStr(rs.Fields("au_lname").Value) & _
      ", " & CStr(rs.Fields("au_fname").Value))
    rs.MoveNext()
  Loop

  rs.Close()
  Marshal.ReleaseComObject(rs)

End Sub
```

When this code is run, it will populate the ListBox control with a list of the names of authors from the pubs database. For the most part, this code should look quite familiar to anyone used to working with ADO.

Gaining access to the data in each row is a bit different, however, since we are explicitly using the Value property from each Field object. This is required since Visual Basic .NET doesn't work with default properties in the same way as VB6, and so the Value property is not treated as a default property. Instead, we must explicitly reference the Value property to gain access to the data in each field.

Of course, the Fields property is the default property for the Recordset object, and since it is a property array we could use it without problem, rewriting the code as follows:

```
ListBox1.Items.Add(CStr(rs("au_lname").Value) & _
    ", " & CStr(rs("au_fname").Value))
```

The only other change is that each method call must have parentheses, just like any other method in Visual Basic .NET.

Of course, at the end we call the ReleaseComObject() method to immediately release our reference to the Recordset object, allowing COM to clean it up as expected.

DCOM

Many existing VB applications make use of COM components that are actually running on other machines across the network. They interact with these components using Distributed COM (DCOM). As we discussed in Chapter 9, the .NET platform uses either Web Services or the .NET Remoting technology to interact with assemblies running on other machines – not DCOM.

However, DCOM is still available for our use when we are writing .NET applications that require access to COM components running on other machines. This is due less to .NET than to COM itself. One of the major strengths of COM and DCOM is that they provide us with **location transparency**. This is the concept that our code can't tell the difference between interacting with a component running on our machine or running on another machine. Either way, the client code is identical.

In VB6 we might write the following code to interact with a COM component:

```
Dim obj As Aclass

Set obj = New Aclass
obj.DoSomething
```

Looking at this code, there is no way to tell if Aclass is included in our application, is loaded into our application from a DLL, is running in MTS or COM+ on our machine, or is running on another machine somewhere on the network. In fact, with no changes to this client code at all, we can reconfigure the application into any of those scenarios and the code will still work. This is location transparency.

We have already seen how Visual Basic .NET allows us to interact with COM components by simply adding a reference to the component from within our project. This same location transparency benefit extends to us in .NET as it did in VB6. Since the .NET runtime relies on COM itself to handle the COM component, we can communicate with a remote COM component as easily as with one running on our local machine.

To invoke a DCOM component from .NET, the component must be installed on the remote machine and registered on the local workstation as a remote component. This process is no different from what we'd do with VB6 to make a remote component available.

Beyond this configuration process, interacting with a DCOM component is identical to interacting with any other COM component as we discussed earlier in the chapter. The Visual Studio .NET IDE provides the component with a .NET wrapper class, and our code interacts with this class just as if the component were native to the .NET platform.

As before, the remote component will be released when the .NET garbage collection process terminates the wrapper object, so it is very important to make sure to call `Marshal.ReleaseComObject()` when working with COM objects through DCOM.

Also, keep in mind that when .NET interacts with a component through DCOM, it must marshal all method and property calls from the .NET environment to the COM environment – incurring the performance penalties that we discussed earlier. Of course that is in addition to the normal overhead of using DCOM to communicate across a network connection between two computers. However, this technique is powerful, in that it can allow our .NET applications to make use of COM components running on other machines on the network in MTS or COM+.

Using ActiveX Controls from Windows Forms

The Windows Forms technology used by Visual Basic .NET to create Windows applications provides its own mechanism for creating and managing controls – different from the ActiveX controls we are used to in VB6. This was discussed in more detail in Chapter 5.

It is possible to use ActiveX controls on a form created using Windows Forms in a similar way to how we can use COM components directly from code. The Visual Studio .NET IDE allows us to add an ActiveX control to the Toolbox so we can use it on our forms.

When an OCX file is added to the Toolbox, Visual Studio .NET automatically creates .NET wrapper classes for each control in the file. These wrapper classes are based on the AxHost class, which provides the ActiveX control with the illusion that it is running in an ActiveX container, and provides the actual Windows Forms host with the illusion that the ActiveX control is a Windows Forms control.

Of course Visual Basic .NET uses COM interoperability to interact with ActiveX controls, since those controls are just specialized COM components. As with a regular COM component, a wrapper class is created that makes the ActiveX control appear as a .NET Windows Forms control to our .NET code. However, this wrapper is much more sophisticated than a normal RCW, since it also emulates a COM control container, giving the ActiveX control the illusion that it is running in a normal COM container such as a VB6 form.

This means that we have the same performance issues with ActiveX controls as we do with COM components in general, in that all property and method calls to a control are marshaled from the .NET environment into the COM environment.

Typically the performance impact of the marshaling between .NET and COM is immaterial for controls. ActiveX controls are typically used as part of a user interface on a client machine and so the performance difference won't even be visible to the naked eye. It may be that setting a property on an ActiveX control takes twice as long as setting a property on a .NET Windows Forms control, but we're talking twice the *milliseconds*, so in most cases it won't matter to the end user.

Adding a Tab to the Toolbox

While not strictly necessary, it is nice to put any imported ActiveX controls on their own tab within the Toolbox to keep things organized.

Adding a tab to the Toolbox is straightforward. Just right-click on the Toolbox and choose the Add Tab menu option. A new tab will be added, with the cursor placed in the name field. Enter a name for the tab – such as ActiveX – and click on the new tab to open it.

Adding an ActiveX Control to the Toolbox

Adding a control to the Toolbox is equally simple. Just right-click on the Toolbox and choose the Customize Toolbox... menu option. Click the checkbox next to the control to be imported and when you click OK, the IDE will import the OCX and create a .NET assembly containing wrapper classes for each control within the OCX, placing the controls on the open tab in the Toolbox.

As with the assemblies that contain the RCW for a regular COM component, these assemblies are added to our project, but are hidden from view by default. We can click the Show All Files button in the Solution Explorer to see the DLLs in the bin directory if desired.

If the ActiveX control's interface (properties, methods, and events) is changed later we'll need to re-import the control so that Visual Studio .NET can create an updated wrapper class. This is particularly important to keep in mind when importing VB6 UserControls that we may be altering later, just as it was when working with UserControls in VB6.

Using the ActiveX Control

Once the control has been added to the Toolbox we can use it like any other control, either using a double click or drag-and-drop approach to adding instances of the control to a form.

From the .NET perspective we are working with what appears to be a .NET control, which means we can use features like docking and anchoring of the control. Of course behind the scenes we know that the .NET wrapper is delegating all our method calls down to an actual ActiveX control.

Once the control is on a form, we can write code to interact with the control, and the user can interact with the control when the program is running. For instance, we might have code in our form similar to the following:

```
Private Sub Form1_Load(ByVal sender As System.Object, _
    ByVal e As System.EventArgs) Handles MyBase.Load

    AxWebBrowser1.Navigate("http://www.wrox.com")

End Sub
```

This code causes the browser control to display the Wrox home page. This is basically the same code we'd write in VB6 to use this control as well, with the addition of some extra parentheses.

Notice that the default name for any ActiveX control will start with Ax to differentiate them from native Windows Forms controls.

Invoking .NET Components from COM

We have seen how easy it is to invoke a COM component from within .NET. We can also do the reverse – invoking a .NET assembly from within the COM environment. This process is nearly as easy, since it is fully supported by the Visual Studio .NET IDE. There is a bit of extra code required in our .NET class to properly expose it for use by COM, however.

A .NET assembly is made available for use from COM-based applications by creating a **COM-callable wrapper** (**CCW**). The assembly containing the CCW is created by Visual Studio .NET when we check the appropriate option in our project's properties dialog.

> *Alternatively, we can create it by using the* `tlbexp.exe` *and* `Regasm.exe` *command line utilities. See Professional Visual Basic Interoperability: COM and VB6 to .NET for more information.*

Either way, an assembly containing the code for the CCW is created, and then registered in the system registry so it *appears* to be a COM component. At this point, the assembly will appear as a COM component on the machine – meaning we can add a reference to it from within the VB6 IDE.

One key thing to bear in mind is how .NET finds assemblies for an application. By default, .NET assemblies are local to each application and the runtime locates them by searching in the same directory or the directory tree. For an assembly to be available to all applications it must be somehow made available to the COM client application.

For COM to interact with an assembly, it must be able to find the assembly. There are two options at our disposal. We can either place the CCW assembly in the GAC, which is somewhat like registering a .NET assembly, or we can use the `/codebase` switch on the `tlbexp` command line utility. This latter approach is simplest, since it leaves the .NET assembly where it is and COM uses it from there.

Visual Studio .NET uses this second approach, keeping things as simple and straightforward as possible. When Visual Studio .NET compiles an assembly that is marked for use through COM interop, it automatically registers the assembly with COM using the `/codebase` switch – making the assembly available to any COM client application without having to 'register' the assembly in the .NET GAC.

It is important to keep in mind, however, that while a .NET DLL can be installed in several directories on a machine – so that it is available to several .NET applications – it can only be registered in *one directory* for use by COM. This is because there is only one registry entry for a given component under COM. Again, any time our .NET code needs to interact with COM we must conform to the rules of COM – and this is a perfect example of how our .NET code must accommodate extra restrictions to work across platforms.

Earlier in the chapter, we discussed how data is marshaled between COM and .NET when a COM component is called from .NET. This marshaling process also occurs when a .NET assembly is called from COM, and so many of the rules and best practices we discussed earlier apply equally in this case:

- ❏ Provide version and locale information in the assembly
- ❏ Use only data types supported by OLE Automation
- ❏ Use types common to both COM and .NET (isomorphic types)

❑ Avoid chatty interfaces

❑ Name enums and structures clearly – these names carry through

❑ Explicitly free resources

❑ Don't use methods with the same names as methods in the `System.Object` class in .NET

Creating a .NET Assembly for COM

For the sake of symmetry, let's create a Visual Basic .NET class that acts as a mirror image to the COMClass we created earlier in this chapter to demonstrate calling into COM from .NET. Create a Class Library package in Visual Basic .NET. Name the project NETServer, and rename Class1 to NETClass. Then add the following methods to NETClass:

```vb
Public Class NETClass

  Public Function GetValue(ByVal Data As String) As String
    Return "The data is " & Data
  End Function

  Public Function GetNumber() As Integer
    Return 42
  End Function

  Public Function GetArray() As Short()
    Dim a() As Short = {0, 1, 2, 3, 4, 5}

    Return a
  End Function

  Public Function GetDate() As Date
    Return Now
  End Function

  Public Function GetVar() As Object
    Return Now
  End Function

End Class
```

This code is equivalent to the code we wrote earlier in COMClass, returning a variety of data types for use by our COM client application. Notice for instance, that the integer data types are the .NET equivalents of their COM counterparts as we discussed in Chapter 4.

The <ComClass()> Attribute

Now we need to add just a bit of code to properly expose this class for use by COM clients. This is done by adding an attribute to the class:

```vb
<ComClass()> _
Public Class NETClass
```

This attribute will cause interface and class information to be exported to COM in a way that will make this class appear as though it were generated by VB6. Thus, we will have maximum transparency when using this class from VB6.

Other options and attributes exist, which allow more flexibility and control over the process. For details on these, refer to *Professional Visual Basic Interoperability*.

Exporting to COM

Now that our code is ready for exporting to COM, we need to set a property in our project so Visual Studio .NET will actually do the export process – creating the assembly containing the CCW and registering it in the System Registry.

To do this, right-click on the project in the **Solution Explorer** window and choose **Properties**. In the resulting **Properties** dialog, choose the **Configuration Properties | Build** option in the left-hand pane. Click the **Register for COM Interop** box and this will instruct Visual Studio .NET to create the wrapper assembly and register our code for use by COM when the solution is built.

Build the solution to compile the DLL and export it to COM. At this point, we are ready to build a client application.

Creating a COM Client

The COM client application can be written in any language that can invoke COM components. In this example, we will use VB6 to create the client.

For a client application, just create a standard Windows project named **NETTest** in VB6. Add a **ListBox** control to the form and add the following code to manage the size of the **ListBox** control:

```
Private Sub Form_Resize()
  List1.Move 0, 0, ScaleWidth, ScaleHeight
End Sub
```

Now we can move on to the real work.

Adding a Reference to the Assembly

We can make use of the assembly via late binding or early binding. Obviously, performance will be better through early binding. Let's now add a reference to the assembly to our project, using the **Project | References...** menu option and selecting the **NETServer** entry. With this reference added, our application is ready to use the assembly.

Again, this is the procedure you would follow if your COM environment is on the same machine as your .NET runtime. If this is not the case, then your VB6 machine will need to have at least the .NET Redistributable installed, and you will need to register the assembly on that machine using `regasm.exe`*.*

Using the Object

To use the `NETClass` object, add the following code:

```
Private Sub Form_Load()
  Dim obj As NETServer.NETClass
  Dim a() As Integer
```

```
    Dim val As Variant

    Set obj = New NETServer.NETClass

  List1.AddItem obj.GetValue("sample data")
    List1.AddItem obj.GetNumber
    List1.AddItem "The date is " & obj.GetDate

    List1.AddItem "The array contains"
    a = obj.GetArray
    For Each val In a
      List1.AddItem val
    Next

    List1.AddItem "The date is " & obj.GetVar

    Set obj = Nothing

  End Sub
```

This code is functionally equivalent to the client code we created in .NET earlier when working with the COMClass object. It just calls each of the methods we created, displaying the results into the ListBox control on the form.

The result should be a display similar to the previous example when we used a COM component in a Visual Basic .NET project.

Calling a .NET assembly from COM is nearly as simple as doing the reverse. We can easily pass most common data types between the two environments – providing solid interoperability between the new .NET platform and the COM platform.

Calling Windows APIs

Though the .NET system class libraries are quite comprehensive, there may be times when we need to directly call Win32 API functions from our application. It is preferable to make use of any .NET functionality whenever possible, but the .NET Framework does include provisions for calling native operating system API functions when needed.

API functions are stored in static DLL files and may have been written by Microsoft, third party vendors, or others. Since, at its core, much of the .NET system class library interacts with the Win32 API, there is obviously a very good mechanism built into the .NET Framework for interacting with these DLL functions.

Using the Platform Invocation Services

The technologies used to access APIs are called the Platform Invocation Services, or **PInvoke** for short. PInvoke takes care of locating the appropriate DLL, loading it into our process memory, locating the function address, and making the call. This typically also includes marshaling data from the .NET environment to the unmanaged API and back again.

This may sound familiar, since it is the same basic process followed when we interact with an existing COM component. In fact, the general process for invoking an API function is the same as for a COM method, though the actual code within our Visual Basic .NET application is somewhat different when calling an API since Visual Studio .NET doesn't automatically wrap API calls the way it does with COM components.

PInvoke is very powerful. It not only handles the marshaling, but it has a great deal of intelligence in terms of locating the API function we want to invoke. It uses fuzzy name matching to find the right API. Fuzzy name matching is particularly important when we look at all the APIs that support both ANSI and Unicode text. In these cases there is an API ending in the letter A that handles the ANSI call, and one ending in W for the Unicode call. Fuzzy name matching allows PInvoke to automatically use the right one based on whether we indicate we're passing an ANSI or Unicode data type – entirely eliminating our need to worry about which API to invoke.

We will discuss this later, but first let's look at a simple example.

Calling a Simple API Function

We can use the VB6 syntax to declare and use API functions, in which case Visual Basic .NET will use PInvoke to make the call behind the scenes. We can also use a new .NET syntax to declare API functions. This new syntax can provide some benefits in terms of flexibility as we use the API methods, and that's what we will use here.

For our first example, we will call the MessageBox API, which is located in the user32.dll.

Normally of course, we would simply use the VB MsgBox() function or call the .NET MessageBox class rather than directly calling the API.

To keep our code shorter, it is also a good idea to import the interoperability namespace:

```
Imports System.Runtime.InteropServices
```

This will save a lot of typing and make our code more readable.

Declaring an API in Visual Basic .NET

Before we can use an API function within our application we need to declare it. Basically, what we're doing is creating a function wrapper in Visual Basic .NET that describes the function within the .NET environment. Using attributes, we also provide metadata that PInvoke can use to locate the actual function on the system. When an application invokes our wrapper function, PInvoke automatically transfers the function call to the appropriate function in the appropriate DLL.

Conceptually, this function wrapper is comparable to the one Visual Studio .NET creates for a COM component, though it is created in memory – no extra .NET assembly is created. However, static DLLs have no type library or other self-description mechanism and so it is not possible to automatically generate the wrapper. Therefore we end up creating the wrapper ourselves.

To be fair, the most useful and commonly used APIs are already wrapped – via the .NET system class library. Only when we want to interact with a less common API such as DirectX or with a DLL created by a third party will this issue come into play.

An API function is declared in Visual Basic .NET just like any other function – with the addition of the DllImport attribute. Start a new **Windows Application** project and add a class to it, calling it **API**. Then declare the MessageBox API by adding the following code to the class:

```
Imports System.Runtime.InteropServices

Public Class API
```

```
<DllImport("user32.dll")> _
Public Shared Function MessageBox( _
  ByVal Hwnd As Integer, ByVal Text As String, _
  ByVal Caption As String, ByVal Type As Integer) As Integer
End Function
```

```
End Class
```

On the surface, this is just a function with no implementation. We have both `Function` and `End Function` statements to form a complete block – but no code inside. No code is allowed either – if we try to place code in this block, we will get a compile error. Instead, the declaration uses the `DllImport` attribute:

```
<DllImport("user32.dll")>
```

`DllImport` can accept a number of parameters, but typically, we just need to specify the actual static `DLL` where the function is located. PInvoke will take care of locating that DLL and calling the specified function inside.

For this to work properly, our declaration of the `MessageBox()` function must have exactly the same parameters as the actual API function – matching in order, data type, and quantity. If they don't match the API call will fail at run-time with an error. Also note that Visual Basic .NET doesn't support the `As Any` syntax of previous versions of VB, so we must provide matching data types for all parameters.

Calling the API Function

We can now write code behind a button on the form to call the function. Add a **Button** and the following code to **Form1**:

```
Private Sub Button1_Click(ByVal sender As System.Object, _
  ByVal e As System.EventArgs) Handles Button1.Click

  API.MessageBox(0, "Hello world", "Hi", 0)

End Sub
```

This is no different from calling any other `Shared` method on a class – we have entirely hidden the fact that the function is actually using a Win32 API.

Aliasing a Function

Sometimes we don't want to use the actual name of the API function within our application. This may be to avoid a naming conflict or to increase the readability of our application.

We can alias an API function by adding an extra parameter to the `DllImport` attribute. For example, we could rename the `MessageBox()` function to `PopUp` with the following declaration in our API class:

```
<DllImport("user32.dll", EntryPoint:="MessageBox")> _
Public Shared Function PopUp( _
  ByVal Hwnd As Integer, ByVal Text As String, _
  ByVal Caption As String, ByVal Type As Integer) As Integer
End Function
```

We just renamed the function name to `PopUp` and added the `EntryPoint` parameter to the `DllImport` attribute. Now throughout our application we can refer to this function as `PopUp` instead of `MessageBox`.

Hiding an API Interface

At times we may not like the parameter list required by an API. For instance, perhaps in our newly renamed `PopUp()` method we don't want to require the user to provide the `Hwnd` or `Type` parameters. While we can't change the signature of the API method declaration itself, we can provide a surrogate implementation, which just calls the actual API method.

To do this, we can change the code in the `API` class as follows:

```
<DllImport("user32.dll")> _
Private Shared Function MessageBox( _
  ByVal Hwnd As Integer, ByVal Text As String, _
  ByVal Caption As String, ByVal Type As Integer) As Integer
End Function
```

```
Public Shared Function PopUp(ByVal [Text] As String, _
  ByVal Caption As String) As Integer

  Return MessageBox(0, [Text], Caption, 0)

End Function
```

We have change the API declaration back to its original form and, more importantly, declared it as `Private` in scope. This means the API function can't be directly called by code outside our class.

The `PopUp()` function has been changed to be a regular Visual Basic .NET function that accepts only the parameters we want the user to provide. The call is then delegated to the `Private` API function to do the actual work. In this way we can change the external interface for an API function into whatever form makes sense for our application.

Using Automatic ANSI/Unicode Location

As we mentioned earlier, PInvoke can automatically invoke the appropriate API function when faced with a choice between the ANSI version (ending in `A`) and the Unicode version (ending in `W`). For instance, to retrieve the system directory path, we can call the `GetSystemDirectory` API. However, in reality, there is no `GetSystemDirectory` API – instead there are the two flavors; `GetSystemDirectoryA` and `GetSystemDirectoryW`.

Due to the way PInvoke uses fuzzy name matching, however, we can declare the `GetSystemDirectory` API in Visual Basic .NET as follows:

```
<DllImport("kernel32")> _
  Public Shared Function _
    GetSystemDirectory(ByVal Buffer As StringBuilder, _
    ByVal Size As Integer) As Integer
  End Function
```

Here, we are specifying neither the A nor W version of the API. Rather, we are allowing PInvoke to determine which version to call as appropriate, based on the underlying operating system and whether it supports ANSI or Unicode strings in the API.

Note that we are using the `StringBuilder` class to provide the buffer. This class comes from the `System.Text` namespace, so we should import it at the top of our code module.

We can then call this method from the form (again importing the `System.Text` namespace) using the following code:

```
Private Sub Button1_Click(ByVal sender As System.Object, _
    ByVal e As System.EventArgs) Handles Button1.Click

  Const MAX_PATH As Integer = 256
  Dim str As New StringBuilder(MAX_PATH)

  API.GetSystemDirectory(str, MAX_PATH)

  MsgBox(str.ToString)

End Sub
```

The appropriate API will automatically be called by PInvoke, without our having to worry about which version is appropriate.

Passing Structures as Parameters

Some API functions require complex structures as parameters. In Chapter 4, we discussed how to declare a `Structure` in Visual Basic .NET. The trick with these structures is that we don't know exactly how they are stored in memory, so, when passing them to an API function, they must be laid out in memory in such a way that the API can write into them.

To ensure a structure is stored in memory appropriately, we need to use attributes when declaring the structure. As an example, consider the API that generates a GUID value – `CoCreateGuid`. This API fills in a structure composed of a set of numeric values, which we can then use to create an object of type `System.Guid`.

> *Again, it is preferable and easier to use the built-in* `Guid.NewGuid()` *method to generate a* `Guid`, *but this API is a good example of using a structure as a parameter.*

The structure we will pass as a parameter can be declared in our `API` class as:

```
<StructLayout(LayoutKind.Sequential)> _
Private Structure GUIDstruc
  Public Guid1 As Int32
  Public Guid2 As Int16
  Public Guid3 As Int16
  Public Guid4a As Byte
  Public Guid4b As Byte
  Public Guid4c As Byte
  Public Guid4d As Byte
```

```
        Public Guid4e As Byte
        Public Guid4f As Byte
        Public Guid4g As Byte
        Public Guid4h As Byte
    End Structure
```

The key here is the StructLayout attribute:

```
    <StructLayout(LayoutKind.Sequential)>
```

This attribute indicates that the structure should be stored sequentially in memory, preventing the .NET runtime from storing the various parts of the structure in different locations in memory. This is critical since the API doesn't write the data field by field, but rather writes a stream of bytes into a contiguous section of memory. If our structure wasn't all stored in the same spot, who knows what the API might overwrite?

Given this structure declaration, we can declare the CoCreateGuid API as follows:

```
    <DllImport("OLE32.DLL")> _
    Private Shared Function CoCreateGuid( _
      ByRef Buffer As GUIDstruc) As Integer
    End Function
```

The parameter we provide to this function is of type GUIDstruc, allowing the API to populate the structure appropriately. Notice that this function is declared as Private. For ease of use, we can create a Public function that returns a variable of type Guid:

```
    Public Shared Function NewGuid() As Guid
      Dim Buffer As GUIDstruc
      Dim result As Long
      Dim g As Guid
      Const S_OK As Integer = 0

      result = CoCreateGuid(Buffer)

      If result = S_OK Then
        g = New Guid(Buffer.Guid1, Buffer.Guid2, _
          Buffer.Guid3, Buffer.Guid4a, Buffer.Guid4b, _
          Buffer.Guid4c, Buffer.Guid4d, Buffer.Guid4e, _
          Buffer.Guid4f, Buffer.Guid4g, Buffer.Guid4h)

        Return g
      Else
        err.Raise(1, "GUIDgen", "Unable to create GUID value")
      End If
    End Function
```

This function calls the CoCreateGuid() method, passing in a GUIDstruc parameter. If the API completes successfully, the elements of the structure are provided to the constructor of the Guid class to create a new object.

451

To use this new function we could write code in our UI such as:

```
MsgBox(API.NewGuid()).ToString
```

As with our previous examples, we've entirely hidden the complexity of the API call within our .NET class.

Using the Migration Wizard

Given all of the differences between Visual Basic .NET and VB6, it is obviously not trivial to migrate an existing application from VB6 into the Visual Basic .NET environment. Microsoft provides a **Migration Wizard** to assist with this process. It will be a rare project that can be automatically migrated without any intervention on our part, but the wizard does help by handling much of the drudge work that we'd otherwise have to do by hand.

It converts common data type names, properties, and methods to the new syntax, adds parenthesis where needed, and adds references to ADO and to any ActiveX controls. In short, it does all the things that are relatively straightforward for conversion.

There are many things that are not so straightforward of course. If we used arrays with a lower bound of one for instance, and then did calculations to generate array indexes in our code there's not much the wizard can do for us. In these cases it flags suspicious code for later attention.

The Migration Process

The Migration Wizard is automatically invoked when we attempt to open a VB6 project in the Visual Basic .NET IDE. It will run through the code in the original project, generating a new Visual Basic .NET project. The new project will be partially upgraded and will have comments where the wizard was unable to upgrade the code. The wizard will also generate an upgrade report listing any problems that it was unable to address.

When run against a VB6 project group, only the first project in the group is migrated.

Running the Wizard

The first page you will see when you run the Wizard is a welcome page. Next, the wizard automatically detects the type of project being upgraded – whether it is an ActiveX EXE or ActiveX DLL, for instance. Based on this information, it creates the appropriate target project type. At the third step, we are asked where the new Visual Basic .NET project should be created. By default, the new project will be created in a subdirectory beneath the existing project directory.

> **Remember that .NET applications cannot typically be run from a network drive without changing security settings, so ensure that the target directory is located on a drive local to the development workstation.**

If the target directory doesn't exist, we will be prompted to create it. Once the target directory is specified and created, the wizard will confirm that we want to do the upgrade.

If you click on Next, the wizard will then run through the VB6 project, converting it to a Visual Basic .NET project. At this point, we will be in a position to work with the newly created Visual Basic .NET project. The project should contain files corresponding to each of the original code files in the VB6 project, along with an upgrade report.

The Upgrade Report

The upgrade report is presented as a DHTML page included as a file in the project. This page includes information about the upgrade process, including a list of the files upgraded along with the status of each. The following report shows the results of upgrading COMClass from earlier in the chapter. To make it more interesting, this version of COMClass includes a one-based array:

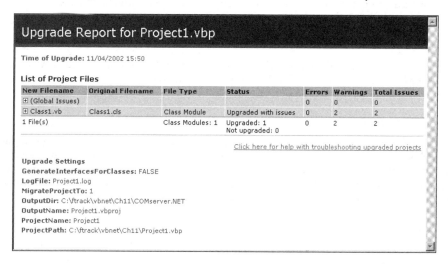

```
Upgrade Report for Project1.vbp

Time of Upgrade: 11/04/2002 15:50

List of Project Files
```

New Filename	Original Filename	File Type	Status	Errors	Warnings	Total Issues
⊞ (Global Issues)				0	0	0
⊞ Class1.vb	Class1.cls	Class Module	Upgraded with issues	0	2	2
1 File(s)		Class Modules: 1	Upgraded: 1 Not upgraded: 0	0	2	2

Click here for help with troubleshooting upgraded projects

```
Upgrade Settings
GenerateInterfacesForClasses: FALSE
LogFile: Project1.log
MigrateProjectTo: 1
OutputDir: C:\ftrack\vbnet\Ch11\COMserver.NET
OutputName: Project1.vbproj
ProjectName: Project1
ProjectPath: C:\ftrack\vbnet\Ch11\Project1.vbp
```

The wizard also places comments in our code where it found issues it couldn't fully resolve, or can't guarantee were resolved adequately. For instance, where we had a one-based array we get this warning:

```
Public Function GetArray() As Short()
    'UPGRADE_WARNING: Lower bound of array a was changed from 1 to 0.
    'Click for more:
    ' 'ms-help://MS.VSCC/commoner/redir/redirect.htm?keyword="vbup1033"'

    Dim a(5) As Short

    a(1) = 1
    a(2) = 2
    a(3) = 3
    a(4) = 4
    a(5) = 5
    GetArray = VB6.CopyArray(a)
End Function
```

Notice that the comment also includes a link to the online help where we can get more information about the warning and possible resolutions.

General Wizard Activities

The wizard performs a variety of activities during the upgrade process. The following is a summary of some of the most important tasks.

Syntax Changes

Most of the syntax changes – such as how a `Property` routine is built, or the change from `Long` to `Integer` data types – can be easily accommodated by the upgrade wizard and will occur automatically.

The wizard converts `UDT` declarations to `Structure` declarations and removes the `Set` statements where object assignments occur. Most other simple syntax or code structure changes are handled automatically.

Data Access

Data access is another area of concern. Most existing VB6 applications make use of ADO for data access. The Migration Wizard uses COM interoperability to allow the upgraded code to continue to use ADO. If we want to upgrade our code to use ADO.NET, we will have to make those changes manually.

Form-based Applications

VB6 graphical forms are a bit trickier. While some of the standard VB controls can be migrated to Windows Forms counterparts, there are many controls that can't be automatically migrated. While this includes most third-party controls, it also includes a number of standard controls that don't have counterparts in Visual Basic .NET, such as the `Shape` control. Where no Windows Forms control exists, the ActiveX control is referenced into the project and is used.

ActiveX DLL Projects

In general, upgrading an ActiveX DLL project is easier than upgrading a forms-based application. Most DLL projects are composed of a set of class modules that perform business processing or data access. This type of code can generally be upgraded to Visual Basic .NET with minimal effort on our part. We can, however, run into issues with arrays, or VB6 keywords that are no longer supported in Visual Basic .NET, if those features are used in the ActiveX DLL code.

Summary

As we move into the world of .NET, we will need to continue to support and interact with existing COM applications. Visual Basic .NET makes it very easy to write .NET applications that call into COM components, whether they are DLLs on the local machine or running in MTS or COM+ on a remote machine. The same is true with ActiveX controls, which can be directly hosted within a Windows Forms application or even used within a Web Forms application.

Likewise, .NET assemblies can be made available for use by COM applications, allowing existing applications to be enhanced to interact with new .NET applications as they are created.

The .NET Framework also includes the PInvoke services, which provide very strong support for calling into Win32 API functions or other functions exported from static DLLs. While most common API functionality is already built into the .NET system class library, when we need to we can easily call into the API functions directly.

Obviously, there will also be a need to upgrade some existing VB6 applications into Visual Basic .NET. This process will never be painless, but Microsoft provides a Migration Wizard that helps ease the process.

With the strong interoperability support built into .NET, upgrading applications may not be terribly critical in the short term, since we can instead choose to build new .NET applications that make use of existing code. This is a powerful and cost-effective overall strategy.

Index

A Guide to the Index

The index is arranged hierarchically, in alphabetical order, with symbols preceding the letter A. Most second-level entries and many third-level entries also occur as first-level entries. This is to ensure that users will find the information they require however they choose to search for it

#End Region directive, 66
#Region directive, 66
.NET Class Framework
  see base classes
.NET Enterprise Servers, 13, **31-32**
  BizTalk Server, 31
  Commerce Server, 31
  Exchange Server, 31
  Host Integration Server, 31
  Internet Security and Acceleration Server, 31
  SharePoint Portal Server, 31
  SQL Server, 31
.NET Framework, **11-21**, **29-59**
  .NET Enterprise Servers, **31-32**
  advantages, 55-56
  ASP.NET, **248**
  assemblies, **443-46**
  asynchronous processing, **365-68**
  base classes, **49-51**
  C#, 11
  CLR, 12, **36-49**
  COM and, 54-55
  common type system, **41-44**
  compared to Windows DNA, 11, 55
  description, **35-36**
  disadvantages, 56
  DTC, 19
  Enterprise Services, **349-53**
  installation and configuration, **19-21**
    configuring remote IIS Server, **21**
    configuring samples, 20
    running samples from other machines, 20-21
  introduction, **30-31**
  libraries, **59**
  mapped network drives and, 16-19
  marshaling between .NET and COM, **432-33**
  metadata, **39-41**
  MSMQ, 19
  multi-language integration and support, **41**
  namespaces, **44-45**, **96-100**
  origins of .NET, **34-35**
  security, 16
  SQL Server, 19
  system requirements, **13-16**
    application server requirements, 14
    developer requirements, 15-16
    end user requirements, 14
    web server requirements, 14
  threads, **357-72**
  Visual Basic .NET, 11
  Visual Studio .NET, 12, **56-57**
  Web Forms, 36, **52-53**, **243-71**
  Web Services, 36, **271-77**
  Windows DNA and, 11, 55
  Windows Forms, 36, **51-52**, **137-85**
  XML, **54**
.NET Framework Configuration Tool, 393
.NET Framework Redistributable
  see .NET runtime
.NET remoting
  see remoting
.NET runtime, 13
  installation, **399**

A

Abort method, Thread class, 362
abstract base classes, **229-33**
  compared to interfaces, 230
abstract methods, 229
abstraction, 188
AcceptButton property, Form class, **144**
AcceptChanges method, ADO.NET DataRow class, 302
AcceptChanges method, ADO.NET DataTable class, 299
AccessibleDescription property, Control class, 156
AccessibleName property, Control class, 156
AccessibleRole property, Control class, 156
ActiveX controls
  Migration Wizard, 454
  Windows Forms and, **441-42**
    using ActiveX control, 442
Add method, Controls collection, 157
Add References dialog, 78-79
Add Web Reference option, 275
AddHandler method, 131
AddOwnedForm method, Form class, **152**
AddressOf operator, 132-33

ADO, 281, **330-31**, **439-40**
  compared to ADO.NET, 282-83, **330-31**
  pessimistic concurrency, 330
  RDS, 281
  Recordset object, 284
  server-side cursors, 331
  using ADO from Visual Basic .NET, **439-40**
ADO.NET
  accessing XML through ADO.NET, **326-28**
  business tier and, 330
  Command classes, 291-92
  compared to ADO, 282-83, **330-31**
  Connection classes, 290
  Constraints collection, 303
  data access, **297**
  data providers, **287-97**
  DataAdapter classes, 295-97
  DataColumn class, 300
  DataReader classes, 284, 293-95
  DataRelation class, 304-6
  DataRow class, 301-3
  DataSet class, 284-86, **298-316**
  DataTable class, 299-304
  DataView class, **317-19**
  Exception classes, **323-24**
  ForeignKeyConstraint class, 303
  history, 281
  introduction, **283-86**
  optimistic concurrency, 330
  stored procedures, **321-23**
  System.Data namespace, 284
  System.Data.OleDb namespace, 284
  System.Data.SQLClient namespace, 284
  UniqueConstraint class, 303
AdRotator server control, Web Forms, 258
aggregation
  has-a relationship, 214
aliases, APIs, **448-49**
aliases, namespaces, 99
AllowDBNull property, ADO.NET DataColumn class,
  300
Anchor property, Control class, 141, 154-55
AndAlso statements, 116
ANSI version API
  compared to Unicode version, 449-50
APIs, 446-52
  aliases, **448-49**
  calling simple API, **447-48**
  CoCreateGuid API, 450
  declaring API in Visual Basic .NET, 447-48
    DllImport attribute, 447
  hiding API interface, **449**
  MessageBox API, 447
  parameters, **450-52**
  PInvoke, **446-52**
    automatic choice between ANSI and Unicode API
    versions, 449-50
AppDomain class, System namespace
  AssemblyResolve event, 422
  CurrentDomain property, 422
  GetCurrentThreadID method, 357
  threads, 357
application configuration files
  launching .NET programs from URLs, 415
Application events, Web Forms, 253
Application property, Page class, 250

application server requirements, .NET, 14
arithmetic operators, 116
ArrayList class, System.Collections namespace, 113
arrays, 109-11
  declaring an array, **110**
  fixed arrays, **111**
  property arrays, 196
  ReDim statements, **110-11**
    Preserve keyword, 111
  zero based arrays, **109-10**
ASP
  Global.asa file, 253
  problems with, 32, **242-43**
ASP.NET, 248
  Global.asax file, 253
  rendering output as HTML, 248
  security, **269-70**
  server controls, **257-58**
  Setup Wizard, **411-14**
  System.Web.UI namespace, 248
  virtual directory, 402, 413
  Web.config file, **268-71**
  XCOPY deployment, **401-3**
assemblies, 45-46, 443-46
  creating assembly for COM, **444-45**
    ComClass attribute, 444
    exporting .NET assembly to COM, 445
    using assembly, **445-46**
  invoking .NET assemblies from COM, **443-46**
  manifests, 46
  modules, 46
  namespaces and, 96
  references, **445**
  types, 46
Assembly Binding Log Viewer, 392
Assembly Cache Viewer, 392
Assembly class, System.Reflection namespace
  CreateInstance method, 420
  EntryPoint property, 417
  LoadFrom method, 417, 420
Assembly Generation Utility, 392
Assembly Registration Tool, 392
AssemblyInfo file, 79-80
  AssemblyVersion attribute, 80
  Guid attribute, 80
AssemblyResolve event, AppDomain class, 422
AssemblyVersion attribute, 80
asynchronous processing, 365-68
  IP sockets, 368-72
  thread pool, 365
asynchronous queued messaging
  MSMQ, **353-57**
attributes, 134-35
  AssemblyVersion attribute, 80
  Guid attribute, 80
Authentication section
  Web.config file, 269-70
Authorization section
  Web.config file, 269-70
AutoIncrement property, ADO.NET DataColumn class,
  300
**AutoIncrementSeed property, ADO.NET DataColumn
  class**, 300
**AutoIncrementStep property, ADO.NET DataColumn
  class**, 300

automatic deployment, 414-26
  launching .NET programs from URLs, **415-18**
    Windows applications, **416-18**
  security, 414, **423-26**
  shell program for deployment, **419-23**
Autos window, 91
AutoScroll property, ScrollableControl class, 141
AutoScrollPosition property, ScrollableControl class,
  141

B

base classes, **49-51**, 64, 67, 213
  abstract base classes, **229-33**
  description, **49-51**
  MyBase keyword, 67, **223-24**
  Visual Basic .NET, **236-37**
BeginEdit method, ADO.NET DataRow class, 301
BeginReceive method, Socket class, 369, 370
bin directory, 391-95
binary compatibility
  designing COM components for .NET, **433-34**
binding, objects, 207-9
  early binding, 207
  late binding, 207
  Object data type, **207-8**
BitArray class, System.Collections namespace, 113
BitVector32 structure, System.Collections.Specialized
  namespace, 113
BizTalk Server, 31
block-level scope, 109
Body property, Message class, 355
Boolean data type, 43
Breakpoints window, 91
BringToFront method, Control class, 145
browser based applications
  compared to client applications, 51
buddy controls, 162
business tier
  ADO.NET and, 330
Button server control, Web Forms, 246, 257, 264
  Click event, 267
ByRef keyword, 126-27, 194
Byte data type, 43, 103, 104
bytecode
  see MSIL
ByVal keyword, 126-27
  passing by value default in Visual Basic .NET, 127

C

C#, 11
  compared to Visual Basic .NET, 11
  subclasses, **237-38**
Cab file
  deployment and installation, Visual Basic .NET, 404
Calendar server control, Web Forms, 258
Call Stack window, 91
CancelButton property, Form class, 144
CancelEdit method, ADO.NET DataRow class, 301
CanPauseAndContinue property, ServiceBase class,
  383

Caption property, Visual Basic controls, 169
casting, 208
Catch blocks, 121, 122
CCW (COM-callable wrapper), 443
  registering CCW, 443
Certificate Creation Utility, 394
Certificate Manager Utility, 393
Certificate Verification Utility, 394
Changed event, FileSystemWatcher class, 390
channels, remoting, 335
  specifying for host applications, 345
Char data type, 43, 104
CheckBox server control, Web Forms, 257
CheckBoxList server control, Web Forms, 258
Checked property, MenuItem class, 160
CheckedListBox controls, Windows Forms, 163
child classes
  see subclasses
child forms, MDI, 171
child windows, MDI, 171
Class keyword, 191
class libraries, 334-49
  C# class libraries, **237**
Class View window, 80-83
Class_Initialize event, Visual Basic, 197, 198
  compared to New method, 198
Class_Terminate event, Visual Basic, 197, 202
classes, 62-64, **189-97**
  see also objects
  abstract base classes, **229-33**
  base classes
    Visual Basic .NET, **236-37**
  creating, **190-91**
  events, **197, 212**
    shared events, **212**
  inheritance, 64, 188, **212-33**
    base classes, 64, 67, 213
    subclasses, 213
  Me keyword, **222-23**
  methods, **193-94**
    abstract methods, 229
    constructor methods, **67, 226**
    overloading, **194-95**
    overriding, **219-26**
    shadowed methods, **226-29**
    shared methods, **209-10**
    virtual methods, **220-22**
  MyClass keyword, **224-26**
  namespaces and, **191-92**
  nested classes, **192-93**
  properties, **195**
    default properties, **195-97**
  shared variables, **210-12**
Clear method, ADO.NET DataTable class, 300
Click event, Button server control, 267
client applications
  compared to browser based applications, 51
  configuration file, **348**
  cross-language inheritance, **238-39**
  implementing remoting, **346-49**
  programmatic configuration, **348**
client applications, COM, 445-46
  referencing .NET assembly, **445**
  using .NET assembly, **445-46**
ClientTarget property, Page class, 251
Clipboard Ring tab, Toolbox window, 85

Close method, ADO.NET Connection class, 290
CLR (Common Language Runtime), 12, 36-49
  memory management, 37, 47-49
  MSIL, 47
  multi-language integration and support, 38
  scalability, 39
  XCOPY deployment, 38-39
CoCreateGuid API, 450
Code Access Security Policy Utility, 393
code fragments and Toolbox window, 85-86
code groups
  security, 17
code-behind module, Web Forms, 250
Collection class, Microsoft.VisualBasic namespace, 113
CollectionBase class, System.Collections namespace, 115
collections, 112-15
  custom collections, 114-15
  System.Collections namespace, 113-14
  System.Collections.Specialized namespace, 113
COM
  see also COM+
  .NET Framework and, 54-55
  cross-language integration issues, 33
  DCOM, 440-41
  exporting .NET assembly to COM, 445
  interoperability, 430-46
    invoking .NET assemblies from COM, 443-46
    invoking COM components from .NET, 430-42
  limitations, 32-34
  marshaling between .NET and COM, 432-33
  Visual Basic in COM/DNA, 33-34
COM components, 188-89
  calling COM components from Visual Basic .NET, 434-38
    referencing a component, 435-36
    using component, 436-38
  client applications, 445-46
  creating a component, 434-35
  DCOM, 440-41
  designing COM components for .NET, 430-34
    binary compatibility, 433-34
    data types, 431
    garbage collection, 433
    type libraries, 432
  invoking components from .NET, 430-42
  marshaling between .NET and COM, 432-33
  using ActiveX controls in Windows Forms, 441-42
  using ADO from Visual Basic .NET, 439-40
COM+
  see also COM
  Enterprise Services and, 349
ComboBox controls, Windows Forms
  data binding, 324-25
    binding to collection of objects, 325
  DisplayMember property, 325
  ValueMember property, 325
COM-callable wrapper
  see CCW
ComClass attribute
  creating assembly for COM, 444
Command classes, ADO.NET, 291-92
  connected operations and, 292
  methods, 291
  properties, 291
  using stored procedures with commands, 321-22

command line options, 390-91
  vbc command, 390-91
Command window, 89
  compared to Visual Basic Immediate window, 89
CommandText property, ADO.NET Command class, 291
CommandType property, ADO.NET Command class, 321
comments, 88
  custom comments, 88
  TODO comments, 67, 88
Commerce Server, 31
Common Language Runtime
  see CLR
Common Language Runtime Debugger, 394
Common Language Runtime IL Assembler, 395
Common Language Runtime Minidump Tool, 395
Common Language Runtime XML Schema Definition Tool, 393
common type system, 41-44
  objects, 43
CommonDialog class, System.Windows.Forms namespace, 375
CompareValidator control, Web Forms, 259
Component class, System.ComponentModel namespace, 337
component trays, 76-77
composite controls, Windows Forms, 184
concurrency
  optimistic concurrency, 330
  pessimistic concurrency, 330
configuration files
  client applications, 348
  host applications, 343-45
  Web.config file, 341
connected operations
  Command class and, 292
Connection classes, ADO.NET, 290
  Close method, 290
  Open method, 290
Connection property, ADO.NET Command class, 291
console applications, 53, 372-75
  Console class, System namespace, 373-75
Console class, System namespace, 373-75
  OpenStandardError method, 374
  OpenStandardInput method, 374
  OpenStandardOutput method, 374
  Read method, 374
  ReadLine method, 374
  Write method, 373
  WriteLine method, 98, 373
constants, 108
Constraints collection, ADO.NET, 303
  ForeignKeyConstraint class, 303
  UniqueConstraint class, 303
construction, objects, 198-201
  controlling object creation, 199-201
  Main procedure, 201
  New method, 198-99
constructor methods, 67
  see also New method
  overriding, 226
ContainerControl class, System.Windows.Forms namespace, 141
ContextMenu controls, Windows Forms, 161-62

ContextUtil class, System.EnterpriseServices namespace, 352-53
  SetAbort method, 353
  SetComplete method, 353
control arrays, Visual Basic, 169-70
Control class, System.Windows.Forms namespace, 140-41
  AccessibleDescription property, 156
  AccessibleName property, 156
  AccessibleRole property, 156
  Anchor property, 154-55
  BringToFront method, 145
  building new control from Control class, **185**
  Dock property, 155
  Height property, 145
  Left property, 145
  Location property, 145
  SendToBack method, 145
  Size property, 145
  Top property, 145
  Width property, 145
controlling object creation, 199-201
  Visual Basic compared to Visual Basic .NET, 199
Controls collection, Form class, 157
  Add method, 157
controls, Web Forms
  see server controls
controls, Windows Forms, 153-70
  adding a control at run time, **156-57**
  CheckedListBox controls, 163
  ComboBox controls, 324-25
  compared to Visual Basic controls, 157-58
  custom controls, **182-85**
  data binding, 169, **324-26**
    binding to any property of any control, 326
    binding to collection of objects, 325
  DataGrid controls, 168
  DateTimePicker controls, **163-64**
  default names, 169
  extender provider controls, **166-68**
  GroupBox controls, **164**
  invisible controls, **143-44**
  Items collection, 169
  LinkLabel controls, **162**
  ListBox controls, 324-25
  locked controls, **144**
  menu controls, **158-62**
  MonthCalendar controls, **164**
  multiple controls, **146**
  Panel controls, **165**
  PictureBox controls, 169
  positioning and layout, **145-46**
  PrintDocument controls, 168
  SelectedIndex property, 169
  setting scope for controls, **156**
  Text property, 169
  TrayIcon controls, **165**
  UpDown controls, 162-63
ControlToValidate property, validation controls, 259
Create method, MessageQueue class, 354
Created event, FileSystemWatcher class, 390
CreateInstance method, Assembly class, 420
CreateObject method, Visual Basic, 198
cross-language inheritance, 236-39
  C# subclass, **237-38**
  client application, **238-39**
  Visual Basic .NET base class, **236-37**

cross-language integration issues, 33
  multi-language integration and support, 38
CType statements, 107, 208-9
  casting, 208
  Object data type and, 107
Currency data type, 104
  not available in Visual Basic .NET, 104
CurrentDomain property, AppDomain class, 422
CurrentThread property, Thread class, 362
custom collections, 114-15
custom comments, 88
custom controls, Web Forms, 260-63
  extending existing control, 263
  Render method, 261-63
custom controls, Windows Forms, 182-85
  building new control from Control class, **185**
  composite controls, **184**
  inheritance from existing control, **183-84**
CustomValidator control, Web Forms, 259

D

DAO, 281
data access, 281-331
  accesssing XML through ADO.NET, **326-28**
  ADO, **330-31**
  ADO.NET, **297**
  data binding, **324-26**
  data providers, **287-97**
  DataSet class, 285-86, **298-316**
  DataView class, **317-19**
  early history, **281-82**
  Exception classes, **323-24**
  Migration Wizard, **454**
  stored procedures, **321-23**
  typed DataSets, **319-21**
Data Access Objects
  see DAO
data binding, 324-26
  Web Forms, 263-64
  Windows Forms controls, 169, **324-26**
    binding to any property of any control, 326
    binding to collection of objects, 325
data providers, ADO.NET, 287-97
  Command classes, 291-92
  Connection classes, 290
  DataAdapter classes, 295-97
  DataReader classes, 293-95
  different providers cannot be mixed, 289
  OLE DB data provider, 287, 288
  SQL Server data provider, 287, 288
  table of classes, 288
  using wizards with, 289
data types, 102-7
  arrays, **109-11**
  collections, **112-15**
  common type system, **41-44**
  designing COM components for .NET, **431**
  reference types, **41-43**
  table of primitive data types, 43-44
  user defined types, **112**
  value types, **41-43**

DataAdapter classes, ADO.NET, 295-97
creating DataSet using DataAdapter, 295-97
DeleteCommand property, 322
Fill method, 295
InsertCommand property, 322
SelectCommand property, 323
Update method, 323
UpdateCommand property, 323
using stored procedures with DataAdapters, 322
DataAdapter Wizard
creating DataSet using DataAdapter Wizard, **309-16**
Web Forms, 315-16
Windows Forms, 310-15
DataColumn class, ADO.NET, 300
properties, 300
DataGrid controls, Windows Forms, 168
creating DataSet using DataAdapter Wizard, 312
DataGrid server control, Web Forms, 258
creating DataSet using DataAdapter Wizard, 315
DataList server control, Web Forms, 258
DataReader classes, ADO.NET, 293-95
creating, 293-95
guidelines for using, 329
Read method, 293
replacing Recordset by, 284
DataRelation class, ADO.NET, 304-6
DataRow class, ADO.NET, 301-3
adding rows to datatable, 306
Delete method, 308
deleting rows from datatable, 307-8
different versions of data, 302-3
finding row in datatable, 307
GetChildRows method, 305
Item property, 301
methods for changing data, 301-2
RowState property, 308
DataSet class, ADO.NET
accessing XML through ADO.NET, **326-28**
adding rows to datatable, 306
creating DataSet manually, **308-9**
creating DataSet using DataAdapter, 295-97
creating DataSet using DataAdapter Wizard, **309-16**
data access, 285-86
DataRelation class, 304-6
DataTable class, 299-304
deleting rows from datatable, 307-8
description, 284-85, **298-306**
finding row in datatable, 307
guidelines for using, 329
ReadXML method, 326
replacing Recordset by, 284
typed DataSets, **319-21**
using, **306-8**
WriteXML method, 327
DataTable class, ADO.NET, 299-304
adding rows to datatable, 306
Constraints collection, 303
DataColumn class, 300
DataRow class, 301-3
deleting rows from datatable, 307-8
finding row in datatable, 307
methods, 299
properties, 299
DataType property, ADO.NET DataColumn class, 300

DataView class, ADO.NET, 317-19
RowFilter property, 317
RowStateFilter property, 317
Sort property, 318
Date data type, 44
DateTimePicker controls, Windows Forms, 163-64
DCOM, 334-36, **440-41**
compared to remoting, 334-36
using DCOM in .NET applications, **440-41**
Debug class, System.Diagnostics namespace, 89
WriteLine method, 89
Debug configuration, Visual Studio .NET, 398-99
compared to Release configuration, 398
debugging
Breakpoints window, 91
Call Stack window, **91**
IDE, **90-91**
value display windows, 91
Watch window, 91
Decimal data type, 44, 104
new in Visual Basic .NET, 104
declarations
arrays, **110**
variables, **68**
deep serialization, 337
Default keyword, 120, 196
default properties, **120**, **195-97**
DefaultItem property, MenuItem class, 160
DefType statements, 132
not available in Visual Basic .NET, 132
Delegate keyword, 133
delegates, **132-34**
threads, 359
Delete method, ADO.NET DataRow class, 308
DeleteCommand property, ADO.NET DataAdapter class, 322
Deleted event, FileSystemWatcher class, 390
deployment and installation, Visual Basic .NET, **397-427**
automatic deployment, **414-26**
Cab file, 404
Setup Wizard, 404
Web applications, **411-14**
Windows applications, **405-11**
web server deployment, 404
Windows System Installer, 404
XCOPY deployment, **400-403**
dereferencing, objects, **206**
designers
see graphical designers
DesktopBounds property, Form class, 145
DesktopLocation property, Form class, 146
deterministic finalization, 48, 202
developer requirements, .NET, 15-16
dialog boxes, Windows Forms, 146-50
DialogResult property, Form class, 148-50
DictionaryBase class, System.Collections namespace, 115
direct addressing, namespaces, 97-98
disabling state management, Web Forms, 254
DispayMember property, ComboBox controls, 325
DispayMember property, ListBox controls, 325
Display property, validation controls, 260
Dispose method, 67-68, 197, **203-12**
IDisposable interface, 203

Distributed Transaction Coordinator
  see DTC
DLL Hell, 33
DllImport attribute, 447
  aliasing APIs, 448
DLLs, **334-49**
  Migration Wizard, 454
  registration issues, 33
DNA
  see Windows DNA
Dock property, Control class, 141, 155
docking windows, IDE, **73-74**
DOM (Document Object Model)
  accessing XML through DOM, 328
DomainUpDown controls, 163
Double data type, 44, 103
DropDownList server control, Web Forms, 258
DTC (Distributed Transaction Coordinator), 19, 349
Dynamic Help window, **83-84**

E

early binding, 207
  compared to late binding, 207
Elapsed event, Timer class, 384, 385
Enabled property, MenuItem class, 160
Enabled property, Timer class, 384
Enabled property, validation controls, 260
EnableViewState property, Page class, 255
EnableViewState property, Web Forms controls, 254
encapsulation, 188
End Class statements, 191
end user requirements, .NET, 14
EndEdit method, ADO.NET DataRow class, 302
EndReceive method, Socket class, 370
Enterprise Servers
  see .NET Enterprise Servers
Enterprise Services, **349-53**
  COM+ and, 349
  System.EnterpriseServices namespace, 349
  Transactional attribute, 349
  transactional components, **349-53**
EntryPoint property, Assembly class, 417
Equals method, Object class, 43
Err class
  GetException method, 123
error handling
  exception handling, 121
  structured error handling, **120-25**
error messages, Web Forms, 260
ErrorPage property, Page class, 251
ErrorProvider controls, Windows Forms, **167**
errors
  Exception class, **123**
  On Error Goto statements, **123-25**
  On Error Resume Next statements, **125**
  structured error handling, **120-25**
  Try blocks, **121-25**
    Catch blocks, **121**, **122**
    Exit Try statements, **122-23**
    Finally blocks, 121-22
Errors collection, ADO.NET Exception class, 323

event handlers, **69-71**, **129-30**
  AddHandler method, **131**
  Handles clause, 71, 130
  multiple events, **130-31**
  parameters, 70
  syntax, 71
  Visual Basic compared to Visual Basic .NET, 70, 71
  Web Forms, performance issues, 252
Event keyword, 197
EventLog class, System.Diagnostics namespace, 383
events, **69-71**, **129-30**, 197
  Application events, 253
  Handles keyword, 71, 130
  inheritance, **212**
  multiple events, **130-31**
  non-postback events, 252
  postback events, 252
  RaiseEvent statements, 129, 197
  Session events, 253
  shared events, **212**
  Web Forms, **251-55**
  WithEvents keyword, 129
Exception class, System namespace, **123**, 323
Exception classes, ADO.NET, **323-24**
  Errors collection, 323
exception handling
  Exception class, **123**
Exchange Server, 31
ExecuteNonQuery method, ADO.NET Command class, 291, 322
ExecuteReader method, ADO.NET Command class, 291, 322
ExecuteScalar method, ADO.NET Command class, 291, 322
ExecuteXMLReader method, ADO.NET Command class, 292
Exists method, MessageQueue class, 354
Exit Try statements, **122-23**
extender provider controls, Windows Forms, **166-68**
  ErrorProvider controls, **167**
  HelpProvider controls, **166-67**
  ToolTip controls, 166
  using, 167-68
extensions, file names, **78**

F

File Signing Utility, 394
FileSystemWatcher class, System.IO namespace, 389-90
  Changed event, 390
  Created event, 390
  Deleted event, 390
  Renamed event, 390
Fill method, ADO.NET DataAdapter class, 295
Finalize method, 197, **203**
Finally blocks, 121-22
fixed arrays, **111**
floating point numbers, **103-4**
ForeignKeyConstraint class, ADO.NET, 303

Form class, System.Windows.Forms namespace, 64, **141-42**
    AcceptButton property, **144**
    AddOwnedForm method, **152**
    CancelButton property, **144**
    Controls collection, 157
    DesktopBounds property, 145
    DesktopLocation property, 146
    DialogResult property, **148-50**
    MaximumSize property, 146
    MinimumSize property, 146
    Opacity property, 151
    OwnedForms property, **153**
    Owner property, **152**
    Region property, 150-51
    RemoveOwnedForm method, 153
    ShowDialog method, **148**
    TopMost property, **153**
    TransparencyKey property, 152
forms, 62-69
    constructor methods, **67**
    Dispose method, 67-68
    form-based applications and Migration Wizard, 454
    inheritance, 64
    InitializeComponent method, **68-69**
    Visual Basic compared to Visual Basic .NET, 63
    Visual Basic forms, **142-57**
    Visual Studio .NET IDE, **65-69**
    Web Forms, 142, **243-71**
    Windows Forms, **137-85**
        MDI forms, **170-73**
        owned forms, **152-53**
FormsAuthentication class, System.Web.Security namespace
    RedirectFromLoginPage method, 270
Friend keyword, 189, 193, 194, 217
Friend scope, Windows Forms controls, 156
fully qualified names, 97
Function keyword, 193
functions
    see procedures

G

garbage collection, 202-3
    designing COM components for .NET, **433**
    nondeterministic finalization, 202
GDI+, **176-82**
    Windows Forms, **178-80**
generalization
    see inheritance
Get blocks, 119
    read only properties, 119
    scope, 119
GetChildRows method, ADO.NET DataRow class, 305
GetCurrentThreadID method, AppDomain class, 357
GetErrors method, ADO.NET DataTable class, 300
GetException method, Err class, 123
GetHashCode method, Object class, 43
GetObjectContext function, Visual Basic, 352
GetType method, Object class, 43
Global Assembly Cache Utility, 392
global variables, **212**
Global.asa file, ASP, 253

Global.asax file, ASP.NET, 253
Gosub keyword, **131-32**
    not available in Visual Basic .NET, 131
graphical designers, 75-77
    component tray, **76-77**
    tabbed navigation, 76
Graphics class, System.Drawing namespace, **177-79**
    Windows Forms, **178-80**
Graphics Device Interface
    see GDI+
graphics paths
    changing shape of form, 150
Graphics property, PrintPageEventArgs object, 378
GraphicsPath class, System.Drawing.Drawing2D namespace, 181
grid layout, Web Forms, 255-56
GroupBox controls, Windows Forms, **164**
Guid attribute, 80
Guid class, System namespace, 450
    NewGuid method, 450
GUID data type, 44

H

Handles clause, 71, 130
    multiple events, **130-31**
has-a relationship
    aggregation, 214
    compared to is-a relationship, 214
HasErrors property, ADO.NET DataTable class, 299
Hashtable class, System.Collections namespace, 113
HasMorePages property, PrintPageEventArgs object, 379
HasVersion method, ADO.NET DataRow class, 303
Height property, Control class, 145
HelloWorld project, **21-26**, 62-71
HelpProvider controls, Windows Forms, **166-67**
home page, IDE, **72-73**
host applications
    configuration file, **343-45**
    implementing remoting, **342-46**
    programmatic configuration, **345-46**
    specifying channels, 345
    testing, **346**
Host Integration Server, 31
HTML forms
    compared to Web Forms, 243
HTML template, Web Forms, 249-50
HtmlTextWriter class, System.Web.UI namespace, 263
HTTP protocol, 335
    limitations, 32
HttpResponse class, System.Web namespace, 262
    Output property, 262
HybridDictionary class, System.Collections.Specialized namespace, 113
Hyperlink server control, Web Forms, 258

I

IDE (Integrated Development Environment), 65-69, 72-91
  Class View window, **80-83**
  Command window, **89**
  debugging, **90-91**
  docking windows, **73-74**
  Dynamic Help window, **83-84**
  graphical designers, **75-77**
  home page, **72-73**
  macros, **90**
  Output window, **88-89**
  Properties window, **80**
  regions, 65-68
  Server Explorer window, 77, **86-87**
  Solution Explorer window, **77-79**
  Task List window, **87-88**
  Toolbox window, **84-86**
IDisposable interface
  Dispose method, 203
If...Then statements
  short-circuiting, **116-17**
IIS
  configuring remote IIS Server, **21**
  implementing remoting, 340-41
    Web.config file, 341
IL (Intermediate Language)
  see MSIL
Image controls, Visual Basic controls, 169
Image server control, Web Forms, 257, 258
ImageButton server control, Web Forms, 258
Immediate window, Visual Basic, 89
  compared to Command window, 89
implementation inheritance, 213
  compared to interface inheritance, 213
  is-a relationship, 213
Implements keyword, 189, 233, 234-36
Imports keyword, 79, **98**
inheritance, 64, 188, **212-33**
  base classes, 64, 67, 213
    MyBase keyword, 67
  constructor methods, **226**
  cross-language inheritance, **236-39**
  events, **212**
  implementation inheritance, 213
  Me keyword, **222-23**
  MyBase keyword, **223-24**
  MyClass keyword, **224-26**
  overriding methods, **219-26**
  preventing inheritance, **216-17**
  scope, **217-18**
  shadowed methods, **226-29**
  subclasses, 213
    creating subclasses, 214-16
    overloading methods in subclasses, **218-19**
  virtual methods, **220-22**
  visual inheritance, **239**
    Windows Forms, **173-74**
  Windows Forms custom controls, **183-84**
inheritance picker
  Windows Forms, **174-76**
Inherits keyword, 25, 64, 189, 216, 232
InitializeComponent method, **68-69**

InsertCommand property, ADO.NET DataAdapter class, 322
installation, Visual Basic .NET
  see deployment and installation, Visual Basic .NET
Installer class, System.Configuration.Install
  namespace, 385
Installer Utility, 392
  installing service, 387
installutil.exe
  see Installer Utility
Integer data type, 44, 103
interface inheritance
  see also multiple interfaces
  compared to implementation inheritance, 213
Interface keyword, 233
interfaces, **233-36**
  compared to abstract base classes, 230
  implementing an interface, **234-35**
  multiple interfaces, **235-36**
  overloading methods, **234**
  user interfaces, **51-54**
Intermediate Language (IL)
  see MSIL
Internet, **58**
  see also Web Forms, Web Services
Internet Information Services
  see IIS
Internet Security and Acceleration Server, 31
interoperability
  APIs, **446-52**
  COM, **430-46**
    invoking .NET assemblies from COM, **443-46**
    invoking COM components from .NET, **430-42**
    marshaling between .NET and COM, **432-33**
  using ActiveX controls in Windows Forms, **441-42**
  using ADO from Visual Basic .NET, **439-40**
Interval property, Timer class, 384
invisible controls, Windows Forms, **143-44**
Invoke method
  calling delegates, 133, 358
  MethodInfo class, 417
  Windows Forms, 358
IP socket, asynchronous processing, 368-72
is-a relationship
  compared to has-a relationship, 214
  implementation inheritance, 213
IsMissing statements, 127-28
  not available for Visual Basic .NET, 128
Isolated Storage Utility, 392
IsPostBack property, Page class, 251
IsValid property, Page class, 251
Item property, ADO.NET DataRow class, 301
Items collection, Windows Forms controls, 169

J

JIT (just-in-time) compilers, 47

L

Label server control, Web Forms, 245, 246, 257, 264
late binding, 207
  compared to early binding, 207
  Reflection, *208*

LBound statements, 110
Left property, Control class, 145
libraries, 59
  class libraries, **334-49**
  type libraries, **432**
linear layout, Web Forms, 255
LinkButton server control, Web Forms, 258
LinkLabel controls, Windows Forms, **162**
List collection, Visual Basic controls, 169
ListBox controls, Windows Forms
  data binding, 324-25
    binding to collection of objects, 325
  DisplayMember property, 325
  ValueMember property, 325
ListBox server control, Web Forms, 257
ListDictionary class, System.Collections.Specialized
  namespace, 114
ListIndex property, Visual Basic controls, 169
Literal server control, Web Forms, 258
Load event, UserControl class, 142
LoadControl method, Page class, 251
LoadFrom method, Assembly class, 417, 420
Locals window, 91
Location property, Control class, 145
location transparency, 440
locked controls, Windows Forms, **144**
Long data type, 44, 103

M

macros, Visual Studio .NET, **90**
Main procedure, **201**
MainMenu controls, Windows Forms, **158-59**
managed code
  see MSIL
Management Strongly Typed Class Generator, 395
manifests, 46
mapped network drives
  .NET Framework and, 16-19
  security, 16
MarginBounds property, PrintPageEventArgs object, 379
Marshal class, System.Runtime.InteropServices
  namespace, 433
  ReleaseComObject method, 433, 438, 440, 441
MarshalByRefObject class, System namespace, 338, 339
MarshalByValueComponent class, System.ComponentModel namespace, 338
Math class, System namespace
  Sqrt method, 50
MaximumSize property, Form class, 146
MDI forms, **170-73**
  child forms, **171**
  child windows, 171
  example in Visual Basic .NET, **171-73**
  parent forms, **170-71**
MDIList property, MenuItem class, 160
Me keyword, **222-23**
memory management, 37, **47-49**

menu controls, Windows Forms, **158-62**
  ContextMenu controls, 161-62
  MainMenu controls, **158-59**
MenuItem class, System.Windows.Forms namespace, 158-61
MergeOrder property, MenuItem class, 160
MergeType property, MenuItem class, 160
Message class, System.Messaging namespace, **355-57**
  Body property, 355
Message Queuing Services
  see MSMQ
MessageBox API, 447
MessageBox class, System.Windows.Forms namespace, 71
MessageQueue class, System.Messaging namespace, 354
  Create method, 354
  Exists method, 354
  Receive method, 355-56
  Send method, 355
messages
  see MSMQ
metadata, **39-41**
  multi-language integration and support, 41
  Reflection and, 40
method signature, 194
MethodInfo class, System.Reflection namespace
  Invoke method, 417
methods, **193-94**
  see also procedures
  abstract methods, 229
  constructor methods, **67**, **226**
  Dispose method, 67-68
  InitializeComponent method, **68-69**
  overloading methods, **194-95**
    interfaces, **234**
    subclasses, overloading methods in, **218-19**
  overriding methods, **219-26**
  parameters, 194
    optional parameters, 198
  scope, **217-18**
  shadowed methods, **226-29**
    arbitrary shadowing, 228-29
  shared methods, **209-10**
  virtual methods, **220-22**
Microsoft .NET Framework IL Disassembler, 395
Microsoft CLR Debugger, 394
Microsoft.Data.ODBC namespace
  ODBC data provider, 287
Microsoft.VisualBasic namespace, **100**
  Collection class, **113**
  MsgBox class, 71
middle tier components, **334-57**
  Enterprise Services, **349-53**
  remoting, **334-49**
Migration Wizard, **452-54**
  ActiveX DLL projects, 454
  data access, 454
  form-based applications, 454
  syntax changes, 454
  upgrade report, 453-54
MinimumSize property, Form class, 146
modules, 46
MonthCalendar controls, Windows Forms, **164**
MsgBox class, Microsoft.VisualBasic namespace, 71

MSIL (Microsoft Intermediate Language), 39, 47, 56
MSMQ, 19, 334, **353-57**
  asynchronous queued messaging, **353-57**
  messages
    receiving a message, **355-57**
    sending a message, **355**
  queues, **354-55**
  System.Messaging namespace, 19, **353-57**
MTS (Microsoft Transaction Server), 349-50
multi-language integration and support, 38, **41**
  metadata, 41
multiple controls, Windows Forms, 146
multiple events, **130-31**
multiple interfaces, **235-36**
  see also interface inheritance
multiple variables
  declaring variables, 107
MustInherit keyword, **229**
MustOverride keyword, **229**
MyBase keyword, 67, **223-24**
MyClass keyword, **224-26**

N

NameObjectCollectionBase class,
  System.Collections.Specialized namespace, 115
Namespace keyword, **100**
namespaces, 44-45, **96-100**
  aliases, **99**
  assemblies and, 96
  classes and, **191-92**
  creating a namespace, **99-100**
  direct addressing, **97-98**
  Imports keyword, **98**
  root namespaces, **99-100**, 192
  using, **97-99**
NameValueCollection class,
  System.Collections.Specialized namespace, 114
Native Image Generator Tool, 392
Navigate method, Page class, 251
nested classes, **192-93**
nested Try blocks, 124
New keyword
  using to declare object variable, 108
New method, 67, 197, **198-99**, **204-6**
  see also constructor methods
  compared to Class_Initialize event, Visual Basic, 198
NewGuid method, Guid class, 450
NewRow method, ADO.NET DataTable class, 300, 306
nondeterministic finalization, 202
non-postback events, Web Forms, 252
  compared to postback events, 252
NonSerializable attribute, 337
NotifyIcon controls, Windows Forms, **165**
NotInheritable keyword, 216-17
NotOverridable keyword, 220
NumericUpDown controls, Windows Forms, 163

O

Object class, System namespace, 43, 106
  Equals method, 43
  GetHashCode method, 43
  GetType method, 43
  RCW derived from, 432
  ToString method, 43
Object data type, 106, **207-8**
  CType statements and, 107
  Option Strict statements and, 106, 107
  replacing Variant type with Object type, 106
  storing object references, 107
object oriented programming, **187-239**
  abstraction, 188
  classes, **189-97**
    events, **197**, **212**
    methods, **193-94**
    properties, **195**
  encapsulation, 188
  inheritance, 188, **212-33**
    cross-language inheritance, **236-39**
    visual inheritance, **239**
  interfaces, **233-36**
  polymorphism, 188
objects, 43, **197-212**, **204-9**
  see also classes
  binding, **207-9**
  construction, **198-201**
    controlling object creation, 199-201
    Main procedure, **201**
    New method, **198-99**
  declaration and instantiation, 204-6
  dereferencing, **206**
  New statements, **204-6**
  references, **336-39**
  Reflection, **208**
  remote access, **336-39**
    default of no remote access, 336-37
    passing objects by reference, 338-39
    passing objects by value, 337-38
  termination, **202-12**
    Dispose method, **203-12**
    Finalize method, **203**
    garbage collection, **202-3**
ODBC data provider
  Microsoft.Data.ODBC namespace, 287
OLE DB data provider, 287, 288
  System.Data.OleDb namespace, 287
  table of classes, 288
  using wizards with, 289
OleDbCommand class
  see Command classes, ADO.NET
OleDbConnection class
  see Connection classes, ADO.NET
OleDBDataAdapter class
  see DataAdapter classes, ADO.NET
OleDbDataReader class
  see DataReader classes, ADO.NET
OleDbException class
  see Exception classes, ADO.NET

On Error Goto statements, 123-25
Resume statements, 124-25
On Error Resume Next statements, 125
compared to structured error handling, 125
OnContinue method, ServiceBase class, 383
OnLoad method, UserControl class, 142
OnPause method, ServiceBase class, 383
OnStart method, ServiceBase class, 383
OnStop method, ServiceBase class, 383
Opacity property, Form class, 151
Open method, ADO.NET Connection class, 290
OpenStandardError method, Console class, 374
OpenStandardInput method, Console class, 374
OpenStandardOutput method, Console class, 374
operators
arithmetic operators, 116
optimistic concurrency, ADO.NET, 330
Option Base statements
not available in Visual Basic .NET, 101
Option Compare statements, 101
Option Explicit statements, 101
Option keyword, 101
Option Strict statements, 101, 106, 207
new in Visual Basic .NET, 102
Object data type and, 106, 107
Optional keyword, 128, 198
optional parameters, 127-28, 198
OrElse statements, 116
Output property, HttpResponse class, 262
Output window, 88-89
overloading methods, 194-95
interfaces, 234
method signature, 194
subclasses, overloading methods in, 218-19
Overridable keyword, 219, 224
Overrides keyword, 220
overriding methods, 219-26
compared to shadowed methods, 226
constructor methods, 226
owned forms, 152-53
OwnedForms property, Form class, 153
Owner property, Form class, 152
OwnerDraw property, MenuItem class, 161

P

Page class, System.Web.UI namespace, 250-51
EnableViewState property, 255
PageSettings class, System.Drawing.Printing namespace, 381-82
PageSetupDialog class, System.Windows.Forms namespace, 381-82
ShowDialog method, 382
Paint event, Form class, 178, 179
Panel controls, Windows Forms, 165
parameters
APIs, 450-52
event handlers, 70
methods, 194
optional parameters, 127-28, 198
procedures, 126-28
Parameters collection, ADO.NET Command class, 321

parent classes
see base classes
parent forms, MDI, 170-71
child windows, 171
parentheses
required on procedure calls, 126
passing objects by reference, 338-39
passing objects by value, 337-38
Serializable attribute, 337
serialization, 337
path variable
adding deployment application to path variable, 418
Permissions View Utility, 394
pessimistic concurrency, ADO, 330
PEVerify Tool, 394
PictureBox controls, Windows Forms controls, 169
PInvoke (Platform Invocation Services), 446-52
automatic choice between ANSI and Unicode API versions, 449-50
calling simple API, 447-48
Point structure, System.Drawing namespace, 177
polymorphism, 188
pop-up menus, 161
postback events, Web Forms, 252
compared to non-postback events, 252
Preserve keyword, 111
PrimaryKey property, ADO.NET DataTable class, 299
primitive data types, table of, 43-44
Print method, PrintDocument class, 376, 377
PrintDialog class, System.Windows.Forms namespace, 380
ShowDialog method, 381
PrintDocument class, System.Drawing.Printing namespace, 375, 377
Print method, 376, 377
PrintPage method, 376, 377
PrintDocument controls, Windows Forms, 168
Printer object, Visual Basic, 375
printing, 375-82
example, 377
implementing, 376-82
print preview, 376
rendering output, 377-80
System.Drawing.Printing namespace, 375
System.Windows.Forms namespace, 375
PrintPage method, PrintDocument class, 376, 377
PrintPageEventArgs object, System.Drawing.Printing namespace, 378
Graphics property, 378
HasMorePages property, 379
MarginBounds property, 379
Private keyword, 193, 217
Private scope, Windows Forms controls, 156
procedures, 126-29
see also methods
delegates, 132-34
Main procedure, 201
names of procedures, 117
parameters, 126-28
optional parameters, 127-28
parentheses required on calls, 126
Return keyword, 128-29
programming models, Visual Basic .NET, 58

project groups, Visual Basic, 77
  compared to solutions, 77
projects
  AssemblyInfo file, 79-80
  references, **78-79**
properties, **195**
  default properties, **120**, **195-97**
  Get blocks, 119
  read only properties, **119**
  scope, 119, **217-18**
  Set blocks, 119
  write only properties, **120**
Properties window, **80**
property arrays, **196**
Property Get routines, **195**
Property Let routines, **195**
  not available in Visual Basic .NET, 119
Property Set routines
  not available in Visual Basic .NET, 118
Protected Friend keyword, **218**
Protected keyword, 194, **218**
Protected scope, Windows Forms controls, 156
Public keyword, 194, 217
Public scope, Windows Forms controls, 156
pure virtual functions
  see abstract methods

Q

quantum, threads, 364
Queue class, System.Collections namespace, 113
queues, MSMQ, **354-55**

R

RadioButtonList server control, Web Forms, 258
RadioCheck property, MenuItem class, 161
RaiseEvent statements, 129, 197
RangeValidator control, Web Forms, 259, 265
RCW (runtime-callable wrapper), 432
  derived from Object class, System namespace, 432
  referencing COM component, 436
RDO, 281
RDS (Remote Data Services), 281, 335
Read method, ADO.NET DataReader class, 293
Read method, Console class, 374
read only properties, **119**
ReadLine method, Console class, 374
ReadOnly keyword, 119
ReadOnly property, ADO.NET DataColumn class, 300
ReadOnlyCollectionBase class, System.Collections
  namespace, 115
ReadXML method, ADO.NET DataSet class, 326
Receive method, MessageQueue class, 355-56
Recordset object, ADO
  replaced by DataSet and DataReader, 284
ReDim statements, **110-11**
  Preserve keyword, 111
RedirectFromLoginPage method, FormsAuthentication
  class, 270
reference types, **41-43**
  compared to value types, 42

references
  .NET assemblies, **445**
  COM components, **435-36**
  objects, **336-39**
  projects, **78-79**
Reflection, **208**
  metadata and, 40
  System.Reflection namespace, 208
Region property, Form class, 150-51
regions, 65-68
RegisterWellKnownClientType method,
  RemotingConfiguration class, 349
RegisterWellKnownServiceType method,
  RemotingConfiguration class, 346
regular expressions, 259-60
RegularExpressionValidator control, Web Forms, 259,
  266
  regular expressions, 259-60
RejectChanges method, ADO.NET DataRow class, 302
RejectChanges method, ADO.NET DataTable class,
  300
Release configuration, Visual Studio .NET, **398-99**
  compared to Debug configuration, 398
ReleaseComObject method, Marshal class, 433, 438,
  440, 441
Remote Data Objects
  see RDO
Remote Data Services
  see RDS
remoting, **334-49**
  channels, 335
  client applications, **346-49**
    configuration file, **348**
    programmatic configuration, **348**
  compared to DCOM, 334-36
  host applications, **342-46**
    configuration file, **343-45**
    programmatic configuration, **345-46**
    testing, **346**
  implementing remoting, **339-49**
    IIS, 340-41
  System.Runtime.Remoting namespace, 342, 346
RemotingConfiguration class,
  System.Runtime.Remoting namespace
  RegisterWellKnownClientType method, 349
  RegisterWellKnownServiceType method, 346
RemoveOwnedForm method, Form class, 153
Renamed event, FileSystemWatcher class, 390
Render method, Web Forms custom controls, 261-63
Repeater server control, Web Forms, 258
Request property, Page class, 251
RequiredFieldValidator control, Web Forms, 246, 259
reserved words, **117**
Resize event, Visual Basic forms, 154
Resource File Generator Utility, 393
Response property, Page class, 251
Resume statements, **124-25**
  not available in structured error handling, 124
Return keyword, **128-29**
  new in Visual Basic .NET, 128
root namespaces, **99-100**, 192
RowFilter property, ADO.NET DataView class, 317
RowState property, ADO.NET DataRow class, 308
RowStateFilter property, ADO.NET DataView class,
  317

469

RunInstaller attribute
  installing service, 385
runtime-callable wrapper
  see RCW

S

Sbyte data type, 44
scalability, **39**
scope
  Friend keyword, 217
  inheritance, **217-18**
  Private keyword, 217
  properties, **119**
  Protected Friend keyword, **218**
  Protected keyword, **218**
  Public keyword, 217
  variables, **109**
    block-level scope, 109
  Windows Forms controls, **156**
ScrollableControl class, System.Windows.Forms namespace, **141**
Secure Sockets Layer (SSL), 277
security
  automatic deployment, 414, **423-26**
    launching .NET programs from URLs, 415
  code groups, 17
  mapped network drives, 16
  running samples from other machines, 20
  table of security zones, 423
  Web Services, **277**
  Web.config file, **269-70**
Secutil Utility, 394
Select method, ADO.NET DataTable class, 307
SelectCommand property, ADO.NET DataAdapter class, 323
SelectedIndex property, Windows Forms controls, 169
Send method, MessageQueue class, 355
SendToBack method, Control class, 145
Serializable attribute
  passing objects by value, 337
  shell program for deployment and, 421-22
serialization, 337
  deep serialization, 337
  shallow serialization, 337
server controls, Web Forms, 52-53, 248, **256-63**
  ASP.NET, **257-58**
  Button control, 246, 264
  custom controls, **260-63**
  EnableViewState property, 254
  Label control, 245, 264
  list of controls, 257-58
  reasons for using, 256
  TextBox control, 246, 264
  validation controls, **258-60**
Server Explorer window, 77, **86-87**
Server property, Page class, 251
server-side cursors, ADO, 331
ServiceBase class, System.ServiceProcess namespace, 383
  CanPauseAndContinue property, 383
  OnContinue method, 383
  OnPause method, 383
  OnStart method, 383
  OnStop method, 383

ServicedComponent class, System.EnterpriseServices namespace, 349
Services Registration Tool, 392
Session events, Web Forms, 253
Session property, Page class, 251
sessionState section
  Web.config file, 271
Set blocks, 119
  scope, 119
  write only properties, 120
Set keyword, **117-19**, 206
  not available in Visual Basic .NET, 117, 206
Set Registry Utility, 394
SetAbort method, ContextUtil class, 353
SetComplete method, ContextUtil class, 353
Setup Wizard, 404
  Web applications, **411-14**
    building project, 413
    running setup program, **413-14**
    setting project properties, 412
    using Setup Wizard, **412-13**
  Windows applications, **405-11**
    building project, 408-9
    icon, adding, 408
    running setup program, **410-11**
    setting project properties, 408
    using Setup Wizard, **406-9**
shadowed methods, **226-29**
  arbitrary shadowing, 228-29
  compared to overriding methods, 226
shadowed variables, 222
Shadows keyword, 227
shallow serialization, 337
shared events, **212**
Shared keyword, 210-11
shared methods, **209-10**
shared variables, **210-12**
  global variables, **212**
SharePoint Portal Server, 31
shell program for deployment, **419-23**
  deploying DLL to Server, 422
  Serializable attribute and, 421-22
  System.Reflection namespace, 420
  Windows applications, **419-23**
    creating child form, 422
Short data type, 44, 103
Shortcut property, MenuItem class, 161
shortcut, creating
  launching .NET programs from URLs, 418
shortcuts, operators, 116
ShowDialog method, Form class, **148**
ShowDialog method, PageSetupDialog class, 382
ShowDialog method, PrintDialog class, 381
ShowMessageBox property, ValidationSummary control, 260
ShowShortcut property, MenuItem class, 161
Single data type, 44, 103
Size property, Control class, 145
Sleep method, Thread class, 362-63
SOAP (Simple Object Access Protocol), **272-73**, 334
Soapsuds, 395
Socket class, System.Net.Sockets namespace, 369
  BeginReceive method, 369, 370
  EndReceive method, 370
sockets
  IP sockets, 368-72
  TCP sockets, 335

Software Publisher Certificate Test Utility, 394
Solution Explorer window, 77-79
  Add References dialog, 78-79
solutions, Visual Basic .NET, 77
  compared to project groups, 77
Sort property, ADO.NET DataView class, 318
SortedList class, System.Collections namespace, 113
SQL Server, 19, 31
SQL Server data provider, 287, 288
  System.Data.SQLClient namespace, 287
  table of classes, 288
  using wizards with, 289
SqlCommand class
  see Command classes, ADO.NET
SqlConnection class
  see Connection classes, ADO.NET
SqlDataAdapter class
  see DataAdapter classes, ADO.NET
SqlDataReader class
  see DataReader classes, ADO.NET
SqlException class
  see Exception classes, ADO.NET
Sqrt method, Math class, 50
SSL (Secure Sockets Layer), 277
Stack class, System.Collections namespace, 113
state management, Web Forms, 253-55
  disabling state management, 254
  Web.config file, 270-71
stored procedures, 321-23
  using stored procedures with commands, 321-22
  using stored procedures with DataAdapters, 322
String class, System namespace, 104
String data type, 104-5
  concatenating string, 105
StringBuilder class, System.Text namespace, 450
  concatenating string, 105
StringCollection class, System.Collections.Specialized
  namespace, 114
StringDictionary class, System.Collections.Specialized
  namespace, 114
Strong Name Utility, 394
StructLayout attribute, 451
Structure keyword
  user defined types, 112
structured error handling, 120-25
  compared to On Error Resume Next statements, 125
  Resume statements not available, 124
Sub keyword, 193
subclasses, 213
  see also inheritance
  C# subclasses, 237-38
  creating subclasses, 214-16
  overloading methods in, 218-19
superclasses
  see base classes
synchronization mechanisms
  System.Threading namespace, 360
SyncLock keyword, 359-60
  SyncRoot property and, 360
SyncRoot property
  SyncLock keyword and, 360
syntax changes, Migration Wizard, 454
System namespace, 50
  AppDomain class, 357, 421
  Console class, 98, 373-75

Exception class, 123, 323
  Guid class, 450
  MarshalByRefObject class, 338, 339
  Math class, 50
  Object class, 43, 106
  String class, 104
  Type class, 43
System.Collections namespace, 50, 113-14
  base classes, 114
System.Collections.Specialized namespace, 113
System.ComponentModel namespace
  Component class, 337
  MarshalByValueComponent class, 338
System.Configuration.Install namespace
  Installer class, 385
System.Data namespace, 50, 284
  Constraints collection, 303
  DataColumn class, 300
  DataRelation class, 304-6
  DataRow class, 301-3
  DataSet class, 298-316
  DataTable class, 299-304
  DataView class, 317-19
  ForeignKeyConstraint class, 303
  UniqueConstraint class, 303
System.Data.dll assembly, 350
System.Data.OleDb namespace, 284
  OLE DB data provider, 287
  table of classes, 288
System.Data.SQLClient namespace, 284
  SQL Server data provider, 287
  table of classes, 288
System.Diagnostics namespace, 50
  Debug class, 89
  EventLog class, 383
System.dll assembly, 390
System.Drawing namespace, 176-77
  compared to Visual Basic, 182
  Graphics class, 177-79, 178-80
  Point structure, 177
System.Drawing.Drawing2D namespace, 181
  GraphicsPath class, 181
System.Drawing.Imaging namespace, 181
System.Drawing.Printing namespace, 375
  PageSettings class, 381-82
  PrintDocument class, 375, 377
  PrintPageEventArgs object, 378
System.Drawing.Text namespace, 181-82
System.EnterpriseServices namespace, 349
  ContextUtil class, 352-53
  ServicedComponent class, 349
System.IO namespace, 50
  FileSystemWatcher class, 389-90
System.Math namespace, 50
System.Messaging namespace, 353-57
  Message class, 355-57
  MessageQueue class, 354
  MSMQ, 19
  XmlMessageFormatter class, 356
System.Messaging.dll assembly, 353
System.Net.Sockets namespace, 368
  Socket class, 369
  TCPListener class, 372
System.Reflection namespace, 50, 208
  Assembly class, 417, 420
  MethodInfo class, 417
  shell program for deployment, 420

System.Runtime.InteropServices namespace
  calling API function, 447
  Marshal class, 433, 438
  using ADO from Visual Basic .NET, 439
  using COM component in .NET, 437
System.Runtime.Remoting namespace, 342, 346
  RemotingConfiguration class, 346, 349
System.Security namespace, 50
System.ServiceProcess namespace
  ServiceBase class, 383
System.Text namespace
  StringBuilder class, 105, 450
System.Threading namespace, 357
  synchronization mechanisms, 360
  Thread class, 361
  ThreadPool class, 366
System.Timers namespace
  Timer class, 384
System.Web namespace
  HttpResponse class, 262
System.Web.Security namespace
  FormsAuthentication class, 270
System.Web.UI namespace, 248
  HtmlTextWriter class, 263
  Page class, **250-51**
System.Web.UI.WebControls namespace
  WebControl class, 261
System.Windows.Forms namespace, 51, 138, **140-42**
  CommonDialog class, 375
  ContainerControl class, **141**
  Control class, **140-41**
  Form class, 64, **141-42**
  MenuItem class, 158-61
  MessageBox class, 71
  PageSetupDialog class, **381-82**
  PrintDialog class, **380**
  ScrollableControl class, **141**
  UserControl class, **142**
  Windows Forms, 51
System.Windows.Forms.dll assembly, 391
System.Xml namespace
  accessing XML through DOM, 328

T

Table server control, Web Forms, 258
TableCell server control, Web Forms, 258
TableRow server control, Web Forms, 258
TargetTypeNames property, XmlMessageFormatter class, 356
Task List window, 87-88
  comments, **88**
TCP sockets, 335
TCPListener class, System.Net.Sockets namespace, 372
termination, objects, 202-12
  Dispose method, **203-12**
  Finalize method, **203**
  garbage collection, **202-3**
Text property, MenuItem class, 161
Text property, Windows Forms controls, 169
TextBox server control, Web Forms, 246, 257, 264
this keyword
  compared to Me keyword, 222

Thread class, System.Threading namespace, 361
  Abort method, 362
  CurrentThread property, 362
  Sleep method, 362-63
thread pool
  asynchronous processing, 365
ThreadPool class, System.Threading namespace, 366
threads, 357-72
  AppDomain class, System namespace, 357
  asynchronous processing, **365-68**
  creating a thread, **361-62**
  creating worker threads for service, 384-85
  delegates, 359
  lifetimes, **362**
  passing data to thread, **363-65**
  quantum, 364
  SyncLock keyword, **359-60**
  System.Threading namespace, 357
  Windows Forms, **358-59**
  worker method, 360-61
threadsafe code, 358, 359
Timer class, System.Timers namespace, 384
  Elapsed event, 384, 385
  Enabled property, 384
  Interval property, 384
TODO comments, 67, 88
Toolbox window, 84-86, 442
  Clipboard Ring tab, 85
  code fragments and, 85-86
  tabs, 84-85
  using ActiveX controls in Windows Forms, 442
ToolTip controls, Windows Forms, 166
Top property, Control class, 145
TopMost property, Form class, **153**
ToString method, Object class, 43
Transactional attribute, 349
transactional components, 349-53
  transactional web service, 350-53
transactional web service, 350-53
TransparencyKey property, Form class, 152
Try blocks, 121-25
  Catch blocks, **121**, **122**
  Exit Try statements, **122-23**
  Finally blocks, 121-22
  nested Try blocks, 124
Type class, System namespace, 43
Type keyword
  user defined types, 112
type libraries
  designing COM components for .NET, **432**
Type Library Exporter, 393
Type Library Importer, 393
typed DataSets, 319-21
types
  see data types
types, assemblies, 46

U

UBound statements, 110
UDTs
  see user defined types
Unicode version API
  compared to ANSI version, 449-50

Unique property, ADO.NET DataColumn class, 300
UniqueConstraint class, ADO.NET, 303
Update method, ADO.NET DataAdapter class, 323
UpdateCommand property, ADO.NET DataAdapter class, 323
UpDown controls, Windows Forms, 162-63
  DomainUpDown controls, 163
  NumericUpDown controls, 163
upgrade report, Migration Wizard, 453-54
URLs
  launching .NET programs from URLs, **415-18**
    Windows applications, **416-18**
user defined types, **112**
  Structure keyword, Visual Basic .NET, 112
  Type keyword, Visual Basic, 112
user interfaces, **51-54**
  console applications, 53
  Web Forms, **52-53**
  Web Services, **53-54**
  Windows Forms, **51-52**
User property, Page class, 251
UserControl class, System.Windows.Forms namespace, **142**

V

validation controls, Web Forms, **258-60**
  ControlToValidate property, 259
  Display property, 260
  Enabled property, 260
  error messages, **260**
  list of controls, 259
  RangeValidator control, 265
  regular expressions, 259-60
  RegularExpressionValidator control, 266
  RequiredFieldValidator control, 246
  ValidationSummary control, 266
ValidationSummary control, Web Forms, 259, 266
  ShowMessageBox property, 260
Validators property, Page class, 251
value types, **41-43**
  compared to reference types, 42
ValueMember property, ComboBox controls, 325
ValueMember property, ListBox controls, 325
variables
  constants, 108
  declaring a variable, **68**, **107-9**
    New keyword, 108
  initial values, 108
  multiple variables, 107
  scope, **109**, **217-18**
  shadowed variables, 222
  shared variables, **210-12**
Variant data type, 106
  not available in Visual Basic .NET, 106
  replacing Variant type with Object type, 106
  storing object references, 107
vb file name extension, 78
vbc command, **390-91**
virtual directory, 402, 413
virtual methods, **220-22**
Visible property, MenuItem class, 161

Visual Basic
  binary compatibility, **433-34**
  COM components, 188-89
  compared to System.Drawing namespace, 182
  compared to Visual Basic .NET, 24, 57
    controlling object creation, 199
    event handlers, 70, 71
    forms, 63
  controls
    Caption property, 169
    compared to Windows Forms controls, 157-58
    List collection, 169
    ListIndex property, 169
  deterministic finalization, 48
  forms, **142-57**
    compared to Web Forms, 245
    Resize event, 154
  GetObjectContext function, 352
  Immediate window, 89
  limitations in COM/DNA, 33-34, 57
  migrating from Visual Basic to Visual Basic .NET, **452-54**
  object lifecycle, 197
  Printer object, 375
  project groups, 77
  Type keyword, 112
Visual Basic .NET, 11
  Add Web Reference option, 275
  base classes, **236-37**
  Call Stack window, **91**
  calling COM components from Visual Basic .NET, **434-38**
  classes, 62-64, **189-97**
  command line options, **390-91**
  Command window, **89**
  compared to C#, 11
  compared to Visual Basic, 24, 57
    controlling object creation, 199
    event handlers, 70, 71
    forms, 63
  component tray, **76-77**
  constructor methods, **67**
  creating assembly for COM, **444-45**
  data types, **102-7**
  Debug configuration, **398-99**
  declaring API in Visual Basic .NET, 447-48
    DllImport attribute, 447
  deployment and, 59, **397-427**
  Dispose method, 67-68
  error handling, **120-25**
  event handlers, **69-71**
  exception handling, 121
  forms, 62-69
  HelloWorld project, **21-26**, **62-71**
  Internet, **58**
  MDI forms example, **171-73**
  migrating from Visual Basic to Visual Basic .NET, **452-54**
  object lifecycle, 197
  Option statements, **101-2**
  passing by value default in Visual Basic .NET, 127
  programming models, 58
  Release configuration, **398-99**
  solutions, 77
  Structure keyword, 112
  SyncLock keyword, **359-60**
  using ADO from Visual Basic .NET, **439-40**

Visual Basic .NET (continued)
Web Services
consuming Web Service in Visual Basic .NET, **275-76**
consuming Web Service in Windows application,
276-77
creating Web Service in Visual Basic .NET, **273-75**
Windows Service, **382-88**
Visual Designer
using for Windows Forms, **143-44**
visual inheritance, 239
Web Forms, 239
Windows Forms, **173-74**, 239
inheritance picker, **174-76**
Visual Studio .NET, 12, **56-57**
DataAdapter Wizard, **309-16**
docking windows, **73-74**
formal installation options, **403-14**
HelloWorld project, **21-26**, **62-71**
IDE, **65-69**, **72-91**
macros, **90**
must be installed to physical local drive, 16
regions, 65-68

W

Watch window, 91
Web applications
Setup Wizard, **411-14**
building project, 413
running setup program, **413-14**
setting project properties, 412
using Setup Wizard, **412-13**
Web Forms example, **264-68**
Web.config file, **268-71**
XCOPY deployment, **401-3**
Web Forms, 36, **52-53**, 142, **243-71**
ASP.NET, **248**
code-behind module, **250**
compared to HTML forms, 243
compared to Visual Basic forms, 245
compared to Windows Forms, 142, 245
creating DataSet using DataAdapter Wizard, 315-16
data binding, 263-64
error messages, **260**
events, **251-55**
Application events, 253
non-postback events, 252
order of events, 252
performance issues, 252
postback events, 252
Session events, 253
grid layout, 255-56
HTML template, **249-50**
linear layout, 255
rendering output as HTML, 248
server controls, 52-53, 248, **256-63**
custom controls, **260-63**
validation controls, **258-60**
simple example, **244-47**
state management, **253-55**
System.Web.UI namespace, 248
visual inheritance, 239
Web application example, **264-68**
Web.config file, **268-71**
web server deployment, 404
web server requirements, **.NET**, 14

Web Services, 36, **53-54**, **271-77**
consuming Web Service in Visual Basic .NET, **275-76**
consuming Web Service in Windows application,
276-77
creating Web Service in Visual Basic .NET, **273-75**
reasons for using, **271-72**
security, **277**
SOAP, **272-73**
transactional web service, 350-53
WebMethod attribute, 274
Web Services Description Language
see WSDL
Web Services Description Language Tool
see WSDL.exe
Web Services Discovery Tool, 395
Web.config file, **268-71**
Authentication section, 269-70
Authorization section, 269-70
implementing remoting, 341
security, **269-70**
sessionState section, 271
state management, Web Forms, **270-71**
WebControl class, System.Web.UI.WebControls
namespace, 261
WebMethod attribute, 274, 350, 352
Width property, Control class, 145
Windows APIs
see APIs
Windows applications
consuming Web Service in Windows application,
276-77
launching .NET programs from URLs, **416-18**
adding deployment application to path variable, 418
creating shortcut, 418
deploying test application, 417
Setup Wizard, **405-11**
building project, 408-9
icon, adding, 408
running setup program, **410-11**
setting project properties, 408
using Setup Wizard, **406-9**
shell program for deployment, **419-23**
creating child form, 422
deploying DLL to Server, 422
System.Reflection namespace, 420
XCOPY deployment, **400-401**
Windows DNA
.NET Framework and, 55
compared to .NET Framework, 11
cross-language integration issues, 33
limitations, **32-34**
Visual Basic in COM/DNA, 33-34
Windows Forms, 36, **51-52**, **137-85**
ActiveX controls and, **441-42**
using ActiveX control, 442
architecture, **140-42**
changing shape of form, **150-51**
graphics paths, 150
compared to Visual Basic forms, **142-57**
compared to Web Forms, 142, 245
consuming Web Service in Windows application,
276-77

Windows Forms (continued)
controls, **153-70**
  adding a control at run time, **156-57**
  custom controls, **182-85**
  invisible controls, **143-44**
  locked controls, **144**
  multiple controls, 146
  positioning and layout, **145-46**
creating DataSet using DataAdapter Wizard, 310-15
dialog boxes, **146-50**
GDI+, **178-80**
inheritance picker, **174-76**
introduction, **139-40**
Invoke method, 358
MDI forms, **170-73**
owned forms, **152-53**
reasons for using, **138-39**
System.Windows.Forms namespace, 51, 138, **140-42**
threads, **358-59**
using Visual Designer, **143-44**
visual inheritance, **173-74**, 239
Windows Forms ActiveX Control Importer, 393
Windows Forms Class Viewer, 395
Windows Forms Resource Editor, 393
Windows Service, 382-88
creating Windows Service, **382-85**
creating worker threads for service, 384-85
installing service, **385-88**
  Installer Utility, 387
  RunInstaller attribute, 385
Windows System Installer
deployment and installation, Visual Basic .NET, 404
windows, docking in IDE, 73-74

WithEvents keyword, 129
WndProc method, Control class, 141
worker method, threads, 360-61
Write method, Console class, 373
write only properties, 120
WriteLine method, Console class, 98, 373
WriteLine method, Debug class, 89
WriteOnly keyword, 120
WriteXML method, ADO.NET DataSet class, 327
WSDL (Web Services Description Language), 272
WSDL.exe, 395

X

XCOPY deployment, 38-39, **400-403**
  Web applications, **401-3**
  Windows applications, **400-401**
XML, 54
  accessing XML through ADO.NET, **326-28**
  accessing XML through DOM, 328
XML server control, Web Forms, 258
XmlMessageFormatter class, System.Messaging namespace, 356
  TargetTypeNames property, 356

Z

zero based arrays, 109-10

wrox

Programmer to Programmer™

Registration Code: 7124RA9W710RYF01

Wrox writes books for you. Any suggestions, or ideas about how you want information given in your ideal book will be studied by our team. Your comments are always valued at Wrox.

Free phone in USA 800-USE-WROX
Fax (312) 893 8001

UK Tel.: (0121) 687 4100   Fax: (0121) 687 4101

Fast Track Visual Basic .NET – Registration Card

Name _____

Address _____

_____

_____

City _____ State/Region _____

Country _____ Postcode/Zip _____

E-Mail _____

Occupation _____

How did you hear about this book?

❐ Book review (name) _____

❐ Advertisement (name) _____

❐ Recommendation _____

❐ Catalog _____

❐ Other _____

Where did you buy this book?

❐ Bookstore (name) _____ City _____

❐ Computer store (name) _____

❐ Mail order _____

❐ Other _____

What influenced you in the purchase of this book?

❐ Cover Design ❐ Contents ❐ Other (please specify):

_____

How did you rate the overall content of this book?

❐ Excellent ❐ Good ❐ Average ❐ Poor

What did you find most useful about this book? _____

What did you find least useful about this book? _____

_____

Please add any additional comments. _____

_____

What other subjects will you buy a computer book on soon?

_____

What is the best computer book you have used this year?

_____

Note: This information will only be used to keep you updated about new Wrox Press titles and will not be used for any other purpose or passed to any other third party.

wrox

Programmer to Programmer™

Note: If you post the bounce back card below in the UK, please send it to:

Wrox Press Limited, Arden House, 1102 Warwick Road,
Acocks Green, Birmingham B27 6HB. UK.

Computer Book Publishers

BUSINESS REPLY MAIL

FIRST CLASS MAIL   PERMIT#64   CHICAGO, IL

POSTAGE WILL BE PAID BY ADDRESSEE

**WROX PRESS INC.,
29 S. LA SALLE ST.,
SUITE 520
CHICAGO IL 60603-USA**